The Rise of Massive Resistance

THE RISE OF
MASSIVE
RESISTANCE

Race and Politics in the South During the 1950's

NUMAN V. BARTLEY
With a New Preface by the Author

LOUISIANA STATE UNIVERSITY PRESS   BATON ROUGE

Louisiana Paperback Edition, 1999
00 02 04 06 08 07 05 03 01 99
1 3 5 4 2

Designed by Robert L. Nance
Compilation by St. Catherine Press, Ltd., Bruges, Belgium

Library of Congress Catalog Card Number 76-80041
ISBN 0-8071-2419-2

The paper in this book meets the guidelines for permanence and durability
of the Committee on Production Guidelines for Book Longevity of the
Council on Library Resources. ∞

To Rosa

PREFACE TO THE PAPERBACK EDITION

While *The Rise of Massive Resistance* was being researched and written in the mid-to-late 1960s, the United States faced a crisis in race relations. The civil rights movement elevated the expectations of black Americans, but continuing white opposition precluded rapid advancement of their cause. Against the backdrop of an unpopular war in Southeast Asia, the frustrations of some African Americans exploded in massive rioting, beginning with the Watts riot in the summer of 1965. The federal government responded with a "war on poverty" that was oriented toward the restive inner-city ghettos, while journalists wrote of a growing "white backlash" and the presidential campaign of George C. Wallace, the segregationist former governor of Alabama, fanned the flames of discord.

Witnessing these events, I was intrigued by the extent of white hostility. I completed the manuscript for this book before the advent of affirmative action and before "forced busing" of schoolchildren was a factor outside the rural-town South, which was the only substantial area in the nation where residential patterns were diverse enough to produce widespread school integration. Cities and suburbs, South and North, practiced "freedom of choice" or "open enrollment" policies that perpetuated what the United States Commission on Civil Rights in 1967 termed "racial isolation in the public schools." For the vast majority of white citizens, civil rights for blacks had required rather few changes. Yet during the years following World War II, many whites viewed black civil rights with reluctance or with outright hostility.

Prior to the mid-1960s, observers usually identified the South as the crux of "the Negro problem." The spread of the civil rights movement outside the South and the urban rioting that shook numerous northern and western cities nationalized racial issues, but the South remained the center of overt race-based proscription. Given the region's history and its social conventions, it is not surprising that few whites welcomed desegregation. But the extent and the belligerence of the opposition struck me as remarkable. It also seemed to me—writing in the backwash of ghetto upheavals—that of many past opportunities lost, the 1950s was a particularly bereft decade. Now, thirty years later, that view still seems to me to be accurate. The struggle against southern *de jure* segregation absorbed the nation's idealism, while many of the more fundamental problems of African Americans continued to fester.

My original interest in the regional policy of massive resistance to social change was an effort to understand why it happened, why the political South behaved as it did. But there was also a corollary question: what effect did court decisions, federal intervention, and an emerging black protest movement have on the South? Scholars studying the region had usually located a strong relationship between white racism and political conservatism. The demise of Jim Crow, much of this literature suggested, might free what V. O. Key in his classic *Southern Politics in State and Nation* referred to as the "underlying liberal drive [that] permeates southern politics." Preparing this manuscript at a time when sectionalism was an important theme in the interpretation of American history, I hoped to evaluate the impact of social change on political tendencies in the South. My conclusions leaned toward the pessimistic side, and I have discovered no reasons to alter my views.

During the late 1950s and the 1960s, the intransigent behavior of white southern conservatives intrigued many scholars and journalists. A spate of publications (most of which are included in the bibliography of this book) endeavored to explain the region's aberrant behavior. Thereafter, the focus of scholarly inquiry shifted—quite understandably in the backwash of the civil rights movement—to the struggles of black southerners and their drive for equality. Only recently have students of the modern South demonstrated a renewed interest in the conservative defenders of the social status quo. As a result, this book is being reissued in a paperback edition.

Were I writing *The Rise of Massive Resistance* today rather than three decades ago, I would make few changes. Perhaps I am being myopic, but I think it has held up rather well.

NUMAN V. BARTLEY

Fall 1999

PREFACE

For several decades the South has been absorbing sweeping demographic and economic changes. At the same time, southern politics have reflected the region's attachment to traditional values. The emergence of what some contemporary historians have called the Second Reconstruction brought to a head this conflict between change and continuity. President Harry S. Truman's civil rights program and a series of United States Supreme Court decisions culminating in the 1954 school desegregation ruling struck directly at the institutionalized framework of the southern social system. These events sparked a white reaction that sought to restore and protect time-honored conventions. The movement in defense of southern rural small-town values offered "massive resistance" to social innovation, and it dominated southern politics during much of the 1950's.

The following pages are an attempt to describe and evaluate the rise of massive resistance to public school desegregation. I have tried to view southern politics and race relations broadly, searching for basic patterns while at the same time recognizing the immense variety of the region. Nevertheless, there are several limitations of which the reader should be aware. As an examination of the opposition to social change, this study focuses on the more conservative aspects of southern politics. Progressive tendencies and alternative programs have not been ignored, but the approach used here stresses the role of the defenders of white supremacy. Similarly, Negro political participation has been dealt with in a relatively cursory manner since nonwhite voter registration was too small to exercise more than limited influence on the course of southern politics during the 1950's. Finally, this work is a study of politics and race relations in the South. I would have few quarrels with those who would argue that many of the flaws of southern politics are also the flaws of American politics generally. Yet, only the eleven states of the former

Confederacy enacted legislation to prevent or hamper enforcement of the 1954 school desegregation decision, and these states have been the subject of my investigation.

In dealing with the controversial and often emotional issues involving social change in the South, I have attempted an objective and interpretive appraisal. I have endeavored to understand the attitudes that led a significant number of white southerners to endorse massive resistance. But I lay no claim to neutrality in the field of human relations. An underlying assumption of this work is that elementary human equality and human dignity are essential parts of the American creed.

Many factors and many people have contributed to my understanding and knowledge of the subject matter in this book. Not all of these, of course, can be singled out for acknowledgments, but I would be remiss if I did not make an attempt to do so.

I am indebted first of all to the people of my hometown in East Texas, who instructed me in "the southern way of life." The storeowner who sternly explained to me and my young companions that we should not play baseball with other youngsters because they were Negroes; the farmhands—older, stronger, and wiser than I—who worked with me in the hayfields and called me "Mister" because I was white of skin and they were not; the otherwise kind and generous friends and relatives who talked of "Nigger Bob" and "Nigger Tom" and generally made clear that there were two distinct types of homo sapiens; the neighboring town which had, arched over its major highway entrances, large signs reading "The Blackest Land—The Whitest People"—these and other people and events taught me much about the nature of southern small-town race relations.

Later, I was fortunate enough to begin my study of southern history under the tutelege of Professor Jack Scroggs of North Texas State University. I had worked in other subjects as an undergraduate and entered the Graduate School of History at North Texas State with virtually no training in history or in any associated field. In Professor Scroggs' seminars, I was introduced to and became absorbed in the fascinating complexities of the southern past. Professor Scroggs suggested the topic for this book, and, in one of his seminars, I first investigated the southern response to the 1954 school desegregation decision.

In an earlier draft, this book was my Ph.D. dissertation written under the direction of Professor Dewey W. Grantham at Vanderbilt University. It now seems presumptuous for me to dismiss in a few words my profound indebtedness to Professor Grantham. His criticisms, suggestions, and encouragement contributed mightily to whatever merit this work possesses. While any errors of fact or mistakes of judgment are exclusively mine, they are substantially less numerous than they would have been had not Professor Grantham shared with me his vast knowledge of the modern South.

Much of the research for this study was undertaken at the Southern Education Reporting Service in Nashville and the Southern Regional Council in Atlanta. I am deeply grateful to Reed Sarratt, Jim Leeson, Bill Griffitts, and the other staff members of the Southern Education Reporting Service, and to Paul Anthony, Bernice Morrison, and other members of the Southern Regional Council staff, all of whom contributed more than they perhaps realize to making the research for this work a pleasant and personally rewarding experience. I was able to put in a full year of uninterrupted research at the Southern Education Reporting Service because of grants from the Ford Foundation's Small-Grants-in-Aid program and from Vanderbilt University. A grant from the Georgia Tech Foundation was extremely helpful in preparing this study for publication.

Glenda Bartley, who supervises the research department at the Southern Regional Council, generously contributed time and effort above and beyond the call of duty and more than a few of her observations and suggestions have found their way into the pages that follow. Professor Henry L. Swint of Vanderbilt University read and perceptively criticized the entire manuscript. Mrs. Crickett C. Waldroup of the Louisiana State University Press made a substantial contribution to the book's readability. Constance Curry, Winifred Green, and Professor H. Glyn Thomas read and commented on portions of this work. Mrs. Verna Chambless maintained her good humor while doing the typing chores through several draft copies.

And the pleasant evenings spent "talking politics" with Miss Curry, director of the Southeastern Office of the American Friends Service Committee; Miss Green, fieldworker for the American Friends Service Committee; Glenda Bartley; Professor Thomas of the Georgia Institute of Technology; Al Ulmer, then a fieldworker for the Southern Regional Council; Joan Browning of the Federation of Southern Co-operatives; George Anderson, formerly with the Westinghouse VISTA Training Program; and others did more to broaden my understanding of the New South than I can adequately convey.

N.V.B.

CONTENTS

ILLUSTRATIONS

The Rise of Massive Resistance

CHAPTER I

THE SOUTH AT MID-CENTURY

By any rational standard of measurement, mid-twentieth century America seemed an alien habitation for an extensive system of racially segregated public schools. The foundations for institutionalized white supremacy belonged to the past. Jim Crow appeared as anachronistic as slavery had been a century before.

Racial segregation no longer possessed the intellectual respectability that had accompanied Social Darwinism, biological determinism, and justifications for imperialism. A new school of anthropology and a changed intellectual atmosphere made a mockery of white supremacy, while American pretensions to world leadership added the insult of hypocrisy. Negroes could no longer be excluded from the mainstream of American life because of their "inferiority." As Gunnar Myrdal concluded in 1944, *"the gradual destruction of the popular theory behind race prejudice is the most important of all social trends in the field of interracial relations."*[1]

This tendency toward acceptance of human equality, which coincided with vast changes caused by the Depression, the New Deal, World War II, and the Cold War, had penetrated American thought deeply by the post-World War II period. President Franklin D. Roosevelt's executive order creating the Fair Employment Practices Committee marked a limited but nevertheless significant change in the policy of the federal government. President Harry S. Truman went much further, shifting executive power and the national Democratic Party to the support of civil rights, an act which Leslie W. Dunbar, former executive director of the

---

[1] Gunnar Myrdal, *An American Dilemma: The Negro Problem and Modern Democracy* (New York, 1944), II, 1003 (Myrdal's italics). This work, written by a Swedish social scientist, is the most important study of American race relations thus far published.

3

Southern Regional Council, summed up as the repeal of the Compromise of 1877.[2] Although southern influence in Congress long delayed civil rights legislation, executive authority was sufficient to broaden the fair employment program and to abolish segregation in the armed services.

In assuming leadership of the national civil rights movement, Truman was voicing a substantial nonsouthern consensus that reflected the world-wide reevaluation of human rights. The postwar period witnessed a surge of popular feeling against Jim Crowism. Several northern and western states enacted fair employment practices legislation, open-occupancy laws in public housing, and other civil rights measures. New Jersey voters ratified a constitutional revision stating specifically that discrimination in public schools was illegal, and a special legislative session enacted imple-menting laws. In 1949 the Indiana legislature prohibited permissive segregation in schools, and Illinois legislators in the same year banned the use of state money in school districts maintaining Jim Crow classrooms. In Arizona voters defeated an initiative measure abolishing racial separa-tion in education; nevertheless, the state legislature rewrote the statute to eliminate requirements for a mandatory dual school system, and a number of communities desegregated. These states and others demon-strated a revival of the abolitionist tradition in the North and beyond.[3]

Nowhere was the new mood more evident than in the decisions of the United States Supreme Court. Just as an earlier Court had been in the van of the Social Darwinist stampede to nullify the work of Radical Republicanism, a new Court was the precursor in revitalization of the equal protection clause of the Fourteenth Amendment. Under four different Chief Justices, the Court moved steadily toward a realistic view of the "separate but equal" formula and the whole system of forced segregation that rested upon it. In numerous cases centering around voting and education but overlapping other areas, the Supreme Court under-took the task of restoring equality before the law. The new trend in jurisprudence was indicated clearly in *Gaines v. Canada* in 1938. Missouri, like most southern states, maintained a law school for whites but none for Negroes, providing instead out-of-state tuition for those who wished to study law elsewhere. Lloyd Gaines was denied admission to the

---

[2] Leslie W. Dunbar, "The Changing Mind of the South: The Exposed Nerve," *Journal of Politics*, XXVI (February, 1964), 14.

[3] Harry S. Ashmore, *The Negro and the Schools* (Chapel Hill, 1954), 66–94; and see generally Robin W. Williams, Jr., and Margaret W. Ryan, *Schools in Transition: Community Experiences in Desegregation* (Chapel Hill, 1954).

University of Missouri Law School because of race. When Gaines, with the backing of the National Association for the Advancement of Colored People, brought suit, the Supreme Court ruled that equal protection of the laws required that Missouri either provide a "separate but equal" law school or admit Gaines to the white school.[4] A decade later the Supreme Court reaffirmed the *Gaines* decision in *Sipuel v. Board of Regents* (1948), a similar case involving the University of Oklahoma Law School. Neither of these decisions questioned segregation per se, but by the end of the 1940's the judicial stage had been set and the NAACP had shifted its legal attack to a direct challenge of the separate but equal doctrine itself.[5] In late 1949 the Court voted to review cases stemming from the University of Texas and the University of Oklahoma.

Sweatt v. Painter was widely recognized as a crucial case. Heman Sweatt applied to the University of Texas Law School, and his application was rejected because of race. Unlike Missouri, which had provisions for payment of out-of-state tuition, and Oklahoma, which had had no provisions for Negro law students at all, Texas proceeded to create a Negro law school. Sweatt's lawyers, in addition to attacking segregation per se, argued that the Negro law school was inferior and that Sweatt's constitutional right of equal protection of the laws could be satisfied only by admission to the state university. Since virtually all Negro schools in the South were inferior to the corresponding white institutions, this case obviously involved a basic threat to the whole separate but equal concept in education. The attorneys general of all the former Confederate states entered friends-of-the-court briefs defending the separate but equal formula, while the United States Attorney General and a committee of law professors submitted *amici curiae* briefs in support of the arguments of the NAACP.[6]

Working within a separate but equal framework, the Court determined that the Negro law school was not equal to its white counterpart, observing that "the University of Texas Law School possesses to a far greater

[4] *Missouri ex rel. Gaines v. Canada,* 305 U.S. 337. On the Fourteenth Amendment, see Robert J. Harris, *The Quest for Equality: The Constitution, Congress and the Supreme Court* (Baton Rouge, 1960); Joseph B. James, *The Framing of the Fourteenth Amendment* (Urbana, Ill., 1956); and Bernard H. Nelson, *The Fourteenth Amendment and the Negro Since 1920* (New York, 1946).

[5] *Sipuel v. Board of Regents,* 332 U.S. 631; Walter White, *How Far the Promised Land?* (New York, 1955), 37.

[6] *Sweatt v. Painter,* 339 U.S. 629; Albert P. Blaustein and Clarence Clyde Ferguson, Jr., *Desegregation and the Law: The Meaning and Effect of the School Segregation Cases* (2nd ed. rev.; New York, 1962), 95–113.

degree those qualities which are incapable of objective measurement but which make for greatness in a law school."[7] By viewing segregation realistically and including such intangibles as prestige of faculty and alumni in evaluating the quality of separate facilities, the Court questioned a fiction and thereby came close to destroying it. The Court ordered the admission of Sweatt to the white law school.

The ruling in *McLaurin v. Board of Regents* was handed down on the same day. After the *Sipuel* case, the University of Oklahoma had retreated to a second line of defense. The institution began to accept Negro applicants to graduate and professional schools but, while dropping racial bars to admission, stanchly maintained the principle of separation within the university. G. W. McLaurin, a student in the Graduate School of Education, was segregated in the cafeteria, provided a Jim Crow table in the library, and even seated in a Jim Crow classroom where he could hear, through an open door, lectures being delivered in an adjoining room to his white classmates. McLaurin charged that this arrangement denied equality before the law. In upholding McLaurin's plea, the Court once again turned to intangible factors, pointing to the lack of opportunity for intellectual exchange with other students.[8]

The *Sweatt* and *McLaurin* decisions left the separate but equal concept with only a shadow of legality, and, as if to underline this point, the Court handed down a third decision on that same day, June 5, 1950, prohibiting segregated arrangements on railway dining cars. Since the original legal basis for the separate but equal doctrine stemmed from Jim Crow on the railroads, *Henderson v. United States*, combined with the rest of the day's work, seemed to point clearly toward the hopeless future of institutionalized white supremacy.[9] "After 1950," one legal scholar has written, "every careful student of constitutional law knew that, given the climate of judicial—as well as national—opinion, the 'separate but equal' formula was doomed."[10]

---

[7] *Sweatt v. Painter*, 339 U.S. 634.

[8] *McLaurin v. Board of Regents*, 339 U.S. 637.

[9] *Henderson v. United States*, 339 U.S. 816. *Plessy v. Ferguson*, 163 U.S. 537 (1896), was, of course, the case in which the Supreme Court first accepted the "separate but equal" concept.

[10] Walter F. Murphy, *Congress and the Court: A Case Study in the American Political Process* (Chicago, 1962), 80. Among several studies dealing with the legal background of segregation and desegregation, Blaustein and Ferguson, *Desegregation and the Law;* United States Commission on Civil Rights, *Equal Protection of the Laws in Public Higher Education* (Washington, 1960); Jack Greenberg, *Race Relations and American Law* (New York, 1959); and Harris, *The Quest for Equality*, are helpful.

Several states in the South quietly accepted the decisions. Texas admitted two Negro students to the state university, and Kentucky altered its segregation laws to allow limited college integration. When the admission policy of the University of Virginia was challenged in the federal courts, Virginia did not bother to plan a defense. Louisiana followed when Louisiana State University desegregated its law school under court order during 1950. Arkansas had already desegregated the university law school after the *Sipuel* decision in 1948. Various private and religious colleges and universities, a few in the Deep South, voluntarily admitted Negroes. The Southern Regional Council counted twenty such colleges in 1951, including two in Louisiana, one in Georgia, one in Virginia, and four in Texas.[11] Such changes were "token," however; outside of a few Negro students in a limited number of "white" graduate and professional schools, Jim Crow remained intact in southern education.

The most obvious manifestation of shifting race relations in the South was Negro participation in politics. In this area, too, the federal courts demonstrated a growing tendency to look behind the legal sophistries that served as cloaks for white supremacy. A series of cases challenging the constitutionality of the widespread practice that excluded Negroes from southern primary elections culminated in *Smith v. Allwright* (1944), which decreed a judicial funeral for the white primary.[12] The decision legally opened the way for large-scale Negro voter registration and the reentry of nonwhite citizens into the southern political process.

Yet *Smith v. Allwright* did not mark the emergence of a large reservoir of votes to support racially liberal politicians. In 1944 approximately 250,000 Negroes, about 5 percent of the almost five million Negroes of voting age in the former Confederacy, were registered as voters. The number gradually increased for several years, reaching something over

[11] *New South*, August–September, 1951. See also the figures in Alexander Heard, *A Two-Party South?* (Chapel Hill, 1952), 294.

[12] In *Nixon v. Herndon*, 276 U.S. 536 (1927), the United States Supreme Court held against exclusion of Negroes from Texas primary elections. Texas altered its primary election laws, although still continuing to bar Negroes, but the Supreme Court again ruled against political white supremacy in *Nixon v. Condon*, 286 U.S. 73 (1932). Texas returned to the law offices and came up with yet another scheme both to satisfy the Court and to thwart Negro suffrage. This time the Court, in *Grovey v. Townsend*, 295 U.S. 45 (1935), acquiesced in Texas conniving and left Democratic elections to the white man. The respite was temporary, however, and the Court shifted back to the spirit of earlier decisions in *Smith v. Allwright*, 321 U.S. 664, which also originated in Texas. See additionally, *United States v. Classic*, 313 U.S. 299 (1941) and *Terry v. Adams*, 345 U.S. 461 (1953).

one million—approximately 20 percent of potential Negro registrants—
by 1952. After this the rate of increase fell by almost half. The estimated
1960 figure was 1,414,000, representing 28 percent of the Negro population of voting age. Since approximately 60 percent of white adults were
registered, Negroes represented less than 20 percent of total registration
in all southern states throughout the 1950's.[13]

Furthermore, not all Negro ballots went into opposition to the status
quo. In smaller cities and rural areas, the increasing Negro vote was
often absorbed into the existing local power structure. Lower-class
Negroes, Florida investigators found, were primarily interested in fair
and friendly law enforcement and in white laissez faire toward "impulse
freedom" in the Negro community. Middle-class Negroes were more
conscious of abstract considerations in voting, but they were also more
often open to economic reprisals from the white community.[14] Similar
conclusions resulted from a study of Negro voting in rural and semirural
East Texas.[15]

Nevertheless, Negroes were registering in the South, and in some
states they represented a significant vote. By 1956 more than 200,000
nonwhites were on the registration rolls of Texas, while both Georgia
and Louisiana had more than 150,000 and Florida and North Carolina
each numbered above 100,000.[16] This voting strength gave Negro leaders
influence, at least "in the private places where campaign strategy is
plotted,"[17] but in the Deep South the candidate favored by Negro voters
in a first primary faced the charge of being the NAACP candidate in a
second primary.

[13] Margaret Price, *The Negro Voter in the South* (Atlanta, 1957), 1–5; Price, *The Negro
and the Ballot in the South* (Atlanta, 1959); Donald R. Matthews and James W. Prothro,
"Negro Voter Registration in the South," in Allan P. Sindler (ed.), *Change in the Contemporary South* (Durham, 1963), 119–49. The latter is a good study of the decline in the
rate of Negro voter registration after 1952. After 1960 there was another upward spurt
in the rate of Negro voter registration. For recent figures, see Voter Education Project,
Southern Regional Council, *Voter Registration in the South: Summer, 1966* (Atlanta, 1966).
[14] Alfred B. Clubok, John M. DeGrove, and Charles D. Farris, "The Manipulated
Negro Vote: Some Preconditions and Consequences," *Journal of Politics*, XXVI (February,
1964), 112–29.
[15] James R. Soukup, Clifton McCleskey, and Harry Holloway, *Party and Factional
Division in Texas* (Austin, 1964), 108–26. Pat Watters and Reese Cleghorn, *Climbing
Jacob's Ladder: The Arrival of Negroes in Southern Politics* (New York, 1967), 331–58, is a
thoughtful discussion of the impact of Negro voting in the South; Donald R. Matthews
and James W. Prothro, *Negroes and the New Southern Politics* (New York, 1966), is an
in-depth analysis of this subject.
[16] Price, *The Negro Voter in the South*, 5.
[17] Harry S. Ashmore, *An Epitaph for Dixie* (New York, 1958), 23.

With growing Negro voting strength, Negro officeholders became increasingly less rare. In 1951 thirty nonwhites sought city political offices, and five were successful. In 1952, for the first time since Reconstruction, a Negro was elected to public office in Georgia, and in the following year Dr. Rufus Clement, president of Atlanta University, carried forty of Atlanta's fifty-eight precincts to win a place on the city school board.[18] Negro political strength was also demonstrated by the growing number of Negro policemen who patrolled newly paved streets in the Negro districts in an increasing number of southern cities.[19] Yet, Negro officeholding was entirely an urban phenomenon in the 1950's; state politics remained the white man's domain.

In June, 1951, for the first time in thirty-one years, the NAACP, undisputed leader of the Negro civil rights movement, held an annual meeting in the South. In Atlanta the legal strategy board promised delegates from forty-two states an all out attack on discrimination in all forms, with top priority on segregation in education.[20] Several months before, an NAACP-supported suit demanding equal public school facilities for Negro students in Clarendon County, South Carolina, had been dropped, and in its place had been substituted a suit attacking the separate but equal concept in public education.[21] By this time the legal fate of institutionalized white supremacy in the South was centered around the schools, and against a judicial background of *Sweatt* and *McLaurin*, public school segregation obviously faced a "clear and present danger."

These threats to white supremacy emerged during a period of economic and demographic change. Industry and mechanization were at last transforming southern society. In the black belts, where history had given the white man both cotton and Negroes to pick it, modern farm machinery, acreage allotments, and other factors were making cheap labor dispensable. The Negro population was moving to the cities—migrating to established industrial centers of the North or joining the general movement

---

[18] *New South*, October–November, 1952.

[19] John N. Popham, in *New York Times Magazine*, December 1, 1957. Most of the newspaper research for this study was done at the Southern Education Reporting Service in Nashville and the Southern Regional Council in Atlanta. These libraries identify news clippings only by date and newspaper. Stories from weekly newspaper magazines, like the *New York Times Magazine*, are filed in the same fashion. Consequently, newspaper references will be identified by newspaper and date only.

[20] New York *Times*, June 27, 1951.

[21] Howard H. Quint, *Profile in Black and White: A Frank Portrait of South Carolina* (Washington, 1958), 13.

toward urbanization in the South. Segregation had been the social organization for a staple-crop economy, but by 1950 almost half of all southerners lived in cities, and the income from industry and services dwarfed that from cotton and tobacco. These trends toward urbanization, industrialization, and rising per capita income in the South have been amply documented in a number of studies.[22]

Such changes were of obvious importance, but, at the same time, care should be taken not to exaggerate their immediate social and political significance. The South remained more rural in outlook than economic and demographic reality justified. Urbanization came late to the South. Sociologist Leonard Reissman has made a strong argument that not before 1940 did urbanization make a major impact on the region. "Prior to 1940," he stated, "the South could fairly be described, with one or two states excepted, as a predominantly rural region here and there dotted with cities," themselves to a considerable degree dependent economically on the agricultural economy.[23] Migration to the city did not blot out the rural backgrounds of many urban residents, particularly since the automobile—and consequently suburbia—came to the South before urbanization. There was a tendency for white migrants from the countryside to move "more or less directly from the older agrarian way of living to the new metropolitan way, without passing through the phase of centripetal urbanization which other parts of the nation have experienced. . . ."[24] Southerners were not only close to the land in point of time, but many of them moved from farm to housing development and thus circumvented the urbanizing process.

Growing per capita personal income, by 1950 just under 70 percent of the national average, represented a real rise in living standards. But

[22] Thomas D. Clark, *The Emerging South* (New York, 1961); John M. Maclachlan and Joe S. Floyd, Jr., *This Changing South* (Gainesville, Fla., 1956); John C. McKinney and Edgar T. Thompson (eds.), *The South in Continuity and Change* (Durham, 1965); Hammer and Company, *Post-War Industrial Development in the South* (Atlanta, 1956); William H. Nicholls, *Southern Tradition and Regional Progress* (Chapel Hill, 1960); Melvin L. Greenhut and W. Tate Whitman (eds.), *Essays in Southern Economic Development* (Chapel Hill, 1964); Rupert B. Vance and Nicholas J. Demerath (eds.), *The Urban South* (Chapel Hill, 1954); Joseph J. Spengler, "Demographic and Economic Change in the South, 1940–1960," in Sindler (ed.), *Change in the Contemporary South*, 26–63.

[23] Leonard Reissman, "Urbanization in the South," in McKinney and Thompson (eds.), *The South in Continuity and Change*, 79. Other studies, however, have stressed the long-term growth of southern urbanization. For example, see generally Vance and Demerath (eds.), *The Urban South*. On the persistence of rural attitudes, see Alfred O. Hero, Jr., *The Southerner and World Affairs* (Baton Rouge, 1965), 317, *passim*.

[24] Maclachlan and Floyd, *This Changing South*, 44.

it also resulted in part from the fact that the South was exporting its poverty to the rest of the nation. John M. Maclachlan and Joe S. Floyd, in their intensive study of census data, found a close correlation between increases in per capita income and out-migration.[25] People from poorer southern states were moving in vast numbers to more prosperous areas. By 1960 almost ten million southern-born men and women resided outside the region.[26] The South suffered its greatest net-migration losses among both the best educated and the least educated as the North and West attracted substantial numbers of college trained southerners (especially the young and the nonwhite) and greater numbers of poorly educated citizens (many of whom were the human byproducts of the mechanization of southern agriculture and the breakdown of the farm-tenancy system).[27] Jack Patterson of *Business Week* has recently noted that "since about 1945 Mississippi's gains in total income have actually lagged behind the nation; it has improved its position in per capita income only because of its declining population."[28]

A considerable proportion of the South's manufacturing growth was in "soft" industries with low capital-labor ratios and relatively low wages. The apparel, textile, food service, and lumber industries accounted for almost half of all new factories constructed in the South during the post-World War II decade.[29] Approximately 50 percent of southern manufacturing workers labored in industries that ranked in the five lowest of the twenty census-of-manufacturing categories based on value added per employee.[30] Economist Joseph J. Spengler has pointed out that

[25] *Ibid.*, 108, 112. This tendency was also apparent within the region. Southerners moved from poorer states to the wealthier states of Texas, Florida, and Virginia.

[26] C. Horace Hamilton, "Continuity and Change in Southern Migration," in McKinney and Thompson (eds.), *The South in Continuity and Change*, 59. This figure is based on the U.S. Bureau of the Census definition of the South, which includes seventeen states.

[27] James H. Street, *The New Revolution in the Cotton Economy: Mechanization and Its Consequences* (Chapel Hill, 1957), 175-251.

[28] Jack Patterson, "Business Response to the Negro Movement," *New South*, XXI (Winter, 1966), 73.

[29] Hammer and Company, *Post-War Industrial Development in the South*, 7–18. This study, conducted by Hammer and Company for the Southern Regional Council, surveyed all new industrial facilities employing more than twenty-five workers built in the South during the period January 1, 1946, to December 31, 1955. The South here is defined as Kentucky and all the former Confederate states except Florida.

[30] These industries—apparel, textiles, leather, lumber, and furniture—accounted for less than one-fifth of nonsouthern manufacturing employment. U.S. Senate, 84th Cong., 2nd Sess., *Selected Materials on the Economy of the South: Report of the Committee on Banking and Currency* (Washington, 1956), 20. In this study, the South included Kentucky and all the former Confederate states except Texas.

"textiles, apparel, and lumber, among the six lowest-paid manufacturing industries in the South, accounted for about 45 percent of all employment in southern manufacturing in 1954."[31] The annual weekly pay check drawn by a southern nonagricultural worker was approximately 25 percent less than that collected by a nonsouthern employee.[32] Nevertheless, such jobs were relatively lucrative compared to average farm earnings and contributed to the rise in regional per capita income.

Southerners enjoyed an increasing prosperity, but, at the same time, rising per capita income was, in part, a result of the export of numerous lower-class citizens and of poor southerners taking low-paying and low-status factory jobs that improved their incomes without significantly changing their relative social position. The out-migration of young, college educated southerners represented a drain on the region's potential leadership that was only partly compensated by in-migration. These factors combined with the persistence of rural attitudes to mitigate the impact of urbanization and industrialization on the southern social system. They suggested an essentially unrevolutionary side to the sweeping changes taking place in the South.

The environment, ideology, and legal basis for segregation were disappearing; yet white southerners were by no means reconciled to basic alterations in the pattern of race relations. Clinging to past ideas of Dixie customs and traditions, southern whites had changed their racial attitudes and practices very little in terms of day-to-day relationships. And, as Professor James W. Vander Zanden has concluded, "culture, more particularly social norms, is a crucial factor in understanding prejudice and discrimination."[33]

The most intensive examination of white "resistance and readiness" with respect to desegregation during the 1950's was undertaken by Melvin M. Tumin and his associates at Princeton University. Working in Guilford County, North Carolina, which contains the city of Greensboro, the Tumin group chose a locality clearly above the state and regional norm in such things as per capita income and educational attainment. Their study then presumably reflected the viewpoint of southerners living

[31] Joseph J. Spengler, "Southern Economic Trends and Prospects," in McKinney and Thompson (eds.), *The South in Continuity and Change*, 116. Spengler defined the South as the former Confederate states and Kentucky. See also E. William Noland, "Technological Change and the Social Order," in *ibid.*, 167–97.

[32] U.S. Senate, 84th Cong., 2nd Sess., *Selected Materials on the Economy of the South*, 25.

[33] James W. Vander Zanden, *American Minority Relations: The Sociology of Race and Ethnic Groups* (2nd ed.; New York, 1966), 75.

in a more enlightened community. The results of their work, in terms of future civil rights progress, were not very heartening.

The image of the Negro held by the majority of whites pictured a basically inferior being. Almost 73 percent of those interviewed felt that Negroes possessed a less fully developed sense of responsibility than whites. Between 65 and 70 percent found them lacking in morality and ambition, while, perhaps most significant of all, just a fraction under 60 percent believed Negroes inferior to whites in intelligence. Fifty percent of the sampled Guilford County's white citizenry found Negroes beneath Caucasian levels in all four categories—intelligence, ambition, morality, and responsibility—while under 17 percent found them inferior in none.[34]

White preference for segregation followed naturally from these attitudes. Over 75 percent favored separate facilities in public education. When white respondents were asked what action they would take if schools were desegregated, 77.30 percent would amend the United States Constitution, 55.55 percent favored withholding state funds from integrating schools, 43.46 percent wanted to close the schools, and 24.82 percent would use force to prevent the change. Only 17.49 percent were amenable to desegregation without protest.[35]

Another team of researchers probed southern white attitudes in an attempt to determine, among other things, the relative percentages of segregationists, moderates, and integrationists. The substantial majority —64 percent—of Caucasian southerners favored "strict segregation," while only 7 percent expressed a preference for integration. The moderates, those in favor of "something in between," made up 28 percent of the white population.[36] This sampling was undertaken in the early 1960's after some of the emotionalism of massive resistance had ended, at least outside Mississippi and Alabama.

Public opinion polls supported the general findings of the researchers. In 1956 the American Institute of Public Opinion surveyed the feelings of southern whites toward the Supreme Court decision invalidating the

[34] Melvin M. Tumin and others, *Desegregation: Resistance and Readiness* (Princeton, 1958), 34–36. A Southwide survey undertaken in the 1960's confirmed the Tumin group's findings. Louis Harris and his associates discovered that 60 percent of white southerners felt "Negroes have less native intelligence" than whites, and 57 percent agreed to the statement that "Negroes are inferior to whites." William Brink and Louis Harris, *The Negro Revolution in America* (New York, 1964), 140–41.

[35] Tumin, *Desegregation*, 37–46.

[36] Donald R. Matthews and James W. Prothro, "Southern Racial Attitudes: Conflict, Awareness, and Political Change," *Annals of the American Academy of Political and Social Science*, CCCXLIV (November, 1962), 110.

separate but equal formula in public education. The poll found 16 percent approving the decision and 80 percent expressing disapproval. The five states of the Deep South—Georgia, Alabama, Louisiana, Mississippi, and South Carolina—were most united in opposition to school desegregation, with nine out of ten white people disapproving and only one out of seventeen favoring. Outside the southern heartland the percentage expressing approval went up. In Virginia, Arkansas, North Carolina, and Florida, about 20 percent of the white population was favorably disposed toward desegregation, while almost one out of four members of the white citizenry of Texas and Tennessee, as well as Kentucky and Oklahoma, expressed approval of the decision.[37] In numerous polls soliciting the opinion of both white and black southerners, the percentage indicating disapproval of desegregation hovered around 70 percent, while that showing a favorable response fluctuated around 20 percent.[38]

The growth of an urban, impersonal, and dynamic society in the South could hardly avoid undermining eventually a social system that was essentially static.[39] The decline of intellectual theories supporting racism was having its influence on southern attitudes. The long-term trend in public opinion in the South as elsewhere in the nation was clearly toward a growing acceptance of desegregation and an erosion of unfavorable images for the Negro.[40] This situation lent a certain credibility to proponents of gradualism. Long conditioned to stress patience and slow change, southern intellectual liberals found some cause for optimism in the post-World War II era. "A halcyon period for the exponents of gradualism," Hodding Carter III described it.[41] The most distinguished spokesman for gradualism, William Faulkner, both in the character Gavin Stevens in *Intruder in the Dust* and in public statements, developed the theme: "A few of us realize that segregation is going, but the job should be accomplished by choice from within the South."[42]

[37] Birmingham *News*, February 29, 1956.

[38] The Gallup Poll released in October, 1957, gives the results of the first seven surveys of this nature. *Ibid.*, October 6, 1957. An increasing majority of Negro southerners approved the *Brown* decision. *Ibid.*, December 3, 1957.

[39] See Henry Allen Bullock, "Urbanism and Race Relations," in Vance and Demerath (eds.), *The Urban South*, 207–29.

[40] Herbert H. Hyman and Paul B. Sheatsley, "Attitudes Toward Desegregation," *Scientific American*, CXCV (December, 1956), 35–39; Hyman and Sheatsley, "Attitudes Toward Desegregation," *ibid.*, CCXI (July, 1964), 2–9; Sheatsley, "White Attitudes Toward the Negro," *Daedalus*, XCV (Winter, 1966), 217–38.

[41] Hodding Carter III, *The South Strikes Back* (Garden City, 1959), 12. Myrdal, *An American Dilemma*, I, 461–73, is an excellent discussion of traditional southern liberalism.

[42] As quoted in Atlanta *Journal*, March 19, 1956.

Whatever the long-range advantages of social justice by commitment, the immediate prospects for gradualism were disheartening. As suggested earlier, the changes taking place in the South were of a less revolutionary nature than statistics implied. Furthermore, most of the factors relied upon to produce an improved racial climate in the white South—advancing education, prosperity, urbanization, communications—were less influential than had been hoped. Education, for example, had been shown to be directly correlated with racial tolerance; but not until a white southerner had gone beyond high school were the odds better than 1 in 3 that he would be other than a "strict segregationist."[43] Similarly, while a rural southerner was somewhat more likely to be a segregationist than a city dweller, "the fact that one works in a factory or on a farm proved . . . to be of little significance."[44] Improved occupational status and income were positively related to pro-integration sentiment, and the rising and prosperous urban middle class was less likely to be committed deeply to segregation.[45] Yet the southern nonfarm middle class still displayed far more nativistic views on race relations than did its socioeconomic peers outside the southern region.[46] Some evidence further suggested that latent intolerance among the affluent was greater than opinion polls reflected.[47] Sociologist James W. Vander Zanden has clearly demonstrated that racial toleration among those of higher socio-economic standing was not always mirrored by precinct voting returns.[48] The strength of the South's emerging prosperity as a force toward racial justice could be exaggerated. Other factors, such as a declining percentage of Negroes in relation to total white population and increasing mobility, made only limited inroads on segregationist attitudes. Finally, the entrenchment of "the white man's sense of group position," the tendency toward rigidity of the group status quo, pulled against more flexible racial patterns.[49]

[43] Matthews and Prothro, "Southern Racial Attitudes," 113–14. See also Matthews and Prothro, "Negro Voter Registration in the South," 135, and Tumin, *Desegregation*, 100.

[44] Tumin, *Desegregation*, 9. Indeed, some evidence suggests that white members of the southern working class were more likely than southern white farmers to hold extreme pro-segregation views. See Sheatsley, "White Attitudes Toward the Negro," 226.

[45] Tumin, *Desegregation*, 75, 80.

[46] Sheatsley, "White Attitudes Toward the Negro," 226.

[47] Charles H. Stember, *Education and Attitude Change: The Effect of Schooling on Prejudice Against Minority Groups* (New York, 1961).

[48] James W. Vander Zanden, *Race Relations in Transition: The Segregation Crisis in the South* (New York, 1965), 100–17.

[49] Lewis Killian and Charles Grigg, *Racial Crisis in America: Leadership in Conflict* (Englewood Cliffs, 1964), 111.

Most white southerners were displeased with the prospects of desegregation, and there were obviously significant degrees of displeasure.
Generally, the Caucasian South could have been divided into three
broad categories of roughly equal strength. At one extreme were the
bitter-end segregationists. Professor Tumin and his associates found that
this group, "those who would use force" to prevent social change, composed 25 percent of white society. At the other end of white population
were the moderates—those who did not favor integration but who also
had no dogmatic commitment to segregation. and thus were willing to
compromise—and the small minority of racial liberals, who approved
integration. The combined moderates and liberals numbered about one-
third of the white population, although if given a choice between segregation and desegregation, not all would have chosen the latter. Finally,
in the middle, the largest group of whites was committed to "strict
segregation," but its members did not necessarily place racial matters
at the top of their scale of values. In the politics of race and massive
resistance during the 1950's, when it seemed to lay observers that the
white South might succeed in turning back the tide of foreign ideas and
alien court decisions, this group largely supported the defenders of white
supremacy. Yet the middle was amenable to aggressive leadership and
thus could be swayed from complete resistance. More important, as events
proved, a considerable number of segregationists were unwilling in the
end to tear apart the fabric of southern society and commit the region
to anarchy in defense of segregation.[50]

---

[50] The size and diversity of the South make broad generalizations difficult. In many
areas the size of the middle group would have been larger than indicated here. The
Tumin group, summarizing the results of its Guilford County study, stated: "There are
roughly the same percentages at both extremes: on the one side, those who would use
force to prevent desegregation, and on the other those who would do nothing to impede
desegregation, or perhaps would even act to facilitate such desegregation. In between
stand the large majority, those who view desegregation as undesirable but do not seem
prepared actively to impede the process." Tumin, *Desegregation*, 151. Thus, after Virginia
closed the white public high schools in Norfolk to avoid desegregation, a substantial
majority of Norfolk's white citizens favored reopening the schools even on a desegregated
basis. A research team from the University of North Carolina Institute for Research in
Social Science found that approximately 25 percent of white respondents in the city
were "unyielding" segregationists who preferred closed schools to desegregated schools
while some 15 percent positively favored desegregation. Almost 60 percent fell into the
"practical" response category, expressing a preference for segregation "but not if it
means closing the schools." Ernest Q. Campbell with the assistance of Charles E.
Bowerman and Daniel O. Price, *When a City Closes Its Schools* (Chapel Hill, 1960), 56–57.
See also Robert Coles, *The Desegregation of Southern Schools: A Psychiatric Study* (Anti-
Defamation League pamphlet issued by the Southern Regional Council, 1963), 9.

The South at mid-century exemplified the sociological concept of "cultural lag." The southern environment was changing substantially more rapidly than southern attitudes. Most white southerners—whether because of commitment, inertia, or an exaggerated concern over morals, crime and syphilis rates, and intellectual attainment—continued to approve of segregation even though the region was undergoing economic and demographic changes that demanded social adjustments. The North, moreover, had resumed its role as protector of the nation's black minority. Outside intervention and environmental transition too swift for the southern social system to assimilate set the stage for political reaction.

Racial issues dominated southern politics during the 1950's as they had not done for half a century. As Harold C. Fleming, past executive director of the Southern Regional Council, described the southern political mood: "Racial antagonism is a ready outlet for the fears and frustrations bred by economic and social upheaval. The old isolation has broken down, leaving the South unprotected against the influx of people and ideas alien to its once impervious way of life. Seeking to hold on to the familiar, to a sense of continuing identity, many a white Southerner has rallied to the call for solidarity on the segregation issue."[51] Capitalizing on this atmosphere, opponents of southern social and ideological innovation launched a determined program of "massive resistance."

The politicians and political activists who led the massive resistance campaign will be referred to in these pages as neobourbons. Their social, economic, and political outlook was in the tradition of nineteenth century bourbonism, and, as an earlier generation of bourbons sought to end the First Reconstruction, neobourbons strove to crush the Second Reconstruction. Leadership for the massive resistance movement came once again, as it had in past racial crises, from the black belt, and the whites of this area provided neobourbon democracy with its most solid phalanx of support.[52] Neobourbonism was by no means confined to a black-belt habitat, however; it enjoyed support generally in rural areas, especially the small towns and county seats. It also showed varying degrees of strength in the cities, particularly those with an Old South heritage (such as Charleston, New Orleans, Montgomery, and Jackson) and those

[51] *New York Times Magazine*, April 3, 1960.

[52] The term "black belt" is used loosely in this work to designate the belt of rich land and high relative Negro population stretching across the South from Tidewater Virginia to eastern Texas. A number of generalizations made in this paragraph and in later paragraphs in this chapter will be detailed and more fully documented in later chapters.

with special economic and corporate interests that had long-standing business-plantation ties (such as Birmingham and Shreveport).

As the chief beneficiary of malapportionment in state legislatures, bourbon democracy enjoyed an enormous competitive advantage in the conflict for control of the destiny of the South. In every southern state rural and small-town areas generally and black-belt voters specifically were over-represented in at least one house of the legislature. In Alabama some 28 percent of the people elected a majority in both the state senate and the house of representatives, with sixteen black-belt counties containing 13.5 percent of the people electing approximately 28 percent of the lawmakers.[53] Twenty percent of Florida's citizens in 1950 selected a legislative majority; by 1960 only some 14 percent were required. The area most over-represented was rural northern Florida, with its black-belt heritage.[54] Georgia not only loaded the legislature in favor of rural areas, but, with its county unit system, even weighted the votes of small-county citizens in statewide elections. In 1960 Georgia's 121 smaller counties, containing a third of the state's population, could nominate a governor with county unit votes to spare.[55] These figures were based on total population; the fact that most black-belt Negroes did not vote added further weight to the rural white man's ballot.

Black-belt legislators also enjoyed longer tenure than other lawmakers. For various reasons, including the limited number of voters and the lack of a democratic tradition, low-country solons accumulated seniority and prestige that added to their influence. In Virginia, for example, the average tenure for a member of the General Assembly was 8.2 years; for black-belt legislators, it was 12 years.[56] In a study of South Carolina, Ernest M. Lander observed that in 1954 the senate had thirty-three standing committees, twenty-five of which were presided over by low-country chairmen. The four senators representing Dorchester, Bamberg,

[53] James L. Larson, *Reapportionment in Alabama* (University, Ala., 1955), 24–25; Patrick E. McCauley, "Be It Enacted," in Don Shoemaker (ed.), *With All Deliberate Speed: Segregation-Desegregation in Southern Schools* (New York, 1957), 134–36. Malapportionment was, of course, a national rather than a peculiarly southern problem. See Paul T. David and Ralph Eisenberg, *Devaluation of the Urban and Suburban Vote: A Statistical Investigation of Long-Term Trends in State Legislative Representation* (Charlottesville, 1961), and Gordon Baker, *Rural Versus Urban Political Power: The Nature and Consequences of Unbalanced Representation* (Garden City, 1955).

[54] H. D. Price, *The Negro and Southern Politics: A Chapter of Florida History* (New York, 1957), 103–106; William C. Havard and Loren P. Beth, *The Politics of Mis-Representation: Rural-Urban Conflict in the Florida Legislature* (Baton Rouge, 1962), 43.

[55] Louis T. Rigdon II, *Georgia's County Unit System* (Decatur, Ga., 1961), 40.

[56] McCauley, "Be It Enacted," 134–36.

Berkeley, and Darlington, four black-belt counties having no city larger than 10,000, held fifteen chairmanships. The five senators representing counties containing Greenville, Charleston, Spartanburg, Columbia, and Anderson, the state's largest cities, swung nary a gavel.[57]

While not all rural legislators by any means were neobourbons (though black-belt members frequently were), the dynamics of the system tended strongly to strengthen bourbon influence. Professor Dewey W. Grantham has explained: "Adverse economic and demographic forces have baffled and frustrated many rural people, exacerbating their fears of social change and their bitter hostility toward the city. Their declining economic and social status has made them more than ever the great conservators of the South's traditions, and they have lost much of the economic radicalism that once made them the cutting edge of southern reform."[58] "The political South," as a South Carolina author put it, "is far more conservative than are Southerners themselves."[59]

A student of Arkansas politics characterized the planter-banker-merchant mercantile alliance that dominated the political as well as the social, economic, and religious life of the Arkansas southeastern low country in these terms: "It is suspicious of 'progress,' liberal education, Yankees . . .; warns of the threat to state's rights; denounces 'creeping socialism' and the federal bureaucracy; laments the passing of Southern civilization based on cotton and caste; and bemoans the increasing impotency of the South in national politics."[60] This description would apply generally to much of the leadership of the black-belt South, and, with the addition of an element of militancy, would summarize the aims of neobourbonism. Fundamentally, proponents of this doctrine sought to suppress the social and ideological aspects of southern change.

Since the predominant mood in the South during the 1950's leaned toward social reaction, the neobourbons were able to capture the initiative in southern politics and launch their massive resistance program. For a time it seemed, incredibly enough, that they would succeed in annihilating

[57] Ernest McPherson Lander, Jr., *A History of South Carolina, 1865–1960* (Chapel Hill, 1960), 194–95.

[58] Dewey W. Grantham, Jr., *The Democratic South* (Athens, Ga., 1963), 88. A number of the observations made in the following paragraphs were suggested by this work.

[59] Henry Savage, Jr., *Seeds of Time: The Background of Southern Thinking* (New York, 1959), 267.

[60] Boyce Alexander Drummond, Jr., "Arkansas Politics: A Study of a One-Party System" (Ph.D. dissertation, University of Chicago, 1957), 8. For a fuller discussion of the neobourbon rationale, see Chapter 13.

opposition at home and rolling back Yankee versions of morality and progress from abroad.

The neobourbon bid for leadership was not, however, to go unchallenged. As in the past, the "Solid South" was divided. At the risk of oversimplification, the opponents of neobourbonism might be structured into two broad groups. One of these was in the rural-liberal tradition and will be termed neopopulist; the other was in the "New South" tradition and will be referred to as business conservative. Many, perhaps most, southern politicians did not, of course, fit precisely and neatly into such simple patterns; yet, broadly speaking, the main currents of southern politics, particularly as they affected racial issues, revolved around the three doctrines of neobourbonism, neopopulism, and business conservatism. While this study will be primarily concerned with the proponents of massive resistance and thus with the neobourbons, the other major political groups that competed for control of southern policy can by no means be ignored.

Neopopulism represented broadly the same creed that had traditionally —though sporadically—done battle with bourbon concepts of good government. Heir to the scalawag-populist heritage of rural radicalism, neopopulism rested not so much on an articulated philosophy as upon a proclivity toward agrarian individualism and democracy and a feeling of sympathy for the underdog. It was basically "a sort of frontier independence with an inclination to defend liberty and to bait the interests."[61] It manifested an intense dedication to rural democracy, carried sometimes to the point of hostility toward bureaucracy and administrative law.[62] This devotion to democracy frequently extended across color lines, and neopopulist leaders tended to be "conscience Democrats" on racial matters and to favor "bread and butter" issues at the expense of white supremacy. Their lower-class white following was avidly nativist in attitude, however, and this divergence created severe political problems for a number of neopopulist leaders.[63] The neopopulist outlook, as

[61] V. O. Key, Jr., with the assistance of Alexander Heard, *Southern Politics in State and Nation* (New York, 1959), 36. Key was referring here to Alabama.

[62] Ellis Gibbs Arnall, *The Shore Dimly Seen* (New York, 1946), 276. This book is perhaps the best statement of the rural-liberal outlook. W. Bradley Twitty, *Y'All Come* (Nashville, 1962), an uncritical biography of Alabama Governor James E. Folsom, and A. J. Liebling, *The Earl of Louisiana* (New York, 1961), a colorful journalistic portrayal of Governor Earl K. Long, capture the mood of southern neopopulism.

[63] On this point, see Chapter 15. On lower-class white racism, see Seymour Martin Lipset, "Democracy and Working-Class Authoritarianism," *American Sociological Review*, XXIV (August, 1959), 482–501, and Hero, *The Southerner and World Affairs*, 389–93.

William C. Havard and Loren P. Beth noted in their description of "the rural populist" in the Florida legislature, was influenced "by a feeling of personal sympathy with the unfortunate and some recognition of the necessity for governmental intervention to redress the balance of economic forces."[64] Such attitudes led neopopulists to advocate programs aimed toward the achievement of social justice and the alleviation of rural poverty. But on the state level these programs not infrequently centered around higher old-age pensions, veterans' bonuses, free lunches and textbooks for school children, farm-to-market roads, public hospitals, and higher teachers' salaries rather than around solutions to the more fundamental problems of a region faced with runaway urbanization, threatened with automation without having fully acquired the skills necessary to primitive industrialization, and torn by deep social problems. Neopopulists normally showed limited enthusiasm for problems of labor unions and slum dwellers although the urban common man, like his country cousin, often benefited from their programs.[65] Additionally, neopopulism displayed an antimonopoly-oriented hostility to economic and financial concentration, a preference for the decentralized free enterprise of a farmer and small-town tradesman variety, and a tendency toward isolationism.[66] In national politics neopopulists generally supported the national Democratic Party.

Neopopulism was native to the rural South, normally the hill country, where Negroes were few and racial concerns less immediate. This was particularly true in Alabama and Louisiana, where the northern Alabama and central Louisiana hills sheltered resurrected populism in its most genuine form.[67] The tight Republican hold on hill-country voter loyalty in Tennessee, Virginia, and North Carolina diluted neopopulist support in these areas, although occasional leaders like Senator Estes Kefauver of Tennessee managed to kindle the flames of political insurgency. In

[64] Havard and Beth, *The Politics of Mis-Representation*, 112.

[65] Allan P. Sindler, *Huey Long's Louisiana: State Politics, 1920–1952* (Baltimore, 1956), 262; Stan Opotowsky, *The Longs of Louisiana* (New York, 1960), 154; Murray Clark Havens, *City Versus Farm?: Urban-Rural Conflict in the Alabama Legislature* (Tuscaloosa, 1957), 9–19; Twitty, *Y'All Come*, 37–39, *passim;* Soukup, McCleskey, and Holloway, *Party and Factional Division in Texas*, 6–13; Arnall, *The Shore Dimly Seen*, 116.

[66] Opotowsky, *The Longs of Louisiana*, 166–67; Twitty, *Y'All Come*, 138ff.; Soukup, McCleskey, and Holloway, *Party and Factional Division in Texas*, 6–7; Arnall, *The Shore Dimly Seen*, 138, 276.

[67] Key, *Southern Politics*, 36–57, 156–82. On the voting tendencies of hill-country whites, see also Thomas F. Pettigrew and Ernest Q. Campbell, "Faubus and Segregation: An Analysis of Arkansas Voting," *Public Opinion Quarterly*, XXIV (Spring, 1960), 436–47.

style, neopopulists projected a rural, common-man image, and their
campaign techniques often bordered on rabble-rousing, whether expressed by a coonskin cap or a hillbilly band. The declining population
in rural counties and the growing influence of urban voters in statewide
elections forced neopopulist politicians to devote attention to urban
voters, however, and more sophisticated proponents of this creed in the
upper South, Kefauver and Senator Ralph W. Yarborough of Texas,
for example, enjoyed considerable success in broadening the urban base
of their support.[68] In the Deep South neopopulism was sometimes associated with "Buccaneering Liberalism," which included use of the spoils
system, favoritism in assigning state contracts and making state pur-
chases, and haphazard administration.[69]

The business conservatives represented a rising force in southern
politics. The principal adherents of this creed were the urban middle
class, the metropolitan, suburban, larger town business and professional
people who varied little in residence, occupation, and—with only a
modest differential—income from national standards. As indicated earlier,
members of this group tended to be segregationists, more so perhaps than
opinion polls indicated. But they showed signs of having been influenced
by the modern intellectual redefinition of human equality and by their
urban environment. They rarely defended segregation on the basis of
Negro inferiority nor showed a willingness to battle for white supremacy
much beyond pocketbook dictates. Middle-class urbanites, as one student
of southern opinion put it, "tended also to be rather indifferent, for they
were neither in competition with the Negro nor directly responsible for
him."[70] More numerous in the peripheral South than in the Deep South,
business conservatives were apt during periods of racial turmoil to join
with Negro voters in opposition to white supremacy extremism.[71]

"Good government" was the business conservative's political ideal.

---

[68] On Yarborough, see Soukup, McCleskey, and Holloway, *Party and Factional Division
in Texas*, 101–102. Kefauver, in his successful bid for the Democratic nomination in the
1948 senatorial primary election, ran best in the hill–country region north and east of
Chattanooga. There was a general similarity between his vote and the Republican
presidential vote of the same year. Kefauver in later elections greatly expanded his base
of voter support.
[69] See generally Sindler's discussion of the Long faction in his *Huey Long's Louisiana*.
[70] Hero, *The Southerner and World Affairs*, 393.
[71] For example, see Corinne Silverman, *The Little Rock Story* (Rev. ed.; University,
Ala., 1959), 36–38; Norman I. Lustig, "The Relationship Between Demographic
Characteristics and Pro-Integration Vote of White Precincts in a Metropolitan Southern
Community," *Social Forces*, XI (March, 1962), 205–208; and Samuel Lubell, *White
and Black: Test of a Nation* (New York, 1964), 72–77.

THE SOUTH AT MID-CENTURY

This meant honest, efficient, institutionalized government that contributed to a favorable business climate. The conviction that the South's future was the factory lay near the business conservative's heart. Former North Carolina Governor Luther H. Hodges explained in his *A Businessman in the Statehouse:* "Industrialization, then, with all its advantages to the people and to the state, became the number one goal of my administration."[72] To achieve this aim business conservative leaders planned, prepared, and propagandized, devoting part of their terms in office to "industry hunting" tours of the Northeast and even Europe. Essentially, business conservatives sought to apply sound business practices to government and to achieve a good business atmosphere for industrial development.[73]

The basic business conservative ethic was pecuniary, and his primary loyalty was to business.[74] These values were sometimes translated into political attitudes that were very conservative indeed. Broadly applicable to a great many members of the urban middle class was Professor Norman L. Parks's characterization of these elements in Memphis, Tennessee: "Many are incased in the old Bourbon insensitivity to social responsibility. Low income groups are seen as hopeless incompetents or ambitionless loafers recklessly sustained by welfare programs and surplus commodity distribution. The drive and self-sufficiency of the new middle class should not be burdened to support such programs."[75] Business conservatives sometimes showed a distinct antilabor bias and an excessive concern for governmental economy.[76]

Yet the urban middle-class political tradition included a significant strain of Progressivism. Professor George B. Tindall has examined the evolution of pre-World War I southern Progressivism into a more business

[72] Luther H. Hodges, *Businessman in the Statehouse: Six Years as Governor of North Carolina* (Chapel Hill, 1962), 32.

[73] Leslie W. Dunbar raised the rather interesting question: "Southern governors have become the de facto executive directors of the state chamber of commerce, and spend their time competing with each other as supplicants for new plants. We have talked of state socialism and state capitalism, but what do we call governments whose chief affair it is to entice and propitiate business?" "The Changing Mind of the South: The Exposed Nerve," 20. The best statement of the business conservative outlook is Hodges, *Businessman in the Statehouse,* and the best critique is Havard and Beth, *The Politics of Mis-Representation,* 113ff.

[74] Robert J. Steamer, "Southern Disaffection with the National Democratic Party," in Sindler (ed.), *Change in the Contemporary South,* 153.

[75] Norman L. Parks, "Tennessee Politics Since Kefauver and Reece: A 'Generalist' View," *Journal of Politics,* XXVIII (February, 1966), 153.

[76] See, for example, Marian D. Irish, "Political Thought and Political Behavior in the South," *Western Political Quarterly,* XIII (June, 1960), 407–409.

oriented creed that retained its attachment to governmental efficiency
and "the public service concept of government."[77] Business conservatism
of the 1950's was heir to this "business progressivism" of the 1920's. Not
infrequently, business conservative leaders advanced programs of a
moderately reformist nature, particularly when dealing with urban
problems. Such business conservative spokesmen as the Atlanta *Constitution*
and former Governor LeRoy Collins of Florida exemplified the progressive side of business conservatism.

In style business conservatives were often " 'Chamber of Commerce'
types—smooth, outwardly sophisticated, skilled in the modern political
techniques of radio and television."[78] In state politics they were the major
spokesmen for southern cities and frequently did battle for reapportionment, constitutional reform, distribution of state funds on the basis of
population, and other normally hopeless causes. Rural control of the
legislative process not only thwarted urban desires, but in practice it led
city solons to cooperate with the leadership that existed, thus stultifying
the formation of legislative "urban blocs."[79] Apart from homestate
political considerations, some members of this type were concerned about
the national image of the South and strove to salvage an element of
dignity in race relations. This often meant walking a tight rope between
presenting a national image free of bigotry and a home profile that
demonstrated sufficient concern for segregation.[80] In national politics,
business conservative leaders were usually loyal to the national Democratic
Party; their followers frequently voted Republican in presidential races.[81]

Absent from this list of "types"—perhaps noticeably so—were liberals
and independents. Both existed, of course, but their numbers were small
and their influence slight. Independent, using the term narrowly to

[77] George B. Tindall, "Business Progressivism: Southern Politics in the Twenties,"
South Atlantic Quarterly, LXII (Winter, 1963), 93. See also Grantham, *The Democratic
South*, 52ff.

[78] Havard and Beth, *The Politics of Mis-Representation*, 28.

[79] Malcolm E. Jewell, "State Legislatures in Southern Politics," *Journal of Politics*,
XXVI (February, 1964), 188.

[80] See, for example, the report of a strategy conference between Tennessee Governor
Frank G. Clement and his advisors by Fred Travis, in Chattanooga *Times*, November 20,
1956. The central question taken up by the Clement forces at this top-level conference
concerned this issue, i.e., whether the governor should attempt to broaden his Tennessee
following by taking a more positive prosegregation position or whether he should seek
to further his national image by maintaining his moderate position on race relations.

[81] For example, see James W. Prothro, Ernest Q. Campbell, and Charles M. Grigg,
"Two-Party Voting in the South: Class vs. Party Identification," *American Political
Science Review*, LII (March, 1958), 131–39; and Price, *The Negro and Southern Politics:
A Chapter of Florida History*, 88, 100–103.

describe an emancipated intellect and a tendency to visualize problems and programs in long-term perspective, generally described a few leading southern politicians like Senators J. William Fulbright of Arkansas and Albert Gore of Tennessee and Representatives Frank E. Smith of Mississippi and Brooks Hays of Arkansas. Although rarely engaging in racial demagoguery, politicians of this type generally avoided unpopular positions on social issues and directed their attention toward other matters.

The absence of a genuine liberal alternative on the race issue was a signal void in southern politics. The South simply lacked an adequate institutional foundation for a viable liberalism. Basic elements of the New Deal coalition did not exist, and, as political analyst Samuel Lubell has observed, "the dominant trends of economic change were operating to make the South more conservative rather than more liberal politically."[82] The region had no ethnic-religious minority with a liberal Democratic voting tradition.[83] The section had virtually no tradition of urban "machine" politics to stabilize the political process. Southern labor unions, by and large, lacked the strength and influence, and sometimes even the will, to provide an organizational framework for a politics oriented toward economics rather than race.[84] Lower-class whites formed a mainstay of the national Democratic Party's support in the South during the 1950's, and neopopulist politicians sought to appeal to these voters, as well as to Negroes, with programs oriented toward the less affluent. But the lower-class white voters' lack of organizational unity and their devotion to white supremacy made them an uncertain element in southern politics and pulled against the effective expression of the mutual economic interests of poor whites and poor Negroes. Southern business and professional people generally "identified the South's economic future with the interests of business,"[85] thus largely isolating the South's intellectual liberals. Rural-urban cleavages, the threat of de-

[82] Lubell, *White and Black*, 69. See also Lubell's *The Future of American Politics* (2nd ed. rev.; Garden City, 1965), 107–28, and his *Revolt of the Moderates* (New York, 1956), 178–202.

[83] It is probably significant that the San Antonio-South Texas area, with its substantial Latin American minority, and Miami, with its large Jewish population, produced outstanding examples of liberalism during the 1950's. Henry B. Gonzalez, Maury Maverick, Jr., and John B. Orr, Jr., among others, represented parts of these districts. The other major example of a large non-Negro minority was the Louisiana Catholics, whose Old South tradition inclined them to behave in a manner not unlike other Deep South residents.

[84] See Chapter 16.

[85] Lubell, *White and Black*, 69. On this point, see W. J. Cash, *The Mind of the South* (reprint; Garden City, 1954), 415–19.

segregation, and the continuing urban cultural invasion of the countryside undermined liberalism and heightened concern for white supremacy in rural areas.

The lack of an institutionalized two party system contributed substantially to the unstructured nature of southern politics, complicating the election process and undermining the expression of liberal sentiment. The inadequacy of single party politics in expressing clearly and openly even the simplest dialectic has been explored by V. O. Key and Alexander Heard.[86] The "southern one or nonparty system," despite significant diversity from state to state, generally contributed toward encouraging localism, confusing voter comprehension of the relation of candidates to programs, eliminating "party responsibility," inclining campaigns toward contests of personality rather than tests of issues, promoting showmanship in elections and irresponsibility in office, and benefiting the "have's" of society at the expense of the "have not's." During a period of high racial tensions, these tendencies were exaggerated. This situation created an almost unparalleled invitation for demagoguery, further complicating the political analysts' dream of a rational and orderly process. Particularly significant was the inability of governors in most states to control their independently elected administrations. More than one chief executive sought a racial *rapprochement* only to find his attorney general ambitiously spearheading the opposition.

Against this complex background, the massive resistance movement emerged in the late 1940's and early 1950's. Vast economic and demographic change swept through a region that evidenced substantial social and ideological continuity with the past. This profound conflict severely strained a relatively unstructured political system. Despite great state-to-state diversity, the political warfare of massive resistance revolved broadly around three main threads represented by neobourbonism, neopopulism, and business conservatism. Neobourbonism represented southern reaction and aimed at imposing a fixed agrarian social and ideological structure upon an urban-industrial South. Neopopulism represented a tattered southern version of liberalism. Although it, too, was rural and, in a sense, reactionary, neopopulism contained basic elements of true liberalism—democracy, individualism, and concern for social justice. Business conservatives were the southern moderates. They sought a

[86] Key, *Southern Politics*, especially 298–311; Heard, *A Two-Party South?*, especially 3–19.

northern-type, urban-industrial society, with perhaps a New South bias.

Coming to the defense of segregation and southern tradition, neobourbons unfurled the banner of massive resistance. For a time, they enjoyed considerable success. Eventually, however, the tide turned, and, when the situation had so degenerated that the effective choice was token desegregation or anarchy, a sufficient number of neobourbons and their followers—those with a business conservative bent who had joined or acquiesced in the neobourbon crusade or those who merely had a physical and psychological stake in the present—finally opted for moderation, a moderation based on the ethics of cost-accounting rather than human justice.

CHAPTER 2

THE DIXIECRATS
AND THE RISE OF NEOBOURBONISM

During the 1930's a substantial majority of southerners thought of themselves as liberals. More so than the citizens of any other section of the nation, southerners avowed their proliberal orientation and their preference for a liberal party over a conservative one. Events of the 1940's steadily eroded this dedication to a politics of reform, however, and by the 1950's the South had been transformed into a national stronghold of conservatism.[1] The economic liberalism of the New Deal had attracted a broad southern following, but rising prosperity and the growth of conservatism in rural areas undermined support for New Deal policies. More significantly, national and world events shifted the focus of political conflict away from economic issues to the problems of cold war and, most important of all in its influence on southern opinion, minority rights. Regarding these issues, southerners were far less likely to express liberal views. Studies have found nativism, intolerance, and authoritarianism more prevalent among southerners than among other American citizens.[2] With Supreme Court decisions and policies pursued by the Truman administration directly challenging institutional white supremacy, concern for the preservation of "the southern way of life" became a part of the general shift toward conservatism.[3]

During the 1940's a sporadic but growing political reaction emerged in the South. In part this reaction was an expression of anti-New Deal

[1] Hero, *The Southerner and World Affairs*, 369–81.

[2] *Ibid.*, 341–82, and Samuel A. Stouffer, *Communism, Conformity and Civil Liberties: A Cross-Section of the Nation Speaks Its Mind* (Garden City, 1955), 109–30.

[3] On the growth of southern sectional consciousness, see Fletcher M. Green, "Resurgent Southern Sectionalism, 1933-1955," *North Carolina Historical Review*, XXXIII (April, 1956), 222–40.

sentiment, both economic and ideological. During the previous decade the 1936 "grass roots" protest movement and the failure of Franklin Roosevelt's 1938 efforts to "purge" several southern conservative senators had revealed discontent with New Deal policies. In 1944 the stirrings of revolt led to increased anti-Roosevelt maneuvering. At the Democratic national convention, seven southern states gave all or part of their delegate votes to Senator Harry Flood Byrd of Virginia as a protest against Roosevelt's nomination.[4] Southern delegates also played a significant role in defeating Henry A. Wallace's bid for renomination as the vice-presidential candidate.

Following the 1944 convention, electors pledged to vote against Roosevelt appeared in three southern states. After losing a bitter intra-party struggle for control of the state Democratic Party machinery, the Texas Regulars, supported by such conservative stalwarts as former Governor Dan Moody and Senator W. Lee "Pappy" O'Daniel, campaigned unsuccessfully for the election of an anti-Roosevelt ticket of independent presidential electors. A "Southern Democratic" slate of electors pledged to Byrd appeared in South Carolina, though it made only a token showing. The Mississippi state Democratic convention chose anti-Roosevelt electors, but the state legislature reacted by nominating a pro-Roosevelt slate that won the election. An independent ticket of electors narrowly missed appearing on the ballot in Louisiana.[5]

By 1944 the anti-New Deal movement had been reinforced by a more distinctly racial reaction. The 1944 Supreme Court decision in *Smith v. Allwright* pronounced as unconstitutional the barring of Negroes from Democratic primary elections. As Professor Key observed, "The white primary, since it drew the color line sharply and cleanly, appealed . . . strongly to the defenders of white supremacy."[6] Several southern states

---

[4] Louisiana, Mississippi, and Virginia voted en bloc for Senator Byrd. Two rival Texas delegations, one pro- and one anti-New Deal, had been seated at the convention, with the state's vote divided between them; Byrd received some backing from the anti-Roosevelt delegation. Byrd also picked up scattered support from the Alabama, Florida, and South Carolina delegations. He received eighty-nine votes in all. Richard C. Bain, *Convention Decisions and Voting Records* (Washington, 1960), Pt. D. A good discussion of presidential politics in the South in the 1940's is Jasper B. Shannon, "Presidential Politics in the South," in Taylor Cole and John H. Hallowell (eds.), *The Southern Political Scene: 1938–1948* (Gainesville, Fla., 1948), 464–89.

[5] Heard, *A Two-Party South?*, 257–61; Lander, *A History of South Carolina*, 175–76; Key, *Southern Politics*, 243–44; L. Vaughan Howard and David R. Deener, *Presidential Politics in Louisiana, 1952* (New Orleans, 1954), 52–53.

[6] Key, *Southern Politics*, 625.

reacted vigorously to the Court-decreed threat to white political monopoly.

Just after the Supreme Court decision South Carolina Governor Olin D. Johnston called a special legislative session to enact measures calculated to evade the *Smith* decision's effect. Since the Fourteenth and Fifteenth Amendments refer only to state action, the South Carolina legislature simply repealed all state laws pertaining to primary elections, attempting in this fashion to divorce the state from the private actions of a political party. South Carolina voters approved an amendment striking all reference to primaries from the South Carolina constitution. The state's most significant elections, as well as questions of fraud and election corruption, were placed entirely in the hands of a private organization. The federal courts refused to accept this "South Carolina Plan," holding that political parties functioned as state instrumentalities when conducting elections.[7] Palmetto politicians continued the battle throughout the remainder of the 1940's, but they were unable to discover a method that would both put the white primary back together again and pass court inspection.[8]

The Mississippi legislature made administrative changes in the operation of primaries aimed at discouraging Negroes from voting, but the electorate rejected a state constitutional amendment tightening voting qualifications. By 1954 the mood of Mississippi voters had changed, however, and in that year they approved a constitutional amendment strengthening literacy and "understanding" provisions.[9] Alabama added comprehensive "understanding" and "good character" clauses to its constitution. After the slow but persistent federal judicial process overtook this amendment, a sharply divided Alabama legislature endorsed a second "understanding" requirement for voter registration, which the electorate narrowly ratified in December, 1951.[10] In Georgia the death of Governor-elect Eugene Talmadge intervened to prevent a legislative defense of the white primary. However, the Talmadge faction, led by

---

[7] *Rice v. Elmore*, 165 F. 2d 389; *Elmore v. Rice*, 72 F. Supp. 516.

[8] *Baskin v. Brown*, 174 F. 2d 391; *Brown v. Baskin*, 78 F. Supp. 933; O. Douglas Weeks, "The White Primary: 1944–1948," *American Political Science Review*, XLII (June, 1948), 508–10.

[9] United States Commission on Civil Rights, *Voting in Mississippi* (Washington, 1965), 3–8.

[10] *Davis v. Schnell*, 81 F. Supp. 872; Donald S. Strong, *Registration of Voters in Alabama* (University, Ala., 1956).

Herman Talmadge after his father's death, purged new registrants from the voter lists on the local level.[11]

The peripheral South showed a distinct reluctance to battle for an all-white Democratic Party. Arkansas was the only state outside the Deep South to enact new legislation designed to prevent Negro political participation. Prior to 1944 Negroes had voted in primary elections in some areas of Tennessee, Virginia, and North Carolina and to a more limited extent in Florida.[12] These states adopted no official resistance measures despite the efforts of a minority to do so.

Although ill-defined and overlapping, two separate strains of discontent were clearly evident in the South during the 1940's. One view expressed economic and ideological dissent from New Deal liberalism. It did not differ essentially from the more extreme conservative opposition to Roosevelt's programs elsewhere in the nation. The other strain was more distinctively racial and sectional in nature. It represented a kind of instinctive reaction to outside intervention in southern racial practices. To be sure, property rights and white supremacy were closely attuned in some states—notably so in Alabama, with its long-standing black-belt-"Big Mule" alliance, and in Georgia, with the Talmadge faction's blend of social and economic reaction.[13] But the dual nature of the emerging southern protest was apparent. The anti-New Deal movement sometimes differed in origin and in ideology from the outcry in defense of the white primary.

South Carolina demonstrated this point. There Governor Johnston, who rallied the faithful to the suffrage fight, was also widely known as a friend of the New Deal. Johnston had received Roosevelt's backing in the 1938 effort to "purge" incumbent Senator Ellison D. Smith. The purge failed, but, in a second attempt in 1944, Johnston combined white supremacy with a pro-New Deal stand to defeat Smith and became senator. Similarly, Senator Theodore G. Bilbo assisted in preventing the anti-New Deal coup aimed at assigning the Mississippi Democratic label to anti-Roosevelt electors in 1944. Two years later Bilbo won reelection

[11] Joseph L. Bernd and Lynwood M. Holland, "Recent Restrictions upon Negro Suffrage: The Case of Georgia," *Journal of Politics*, XXI (August, 1959), 487–513.

[12] Key, *Southern Politics*, 620–49; Weeks, "The White Primary: 1944–1948," 505. See also Donald S. Strong, "The Rise of Negro Voting in Texas," *American Political Science Review*, XLII (June, 1948), 510–29.

[13] Key, *Southern Politics*, 36–57, 106–29; Sarah McCulloh Lemmon, "The Ideology of Eugene Talmadge," *Georgia Historical Quarterly*, XXXVIII (September, 1954), 226–48.

to the Senate, promising in a bitterly Negrophobic campaign to re-establish political white supremacy.[14]

The Texas Regular movement, on the other hand, was primarily an anti-New Deal phenomenon. Although the *Smith* decision was a factor in bringing on the bolt from the party, "the issue of the split was crystal clear: the New Deal,"[15] and Dan Moody and his allies aimed their campaign primarily at big government and socialistic economic policies. A focal point of anti-Roosevelt sentiment was Senator Byrd of Virginia, yet the Byrd organization showed no inclination toward Negrophobia on the voting issue.[16]

The complex and shifting currents of southern protest were channeled by the Dixiecrat revolt of 1948. In a sense, the appearance of the States' Rights Democrats represented anti-New Deal forces seizing upon the racial issue for political purposes, but such a generalization, while containing an element of truth, misrepresents the nature of the movement. Special economic interests and political expediency played a role in the Dixiecrat revolt, but, more fundamentally, it was a true social, economic, and political upheaval, broadly based and purposeful. Its proponents sought to counter the growing attack on southern social institutions, to restore rural small-town concepts of laissez-faire economics, and to reassert the sovereign rights of states. The Dixiecrat movement established the basic neobourbon nature of the reaction that was to play a central role in southern politics during the following decade. It fixed the broad aims and many of the programs that were to carry over into massive resistance.[17]

Racial fears and prejudices dominated the Dixiecrat movement. For the first time since Reconstruction, the federal government was launching a serious and sustained attack on southern racial practices. The Committee on Civil Rights presented its *Report* to President Truman in October, 1947, and Truman delivered his civil rights recommendations

---

[14] Shannon, "Presidential Politics in the South," 480–81, 488.

[15] Key, *Southern Politics*, 256; and see Heard, *A Two-Party South?*, 257–61.

[16] Benjamin Muse, *Virginia's Massive Resistance* (Bloomington, Ind., 1961), 1–3.

[17] On the Dixiecrat movement generally, see Sarah McCulloh Lemmon, "The Ideology of the 'Dixiecrat' Movement," *Social Forces*, XXX (December, 1951), 162–71; Emile B. Ader, *The Dixiecrat Movement: Its Role in Third Party Politics* (Washington, 1955); Ader, "Why the Dixiecrats Failed," *Journal of Politics*, XV (August, 1953), 356–69; William G. Carleton, "The Fate of Our Fourth Party," *Yale Review*, XXXVIII (March, 1949), 449–59; David M. Heer, "The Sentiment of White Supremacy: An Ecological Study," *American Journal of Sociology*, LXIV (May, 1959), 592–98; Heard, *A Two-Party South?*, 20–38, 159–68, 251–79; and Key, *Southern Politics*, 317–44.

based on this report to Congress in February, 1948. The Democratic National Convention in July, 1948, adopted a positive civil rights plank, prompting the Mississippi delegation and part of the Alabama delegation to walk out. Truman made clear his intention to become the first major party candidate in American history to campaign openly on the proposition that all men "are endowed by their Creator with certain unalienable rights." Already, Truman had taken the first steps toward desegregation of the armed forces and the federal establishment. With institutionalized white supremacy gradually being eroded by developments taking place within the South, these rapidly transpiring events placed segregation in profound jeopardy. The national Democratic Party, pronounced the Dixiecrat platform, "denounced totalitarianism abroad but unblushingly proposed and approved it at home."[18]

The heart of the political rebellion of 1948 was the southern black belt, as Key and Heard have fully demonstrated.[19] The movement was launched and most enthusiastically supported in those states where black-belt whites were most numerous and most influential. Governor Fielding Wright, spokesman for the Mississippi Delta, fathered the movement, converting his inaugural address to the state legislature into a clarion call for a states' rights crusade. South Carolina provided some of the earliest and most dedicated recruits, including the third party standard-bearer J. Strom Thurmond. These two states, of course, contained the highest percentage of Negro population in the nation. They were joined in casting their electoral votes for States' Rights Democrats by Louisiana and Alabama, the states ranking third and fourth in percentages of non-whites to total population. In other southern states, with the exception of North Carolina, the Dixiecrat vote coincided closely with the presence of large numbers of nonvoting Negroes.

The Dixiecrat platform, while denouncing the President, the Supreme Court, and the national Democratic Party for all manner of real or imagined evils, clearly centered on opposition to civil rights. The party promised to oppose the police state and executive usurpation and to promote states' rights and segregation.[20]

[18] Kirk H. Porter and Donald Bruce Johnson (eds.), *National Party Platforms, 1840–1956* (Urbana, 1956), 467; Carleton, "The Fate of our Fourth Party," points out that the Truman civil rights program was far less radical than the Dixiecrats believed, or pretended to believe, and he suggests that Truman's program itself served only as a focus for opposition to changes in the Negro's place in American life generally.

[19] Key, *Southern Politics*, 317–44; Heard, *A Two-Party South?*, 251–79.

[20] Porter and Johnson (eds.), *National Party Platforms*, 466–68.

Also permeating the movement was a strong element of economic reaction. An obvious continuity existed between the anti-New Deal protest of previous years and the States' Rights campaign. Louisiana Dixiecrat spokesmen like former Governor Sam H. Jones and manufacturer John U. Barr were veterans of past battles with the New and Fair Deals.[21] The Texas Regulars of 1944 assumed leadership of the Dixiecrats of 1948, "suggesting," as Alexander Heard phrased it, "that the spokesmen of the two protests were using such votes as they could find and did not arrive at their positions of leadership solely on a ground swell."[22] Senator Byrd of Virginia made no secret of his friendliness toward the Dixiecrats, and significant elements of the Byrd organization maneuvered unsuccessfully to assign Virginia's electoral votes to the Thurmond-Wright ticket.[23] Segregationist champions with New Deal inclinations, such as past associates of Bilbo in Mississippi and Senator Olin Johnston and his political friends in South Carolina, rarely took part in the movement.[24]

The economic traditionalism of the Dixiecrats rested on more than just the continuing efforts of anti-New Deal leaders of the past. Representatives of business and industrial interests, many of whom had previously been inactive in national politics, played a significant role in the States' Rights campaign. Sarah McCulloh Lemmon classified forty-three Dixiecrat leaders by occupation and found "twelve lawyers, . . . twelve associated with banks, oil companies or some similar large business, one planter, . . . [and] one official representative of the National Association of Manufacturers."[25] Vice-presidential candidate Wright was himself a former corporation lawyer and a strong proponent of Mississippi's Balance Agriculture with Industry program.

The political leaders sharing command of the States' Rights movement were primarily state officials. Watching their authority slip away to Washington, many state Democratic politicians seized upon the Dixiecrat revolt as a genuine assertion of states' rights.[26] It was no accident that two

[21] Howard and Deener, *Presidential Politics in Louisiana*, 52–63; Sindler, *Huey Long's Louisiana*, 219.

[22] Heard, *A Two-Party South?*, 259.

[23] Key, *Southern Politics*, 338–39.

[24] *Ibid.*, 340; Lander, *A History of South Carolina*, 168. Bilbo died in 1947 after having been reelected to the United States Senate during the previous year.

[25] Lemmon, "The Ideology of the 'Dixiecrat' Movement," 169–70.

[26] See James McBride Dabbs, *The Southern Heritage* (New York, 1959), 115, and Frank E. Smith, *Congressman from Mississippi* (New York, 1964), 111.

governors headed the ticket and at least five former governors were active in the campaign. For the most part national legislators, with seniority and committee chairmanships to be mindful of, either ignored or opposed the Dixiecrats, although a few, such as Senator James O. Eastland of Mississippi, *plus royaliste que le roi*, did find a place in the movement.

Professor Jasper B. Shannon, writing prior to the 1948 election, described the mood of the "county seat governing class" as it viewed the national Democratic Party and President Truman, himself a former county seat politician: "As the presidential election of 1948 approaches, the elite of county seatdom are ill at ease for they feel betrayed in their household by one of their own kind, and most of all by their own political church, the Democratic party."[27] Especially in black-belt areas where historical loyalty ran deepest, the Democratic Party was as much a part of the southern heritage as was segregation. But the two were no longer compatible. The party had become the vehicle for integration, liberalism, and labor, "an unholy alliance," according to one States' Rights leader, "of leftwingers, pseudo liberals and radicals of as many hues as Joseph's coat."[28] Repulsed by the ideological orientation of the party of Truman and the Americans for Democratic Action, yet loath to abandon the domicile of their fathers—as well as the proven appeal of the Democratic emblem to southern voters—the Dixiecrats were torn by conflicting traditions. They sought to resolve their dilemma by calling themselves the true Democrats and endeavoring to capture control of state party machinery throughout the South. "The significant competition engendered by the Dixiecrats thus occurred *within* the Democratic party rather than *with* it."[29] In only four states, Mississippi, South Carolina, Alabama, and Louisiana, were the Dixiecrats successful in placing their nominees under the Democratic label, and only in these states did Thurmond and Wright gain pluralities.

The States' Rights Democrats sought to resurrect the Compromise of 1877 by winning sufficient electoral votes to deny either major party candidate a majority in the electoral college and thus to place the selection of the President in the House of Representatives. The strategy failed when

[27] Jasper Berry Shannon, *Toward a New Politics in the South* (Knoxville, 1949), 52.
[28] Ader, *The Dixiecrat Movement*, 14, quoting former Alabama Governor Frank Dixon. Matthews and Prothro, *Negroes and the New Southern Politics*, 380–400, is a revealing discussion of this conflict within many white southerners between party identification and socio-ideological outlook.
[29] Heard, *A Two-Party South?*, 23.

Truman won a comfortable majority of electoral votes despite defections from the Deep South. The Dixiecrat appeal in the upper South was inadequate for the accomplishment of their aims. The movement nevertheless represented a substantial regional dissent from national trends. It was in a real sense a premature expression of massive resistance.

Following Truman's victory, the States' Rights protest lost much of its momentum. Failure at the polls undermined both financial backing and popular support, while a general letdown succeeded the enthusiastic crusade in defense of southern tradition. Although notably lenient with its straying miscreants, the Democratic Party purged its National Committee, removing Dixiecrat members from Alabama, Louisiana, Mississippi, and South Carolina, and denied patronage to Senator Eastland and other disloyal congressmen. All of this encouraged caution among southern party professionals.

Despite this decline in fortunes, hard-core Dixiecrats kept the movement alive. The faithful from fourteen states gathered in Jackson, Mississippi, on May 10, 1949, marking the movement's first anniversary, to organize the National States' Rights Committee. With former Arkansas Governor Ben Laney as chairman, the committee announced plans to carry out a program that from the beginning had been dear to Dixiecrat hearts: the establishment of a propaganda center which could undertake lobbying activities in Washington and promulgate nationally information about the South and "the southern way of life." The Dixiecrats hoped in this way to sell the neobourbon creed outside the Deep South. The committee's activities were apparently limited, however, as the decline of Dixiecratism continued. The next annual States' Rights conference, held in May, 1950, was a disappointment, with Georgia absent and other states only nominally represented.[30]

Political trends offered little encouragement to sagging Dixiecrat morale. In most southern states neobourbonism seemed in retreat. South Carolina's Thurmond, titular head of the States' Rights forces, failed in his 1950 effort to unseat Senator Johnston, and Committee Chairman Laney was unsuccessful in his attempt to regain the Arkansas governorship. Alabama loyalist Democrats, led by Senators Lister Hill and John J. Sparkman, broke Dixiecrat control of the state party Executive Committee. In Louisiana, the Longs returned to power in 1948, when Earl K. Long (Huey's brother) defeated Sam Jones, later a Dixiecrat leader,

---

[30] *Ibid.*, 22, 164–65; Ader, *The Dixiecrat Movement*, 15–17.

in the runoff gubernatorial primary, and Russell Long (Huey's son) captured a United States Senate seat.

The leftward drift of southern politics shook the status quo oriented "machines" of the upper South. The gubernatorial candidate of the traditional North Carolina organization fell before Agriculture Commissioner Kerr Scott in the 1948 Democratic primary. Scott's rural-oriented progressivism included support for Fair Deal policies. In 1949 Scott appointed Frank P. Graham, perhaps the South's best-known liberal, to the United States Senate. Even in Virginia the Byrd organization was shaken in 1949 by the most formidable challenge it had yet faced. The anti-organization candidate for governor, Francis Pickens Miller, was finally defeated by Byrd's choice, John S. Battle, after Virginia's Republicans came to the machine's aid.[31] "Boss" Ed Crump's men in Tennessee were less fortunate. Estes Kefauver, a neopopulist-type liberal, and Gordon Browning, a conservative loyalist, defeated the machine candidates for senator and governor respectively. Many observers during this period predicted the approaching demise of the Dixiecrat movement and perhaps "the beginning of the decline of Southern political reaction on the race question."[32]

Like optimistic political predictions about southern politics in the past, this one too was quickly squashed. The economic and intellectual currents pulling the South toward national norms were countered by powerful social and political pressures "tugging hard to keep the South separate and solid from the rest of the nation."[33] The year 1950 terminated the post-Dixiecrat lull in the politics of race.

The Supreme Court decisions in the *Sweatt, Henderson,* and *McLaurin* cases were central issues in the renewed concern over social change. Handed down in June, 1950, they were widely recognized as striking at the heart of institutionalized white supremacy. In Atlanta, Roy V. Harris, a Talmadge lieutenant and later a massive resistance chieftain, explained: "We anticipate that they [the Supreme Court Justices] will go all the way and say there can be no such thing as separate and equal facilities."[34] Most informed observers agreed with Harris, including those on the payroll of the NAACP. In Clarendon County, South Carolina, a

---

[31] Edward T. Folliard, in Washington *Post,* June 19, 1957. A series of articles by Folliard on the Byrd organization appeared in the *Post,* June 9–19, 1957.

[32] Ader, *The Dixiecrat Movement,* 21.

[33] Lubell, *Revolt of the Moderates,* 181–82.

[34] As quoted in *New South,* May–June, 1951.

group of Negro parents dropped an earlier suit petitioning the courts to compel county officials to furnish equal facilities for Negro students and, instead, substituted in December, 1950, a suit attacking the separate but equal concept in public school education. Thurgood Marshall, chief counsel for the NAACP, arrived to direct the first legal frontal assault on the ramparts of segregation in the South. A three-judge federal court gave a split ruling against the plaintiffs in early 1951.[35] While this case was being appealed and reappealed, NAACP attorneys backed a similar legal action in Prince Edward County, Virginia.[36] These two cases, combined with three others, were first argued before the Supreme Court in December, 1952. The Court in June, 1953, ordered further arguments.[37] Beginning in 1950, then, the validity of public school segregation was rather continuously before the federal courts and in the public eye.

At the same time token desegregation in graduate and professional schools continued its slow march through the South. In 1950 the graduate and professional schools of state universities in Arkansas, Texas, Virginia, and Louisiana were accepting Negro applicants, and the University of North Carolina joined the group in 1951.[38]

The threat to segregation was not confined to federal courts and public schools. In Washington the congressional battle over Fair Employment Practices Commission legislation raged through 1949 and 1950. Although the House of Representatives, after harsh and prolonged debate, passed a weak FEPC bill, a southern filibuster prevented Senate action. Twice, in May and July, 1950, Administration Democrats mustered a Senate majority, but not the necessary two-thirds, to limit debate.[39] This bitter congressional wrangle took place against a mounting crescendo of hysteria engendered by the investigations led by Sen. Joseph R. McCarthy (R.-Wis.).

Several issues awaited political exploitation. The federal courts were laying the legal groundwork for destruction of the southern social system, and the FEPC provided the direct link between social separation and property rights. The whole integrationist campaign against segregation, states' rights, and private property emerged hand-in-hand with "Com-

[35] *Briggs v. Elliot*, 98 F. Supp. 529.

[36] *Davis v. County School Board*, 103 F. Supp. 337.

[37] *Brown v. Board of Education*, 345 U.S. 972.

[38] Hugh Talmage Lefler and Albert Ray Newsome, *North Carolina: The History of a Southern State* (Rev. ed.; Chapel Hill, 1963), 592.

[39] New York *Times*, May 20, July 13, 1950.

munist subversion" in government. A vague uneasiness was soon apparent in the behavior of many southern voters, a fact that was soon to make itself felt in politics.

Senators Frank Graham of North Carolina and Claude Pepper of Florida easily ranked among the most liberal and ablest southerners in Congress.[40] Former president of the University of North Carolina, Graham served as a member of Truman's Commission on Civil Rights, where he joined in recommending a broad program of civil rights goals. He was appointed to the Senate in 1949. Pepper, a fourteen-year Senate veteran, combined neopopulism with a courageous approach to race relations, including taboo-shattering votes for antipoll-tax legislation and stricter cloture rules in the Senate. In 1950 both Pepper and Graham suffered primary election defeats that Samuel Lubell has characterized as "the most crushing setbacks Southern liberalism has suffered since the coming of Franklin Roosevelt."[41]

The campaigns that felled the two senators were similar. Political enemies of Pepper united behind George A. Smathers, a personable young United States representative "with strong political ambition and surprising flexibility in his political position."[42] In North Carolina Willis Smith, who narrowly squeezed into a runoff primary against Graham, was the candidate of the traditional state Democratic organization, still smarting from its 1948 trouncing at the hands of Kerr Scott. Smathers and Smith both interspersed generous portions of racist oratory with attacks on their opponents' alleged softness towards Trumanism, communism, and labor bossism. In Florida the last charge was given some outward credibility because of the crude efforts of the CIO's Political Action Committee to promote a mass Negro registration drive on behalf of Pepper.[43] The Smith-Graham election followed by three weeks the *Sweatt*, *Henderson*, and *McLaurin* decisions, and Smith was able to link

---

[40] Based on the Americans for Democratic Action legislative score card for the years 1948–50, Pepper's voting record was approximately 98 percent liberal, and Graham's record (for the years 1949–50) was 90 percent liberal. Kefauver of Tennessee ranked third among southern senators with just above 88 percent. *ADA World*, July, 1948, October 28, 1949, September, 1950. The ADA evaluation is used here and in a few other instances not as a "scientific" indicator of the degree of liberalism possessed by an individual congressman but as a convenient general guide to a legislator's right-left orientation.

[41] Lubell, *The Future of American Politics*, 107.

[42] Price, *The Negro and Southern Politics: A Chapter of Florida History*, 119.

[43] *Ibid.*, 60–61.

Graham's "weakness" on segregation to the threat of public school integration.[44]

Neither Smathers nor Smith personally represented a genuine racial reaction. Past president of the American Bar Association, Smith was conservative, but neither he nor Smathers, whose House voting record was moderately liberal,[45] was ever associated with a neobourbon defense of the southern past. Although conducting the bitterest displays of racial antagonism seen in the peripheral South in years, both men apparently divined the mood of the voting public and sought to capitalize on the fact. Smathers and Smith made heavy inroads on the white rural vote by whipping up racial antagonisms; at the same time they appealed to and won the urban business conservatives with promises to oppose Trumanism and communism as well as integration.[46]

These elections checked the drift of southern politics away from race and reaction. During the 1948–50 period, Scott of North Carolina, Sidney McMath of Arkansas, Kefauver of Tennessee, Earl Long of Louisiana, and Lyndon B. Johnson of Texas had won gubernatorial or senatorial elections over conservative opposition. Each of these candidates had advanced progressive programs in his successful campaign. But the defeat of Graham and Pepper shifted the focus of southern politics. It called the attention of politicians to the dangers of liberalism, and it set the mood for the gradual rise of massive resistance. For 1950 was not only the year when the voters rejected Graham and Pepper, it also marked the election of Herman Talmadge to a full four-year term as governor of Georgia and the election of James F. Byrnes as governor of South Carolina.

Talmadge vigorously insisted that Georgia would accept no further change in the field of race relations. In 1948 Talmadge had conducted a Negro-baiting campaign to win a two-year term as governor in a special election, but not until the following year did he launch an assault on the trends of social evolution in Georgia. A group of Negro parents had petitioned a federal court for equalization of public educational facilities, and Talmadge answered their demand in a statewide radio broadcast in October, 1949. "This litigation," prophesied the governor,

[44] Lubell, *The Future of American Politics*, 110; New York *Times*, June 25, 26, 1950.
[45] On the basis of the ADA score card, Smathers easily rated as the most liberal member of the Florida congressional delegation for the 1948 and 1949 sessions. *ADA World*, July, 1948, October 28, 1949.
[46] Lubell, *The Future of American Politics*, 106–15.

"is the opening wedge to break down segregation in the Southern States."[47] Georgia would have none of it, said Talmadge, promising wholehearted opposition to this invidious effort by "northern agitators" to disrupt race relations. Talmadge was foremost among southerners in denouncing the *Sweatt, Henderson,* and *McLaurin* decisions. "As long as I am Governor," he declared, "Negroes will not be admitted to white schools."[48] In August, 1950, the Georgia Democratic convention commended the governor for his stand and vowed to maintain segregation in the public schools of the state.[49] In discussions with aides during this period, Talmadge often referred to a previous Georgia chief executive, who, some 120 years before, had successfully defied the Supreme Court on an Indian rights question.[50]

In challenging the spread of gradualism, Talmadge became the first major political figure to take a strong segregationist position on college desegregation. The 1951 Georgia appropriations bill stated that funds would be withheld from any state educational institution that mixed the races, whether such action was done voluntarily or under court compulsion.[51] Talmadge legislative leaders also figured prominently in an unsuccessful effort to amend the state constitution to provide for transferring all state schools to a private system.[52]

While seizing leadership of the resurgence of the old order, Herman Talmadge was by no means completely submerged in the past. Unlike his father, he had a sense of urban and industrial economic progress, and his tenure in the governor's office was generally a successful one. Under Talmadge's leadership the Georgia legislature adopted a minimum foundation program for public schools, undertook extensive highway construction, made limited improvements in mental hospitals and state services, and increased the budget for state colleges. Although Talmadge opposed the idea at first, his program made substantial gains in improving Negro schools and equalizing teacher pay. The expenditures were financed largely by a 3 percent sales tax which doubled state income

[47] As quoted in New York *Times,* October 3, 1949; *Davis v. Cook,* 80 F. Supp. 443 (1948).
[48] As quoted in New York *Times,* June 6, 1950.
[49] Reprinted in *Congressional Record,* 81st Cong., 2nd Sess. (September 21, 1950), 15454–55.
[50] New York *Times,* May 28, 1951.
[51] *New South,* July, 1951.
[52] New York *Times,* February 1, 1951.

despite the lowering of state property taxes.[53] This program of expanded state service based on consumer taxes won industrial and business conservative support, and Talmadge soon held the allegiance of a large urban following. At the same time, the patronage and increased spending accompanying the Talmadge program did much to solidify his influence in the more rural counties.

In a real sense Talmadge and his voting coalition were torn between past and present, between agrarian and urban mores. The increasing number of his business conservative adherents approved his "New South" program and his concern for the future; his county strength lay with the poorer Georgia farmers, nurtured on a "Gene" Talmadge blend of racial demagoguery and reaction.[54]

Formidable pressures propelled "Huhman" Talmadge toward the past, however. The Georgia county unit system severely limited the influence of urban voters, who generally approved of states' rights and segregation anyway; it greatly magnified a white rural vote that demanded defense of racial separation. Talmadge had run in 1948 primarily on the basis of the Talmadge name and white supremacy, which appealed mainly to rural areas. The county unit system made it politically imperative that the governor maintain this woolhat voting loyalty. Furthermore, he had not only inherited his father's grass roots support, but also the Talmadge "faction"—the alliance of "gang leaders" who had assisted Eugene Talmadge in his 1946 campaign.[55] In the county unit system the candidate in a primary election winning a plurality in a county carried that county's unit votes. A statewide Georgia primary became 159 separate elections for 159 separate political entities. Under this arrangement, county leaders capable of swaying a few votes were enormously significant in closely contested counties. On the state level energetic and influential leaders became intimately acquainted with the political situation and the personnel in each of Georgia's counties, and, combining this knowledge with the ability to deliver favors in the form of roads and funds, developed

[53] Joseph L. Bernd, *Grass Roots Politics in Georgia: The County Unit System and the Importance of the Individual Voting Community in Bifactional Elections, 1942–1954* (Atlanta, 1960), 14–30; Kenneth Coleman, *Georgia History in Outline* (Athens, Ga., 1960), 102–12; Cabell Phillips, in *New York Times Magazine*, May 20, 1956; Pauli Murray (ed.), *States' Laws on Race and Color* (Cincinnati, 1950), 91–98.

[54] Lemmon, "The Ideology of Eugene Talmadge," 226–48.

[55] Bernd, *Grass Roots Politics in Georgia*, incisively demonstrates the nature of "gang" politics in the state.

political gangs, systems of alliances stretching from the statehouse to the lowliest county.

The most powerful gang leader was Roy V. Harris of Augusta, the most feared man in Georgia politics. Harris had organized successful gubernatorial campaigns for Enrith D. Rivers, Ellis G. Arnall, and Eugene Talmadge and had directed Herman's winning endeavors in 1948 and 1950. He had never backed a loser in a state campaign and seemed able to make or break candidates with ease.[56] Harris was devoted to white supremacy and, because he was Talmadge's leading ally, his prejudices carried no small weight, especially since they coincided with sound political strategy and, probably, the governor's personal convictions.

Talmadge was a political realist, and expediency undoubtedly influenced his tactics; yet, there was never a hint of insincerity in his general aims and program. He consistently opposed democracy, championing states' rights and the county unit system—the latter, he said, a venerable and honorable institution dating "back before the Christian era when people had similar tribe representation."[57] He defended the sacred rights of property, sought to propitiate industry, and vented his hostility toward labor, especially the CIO, which he claimed was in league with the NAACP.[58] He was a states' rights nationalist (most neobourbons were despite the apparent incompatibility of states' rights and nationalism),[59] and he tended to confuse nationalism with orthodoxy and nonconformity with communism. The governor idolized a static society although approving economic change, and he elevated white supremacy to a position of paramount importance, clinging as he did to long-discredited racial interpretations of history.[60] Talmadge possessed an active sense of paternalism, and few questioned his ability. At the same time, however, his values could hardly have been more profoundly neobourbon. "Ol' Gene's" grass roots support and state alliances, the county unit system, the drift to the right by southern voters, and an important part of Herman Talmadge's own ideology pushed the Georgia governor towards defense of the past.

---

[56] *Ibid.*, 7–8, and Key, *Southern Politics*, 124–25, contain good sketches of Harris.

[57] As quoted by Max K. Gilstrap, in *Christian Science Monitor*, June 11, 1954.

[58] Herman E. Talmadge, *You and Segregation* (Birmingham, 1955), 18.

[59] This point is discussed more thoroughly in Chapter 13.

[60] Talmadge, *You and Segregation*, 44. These observations on the Talmadge rationale rest upon this work, Talmadge's only book, and upon Talmadge's public speeches and statements.

Although Talmadge was its first and most vociferous spokesman, South Carolina and Governor James F. Byrnes were perhaps the heart of the revitalized neobourbon protest. Nearing the end of a long career in public life, Byrnes added dignity and a sense of solemn purpose to the segregationist cause. Already one of the most prestigious men in the South, Byrnes could hardly be dismissed as a demagogue playing politics. Elected to the United States House of Representatives in 1910, Byrnes for thirty-five years played a leading role in national affairs, becoming "probably the most influential South Carolina political leader in Washington since John C. Calhoun."[61] Byrnes moved from the House to the Senate in 1930 and was an important Roosevelt administration spokesman during the early 1930's, losing sympathy with the New Deal as it became more socially oriented. In 1941 he was appointed to the Supreme Court but resigned in 1942 to become "assistant President" with an office in the White House during the war years. Byrnes narrowly missed the vice-presidential nomination in 1944; his conversion from Catholicism combined with opposition from labor and civil rights groups to destroy his chances. In 1945 he was appointed Secretary of State by President Truman. Increasingly perturbed by the centralization of power in the federal government and especially by Truman's growing support of civil rights, Byrnes broke with the administration and "returned to South Carolina," as Professor Howard H. Quint put it, "to vent his frustration against the national government and the Democratic Party."[62] In 1950 he sought and easily won the governorship of his native state.

The restoration of states' rights and southern rights, Byrnes seemed to feel, required three things: a broader concept of state responsibility, particularly in regard to the Negro; an adamant stand by individual states against further federal encroachments, especially in matters pertaining to civil rights and school segregation; and cooperative action by the states to counter centralization of authority in Washington. As the first step in this states' rights program, Byrnes declared in his inaugural address: "It is our duty to provide for the races substantial equality in school facilities. We should do it because it is right. For me, that is sufficient reason. If any person wants an additional reason, I say it is wise."[63]

That Byrnes received legislative sanction for an initial $75 million bond

[61] Lander, *A History of South Carolina*, 80.

[62] Quint, *Profile in Black and White*, 15. Byrnes's account of his break with Truman is related in James F. Byrnes, *All in One Lifetime* (New York, 1958), 398–418.

[63] As quoted in New York *Times*, January 17, 1951.

issue and a 3 percent sales tax to finance a broad school construction program designed to equalize Negro-white physical facilities in public education was a tribute to the governor's prestige, since in South Carolina governmental initiative normally rested with the legislature. Although per pupil expenditures based on average daily attendance continued to show a distinct bias in favor of white students, construction funds were allocated heavily in favor of Negro schools.[64] Byrnes also pushed through the legislature a school administrative reorganization plan, an anti-masking bill aimed at the Ku Klux Klan, a right-to-work law, and increased funds (and tuition) for the state colleges.

While building support for his equalization program, Byrnes turned to the second point in his strategy: resistance to the federal government, especially its judicial branch. The Clarendon County case was already before the federal courts at the time of Byrnes' inauguration, adding a note of urgency to protection of the separate but equal formula in public school education. In a series of "preparedness measures," South Carolina made plans to challenge an unfavorable ruling. The legislature authorized local school authorities to sell or lease public school property to private individuals and passed a local pupil assignment law requiring students transferring from one school to another to receive written permission from the superintendents of both schools. To coordinate the state's anti-desegregation planning, the legislature created a fifteen-member committee, headed by State Senator L. Marion Gressette, as the first such strategy-mapping segregation group in the South.[65] The Gressette Committee suggested one further "preparedness measure," the adoption of a constitutional amendment relieving South Carolina of its obligation to provide a free public school system. Byrnes called for action on this recommendation in January, 1952. The legislature acted promptly, and the state's voters approved the amendment in the November, 1952, general election by better than a 2 to 1 majority. The amendment was received most enthusiastically in the black-belt low country; five Piedmont counties cast a majority vote against the change.[66]

In the meantime *Briggs v. Elliot*, the Clarendon County case, was argued before a three-judge federal court in Charleston. Prior to the

[64] Patrick McCauley and Edward D. Ball (eds.), *Southern Schools: Progress and Problems* (Nashville, 1959), 52–54, 114, 142; *Southern School News*, September, 1954; Quint, *Profile in Black and White*, 15–17.
[65] New York *Times*, May 27, 28, 1951.
[66] *New South*, February, 1953.

verdict, Byrnes made clear: "Of only one thing can we be certain. South Carolina will not now, nor for some years to come, mix white and colored children in our schools."[67] He continued by asserting that South Carolina would close its schools before desegregating them. The federal court upheld the validity of the separate but equal doctrine in June, 1951, and the decision was appealed.[68]

The final point in the three-part plan for a revitalized federalism, cooperative state action against continued growth of national power, occupied much of Byrnes's energy during and after his tenure in the governor's office. He included this goal in his 1950 campaign but refused to associate himself officially with the Dixiecrats, apparently hoping during this period to avoid the sectional label of Dixiecratism and to appeal nationally to states' rights advocates. The first active step in this program, which was marked by increasing ambiguity as Byrnes became ever more closely allied with Dixiecrat veterans, was an effort to defeat Harry S. Truman, and the South Carolinian became leader of the "Democrats for Ike" movement in the Southeast.

Talmadge and Byrnes assumed leadership of the emerging opposition to school desegregation. They initiated legislation and programs to protect segregation in the public schools, and they thereby openly challenged the trend in federal court decisions. They were joined, not unpredictably, by political leaders in Mississippi. Governor Wright, former States' Rights Party vice-presidential candidate, pronounced that "We shall insist upon segregation regardless of consequences."[69] These three states, Georgia, Mississippi, and South Carolina, formed the original hard core of resistance to school desegregation. This opposition was to broaden during the years that followed.

[67] As quoted in New York *Times*, March 17, 1951.
[68] *Briggs v. Elliot*, 98 F. Supp. 529.
[69] As quoted in New York *Times*, May 28, 1951.

CHAPTER 3

THE PRESIDENTIAL ELECTION OF 1952
AND SOUTHERN STATE POLITICS

The presidential election of 1952 clarified developing political trends and demonstrated the fact that, while southern voter sentiment generally was swinging to the right, the racial reaction centered in the Deep South. Dwight D. Eisenhower won four southern states and narrowly missed victory in two others. The bulk of Republican strength came from three sources: the urban middle class in the cities and suburbs, which became a decisive regional factor for the first time; the traditionally Republican hill country; and the black-belt South, bedrock of past Democratic unanimity. Like their northern peers, southern business conservatives were concerned about communism, corruption, and Korea and liked the "good government" brand of conservatism that Eisenhower personified. The close correlation between economic status and Republican sympathies has been documented by Donald S. Strong and Samuel Lubell.[1] General Eisenhower swept the upper-South hill country which based its Republican loyalty predominantly on long-dead issues.[2] The most surprising GOP gains in historical terms, however, were tallied in the heartland of Democratic loyalty, the towns and counties containing high percentages of Negro population. Eisenhower ran ahead of the state

---

[1] Donald S. Strong, *The 1952 Presidential Election in the South* (University, Ala., 1955), is the most detailed published analysis of the election. "The case for urban Republicanism" is summed up in Strong's "Durable Republicanism in the South," in Sindler (ed.), *Change in the Contemporary South*, 174–94. Lubell comments on the trends in southern voting in *Revolt of the Moderates*, 176–206; *The Future of American Politics*, 107–36; and *White and Black*, 66–88. Voting statistics used in this analysis were taken from Richard M. Scammon (ed.), *America Votes: A Handbook of Contemporary American Election Statistics* (7 vols.; New York, 1956), I.

[2] On the influence of tradition in determining voting behavior in hill and mountain regions, see Hero, *The Southerner and World Affairs*, 325–33.

average in two-thirds of the black-belt counties. Despite broad, Southwide continuity in Eisenhower's appeal, variations in voting patterns revealed much about the mood of white southerners.

In the upper South, Eisenhower won Viriginia and Tennessee and received well above 40 percent of the vote in North Carolina and Arkansas. Not since 1928 had a Republican presidential candidate even remotely approached such a showing. Yet there was no actual revolution in the GOP gains. Quartile maps comparing Thomas E. Dewey's 1944 showing in the upper South with Eisenhower's 1952 vote were amazingly similar. In both elections the focus of Republican strength was the hill country, where Negroes were few and GOP loyalty rested on events that transpired during the Civil War-Reconstruction period. The main difference between the elections of 1944 and 1952 was that the Republicans got more votes, especially in the cities. Even in urban areas, Eisenhower support was clearly sectional; he ran much better in hill-country cities than he did in lowland cities. In Arkansas, for instance, he won 63.3 percent of the votes in Washington County (Fayetteville), high in the Ozarks; 56.4 percent in Sebastian County (Fort Smith), a bit farther down; 60.1 percent in Garland County (Hot Springs), near the edge of the lowlands; 48.6 percent in Pulaski County (Little Rock), on the dividing line between hills and plains; 41.6 percent in Jefferson County (Pine Bluff), on the edge of the Delta country; and 41.1 percent in Union County (El Dorado), in the flat lands. The same patterns were equally apparent in Tennessee and North Carolina and to a lesser degree in Virginia: Eisenhower dominated hill-country voting and ran poorly in the low country, although he normally did better in the urban areas of the plains than in rural counties. Clearly his upper-South appeal rested heavily on tradition and business conservatism.

Although there were hints that all was not well in the lowlands, only in Virginia did black-belt white dissatisfaction with the national Democratic Party reach substantial proportions. In the Old Dominion, General Eisenhower carried thirteen top quartile Negro counties. Among them were Prince Edward County, where the *Davis v. County School Board* case made racial concerns immediate, and neighboring Southside counties usually high in Democratic loyalty. The revolt was limited, however; most of the white-supremacy conscious Southside counties were in the highest quartile of Democratic support. Compared to elections of the past, the Democratic ticket suffered substantial defections in the counties of high Negro concentration in Tennessee as well as Virginia, and there was an overlapping of counties high in Dixiecrat strength and counties of high Democratic loss in all four states.[3]

Texas and Florida, both of which Eisenhower carried, were least influenced by racial considerations in voting. Of southern states these two were the most urban, had the highest per capita income, and showed the greatest rate of population growth. Both states divided along relatively rational liberal-conservative-traditional balloting lines. The Republican ticket swept the cities of southern Florida and ran poorest in rural "Old South" areas of northern Florida, a north-south, rural-urban cleavage often seen in state contests.[4] In Texas Eisenhower won most of the cities and fared worst in the East Texas piney woods and prairie where the Negro population was most numerous.

The politics of racial protest, hinted at in the upper South, dominated Deep South voting. From Louisiana to South Carolina, the party of Charles Sumner and Thaddeus Stevens won support from whites in counties with high concentrations of Negroes. In South Carolina eight of the eleven counties containing a population 60 percent or more Negro delivered a majority to the Republicans. Eisenhower carried nine of the twenty Mississippi counties with 60 percent or more Negro population and ran well above the state average in nine of the remaining eleven. Louisiana contained only three parishes in the 60 percent or above nonwhite bracket, and all three gave the Republicans a majority. Eleven of the fifteen Louisiana parishes carried by Eisenhower were in the upper half of parishes classified by relative number of Negroes. Of the ten Alabama counties with 60 percent or more nonwhite population, five were in the Republican top quartile. Georgia's black-belt swing to Republicanism was less pronounced; only four of twenty counties 60 percent or more Negro in population were in the Republican top quartile.[5] Throughout the Deep South there was a clear correlation—most pronounced in Georgia, South Carolina, and Louisiana—between counties that had been high in Dixiecrat strength and those that were enthusiastic for Eisenhower.

The Republican ticket also ran well in urban areas of the Deep South. Generally the closer a city was to the black belt, the better the GOP

[3] Strong, The 1952 Presidential Election in the South, 383.

[4] See Havard and Beth, The Politics of Mis-Representation, 14-16, passim.

[5] As Lubell has noted, the Republican vote in the 157 southern counties of 50 percent or more Negro population increased from 19,700 in 1948 to 158,000 in 1952. Revolt of the Moderates, 284.

fared. In South Carolina Eisenhower swept Charleston County with 66.9 percent of the vote, won Richland County (Columbia) with 64.2 percent, carried Greenville County with 54.4 percent, and lost Spartanburg and Anderson by heavy majorities.

General Eisenhower won not a single Deep South state, but the election returns nevertheless demonstrated the depth of southern dissent from Democratic domestic policies. In the five presidential elections prior to 1952, the best Republican showing in South Carolina had been 4.5 percent; Eisenhower received 49.3 percent of the 1952 vote. In Louisiana the best GOP tally in twenty years had been 19.4 percent; Eisenhower lifted this to 47.1 percent. The Mississippi vote for the GOP went up from a twenty-year high of 6.4 percent to 39.6. Alabama and Georgia voters showed similar, though somewhat less dramatic, shifts toward presidential Republicanism. Such massive defection to the once despised GOP was a barometer of Deep South discontent.

Generally the organized push behind the "I like Ike" movement in the South was neobourbon in origin. In many cases, Dixiecrat veterans took up the Eisenhower banner. Such States' Rights Party leaders as Gessner T. McCorvey of Alabama and Leander Perez of Louisiana were among the Republican candidate's earliest southern enthusiasts. A few national Republican leaders, including party chairman Guy Gabrielson and Senator Karl E. Mundt of South Dakota, suggested an open Dixiecrat-Republican southern alliance, but little institutional cooperation was achieved.[6]

Foremost among Eisenhower's southern recruits was Governor Byrnes. In behind-the-scenes maneuvering and in public speeches the South Carolina governor promoted the theme: "If we act in concert with other Southern states on these questions and let the leaders of both political parties know we are no longer 'in the bag' of any political party, we will no longer be ignored."[7] In major addresses before the Virginia General Assembly and the Georgia legislature, Byrnes attacked President Truman and his Fair Deal-civil rights program and called for independent democracy in the South. The time had arrived, Byrnes reiterated, to place principle above party.[8] At home in South Carolina, Byrnes and the ex-

[6] New York Times, January 22, 1950, January 20, 1951; Heard, A Two-Party South?, 165.

[7] As quoted in New York Times, April 17, 1952. Byrnes was speaking before the South Carolina Democratic Convention.

[8] Ibid., February 2, 7, 1952. See also Byrnes, All in One Lifetime, 398ff.

Dixiecrat forces organized and vigorously supported a Democrats for Ike movement. No other man did as much to make Republicanism respectable in the Deep South.

Next to Byrnes the most influential and energetic of those Deep South politicians who liked Ike was Governor Robert F. Kennon of Louisiana. Winning the governorship in 1952 Kennon became head of the anti-Long faction, a business conservative-neobourbon coalition. Among other factors, the governor listed Democratic candidate Adlai E. Stevenson's endorsement of federal control of offshore oil lands and FEPC legislation as reasons for supporting the Republican ticket.[9] Conspicuously associated with Kennon in the Louisiana "Americans for Eisenhower" camp were the old Dixiecrat leaders and the neobourbon wing of the anti-Long faction generally. The fact that Perez's Plaquemines Parish delivered a 93 percent Eisenhower majority was indicative of Dixiecrat enthusiasm. Spokesmen for the progressive, good government wing of the anti-Long coalition were less conspicuous in the "Americans for Eisenhower" leadership. For example, although New Orleans Mayor deLesseps Morrison did not actively campaign, both he and Representative Hale Boggs supported Stevenson. The Republican ticket ran well in the cities, nevertheless, winning approximately 50 percent of the urban vote. Broadly the Eisenhower appeal was to the areas of anti-Long strength, corresponding to the vote received by Kennon in his 1952 runoff primary against Carlos Spaht, the Long candidate.[10]

Farther west Governor Allan Shivers of Texas completed the triumvirate of Eisenhower enthusiasts. The Texas "Democrats for Eisenhower" ideologically represented a continuation of the 1944 anti-New Deal, Texas Regular movement. While there could be little doubt that "Shivercrats" were sincere in their devotion to segregation, states' rights, and a generally neobourbon position, economic issues obviously occupied a position of primary concern. The fact that Eisenhower supported state control of offshore oil was a basic factor leading Shivers, as well as National Democratic Committeeman Wright Morrow, state attorney general and senatorial candidate Price Daniel, and much of the state Democratic Party organization, into the Eisenhower camp. In the election the

[9] New York *Times*, September 7, 1952.
[10] Lubell, *Revolt of the Moderates*, 283; Perry H. Howard, *Political Tendencies in Louisiana, 1812-1952* (Baton Rouge, 1957), 178–90; Howard and Deener, *Presidential Politics in Louisiana, 1952*, pp. 68–92; Sindler, *Huey Long's Louisiana*, 244–45; Steamer, "Southern Disaffection with the National Democratic Party," 161–66.

Republican ticket appealed to the same higher-income areas that voted for Shivers, and ten of the twelve counties that had given more than a 20 percent vote to the Texas Regulars cast a majority for the GOP.[11]

The Byrd machine in Virginia divided in the 1952 presidential contest. Governor John S. Battle, the state party central committee, and a number of organization regulars supported Stevenson. Senator Byrd made plain, however, that he could not support the Democratic ticket, although he did not endorse Eisenhower, and Representative William M. Tuck, also declaring neutrality, hinted clearly his preference for the Republican ticket.[12]

Presumably, southern defections from the Democratic Party would have been even greater had not the national Democratic convention been notably conciliatory toward the South. The convention, to be sure, had its stormy moments of North-South antagonism. Prior to the national gathering, party leaders in six southern states had made plans to hold post-convention meetings to determine whether the national Democratic Party ticket or some other candidates would be the state Democratic Parties' nominees. Most of the delegates from these states—Louisiana, Georgia, Mississippi, South Carolina, Texas, and Virginia—attended the Chicago convention in an uncompromising mood. "The threat of a six-state southern bolt" hung over and to a considerable extent dominated convention maneuvering.[13] Northern moderates sought to pacify the southern leadership, hoping thereby to win the southern electoral votes in the November election. The more militant liberals at the convention were prepared to abandon the southern conservatives and to campaign on an all-out liberal platform. The nomination of Adlai E. Stevenson marked victory for the party unifiers over the sectionalist liberals, and the Democratic convention buried the loyalty-oath issue that had been the focal point of North-South controversy, toned down the civil rights plank (although endorsing fair employment legislation), and chose Senator John Sparkman of Alabama as Stevenson's running mate.[14] The Democratic

[11] Paul T. David, Malcolm Moos, and Ralph M. Goldman (eds.), *The South*, 314–52, Vol. III of *Presidential Nominating Politics in 1952* (5 vols.; Baltimore, 1954); Lubell, *Revolt of the Moderates*, 282; O. Douglas Weeks, *Texas Presidential Politics in 1952* (Austin, 1953), 82–112.

[12] David, Moos, and Goldman (eds.), *The South*, 9–31.

[13] David, Moos, and Goldman (eds.), *The National Story*, 105, Vol. I of *Presidential Nominating Politics in 1952*.

[14] Allan P. Sindler, "The Unsolid South: A Challenge to the Democratic National Party," in Alan F. Westin (ed.), *The Uses of Power: 7 Cases in American Politics* (New York, 1962), 229–83.

Party came out of the convention nominally intact, and the Stevenson-Sparkman ticket appeared under the Democratic emblem in every southern state.

Hardly had the echoes of election oratory died away when a more reasoned and technical debate began before the justices of the United States Supreme Court. In December, 1952, the Court heard argument in the five cases, now grouped under the heading *Brown v. Board of Education,* questioning the separate but equal concept in public school education.[15] Acting as chief counsel for Clarendon County was John W. Davis, Democratic presidential candidate in 1924 and a leading constitutional lawyer. Davis marshaled the defense of yesterday's constitution; Thurgood Marshall of the NAACP was his chief antagonist. Argument was heard, and then all was silent in the federal courts until June, 1953, when the high tribunal, rather than handing down a decision in *Brown v. Board of Education,* ordered instead further argument centered on five questions framed by the Court. Two of the five questions rested on the assumption that the separate but equal formula and the Fourteenth Amendment were incompatible.[16] The nature of these questions, considered in light of *Sweatt v. Painter* and other trend-setting decisions, pointedly indicated that Jim Crow in the classroom was fast approaching a fatal constitutional rendezvous. The Court heard argument on the five questions in December, 1953.

These events again shifted public attention toward segregation and public schools. During the presidential campaign, FEPC legislation, the civil rights issue most clearly dividing the two candidates, had become the center of concern. After the ballots had been tallied, however, FEPC receded to a secondary position, and speculation mounted as informed observers recognized that the decision to rehear argument boded ill for segregated education. Despite state-to-state variations the political mood of the Deep South remained strikingly different from that of the peripheral states, where statements by public officials were less frequent and more restrained. Newspaper comment outside the five Deep South states was generally moderate, advocating a calm and reasoned approach to what-

---

[15] Technically, of course, four cases were in the group headed by *Brown v. Board,* and *Bolling v. Sharpe* was a companion case, since the latter concerned the District of Columbia and therefore involved a different legal question from that in the four other cases brought under the Fourteenth Amendment. Daniel M. Berman, *It Is So Ordered: The Supreme Court Rules on School Segregation* (New York, 1966), 1–79, is a good discussion of the early phases of the *Brown* litigation.

[16] *Brown v. Board of Education,* 345 U.S. 972.

ever ruling the Court might deliver.[17] Below the Tennessee line, however, state leaders privately and publicly affirmed their determination to maintain dual school systems and made further preparations for evading an unfavorable decision.

In November, 1953, Herman Talmadge proposed to the Georgia legislature a "private school plan" designed to evade an unfavorable Supreme Court decision.[18] The stratagem rested upon a constitutional amendment authorizing the state legislature to convert the public educational system into a private one and to channel state funds into tuition grants for students attending private schools. The legislature approved the amendment and authorized its submission to Georgia's voters in the November, 1954, general election.

In another significant action, the legislature created the Georgia Commission on Education, a segregationist strategy group made up of top administrative and legislative officials and prominent private citizens. Talmadge, the commission chairman, swore in members of the group in January, 1954. In his prepared remarks the governor proclaimed his willingness, should such action become necessary, to use the state militia for the maintenance of segregated educational facilities.[19] Durwood Pye, an Atlanta attorney with suitably segregationist views, was named executive secretary. The commission's first task was to participate in the campaign for ratification of the private school amendment.

During 1954 the Talmadge forces worked vigorously for passage of the constitutional change. The governor had met defeat in an effort to expand the county unit system during 1952, and the amendment election, aside from its effect on the future of segregation in Georgia, was deemed essential to Talmadge's prestige. The governor, Lieutenant Governor (and Democratic gubernatorial nominee-elect) Marvin Griffin, and Attorney General Eugene Cook campaigned actively; the state Democratic Party sponsored newspaper and television advertisements; and the Commission on Education spent a reported $13,000 mailing some 90,000 pieces of literature soliciting a favorable vote.[20] To counter this campaign,

[17] Southern Regional Council press surveys may be found in *New South*, May, July, 1953.

[18] New York *Times*, November 17, 1953; *New South*, December, 1953. The plan was not dissimilar to one that Herman Talmadge's lieutenants had unsuccessfully backed in 1951. New York *Times*, February 1, 1951.

[19] New York *Times*, January 19, 1954.

[20] Pat Watters, in Atlanta *Journal*, October 26, 1954; Charles Pou, in *ibid.*, October 27, 1954.

a formidable but poorly organized and financed opposition aired the potential threat the revision posed to Georgia's public schools.[21] The state's voters ratified the private school amendment by a relatively close vote in November, 1954. Generally rural areas favored the proposal, and urban voters opposed, with the former in the majority.[22]

Mississippi, too, made advance arrangements to oppose a judicial threat to segregated education. In late 1953 a special legislative session enacted the long-discussed public school equalization program and then suspended the project until the Supreme Court ruled on the validity of separate but equal arrangements. The lower house of the legislature, after striving to improve the schools, passed by a 2 to 1 majority a proposed constitutional amendment to provide for abolishing them. The amendment was defeated in the senate.[23]

During its regular session in early 1954, the Mississippi legislature, which normally meets every two years, appropriated school funds for only one year, thus assuring that a special session would be called after the Court ruled on the segregation question. The house passed a resolution promising to resist any efforts to force integration upon Mississippi,[24] and the legislature made this threat meaningful by enacting several segregationist measures. The Legal Educational Advisory Committee was created as the Mississippi counterpart to the policy planning groups already established in South Carolina and Georgia. Committee membership encompassed most of the political power structure of the state, including the governor and top administrative officers, legislative leaders, and even the chief justice of the state supreme court.[25] The legislature enacted a pupil placement law, the first of what was to become a popular anti-integration device. It provided for the individual assignment of students to specific schools and for an extended system of administrative remedies available to any pupil objecting to his assignment, thus safely forestalling im-

[21] There were three broad centers of opposition: the "school forces" led by the state superintendent of schools; civic groups led by the League of Women Voters; and a variety of Protestant groups that saw a threat to separation of church and state. *New South*, June, July, 1954; Atlanta *Journal*, October 28, 1954. A majority of Georgia's daily newspapers opposed the amendment, although the two big Atlanta dailies did not take a stand. A survey of Georgia press opinion may be found in Atlanta *Journal*, October 28, 1954.

[22] Lubell, *Revolt of the Moderates*, 181; New York *Times*, November 4, 1954.

[23] Carter, *The South Strikes Back*, 22; New York *Times*, December 14, 1953.

[24] New York *Times*, January 19, 1954.

[25] Chapter 420, Mississippi Legislative Acts, 1954 Sess., in Southern Education Reporting Service (ed.), *Facts on Film*, Roll 3.

mediate, large-scale enrollment changes.[26] Finally, the lawmakers endorsed a constitutional amendment requiring voter applicants to read, write, and understand the state constitution to the satisfaction of county registrars. The amendment was ratified by Mississippi voters in November, 1954.[27]

Elsewhere in the Deep South, South Carolina, having previously enacted extensive "preparedness measures," awaited the Court's decision without further legislative action. Louisiana, despite the widespread concern over threatened social change evidenced by the desertion of black-belt whites from the Democratic Party in the 1952 election, took no advance steps to protect segregation.

In Alabama there was agitation for a belligerent state stand, but action was limited. In the 1953 legislative session Representative Sam Engelhardt, a plantation owner from Macon County (with Tuskegee the county seat), assumed leadership of black-belt segregationists, introducing a constitutional amendment and accompanying legislation to authorize the conversion of the public schools to a private school system. The plan was defeated in the legislature, which contented itself with the establishment of a Joint Interim Legislative Committee on Segregation and Public Schools.[28] The legislature adjourned without further action, leaving the Committee to stand guard over segregated education. In Democratic primary elections in early May, 1954, Alabamians nominated James Folsom for governor and renominated John Sparkman for the Senate, choices hardly dictated by immediate concern for white supremacy. In the senatorial primary Sparkman's opponent, State Representative Laurie C. Battle, conducted an aggressive campaign, promising devotion to segregation and attacking Sparkman because he had been the 1952 vice-presidential candidate on a civil rights platform. The incumbent senator, however, swept to an easy victory.[29]

Moderation dominated the politics of the peripheral South. With Georgia making arrangements for a private education system, Governor Frank G. Clement of Tennessee reiterated in late 1953 his view that "the public schools of Tennessee have been operating since the first flat boat came in and the public schools will continue to operate for the benefit of

[26] Chapter 260, in *ibid.*
[27] *Christian Science Monitor*, November 17, 1954.
[28] *Southern School News*, September, 1954.
[29] New York *Times*, May 6, 1954.

all of our children."[30] In Arkansas Governor Francis Cherry spoke in a similar vein, indicating that his state would comply with whatever decision the Court handed down.[31] Not all public comment in the peripheral South was so accommodating, but nowhere in this region did responsible state officials make belligerent gestures toward the Court.

Throughout Dixie the drive for equalization, the push for equal as well as separate school facilities, continued. Gradualism, firmly checked in the Deep South, made halting progress on the periphery. In the cities Negroes sought and sometimes won local political office. And the Supreme Court pondered the fate of segregation.

During the spring of 1954, two discerning southern journalists delivered speeches in New York City. Jonathan Daniels, editor of the Raleigh *News and Observer*, addressed the National Urban League, optimistically predicting that the South would respond to any decision the Court might announce "with the good sense and goodwill of the people of both races in a manner which will serve the children and honor America."[32] John N. Popham, southern correspondent for the New York *Times*, speaking in the same city only a short time later, pessimistically discussed the belligerent climate of southern opinion, commenting on the "aggressive political action to forestall public school integration" that was taking place in the region.[33] There was considerable truth in the implications of both speeches in the spring of 1954, depending primarily on whether one gazed toward the Deep South or focused on the peripheral South. Events that were to follow, however, were to prove Popham the better prophet.

[30] As quoted in *ibid.*, December 14, 1953.
[31] *Ibid.; New South*, December, 1953.
[32] As quoted in *New South*, April–May, 1954.
[33] As quoted in New York *Times*, April 17, 1954.

CHAPTER 4

THE BROWN DECISION
AND THE FEDERAL GOVERNMENT

The long awaited day of judgment arrived on May 17, 1954, when Chief Justice Earl Warren, speaking for a unanimous Court, read the decision in *Brown v. Board of Education*. "We conclude," said Warren, "that in the field of public education the doctrine of 'separate but equal' has no place. Separate educational facilities are inherently unequal."[1] The legal structure of the southern caste system was left without constitutional foundation. The decision came ninety-one years after the Emancipation Proclamation.

Despite its epic massage, the opinion was not one of the Chief Justice's better efforts. Obviously drafted to attract a Court consensus, the brief document invited some of the criticism later heaped upon it. Warren largely ignored the formidable body of legal precedents that had been accumulating for more than two decades and relied instead upon historical, psychological, and sociological arguments.

The Chief Justice discussed the historical evolution of public schools, noting the great changes that had taken place since Reconstruction and the adoption of the Fourteenth Amendment—changes that had made education not only "perhaps the most important function of state and local governments" but also "the very foundation of good citizenship."[2] Having established the importance of public education in a mass society, he turned to the question of racial separation, concluding that public school segregation, even when "tangible" facilities were equal, generated a feeling of inferiority within the minority group. Citing a number of social and psychological studies, Warren stated that "whatever may have been the extent of psychological knowledge at the time of *Plessy v.*

---

[1] *Brown v. Board of Education*, in *Race Relations Law Reporter*, I (February, 1956), 9.
[2] *Ibid.*, 8.

Ferguson, this finding is amply supported by modern authority."[3] The equal but separate doctrine in education was unequal and therefore was unconstitutional.

The Supreme Court invalidated the principle of institutionalized segregation in the public schools, but, because of the decision's applicability to such wide and varied conditions, the justices delayed issuing an implementation decree. Instead, Warren ordered further arguments concerning the proper method for putting the principle of the decision into practice. All states affected by the decision were permitted to submit briefs and participate in the arguments. During succeeding months six states—Arkansas, Florida, Maryland, North Carolina, Oklahoma, and Texas—accepted the Court's invitation, joining the United States as *amici curiae*. South Carolina, Virginia, Delaware, and Kansas, as well as the NAACP which represented the plaintiffs, were, of course, already involved in the litigation.

Brown v. Board of Education was argued for the third time before the Supreme Court in April, 1955. Although briefs submitted by southern states were composed independently and offered a variety of suggestions and recommendations to the Court, they generally agreed in requesting the least specific and most indirect implementation decree possible. Lawyers for the NAACP took the opposite position, asking for a specific decree with a definite time limit to assure rapid rectification of the constitutional wrongs suffered by their clients. The United States, *amicus curiae* throughout the long period of litigation, took a position closer to the southern one, requesting that the Court provide a flexible equity remedy.[4]

The Supreme Court, not unexpectedly, adopted the substance of the southern position. As a practical matter, the Court could not easily venture beyond the executive department's position in a case involving such complex enforcement problems. The Eisenhower administration had made known its preference on this point in earlier arguments, and Warren's 1954 opinion had referred to "the great variety of local conditions" and the "considerable complexity" of the problem of compliance, thus largely committing the Court to a flexible decree.[5]

[3] *Ibid.*, 9.

[4] Berman, *It Is So Ordered*, 83–121; Blaustein and Ferguson, *Desegregation and the Law*, 158–79.

[5] *Brown v. Board of Education* (1954), in *Race Relations Law Reporter*, I (February, 1956), 9; Berman, *It Is So Ordered*, 118.

Again speaking through the Chief Justice, the Court handed down the second *Brown* decision on May 31, 1955. While reaffirming "the fundamental principle that racial discrimination in public education is unconstitutional," the decision remanded the cases to district courts, which were ordered to ensure "full compliance" with "all deliberate speed."[6] The Court's instructions, recognizing the "varied local school problems" involved, were general in nature and established no time limit.

Since 1955 some writers, noting the slow progress of school integration after the decision, have been critical both of the Court's allowing a year to elapse between the 1954 decision and the 1955 implementation and of the lack of a definite time limit in the decree itself. These analysts point out that the delays allowed time for opinion to crystallize and for southern states to perfect resistance measures.[7] Such speculations seem ill-founded. Lacking effective means to enforce its decrees and bound by the slow and cumbersome judicial process, the Court could do little more than establish the basis for realistic adjustments in race relations. The approach chosen recognized the intransigence of the Deep South and invited progress elsewhere. The policy was substantially successful in the border states; its failure in the South rested on numerous factors, among which was the dearth of leadership in the political branches of national government.

Congress was consistently ineffective during the 1950's, and it made no exception in the field of civil rights. Cohesion, the committee system, and seniority gave southern legislators a strong position in the congressional wing of the Democratic Party, and this fact, combined with support from conservative Republicans, kept Congress deadlocked during most of the decade.[8] In the Senate, the threat of southern filibusters served as a virtual veto on meaningful legislation, while members of the House of Representatives often demonstrated more enthusiasm for measures to censure or embarrass the Court than they did for methods to support the principle of the *Brown* decision.[9] The civil rights laws of 1957 and

---

[6] *Brown v. Board of Education* (1955), in *Race Relations Law Reporter*, I (February, 1956), 11–12.

[7] Among the best works taking this view are Quint, *Profile in Black and White*, 21; John Bartlow Martin, *The Deep South Says "Never"* (New York, 1957), 171; and Loren Miller, *The Petitioners: The Story of the Supreme Court of the United States and the Negro* (New York, 1966), 345–64.

[8] James MacGregor Burns, *The Deadlock of Democracy: Four-Party Politics in America* (Englewood Cliffs, N.J., 1963), is invaluable in this regard.

[9] For detailed discussions of relations between the judicial and legislative branches of government, see Murphy, *Congress and the Court*, and C. Herman Pritchett, *Congress Versus the Supreme Court, 1957–1960* (Minneapolis, 1961).

1960 were most significant perhaps as heralds of important future legislation. Concerned primarily with voting rights, the two acts lacked
adequate enforcement provisions and had little effect on race relations
in the South.[10]

While Congress was rendered inactive by deadlock, the Eisenhower
administration was inactive from choice—as well as from a seemingly
intrinsic inability to come to a decision or take an action in the field of
civil rights.[11] The executive branch continued policies inaugurated by
the Truman administration and offered few new departures. Truman's
attorney general had supported as *amicus curiae* the NAACP assault on
the separate but equal doctrine before the Supreme Court; the Republican administration continued this policy, although President
Eisenhower and most of his cabinet were obviously unenthusiastic about
the decision. The Republicans continued Truman's fair employment
policy but, except in the statements of Vice President Richard M. Nixon,
the Board's accomplishments were meager.[12] The Eisenhower administration effectively enforced desegregation policies in the armed services. But

[10] *Race Relations Law Reporter*, II (October, 1957), 1011; V (Spring, 1960), 237.

[11] Helpful on the Eisenhower administration are: Dwight D. Eisenhower, *The White House Years: Mandate for Change, 1953–1956*, and *The White House Years: Waging Peace, 1956–1961* (Garden City, 1963, 1965); Emmet John Hughes, *The Ordeal of Power: A Political Memoir of the Eisenhower Years* (New York, 1963); Sherman Adams, *Firsthand Report: The Story of the Eisenhower Administration* (New York, 1961); E. Frederic Morrow, *Black Man in the White House: A Diary of the Eisenhower Years by the Administrative Officer for Special Projects, The White House, 1955–61* (New York, 1963); J. W. Anderson, *Eisenhower, Brownell, and the Congress: The Tangled Origins of the Civil Rights Bill of 1956–1957* (University, Ala., 1964). The first three citations following Eisenhower's own reminis-
cences are memoirs by members of the White House staff; the last is an able study of
the administration's dealings with Congress on civil rights matters. The columns of
William S. White are also helpful. See especially his column in Richmond *Times-Dispatch*,
September 21, 1958.

[12] The broad outlines of the federal fair employment program emerged in the following
manner. In 1941 President Roosevelt created by executive order the Committee on Fair
Employment Practices. The committee's existence terminated in 1945 when Congress
severely cut its appropriations. In 1948, President Truman established a Fair Employment Practice Board within the Civil Service Commission (to encourage fair employment
practices in federal governmental agencies); and in 1951 he created the Committee on
Government Contract Compliance (to encourage nondiscrimination on the part of
private businesses with federal governmental contracts). During his last term in office,
Truman and his congressional allies attempted unsuccessfully to win enactment of
legislation institutionalizing a permanent Fair Employment Practices Commission. In
1953 President Eisenhower abolished Truman's Committee on Government Contract
Compliance and established the President's Committee on Government Contracts with
the Vice President as chairman. Two years later Eisenhower replaced the Fair Employment Practice Board with the Committee on Government Employment Policy, an
agency possessing lesser authority but the same mission as Truman's Board. See the
discussion in William Peters, *The Southern Temper* (Garden City, 1955), 241–66.

beyond encouraging the prompt desegregation of public schools in Washington, D.C. (which was accomplished in the fall of 1954), the President made little effort to inspire compliance with the *Brown* decision.

In part, Republican hesitancy in this field flowed from political considerations. Like the Democrats, the Republicans were torn between conflicting strategies. Some GOP leaders looked longingly toward the Negro vote in the northern states and recommended a vigorous civil rights policy. Other party strategists, watching the disintegrating position of the national Democratic Party in the South, visualized further Republican gains among white voters below the Potomac and counseled a cautious approach to the problems of desegregation. This internal dissension helped to sap the party's resolve.[13]

But more fundamentally, the explanation for the lack of presidential leadership seemed to stem back to the President himself. Eisenhower opposed concentrating further power in "the ever-expanding federal government" and sought to avoid infringing upon the rights of states "through overriding Federal law and Federal police methods."[14] His concept of leadership stressed "honesty of purpose, calmness and inexhaustible patience in conference and persuasion, and refusal to be diverted from basic principles."[15] A true conservative in his emphasis upon the gradual nature of social change, Eisenhower distrusted the efficacy of "arbitrary law" in dealing with racial problems. He often called attention to the deep emotional attachment many white southerners felt toward racial segregation, observing that "these great emotional strains and the practical problems" involved in desegregation merited serious consideration.[16] School desegregation, as Eisenhower apparently viewed it, was not so much a part of a sweeping social revolution as it was a question of individual emotions. The basic solution was to allow white southerners to adjust their feelings to a new social situation. Rather than providing leadership for the white South in reaching this accommodation, Eisenhower, seeing the problem as basically emotional rather than rational, sought to ensure that change was sufficiently gradual to prevent law from advancing too far beyond emotional readiness. The adjustment had to

---

[13] See Berman, *It Is So Ordered*, 83–86.

[14] Eisenhower, *The White House Years: Mandate for Change, 1953–1956*, p. 11, and Eisenhower to James Byrnes, August 14, 1953, reprinted in Eisenhower, *The White House Years: Waging Peace, 1956–1961*, p. 682.

[15] Eisenhower, *The White House Years: Mandate for Change, 1953–1956*, p. 193.

[16] As quoted in New York *Times*, November 24, 1954.

come internally—from within a sufficient number of white southerners. Federal pressure would not only be an intrusion into areas that were properly state responsibilities but would deepen emotionalism and compound the problem. On one occasion, when asked at a press conference about a report that he had privately expressed regret that the Court had declared segregation invalid, the President answered that he never commented on Court decisions. "It might have been that I said something about 'slower,' " he said, "but I do believe that we should—because I do say, as I did yesterday or last week, we have got to have reason and sense and education, and a lot of other developments that go hand in hand in this process—if this process is going to have any real acceptance in the United States."[17] From this negative approach, shared more or less by many of the conservative men around Eisenhower, flowed negative policy.[18]

Eisenhower was later to state in his memoirs that the Supreme Court's judgment in the desegregation case was unquestionably correct.[19] During his years in office, however, the President failed to express publically his approval either of the principle enunciated in the *Brown* decision or of the ruling itself. Since the racial question was the dominant domestic issue of the period, he made many comments on the subject. Yet not once did he endorse the desegregation decision or offer support to those struggling to implement its provisions. "I do not believe," the President reiterated, "it is the function or indeed it is desirable for a President to express his approval or disapproval of any Supreme Court decision."[20]

The Eisenhower administration consistently demonstrated a lack of basic forethought and planning. Taking the view that desegregation problems were matters to be resolved by the federal courts, the Republican leadership waited years to formulate elementary plans for dealing with opposition to district court orders. At a time when many southern leaders were belligerently championing the doctrine of interposition and when numerous communities had already experienced mob resistance to desegregation, the federal executive branch seemingly relied upon a vague hope that the problem would go away.

[17] *Ibid.*, August 28, 1958.
[18] The observations made in this paragraph rest upon the sources cited in note 11 and on Eisenhower's press conferences and public comments. Particularly helpful is Hughes, *The Ordeal of Power.*
[19] Eisenhower, *The White House Years: Mandate for Change, 1953–1956*, p. 230. But see also Hughes, *The Ordeal of Power*, 242, 244.
[20] As quoted in *Race Relations Law Reporter*, IV (February, 1959), 5.

In February, 1956, rioters successfully blocked a federal court order for the desegregation of the University of Alabama. Eisenhower's respoose to this challenge of federal judicial authority was to insist that the issue was a state matter, and best handled on the state level.[21] The university remained segregated. The Republican administration was still unprepared when Governor Shivers, responding to community hostility, openly and successfully used Texas Rangers to block court ordered desegregation. Shiver's defiant action was the subject of considerable discussion. The White House staff, after weighing the problem, concluded that there were many "difficult questions ... that we hope will not have to be answered."[22] The executive branch still had no plans for a crisis when Governor Orval E. Faubus called out the National Guard to halt court-approved desegregation in Little Rock in the fall of 1957.

Finally, in 1958, with massive resistance approaching a climax, the administration made some advance preparations. Attorney General William P. Rogers, who had replaced Herbert Brownell, offered the support of federal marshals to local officials attempting to execute court desegregation orders in the face of community hostility and state opposition. Rogers also indicated a more active role for the Justice Department in assisting with legal problems and obtaining injunctions against troublemakers in future desegregation crises.[23]

On one occasion the President did act decisively. In September, 1957, he ordered federal troops to Little Rock to enforce a federal court order and preserve the peace. Emmet John Hughes, the most perceptive chronicler of the Eisenhower years, observed: "The President, so slow to take firm federal action in support of civil rights, could and would respond with dispatch to a public challenge to presidential and constitutional authority. He could never view the first matter as anything but a dubious interpretation of law by the Supreme Court, trespassing close to a defiance of human nature. But the second question stood in no doubt: it was an issue of the dignity of the nation and its sacred founding documents."[24] Eisenhower explained at the time that the soldiers were not in Little Rock to promote a given racial policy, but were simply

[21] Adams, *Firsthand Report,* 338.
[22] Morrow, *Black Man in the White House,* 91–92.
[23] These pronouncements were made concerning the Little Rock desegregation controversy. *Arkansas Gazette,* September 10, 1958. The Justice Department had participated in litigation during controversies at Clinton, Hoxie, Nashville, and Little Rock, but only after being requested to do so by district courts.
[24] Hughes, *The Ordeal of Power,* 244.

filling a vacuum created by the breakdown of normal law enforcement processes.[25]

The President's action at Little Rock saved the federal judiciary from defeat in the South, but one dramatic thrust did not compensate for lack of leadership. On the whole the executive as well as the legislative branches of government left the courts to deal with problems of desegregation.

The Supreme Court declared segregation policies in public schools unconstitutional, and, as careful observers had predicted, the decision brought "down the wrath of all [white] southern society."[26] Public opposition put enormous pressure on southern lower federal court judges, the "fifty-eight lonely men," as Professor J. W. Peltason described them, whose job it was to change the racial policy of a region.[27] Both Peltason and Professor Kenneth N. Vines have examined the plight of these men occupying federal benches in the South. Most of them were native southerners; approximately 90 percent of the district judges had held public offices in the states in which their districts were located.[28] Many were in sympathy with segregation. Torn between professional duties on the one hand and social pressures and often personal desires on the other, federal judges found themselves in a position not unlike that of royal governors in pre-Revolutionary America. While no federal court judge was the victim of physical violence, more than one felt the chilling winds of social ostracism. In this situation, judges wavered, compromised, sometimes failed. Vines found seven district judges who handed down forty-three decisions, all of which were unfavorable to the Negro position.[29] Other judges had a far more prodesegregation judicial record, but the trend in race relations decisions reflected mounting segregationist pressure. By 1957 the courts were accepting even the most nominal of token desegregation plans and by 1958 the district courts were deciding a distinct minority of cases in favor of antisegregation litigants.[30]

Nevertheless, the judiciary successfully defended the principle of the

[25] Eisenhower to Senator John C. Stennis, October 7, 1957, reprinted in Montgomery *Advertiser*, October 24, 1957.
[26] Lubell, *The Future of American Politics*, 132; Hodding Carter, *Southern Legacy* (Baton Rouge, 1950), 89–90.
[27] J. W. Peltason, *Fifty-Eight Lonely Men: Southern Federal Judges and School Desegregation* (New York, 1961).
[28] Kenneth N. Vines, "Federal District Judges and Race Relations Cases in the South," *Journal of Politics*, XXVI (May, 1964), 343.
[29] *Ibid.*, 348–49.
[30] *Ibid.*, 342–49; Peltason, *Fifty-Eight Lonely Men*, 244–54.

Brown decision, expanding the doctrine to encompass transportation and public facilities. Unsupported by the political branches of government, attacked in the North for loyalty-security decisions, assaulted in the South for racial rulings, the federal court system struggled to establish the principle of equality before the law in the South.

CHAPTER 5

THE REACTION
TO THE BROWN DECISION

The 1954 *Brown* decision focused race politics in the South. In news-papers, political rallies, and public statements, on street corners, and in the homes of thousands of parents, the Supreme Court ruling was dis-cussed, attacked, and occasionally defended. Political leaders offered solutions ranging from the constructive to the incredible. Within months the NAACP was sponsoring petitions requesting that local school boards admit Negro students to white schools, while whites of the black-belt South organized to defend sanctioned traditions.

During the uncertain days after May 17, 1954, pronouncements from the South encompassed a broad spectrum of opinion, but much of the political power structure rallied to the defense of the southern past. James O. Eastland and Herman Talmadge unabashedly spoke the sentiments of white supremacy. The Supreme Court Justices, said Eastland, had been "indoctrinated and brainwashed by Left-wing pressure groups."[1] James F. Byrnes, Harry F. Byrd, and Senator Richard B. Russell of Georgia talked in the logical phrases of Burke and Calhoun. Byrnes reasoned that: "If the age of our Constitution is to be held against the soundness of its fundamental principles, what about the age of our religion? If time invalidates truth in one field, will it not do so in another?"[2] Powerful voices questioned the integrity of *Brown v. Board of Education* and the nine men who framed it.

---

[1] *Congressional Record*, 83rd Cong., 2nd Sess. (May 27, 1954), 7254.

[2] This quotation is from a somewhat later speech Byrnes delivered at Rock Hill, South Carolina. The text of the Rock Hill address is reprinted in *The State* (Columbia), December 13, 1955. The New York *Times*, June 7, September 13, 1954, contains charac-teristic Talmadge comments; Byrd's statement concerning the decision is reprinted in the Richmond *Times-Dispatch*, May 18, 1954; Russell's comments are summarized in the New York *Times*, May 18, 1954.

The year that separated the two *Brown* decisions was a year of drift
and decision, of progress and reaction. Border states used the interlude
to make constructive preparations for compliance; the Deep South entrenched itself yet further. The states of the peripheral South in varying
degrees hesitated, watched, waited, searched for leadership. Congress
debated other issues; the President equivocated; and, in Virginia, the Old
Dominion whose border had included the capital of the Confederacy and
Appomattox, a policy began to evolve—a platform upon which Virginia
would offer leadership to the upper South.

The decision became an issue in several primary elections in the
South. In Georgia and South Carolina it was *the* issue, inundating all
others, as politicians maneuvered frantically to occupy the extreme
segregationist position, pushing that position to its outer limits of hyper-
bole. In Texas, Tennessee, and North Carolina, however, efforts to
capitalize on racial reaction achieved little success, while in Arkansas
and Florida political hopefuls largely ignored the matter.

The 1954 Georgia gubernatorial primary was a confused affair. In the
backwash of the *Brown* decision, nine candidates searched for votes in
the labyrinth of race politics and the county unit system. For Marvin
Griffin, the eventual winner, the campaign issue was relatively simple.
"The meddlers, demagogues, race baiters and Communists are determined to destroy every vestige of states' rights," a perfidy Griffin vowed
to prevent, "come hell or high water."[3] Although three other candidates
took relatively moderate positions, only one endorsed the principle of the
Brown decision. Mrs. Grace Wilkey Thomas, an Atlanta Sunday School
teacher who believed in racial justice and wanted to present her case to
Georgia voters, called for compliance with the court ruling. She finished
last among the nine contestants.[4]

When the Georgia Education Commission asked each candidate to
appear at hearings to suggest specific methods for continuing segregation,
the campaign passed from confusion into absurdity. One lesser-known
contender offered the simplest solution of all: abolish the Supreme Court.
But it was Agricultural Commissioner Tom Linder who advanced the
proposal that caught the mood of the election. Linder's census plan would
have compelled state officials to canvass all Georgia, requiring parents of
school-age children to state under oath whether they wanted segregated

---

[3] As quoted in New York *Times*, May 18, 1954.
[4] *Ibid.*, September 5, 9, 1954.

or mixed educational facilities. Those who chose integration under the plan would undoubtedly be "diseased" and could be assigned to the state's mental institutions.[5]

In part the turmoil accompanying the democratic process at work in Georgia resulted from the collapse of dual factionalism. For some years the element of stability in Georgia politics had been the division of the state Democratic party into two relatively identifiable coalitions— Talmadgites and anti-Talmadgites—each appealing with some consistency to certain portions of the electorate. In 1954, however, the antis disintegrated, and the Talmadgites lost whatever real cohesion they had possessed.

Herman Talmadge's policies and personal popularity had extended his faction's base of support into towns and cities, homeland of the opposition. Himself ineligible for reelection, the governor's prestige and the backlash of the *Brown* decision made his faction's candidate an almost certain winner. Consequently, most of the Talmadge lieutenants made known their availability. After much maneuvering and several broken commitments, three candidates—Griffin, Linder, and Fred Hand— emerged from the Talmadge camp. With the opposition thus splintered, leading anti-Talmadge spokesmen backed former Governor Melvin E. Thompson. Charles Gowen's candidacy, however, prevented a unified effort.

Griffin reaped the benefits of Talmadge's governorship. Emerging as the strongest of the Talmadge candidates and receiving unofficial support from the governor himself, Griffin ran well in urban as well as in rural areas, receiving 36 percent of the popular vote, a plurality, and winning almost 75 percent of the county unit ballots. Thompson, with a three-way split in the opposition camp, could do no better than a poor second.[6] Disappointed anti-Talmadgites, including former Governor Ellis G. Arnall, surrendered the field, retiring into private life. Thompson made one more effort by opposing Talmadge for a seat in the United States Senate in 1956, and his dismal showing confirmed the fact that anti-Talmadgism was dead. So, however, was Talmadgism. The 1954 schism, Talmadge's absence from state politics, and the lack of a coherent opposition made that faction an amorphous group of political leaders.

[5] *Ibid.*, June 26, 1954.

[6] *Ibid.*, September 9, 1954; *Christian Science Monitor*, September 9, 1954. On factional politics in Georgia, see Key, *Southern Politics*, 106–29, and Bernd, *Grass Roots Politics in Georgia*, 4–23.

Coincidental with the demise of a rational intraparty cleavage in Georgia was an intensification of primitive dual factionalism in South Carolina. Although by no means a perfect and consistent divorce, the two estranged wings—loyalist and Byrnes-Dixiecrats—were usually at odds when the South Carolina Democratic Party faced major policy questions or important elections. Personal antipathies, especially a long-standing feud between State Senator Edgar A. Brown, a spokesman for the "Barnwell Ring" in the legislature, and former Governor Strom Thurmond, contributed to the division.[7] But more fundamentally, factionalism rested upon ideological differences that eventually evolved into institutionalized form with the establishment of a two-party politics in the 1960's. The Byrnes-Dixiecrat faction was distinctly neobourbon in outlook and favored political independence from the national Democratic Party, revolting in 1948 and supporting Eisenhower in 1952. The some-what unnatural loyalist coalition was less sectionally oriented and re-mained true to the national party throughout the 1950's. Senator Olin Johnston, a loyalist leader, was not notably liberal by northern standards, but he was, nevertheless, far to the left of the Byrnes-Thurmond group. Brown, who shared leadership with Johnston, was considerably more conservative. Both factions, of course, were committed to segregation.

In the 1954 gubernatorial primary Lieutenant Governor George Bell Timmerman, Jr., received support from many of the old Dixiecrats, while Lester Bates, a Columbia businessman, attracted aid from the loyalists. During the election Timmerman popularized the three-school plan. Rather than merely accepting the inefficiency of dual public school systems, Timmerman proposed three separate systems—one for whites, one for Negroes, and one for those who wanted integration. Bates strongly attacked this proposal on the ground that it would permit some de-segregation, and Timmerman, in turn, charged that Bates was nothing but an NAACP candidate anyway. Timmerman won handily.[8]

South Carolina factionalism was sharply delineated in an unexpected and hard-fought senatorial campaign later in the year. During the 1954

[7] The "Barnwell Ring" was the group of veteran legislators closely associated with State Senator Brown and House Speaker Solomon Blatt, both of whom were residents of Barnwell County. Lander, *A History of South Carolina*, 178–93, is the best discussion of factional developments in South Carolina. Also helpful are Quint, *Profile in Black and White*, 128–44, and the stories on South Carolina politics in the New York *Times*, par-ticularly those of June 6, 9, September 4, 8, 1954.

[8] New York *Times*, June 9, 1954.

primary United States Senator Burnet R. Maybank was renominated without opposition. Shortly afterward, Maybank died. The Democratic Executive Committee, over Byrnes's objections, made Brown the Democratic nominee without a primary election. Thurmond, taking advantage of the adverse public reaction to the committee's decision, campaigned as a write-in candidate. Johnston and the loyalist faction supported Brown, and Byrnes and the Dixiecrats campaigned for Thurmond. Running as the champion of "democracy" as opposed to committee "dictation," Thurmond was successful.[9]

With occasional exceptions, such as Thurmond's stirring defense of popular democracy, race overrode all else in both Georgia and South Carolina. In the former, the race issue contributed to making politics a wasteland of conflicting personal ambition; in the latter, a similar fixation accompanied the gradual rise of a meaningful, if proscribed, factionalism. A basic explanation for this anomaly was the Talmadge political skill. By leading the neobourbon quest for the past, he guarded against a revolt by the right; by drawing back from independent political action, he prevented opponents on the left from becoming defenders of the Democratic Party. Griffin, in a less skillful fashion, continued this policy. Byrnes, on the other hand, made regional political independence a major part of his program, while Johnston and his associates refused to do battle with the national party.

Byrnes and Talmadge had led their states to the forefront of resistance to social change. Differing on political strategy, the two men demonstrated equal determination to prevent desegregation. In January, 1955, they turned their political domains over to new management, which was also pledged to defend the past.

Like Germany after Bismarck, however, Georgia and South Carolina found their new leaders far less adept. Timmerman left the South Carolina legislature to run its own affairs, bereft of executive guidance, and Griffin defended his solons from press criticism for being a do-nothing assembly with the explanation that the charges were true "only in the sense you have done nothing to destroy segregation, you have done nothing to weaken the county unit system, you have done nothing to destroy local self government, and you have done nothing to surrender our cherished rights."[10] While Timmerman made clumsy invasions of academic freedom

---

[9] *Ibid.*, November 3, 1954.
[10] As quoted in Atlanta *Constitution*, February 18, 1956.

in South Carolina,[11] the Griffin administration gained a reputation for corruption, attempted to silence criticism from the urban press with a crude legal scheme, and did battle with Georgia Institute of Technology students by trying to prevent their football team from appearing in a postseason game because a Negro athlete played on the opposing team.[12] For the latter action Griffin was hanged in effigy.

Neither governor had a program, if that implies constructive goals, and neither indicated understanding the nature of social, economic, and demographic change in the South. Both seemed to feel that their states contained no ills that could not be cured by greater devotion to white supremacy. Griffin and Timmerman were not lacking, however, in dedication to segregation, and they were energetic proponents of the harsher virtues of the neobourbon creed.[13]

Outside of Georgia and South Carolina there were no major statewide political contests in the Deep South during the period immediately following the *Brown* decision. James Folsom had been nominated for the governorship in Alabama prior to May 17, 1954. Louisiana would choose state officials in 1956, while Mississippi candidates staked out positions for the primary to be held in the summer of 1955.

Among political campaigns in the peripheral South, the most revealing was the North Carolina senatorial primary in 1954. Once again Kerr Scott threw down the gauntlet before the traditional organization, and once again the organization demonstrated its willingness to resort to racial demagoguery when its right to govern was seriously questioned. Upper-class machines of the North Carolina type were particularly prone to these tactics. Dominated by business, commercial, and corporate interests, the organization's ideology centered somewhere between neobourbon reaction and business conservatism. Assured ample campaign funds and a phalanx of support from the economically affluent, it could confidently expect to win any election as long as issues were not sharply defined. The great threat to this comfortable arrangement was an op-

[11] See Chapter 12. Good characterizations of Timmerman are Quint, *Profile in Black and White*, 53, 116–24, and Bob McHugh, in St. Petersburg *Times*, December 7, 1958.

[12] Atlanta *Constitution*, December 3, 1955; Atlanta *Journal*, January 29, 1956, December 17, 1958; Chattanooga *Times*, January 29, 1956.

[13] Apparently sustained racial emotionalism generated a need for men of this caliber. Alabama in 1958 and Mississippi in 1959 elected similar governors, and Louisiana accomplished much the same result in its 1960 gubernatorial election. To a lesser degree Tennessee in 1958 and Florida in 1960 followed somewhat the same pattern.

position candidate who enticed the lower classes to vote their own self-interest, while stirring the progressively oriented of all economic levels. And, of course, the obvious way to defeat such a threat was to obscure the issues with appeals to white supremacy. Thus did Willis Smith fell Frank P. Graham in 1950. Smith died three years later and Governor William B. Umstead, an organization veteran who had defeated a Scott-backed candidate in 1952, appointed Alton A. Lennon to the vacant Senate seat.

The Scott-Lennon contest of 1954 was reminiscent of the 1950 campaign for the same seat. Advertisements and handbills linking the anti-organization candidate to integration appeared near the end of the campaign as they had in 1950. But Scott enjoyed advantages that Graham had not possessed. Agricultural commissioner and then governor, Scott was a professional politician with proven ability and his own cohesive faction. In a vigorous campaign, he denounced McCarthyism and racial intolerance and won the Democratic nomination for the United States Senate.[14] Scott's victory did not prove that North Carolina citizens were less devoted to segregation in 1954 than they had been four years before; it did demonstrate that far more than just a boundary line separated the state from its neighbor to the south.

Tennessee voters also withheld their favor from the champions of racial discord. Both Senator Estes Kefauver and Governor Frank Clement won renomination over segregationist opposition.[15] Texas was the one other state where the *Brown* decision became a major issue in an important statewide election.[16] There Governor Allan Shivers included appeals to racial prejudice in his "uninhibited propaganda campaign which equated the NAACP, the CIO, and the Communist Party," as a critical observer in neighboring Arkansas described his campaign.[17] Shivers won the gubernatorial renomination, but not before challenger Ralph Yarborough had forced him into a bitterly fought runoff primary. Since Shivers had easily won reelection with first-primary victories in 1950 and 1952, his narrow 1954 success was a rather hollow triumph.[18] The incumbent's appeal to

[14] New York *Times*, May 30, 31, 1954; Thomas L. Stokes, in Chattanooga *Times*, March 8, 1955; Lefler and Newsome, *North Carolina*, 649–50.

[15] New York *Times*, August 6, 1954.

[16] The racial issue was also aired in the Florida 1954 gubernatorial campaign between Democrat LeRoy Collins and Republican J. Tom Watson. In this case, however, Watson, who made defense of segregation an important plank in his platform, died prior to election day. *Southern School News*, November, 1954.

[17] Ashmore, *An Epitaph for Dixie*, 142.

[18] O. Douglas Weeks, *Texas One-Party Politics in 1956* (Austin, 1957), 7–8.

racial prejudice was an apparently insignificant factor, particularly since Yarborough also offered opposition to "forced" desegregation. The East Texas region where Negroes were numerous and race feeling was strongest gave Yarborough a majority.[19]

"Intolerable, impractical, and unenforceable"—these were among the adjectives Louisiana solons thought appropriate to describe the *Brown* decision.[20] Alone among southern states, Louisiana's legislature was in session on May 17, 1954. Within days the lawmakers approved a resolution censuring the Supreme Court, created the Joint Legislative Committee to Maintain Segregation to plan strategy, and began drafting laws to counter the threat of school desegregation. State Senator William M. Rainach, chairman of the segregation committee, rapidly emerged as the spokesman for racial reaction. In June, Rainach and his associates offered two bills and a constitutional amendment for legislative consideration. "A vote against these bills," Rainach cautioned, "is an open invitation to the carpet-baggers, scalawags and National Association for the Advancement of the [*sic*] Colored People to integrate our schools."[21] Few Louisiana legislators wanted to proffer such an invitation, nor to be accused of so doing during the next election. All three measures passed the house unanimously and each passed the senate with no more than two opposing votes.[22]

The least offensive was a local pupil assignment law, authorizing parish superintendents to assign individual pupils to public schools and establishing a long and involved system of administrative remedies for parents of children not satisfied with their assignment.[23] The act contained no criteria to guide public school superintendents in making assignments, but shrewd school administrators probably detected a hint of legislative intent from other measures passed on the same day. The "Police Power" bill required segregation in all public schools below the college level, "not on the basis of race but for the advancement, protection and better education of all children of school age in Louisiana regardless of race. . . ."[24] The United States Supreme Court had ruled that "segregation of children in public schools solely on the basis of race" was un-

---

[19] New York *Times*, July 26, 1954; *Southern School News*, September, 1954.
[20] As partially reprinted in New York *Times*, May 27, 1954.
[21] As quoted in *ibid.*, July 7, 1954.
[22] *Ibid.*
[23] Act 556, Louisiana Legislative Acts, 1954 Sess., in *Facts on Film*, Roll 3.
[24] *Race Relations Law Reporter*, I (February, 1956), 239.

constitutional; Louisiana, which, after all, was a part of the Union, promptly quit segregating its children on the basis of race and segregated them racially on the basis of the police power of the state. The tragedy of such nonsense was that the measure's sponsors were serious—violation was made a misdemeanor, and the essential parts of the bill were drafted into a constitutional amendment which passed the legislature at the same time. The amendment was ratified by an overwhelming majority of the voters later in the year.[25]

Louisiana's lawmakers were by no means radically bellicose when compared with other states of the Deep South. Hardly had Chief Justice Warren completed the reading of the *Brown v. Board of Education* decision when segregation strategy committees were devising methods to prevent its enforcement. None of these states accepted the Court's invitation to submit briefs and participate in arguments concerning implementation —either on the grounds that such participation might imply an obligation to comply or that it was futile to debate implementing a decision which was not recognized as valid in the first place.

As state legislatures convened, numerous measures—some of which were ridiculous, more of which were dangerous—became law. Among sundry recommendations of the Georgia Education Commission was a bill making it a felony for any state or local official to spend public funds on an integrated school.[26] The Georgia legislature passed this measure and placed the commission's other legislative proposals on the calendar as a ready reserve for future battles with the federal courts. Lawmakers further broadcast their devotion to white supremacy with various resolutions, including one passed by the house that demanded a return to segregation in the armed services.[27]

In South Carolina the Gressette Committee greeted state legislators with a program that seemed to offer as much threat to the public schools in general as it did to desegregation. Governor Timmerman explained in his inaugural address that a gradual adjustment to desegregated conditions was "cowardly because it seeks to minimize opposition by careful selection of a few victims from time to time."[28] South Carolina solons guarded against such dangers by denying state funds to "any school from

---

[25] *Ibid.*, 239; New York *Times*, November 4, 1954.

[26] Chap. 82, Georgia General Acts and Resolves, 1955 Sess., in *Facts on Film*, Roll 3.

[27] Eugene Cook (ed.), *Compilation of Georgia Laws and Opinions of the Attorney General Relating to Segregation of the Races* (Atlanta, 1956), 50–54.

[28] As quoted in Charlotte *News*, January 18, 1955.

which, and for any school to which, any pupil may transfer pursuant to, or in consequence of, an order of any court,"[29] repealing compulsory attendance laws, authorizing local school boards to lease or sell public school property, broadening assignment authority vested in school officials, and eliminating tenure provisions from teacher contracts.[30]

Mississippi gave ample and ominous warnings of the rift between Deep South whites and reality. Governor Hugh White and the Legal Education Advisory Committee scheduled a conference of Negro and white leaders to allow both groups to endorse continued segregation on a voluntary basis. After consulting with a few conservative Negroes, who agreed to support the plan, White issued the invitations.[31] Held on July 30, 1954, the much-publicized conference opened with proper and paternalistic talks by members of the white hierarchy. Then came the Negroes' turn to pay homage to the mutual advantages of racial separation. But at this point there was a radical departure from the script. To the amazement of white observers, Negro spokesmen with near unanimity insisted upon compliance with the Supreme Court decision. The day of Booker T. Washington had passed. The Legal Education Advisory Committee had endeavored to "learn the true attitude of the Negro leadership of the state," White said later, but it had been "most positively and unexpectedly disappointed."[32] It was becoming harder and harder to learn the "true" sentiment of Negroes in Mississippi.

Governor White called the Legal Education Advisory Committee back into session. The committee then drafted a "last resort" constitutional amendment to relieve the state of the necessity to provide a public school system. The proposed amendment authorized the legislature to abolish the entire public school system, or to permit local school authorities to abolish parts of it, and provided for the payment of tuition grants to school children and the leasing, selling, or renting of school property.[33] A special legislative session approved the amendment in September, 1954, and Mississippi voters ratified the measure by a solid majority in a December election.[34] In another special legislative session in early 1955,

[29] *Race Relations Law Reporter*, I (February, 1956), 241.
[30] *Southern School News*, April–June, 1955; Quint, *Profile in Black and White*, 103–104.
[31] Before the conference convened, however, younger and more militant leaders convinced all but one of these men to support the Court decision. James W. Silver, *Mississippi: The Closed Society* (New York, 1964), 88.
[32] As quoted in New York *Times*, September 8, 1954.
[33] Chap. 39, Mississippi Legislative Acts, 1954 Special Sess., in *Facts on Film*, Roll 3.
[34] *Southern School News*, October, 1954; New York *Times*, December 23, 1954.

Mississippi categorically and positively defined state policy with a law stating:

It shall be unlawful for any member of the white or Caucasian race to attend any school of high school level or below wholly or partially supported by funds of the State of Mississippi which is also attended by a member or members of the colored or Negro race.[35]

Only Alabama, of the Deep South states, avoided the more extreme results of legislative hysteria in the wake of the *Brown* decision. Alabama evidenced no lack of segregationist sentiment among its legislators, but here strong voices called for a sane and moderate approach to racial problems. The fate of such a policy was demonstrated during the years that followed.

Four states of the Deep South banned public school desegregation within their borders, prohibiting social change in the schools in all communities without regard for local preferences, in some cases specifically making it a criminal offense to comply with the *Brown* decision. Each of these states made provisions to abolish, either directly or indirectly by stoppage of funds, all or part of its public school system. In public policy, segregation was a goal that took precedence over local democracy, federal law, and public education itself.

Responsible public officials elsewhere in the South were at first unwilling to lay such sacrifices before the altar of white supremacy. In these states, "local option" became a catchword. Reigning southern governors, meeting in Richmond, Virginia, in June, 1954, unanimously vowed "not to comply voluntarily with the Supreme Court's decision against racial segregation in the public schools."[36] Nevertheless, upper-South governors, directly or by implication, at first accepted the validity of the *Brown* decision, and legislatures refused to pass school-closing bills.

The locally administered pupil assignment plan was the legislative connivance most discussed in the peripheral South. North Carolina and Florida, as well as Alabama and Mississippi, promptly enacted such

[35] Chap. 43, Mississippi Legislative Acts, 1955 Special Sess., in *Facts on Film*, Roll 3.

[36] As reprinted in Richmond *News Leader*, June 11, 1954. The purpose of the conference was to formulate a general southern strategy for dealing with the desegregation decision and for preparing *amici curiae* briefs for the 1955 implementation arguments. Agreement was reached, however, on only a broad statement of protest. Eight of the former Confederate states' governors attended; Arkansas, Tennessee, and Texas sent gubernatorial representatives.

measures. Other states were to do so during following years.[37] The device had two basic elements. It provided for individual assignment of pupils to schools and established prerequisites for local administrators to follow in making placements, and it created a system of administrative remedies for parents displeased with the results. Various criteria were listed to guide local agencies in assigning students, and the words "race" and "Negro" found no place on the list. Instead, administrative problems, physical facilities, sociological and psychological factors, and academic background were among the considerations that school boards were required to take into account. Resulting segregation rested not upon an illegal racial classification but nominally upon weighty and responsible concern for individual students.

The administrative remedies portion of the plan was aimed at parents inadequately appreciative of the state's forethought. A system of appeals, sometimes incredibly long and involved, made unwanted enrollment changes troublesome, time consuming, and expensive. Florida Attorney General Richard Erwin predicted that it would require some two years to exhaust administrative remedies provided by Florida law before a potential Negro litigant could get his case before a federal court.[38] An individual challenging the system found that the burden of proof rested on those who wanted change.

In addition to laws of this type, the legislatures of Florida and North Carolina enacted lesser segregation measures, including acts undermining tenure protection for public school teachers whose social views conflicted with the community norm.[39] The North Carolina program resulted from the recommendations of a Special Advisory Committee. Governor Umstead, who announced that he was "terribly disappointed" with the *Brown* decision, appointed the committee, which included three Negro members—two of whom were selected from the state payroll.[40] Umstead

---

[37] As noted above, Mississippi enacted the first pupil assignment law. Chap. 260, Mississippi Legislative Acts, 1954 Sess., in *Facts on Film*, Roll 3. The best drafted and most widely copied of the early assignment acts, however, was the Alabama law passed in 1955. *Race Relations Law Reporter*, I (February, 1956), 235–37. The Florida assignment law is reproduced in *ibid.*, 237–38; the North Carolina measure in *ibid.*, 240–41. The Florida law particularly was badly drafted and was revised extensively in 1956. *Ibid.*, I (October, 1956), 924–27. The legal aspects of the pupil assignment laws are discussed in Daniel J. Meador, "The Constitution and the Assignment of Pupils to Public Schools," *Virginia Law Review*, XLV (May, 1959), 517–71.

[38] St. Petersburg *Times*, March 18, 1956.

[39] *Southern School News*, May, June, 1955.

[40] *Ibid.*, September, 1954. Governor Umstead is quoted in the New York *Times*, May 18, 1954.

died in November, 1954, and Luther Hartwell Hodges, a businessman and political unknown who had won the lieutenant governorship in 1952, received the committee report. With Hodges' backing the recommendations were approved during the 1955 regular session. In Florida the racial issue became entangled with a bitter legislative reapportionment controversy—a tactic that the defenders of rural domination found helpful in more than one southern state during the 1950's. Governor LeRoy Collins stated that no legislation to protect segregation was needed and urged the lawmakers to concentrate on framing a more equitable system of representation. Ignoring the governor, the legislators passed three segregationist measures, which Collins criticized but also signed into law.[41]

Legislative sessions in Texas and Arkansas produced no segregationist laws at all. Although Shivers made clear his displeasure with the Court decision, he also recommended that no legislative action be taken until the Court had clarified its ruling.[42] Texas lawmakers complied by virtually ignoring the subject. After the second *Brown* decision, Shivers created the Advisory Committee on Segregation in the Public Schools to study the question.[43] Arkansas legislators occupied themselves with the merits and demerits of a tax increase. One segregationist bill, a local pupil assignment proposal, did pass the house but failed in the senate.[44]

The Tennessee legislature, with the exception of Senator Charles A. Stainback, also showed a distinct lack of concern for racial matters. Stainback, a Dixiecrat leader in 1948, represented the only two counties in the state where Negroes were a majority of the population. First elected to the legislature in 1903, the eighty-five-year-old senator came out of retirement following the *Brown* decision to introduce a pupil assignment bill. His fellow senators were wary. The senate calendar committee elected to table the proposal, and Stainback's attempt to force the bill from the committee was voted down on the floor. He introduced an amendment to the general education bill requiring that funds be alloted exclusively to segregated schools, but his amendment was defeated. Finally Stainback redrafted his original proposal into two local bills applicable only to Fayette and Haywood Counties. These bills, along with similar proposals concerning two other West Tennessee counties,

[41] Miami *Herald*, April 6, 1955; *Southern School News*, August, 1955; Frank Trippett, in St. Petersburg *Times*, March 18, 1956.
[42] *Southern School News*, February, 1955.
[43] Dallas *Morning News*, August 2, 1955.
[44] *Southern School News*, April, 1955.

routinely passed the legislature largely unnoticed among other local measures.[45]

Although the acts themselves were relatively harmless, Governor Clement chose to meet firmly the basic issue. He vetoed all four bills, and his veto message to the legislature was a powerful statement of the moderate position: "Segregation is not a political issue to be misused to the detriment of Tennessee and Tennesseans, but it is a significant and far reaching social issue which demands statesmanlike consideration, prayerful thought and legal analysis."[46] The legislature upheld the governor's action.

Virginia officialdom was obviously disconcerted. Just after the Court ruling in May, 1954, Governor Thomas B. Stanley said that he was seeking "a plan which will be acceptable to our citizens and in keeping with the edict of the court."[47] Several days later Stanley conferred with Negro leaders, inviting them to urge the state's black population to ignore the court pronouncement. Stanley learned privately what Mississippians were later to discover publicly—Negroes were no longer willing to endorse the system.[48]

During following weeks members of the Byrd organization, especially spokesmen from the Southside Fourth Congressional District, voiced sharp criticism of desegregation. Stanley soon shifted to this approach. In June he was the host at a meeting of southern governors that resulted in a statement of opposition to the *Brown* decision.[49] Later in the same month he promised to utilize all methods legally available to avoid integration in Virginia.[50] In August he appointed the Commission on Public Education to study the issue. The thirty-two member body was weighted with black-belt representation and was dominated by organization regulars.[51] State Senator Garland Gray, a leading figure in the organization, was chairman. The Supreme Court decision obviously displeased the Byrd hierarchy, but no "nod" came down to the faithful. The Gray Commission looked the matter over, hinting in preliminary reports at a local deter-

[45] Nashville *Tennessean*, March 14–16, 1955; *Southern School News*, February–April, 1955.
[46] As reprinted in Nashville *Tennessean*, March 15, 1955.
[47] As quoted in *Southern School News*, September, 1954.
[48] Robbins L. Gates, *The Making of Massive Resistance: Virginia's Politics of Public School Desegregation, 1954–1956* (Chapel Hill, 1962), 30.
[49] New York *Times*, June 11, 1954.
[50] *Ibid.*, June 26, 1954.
[51] Gates, *The Making of Massive Resistance*, 34–36.

mination approach on the North Carolina model.[52] Senator Gray, however, branded the decision "political and monstrous."[53]

The year separating the two *Brown* decisions confirmed trends already
well established. The Deep South sank deeper into hysterical reaction,
while border states cemented their psychological identification with the
nation, and the peripheral South, like an unstable planet, swayed between
the magnetic attraction of North and South. And the long hot summer
of 1955 lay ahead.

[52] *Southern School News*, February, 1955.
[53] As quoted in *ibid.*, November, 1954.

CHAPTER 6

THE CITIZENS' COUNCILS

Four Negroes were killed by white men in Mississippi during 1955. There were no convictions for any of the four assassinations—despite the fact that one took place on the Lincoln County courthouse lawn in broad daylight. Another, the murder of Emmett Till, remained unsolved after an all-white jury pronounced "not guilty" the two men who admitted abducting Till on the night of the killing. White Mississippians expressed to an exaggerated degree rising racial tensions common to much of the South during late 1955. The mood was not entirely unlike that of 1948, except that the existence of the direct threat of school desegregation, the easily identifiable symbol of the Supreme Court, and the growing militancy of Negroes added greater fury to white resentment. By the end of the year a massive bus boycott raged in Montgomery, Alabama; a broader economic cleavage strangled Orangeburg, South Carolina; and a bitter school desegregation controversy sundered Hoxie, Arkansas. These clashes were among the more publicized manifestations of racial discord during the angry months following the second *Brown* decision.

In so far as there was a focus to white belligerency, it was the appearance of Negro petitioners asking for desegregation of public schools. In June, 1955, the NAACP recommended to its branch organizations that they "file at once a petition with each school board, calling attention to the May 31 decision, requesting that the school board act in accordance with that decision."[1] Some sixty such petitions materialized in the South during the summer of 1955. Similar petitions, though fewer in number, had appeared following the first *Brown* decision in 1954, and although

---

[1] "A Directive to the Branches," excerpts reprinted in Wilson Record and Jane Cassels Record (eds.), *Little Rock, U.S.A.: Materials for Analysis* (San Francisco, 1960), 10.

they had evoked hostility, occasional reprisals, and no redress, they were soon forgotten. When Negroes asked for compliance with federal law in 1955, however, reaction in the Deep South white community was swift and vindictive. Negroes whose names appeared on petitions frequently found themselves without jobs, credit, or even the meager benefits of white paternalism. And sentiment in the white community was crystallizing into stonelike unanimity, a unanimity that was the most fundamental of all forces demanding racial orthodoxy.

The atmosphere of violence, boycott, reprisal, and caste solidarity both set the stage for and announced the arrival of the Citizens' Council movement. The Councils and allied groups provided the organization and inspiration for economic retaliation against active Negro integrationists and any whites who dared to espouse their cause; but burgeoning segregationist organizations were more the result than the cause of the truculent southern mood. The Councils fed on long-developing racial fears and frustrations, and, of course, by feeding on them, heightened them. Fitting the climate of the time, the movement effectively filled a void felt by many white southerners who were often inclined to blame NAACP (and probably communist) organizational superiority for Negro gains and thus tended to view a white man's organization to counter the threat and reestablish "southern" values as the obvious solution to the race problem.[2]

Numerous segregationist groups sprang up throughout the South. An estimated fifty such organizations emerged in the years immediately following *Brown v. Board of Education.*[3] With the rise of the Citizens' Councils, many, though by no means all, of these groups were absorbed into the mainstream of the resistance.

By the end of 1955, the Council movement was the most vocal of all pressure groups in the South. Its period of greatest growth was the year

[2] Helpful on the Citizens' Councils generally are Carter, *The South Strikes Back;* James Graham Cook, *The Segregationists* (New York, 1962); Martin, *The Deep South Says "Never";* Vander Zanden, *Race Relations in Transition;* Paul Anthony, "Resistance!," *Research in Action,* I (November, 1956), 1–6; Frederick B. Routh and Paul Anthony, "Southern Resistance Forces," *Phylon Quarterly,* XVIII (First Quarter, 1957), 50–58; David Halberstam, "The White Citizens Councils: Respectable Means for Unrespectable Ends," *Commentary,* XXII (October, 1956), 293–302; James W. Vander Zanden, "The Citizens' Councils," *Alpha Kappa Deltan,* XXIX (Spring, 1959), 3–9; and Vander Zanden, "A Note on the Theory of Social Movements," *Sociology and Social Research,* XLIV (September-October, 1959), 3–7. See Chapter 10 for a discussion of literature published by the Councils themselves.

[3] Southern Education Reporting Service estimate given in Weldon James, "The South's Own Civil War: Battle for the Schools," in Don Shoemaker (ed.), *With All Deliberate Speed,* 16–17.

following the second *Brown* decision. The movement reached its peak during the early months of 1956, and by 1957 it was already in a gradual decline. At their height the Citizens' Councils and associated groups had perhaps 250,000 members, although a considerably larger number of white southerners probably enrolled at one time or another.[4] But organized segregationists exercised an influence far more pervading than membership rolls implied. Their ranks were the "Jesuits" of the white supremacy creed, the cadres of massive resistance. Effective leadership and organization exploited the movement's position on the popular side of the racial controversy, often allowing Council spokesmen to usurp the voice of the white community. An uneasy but workable alliance with powerful political figures gave its leaders influence on the highest policy levels.[5]

The resistance movement had outposts in every southern state. Citizens' Councils existed in Mississippi, Alabama, Louisiana, South Carolina, Texas, Florida, Arkansas, Tennessee, and Virginia. Allied organizations included the Defenders of State Sovereignty and Individual Liberties in Virginia, the Patriots of North Carolina, the States' Rights Council of Georgia, and the Tennessee and Florida Federations for Constitutional Government. The strength and effectiveness of these groups varied greatly from state to state.

In the opening pages of *Southern Politics*, V. O. Key wrote:

The hard core of the political South—and the backbone of southern political unity—is made up of those counties and sections of the southern states in which Negroes constitute a substantial proportion of the population. . . .

The black belts make up only a small part of the area of the South and—depending on how one defines black belt—account for an even smaller part of the white population of the South. Yet if the politics of the South revolves around any single theme, it is that of the role of the black belts. Although the whites of the black belts are few in number, their unity and their political skill have enabled them to run a shoestring into decisive power at critical junctures in southern political history.[6]

These remarks were fully applicable to the resistance movement. To be sure, the Councils, like the Dixiecrats, were shaped by a complex variety

---

[4] There are no verified resistance membership figures. A Southern Regional Council survey near the end of 1956 estimated membership at approximately 300,000. *Special Report: Pro-Segregation Groups in the South* (Atlanta, 1956). Evidence would seem to indicate that the Southern Regional Council overestimated membership strength in some states, especially those where white supremacy organizations were weakest.

[5] This point is discussed more fully in Chapter 7.

[6] Key, *Southern Politics*, 5–6.

of forces. Yet the basic thrust of the organized resistance and its most solid foundation of support came from whites of the black-belt South.

The first Citizens' Council was formed in July, 1954, in Indianola, Sunflower County, Mississippi, near the heart of the Delta. Robert B. Patterson, a plantation manager, and several local businessmen and political officials were searching for a method to counter the threat posed by the Supreme Court decision when Circuit Judge Tom P. Brady of Brookhaven focused their thinking with a speech delivered in Greenwood in late May. Brady pointed to the need for organized southern resistance, and, following his address, he discussed the project with the Indianola group. Shortly afterward Brady formalized his message in *Black Monday*, a pamphlet that became the handbook of the movement.[7] In July, Patterson and thirteen associates created the original Citizens' Council and devised the organizational structure that served as a model for future local groups. From Indianola an energetic core of proselytizers spread into neighboring counties.[8]

In Mississippi, as in several other southern states, the Councils represented a genuine grass roots movement—the militant reflex of black-belt towns and rural communities, the reaction of the county seat elite, using that term in its broadest sense. Early leadership came from men who, like Patterson, moved out of private life to battle for the "holy cause," and from local politicians, whose occupation for half a century had been the protection and promotion of white supremacy. The movement quickly became an influence in the state legislature, where the powerful Dixiecrat-Old Guard headed by Speaker of the House Walter Sillers of Bolivar County took up its cause. Among politicians appealing to a statewide clientele, the organized resistance found recruiting more difficult. As late as the fall of 1955, State Auditor-elect E. Boyd Golding could claim that he was the only high state official holding membership in the Citizens' Council.[9]

In October, 1954, with some twenty counties organized, Citizens' Council leaders formed a state association to coordinate Council activity and serve as an information center. The association, with Patterson as executive secretary, strove to "organize every town and county in our

---

[7] Judge Tom P. Brady, *Black Monday* (Winona, Miss., 1955). Among several accounts of the origins of the Citizens' Councils, Carter, *The South Strikes Back*, 25–35, is perhaps the best.

[8] Association of Citizens' Councils of Mississippi, *Annual Report* (Winona, Miss., 1955), 1.

[9] Jackson *Daily News*, October 23, 1955.

state and then every state in the South.''[10] The Councils also campaigned for passage of a suffrage restriction amendment to the state constitution, which was approved by heavy majorities in November, and then turned to support of the "last resort" school closing amendment, which was ratified by a comfortable majority in December.[11] By the end of 1954 the Mississippi Association of Citizens' Councils claimed chapters in more than thirty counties, had participated in two winning political campaigns, and was dispatching organizers into neighboring states to spread the resistance.

During 1955 and 1956 the association continued to expand, distending from the rural Mississippi River lowlands into the cities and hill country. The Jackson chapter, formed in early 1955, soon became the hub of state Council activity. Later in the year the association began publication of *The Citizens' Council*, a four-page monthly newspaper edited by William J. Simmons. As Council administrator, Simmons joined Patterson, Brady, and a few others at the top of Mississippi Councildom. Council membership increased rapidly, particularly after NAACP chapters in four Mississippi cities filed desegregation petitions during the summer of 1955. In August, 1955, the state association claimed 60,000 members; by the end of 1956 it claimed a membership of 85,000 with chapters in sixty-five of Mississippi's eighty-two counties.[12] The Mississippi Association was, as Hodding Carter III described it, "the biggest, the most tightly organized, and the most powerful Citizens' Council of them all."[13] Increasingly the Councils dominated the political life of Mississippi. After the inauguration of Ross R. Barnett, a longtime Council member, as governor in 1960, Leslie Dunbar could observe that "Mississippi is experimenting with a Soviet style government, with the Citizens Council paralleling the state machine in emulation of a successful Communist Party."[14]

[10] Association of Citizens' Councils of America, *The Citizens' Council* (Greenwood, Miss., n.d.), 4; Association of Citizens' Councils of Mississippi, *Annual Report* (1955), 2.

[11] *Christian Science Monitor*, November 17, 1954; Kenneth Toler, in Atlanta *Journal and Constitution*, December 26, 1954.

[12] Association of Citizens' Councils of Mississippi, *Annual Report* (1955), 1; *The Citizens' Council*, January, 1957.

[13] Carter, *The South Strikes Back*, 20.

[14] Dunbar, "The Changing Mind of the South," 20. Barnett stated on several occasions that "I am proud that I have been a Citizens' Council member since the Councils' early days." *Strength Through Unity!: Address by Governor Ross R. Barnett to Citizens' Council Rally, New Orleans, March 7, 1960* (Greenwood, Miss., n.d.), 3; Ronald Harry Denison, "A Rhetorical Analysis of Speeches by Segregationists in the Deep South" (Ph.D. dissertation, Purdue University, 1961), 48.

The only state group to rival Mississippi in membership was the Citizens' Councils of Alabama. After a lethargic beginning, the Alabama Council movement mushroomed phenomenally during 1956, numbering perhaps 60,000 members by the middle of that year.[15] The town of Selma in Dallas County, center of the Alabama black belt, spawned the state's first Citizens' Council chapter, which was organized with the aid of Mississippi advisers in October, 1954. The movement gradually spread to nearby rural areas, but further growth was slow. By June, 1955, functioning council chapters existed in only seven counties.[16]

The heavily Negro populated counties of central Alabama remained the center of white supremacy agitation, but the inspiration for an organized resistance emanated from Birmingham as well as from the black belt. The Birmingham-based American States Rights Association, created in early 1954, was the first important white supremacy group in the state. Among its six hundred incorporators were a considerable number of wealthy and prominent citizens. Its board of directors included such business representatives as the chairman of the board of a large Birmingham insurance company and the chairman of the board of a major Birmingham pipe and foundry company. State Senators Sam Engelhardt, Jr., and Walter C. Givhan, both influential black-belt spokesmen, were among board members residing outside the Birmingham area. In addition to other propaganda activities, the American States Rights Association sponsored a radio program featuring Asa Carter of Birmingham as announcer. Members of the association performed an important role in the development of the Alabama Council movement. Carter became a leading Council organizer and, in effect, the movement's unofficial executive secretary, although his intemperate and anti-Semitic public remarks soon led to his dismissal. Engelhardt then became executive secretary and chief Council spokesman, a role Givhan assumed in 1958 when Engelhardt stepped down to campaign unsuccessfully for state office. The American States Rights Association president, Birmingham insurance executive

---

[15] The Citizens' Councils of Alabama claimed 80,000 members in June, 1956. *Southern School News*, July, 1956. Paul Anthony of the Southern Regional Council, in the most thorough study of the Alabama Councils undertaken during the period, estimated their membership "in excess of 60,000 members." "A Survey of the Resistance Groups of Alabama" (unpublished Southern Regional Council field report, 1956), introduction. See also Alabama Council on Human Relations, Inc., "Pro-Segregation Group Trends," *Alabama Council Newsletter*, III (June, 1957), 1–5.

[16] Montgomery *Advertiser*, November 28, 1954; *Southern School News*, December, 1954; Birmingham *News*, November 30, 1954, June 19, 1955.

Olin H. Horton, was a frequent speaker at Council rallies and organizational meetings.[17]

From its inception the Alabama Council movement was deeply intertwined with much of the black-belt political power structure. "Colonel" Alston Keith, chairman of the Dallas County Democratic Executive Committee, and State Senators Givhan of Dallas County and Engelhardt of Macon County were among the original voices of Council sentiment. Keith, a Selma lawyer, was the leading organizer of the state's first Citizens' Council.[18] Givhan, widely considered a spokesman for the State Farm Bureau Federation, was a rising power in the Council and an aggressive organizer sometimes inclined toward "open the bedroom doors of our white women to the Negro men"-type of rabble-rousing.[19] The most influential of all Alabama members was Senator Engelhardt. A planter whose feudal domain spread over 6,500 acres of Macon County and included, along with cotton gin and commissary, some seventy-five Negro families, Engelhardt entered politics in 1950 specifically to counter the growing threat of social change. He provided the movement with effective and dedicated, if unspectacular, leadership.[20] Other spokesmen joined these three in important policy making positions as the organization spread outside the black belt. Luther Ingalls, a Montgomery lawyer, and Dr. John H. Whitley, little-known manager of a drugstore in Tarrant City, an industrial suburb of Birmingham, became the most influential of later recruits. For brief periods, Asa Carter and Leonard Wilson, who won a reputation as a leader of the antidesegregation demonstrations at the University of Alabama, also served as major Council leaders.[21]

The Alabama organization retained a distinctly black-belt character. Even at the height of its power, the movement was dominated at the strategy level by black-belt representatives.[22] Birmingham "Big Mule"

[17] Bem Price, in Louisville *Courier-Journal*, November 21, 1954; Anthony, "A Survey of the Resistance Groups of Alabama," 3–5; Martin, *The Deep South Says "Never"*, 107–13; Birmingham *News*, October 4, November 9, 21, 1955.

[18] Montgomery *Advertiser*, November 28, 1954; Birmingham *News*, November 30, 1954.

[19] *Southern School News*, January, 1955; Birmingham *News*, July 2, 1955; Nashville *Tennessean*, February 18, 1956; Chattanooga *Times*, February 18, 1956.

[20] Martin, *The Deep South Says "Never"*, 105–14.

[21] Anthony, "A Survey of the Resistance Groups of Alabama," 2–9. The Appendix of this work contains biographical sketches of Alabama resistance leaders.

[22] Meetings of the Association of Citizens' Councils were customarily top-heavy with representatives from black-belt counties. See, for example, Montgomery *Advertiser*, August 18, 1956, which reports on an important Citizens' Council strategy meeting. Of sixteen counties represented, only five could not be described as distinctly black-belt.

industrial influence may well have been felt, however, behind the scenes. The American States Rights Association provided a direct link between Birmingham business interests and the Councils. Such spokesman as Sidney W. Smyer and State Senator Albert Boutwell, normally considered to be in close harmony with the wants and desires of Alabama's industrial elite, were enthusiastic Council supporters.[23] Outwardly Birmingham's upper class remained aloof from the Citizens' Councils.

In June, 1955, Council leaders inaugurated a membership drive with a white supremacy rally at Selma, a meeting that revealed a good deal about the movement. Across the rear of the speakers' platform at the rally, twelve state senators, largely from black-belt areas, represented a formidable array of state political influence. A brief speech by Sidney W. Smyer and the presence of Senator Boutwell on the platform implied a reaffirmation of the black-belt-Big Mule coalition. No state leaders were present (unless one so considered Boutwell). More so than in Mississippi, the Alabama Citizens' Councils had difficulty attracting the support of established politicians not directly a part of, or subservient to, the black-belt county seat elite. Featured speakers were from other states, hinting at the organization of an impressive stable of interstate speakers soon to be available for Citizens' Council rallies throughout the South. Herman Talmadge, at his rabble-rousing best, imparted to the five thousand people in the audience sundry tidbits of sage information, including the observation that "the present judges on the supreme court are not fit to empty the waste baskets" of previous justices who upheld the legality of the separate but equal doctrine.[24] Robert Patterson and Judge Brady also spoke, providing Mississippi perspectives for the Alabama listeners.

During following months the Council slowly expanded, spreading into Montgomery and Birmingham. Engelhardt and his associates accomplished the first step toward broader organization with the formation of the Central Alabama Citizens' Council in late 1955. Consolidating county chapters in the black-belt region, the Central Alabama Council, with Engelhardt as chairman, became the nucleus for a statewide organization.[25]

---

[23] Anthony, "A Survey of Resistance Groups of Alabama," Appendix.
[24] As quoted in New York *Times*, June 23, 1955. See also the Birmingham *News*, June 23, 1955.
[25] *Southern School News*, November, 1955. A second regional group, the North Alabama Citizens' Council, was created at the same time. The North Alabama organization, with Asa Carter as executive secretary, did not become a part of the state Council Association.

In December, 1955, the long Montgomery bus boycott began. Two months later rioting prevented the desegregation of the University of Alabama. In this racially tense atmosphere, white Alabamians flocked to join the resistance. Montgomery quickly became a bastion of Council influence. Angered by the Negro community's refusal to accept Jim Crow seating arrangements on city buses, many of the city's white citizens, including the mayor, police commissioner, and other important city officials, became Council members.[26] The organized resistance also made major numerical gains in the industrial suburbs in the Birmingham area. With membership soaring, Council leaders formed a state association of Citizens' Councils in February, 1956. Dr. Whitley was selected as chairman of the state organization, with Engelhardt as its executive secretary and most authoritative spokesman. The association established headquarters in Montgomery, home of the state's biggest and most active county chapter. The bus boycott officially ended late in 1956, however, and after that tempers and Council membership gradually declined. In 1958 the association's central office was shifted to the more hospitable climate of Selma, and Givhan, who lived near Selma, became the Councils' most prominent leader.[27]

In Louisiana the Citizens' Council organization began as (and to a large extent remained) a projection of the Joint Legislative Committee to Maintain Segregation. Throughout the decade Council activity outside the New Orleans area was hardly distinguishable from that of the committee. State Senator William M. Rainach, chairman of the Joint Legislative Committee, was president of the Association of Citizens' Councils of Louisiana. State Representative John Sidney Garrett, committee spokesman in the lower chamber, became president when Rainach stepped down. William M. Shaw, general counsel for the legislative committee, was executive secretary of the state Citizens' Council organization. The result was an interesting example of legislative coercion. Rainach and a few associates, already able to intimidate their peers by questioning their devotion to segregation, invaded with their own organization the bailiwicks of fellow solons. During the latter half of the 1950's, the ambitious

---

[26] *Southern School News*, February-April, 1956.

[27] Robert S. Bird, in St. Louis *Post-Dispatch*, February 28, 1956; Ed Townsend, in *Christian Science Monitor*, May 17, 1956; John N. Popham, in New York *Times*, December 2, 1956; Montgomery *Advertiser*, February 18, 1956; Alabama Council on Human Relations, Inc., "Pro-Segregation Group Trends," 2–5; Fred Taylor, in Birmingham *News*, July 8, 1958.

chairman-president was beyond doubt Louisiana's most powerful legislator.

The Louisiana Citizens' Council movement was organized from the top down to a greater degree than in Mississippi or Alabama. Rainach, Garrett, and Shaw all came from Claiborne, a black-belt parish in the northern part of the state. In Homer, the parish seat, they organized Louisiana's first Council chapter in April, 1955, and tirelessly promoted its expansion, launching a statewide membership drive later in the year.[28] The Councils established close ties with the American Association for the Preservation of State Government and Racial Integrity, a predominantly urban organization that included a number of prominent citizens as sponsors.[29] In January, 1956, with 8,000 members in thirteen parishes, the Councils consolidated on the state level. Officials in the Louisiana Association, in addition to Rainach and Shaw in the two top spots, included Harry P. Gamble, Sr., head of the American Association for the Preservation of State Government and Racial Integrity; J. Stewart Slack, a member of the Louisiana State University Board of Supervisors and an honorary vice president in the American association; Robert G. Chandler, a Shreveport states' rights spokesman; Dr. Emmett L. Irwin, ex-president of the Louisiana Medical Association and president of the Greater New Orleans Citizens' Council; and Malcolm Dougherty, president of the Louisiana Farm Bureau Federation.[30]

The Louisiana Citizens' Councils continued to expand after 1956, although organizations in most other states were declining. In part because of Louisiana's peculiar configuration, four centers of Citizens' Council influence emerged. The Protestant up-country, from Alexandria northward, was the homeland of the resistance. Council recruiting proved most fruitful in the cotton producing areas in the northern Louisiana hills and in the Red and Mississippi river valleys.[31] The Greater New Orleans

---

[28] New Orleans *Times-Picayune*, April 20, 1955; *The Citizens' Council*, June, 1956; Anthony, "Resistance!," 1–6.

[29] Anthony, "Resistance!," 5–6.

[30] New Orleans *Times-Picayune*, January 30, 1956.

[31] Generalizations about the geographical distribution of Council chapters made here and elsewhere in this chapter are based on maps of the eleven southern states constructed in the following manner. Primarily from newspaper reports and Southern Regional Council field reports, lists of counties containing Council chapters were compiled. These lists were compared with the claims of the Councils themselves (for example, *The Citizens' Council*, June, 1956, lists all Louisiana parishes containing active Council chapters). Donald R. Matthews and James W. Prothro of the Institute for Research in Social Science of the University of North Carolina were kind enough to make available to me

Citizens' Council, a vigorous organization and probably the most genuinely grassroots movement in the state, included the city and three parishes to
the south. An intra-Catholic racial feud and the formidable presence of
Leander Perez complicated the politics of race in New Orleans. The
Citizens' Councils established chapters in half a dozen West Florida
parishes (spreading from Baton Rouge to Bogalusa) and in the area
around Lake Charles in the southwestern part of the state. Although the
association claimed up to 100,000 members, such figures were undoubtedly exaggerated.[32] Total membership in all Louisiana chapters never
appeared comparable to that of Mississippi and Alabama.

Compared to Council organizers in other states, resistance leaders in
South Carolina and Virginia placed less emphasis on expanding membership and demonstrated greater concern for proper behavior and sedate
respectability. They made some effort to screen membership applications,
and they showed a more pronounced tendency to avoid activities potentially damaging to institutional prestige. Befitting the older and traditionally more aristocratic eastern seaboard states, the public pronouncements
of resistance spokesmen were normally more erudite and less emotional
in tone than was customary elsewhere. Partly because of this emphasis
on respectability, the major segregationist organizations in South Carolina
and Virginia had little difficulty attracting support from state-level
politicians. Beneath their more sophisticated "style," of course, white
supremacy groups in South Carolina and Virginia differed little in nature
and objective from the organized resistance in other states.[33]

The evolution of a state association of Citizens' Councils in South
Carolina followed patterns similar to those that had appeared in Mississippi, Alabama, and Louisiana. Although a belated arrival, the Council
movement grew rapidly in South Carolina during the period between
the summers of 1955 and 1956. School desegregation petitions in ten
South Carolina communities prompted organization of the state's first
chapters in August, 1955. Predictably, the charter group materialized near

---

a Southwide list of counties containing Council chapters that they compiled in 1960 in
connection with a study of factors influencing Negro voter registration. (Their study is
"Negro Voter Registration in the South," in Sindler [ed.], *Change in the Contemporary
South,* 119–49.) From these sources, the author was able to construct what he believes
to be relatively accurate maps denoting the areas of Council membership.

[32] *The Citizens' Council,* June, 1956.

[33] See Gates, *The Making of Massive Resistance,* 158–63; Muse, *Virginia's Massive
Resistance,* 9–10; and "The Resistance Groups of South Carolina" (unpublished Southern
Regional Council field report, n.d.), 9–11.

the center of the South Carolina black belt in Elloree, Orangeburg County. A group of Elloree civic leaders met with S. Emory Rogers, who was an attorney for Clarendon County during the long years of *Briggs v. Elliot* and the first public advocate of a South Carolina Council movement, and Farley Smith, who represented the "Committee of 52," to organize the state's initial Citizens' Council. The movement quickly spread through the rural communities of the feudal lowlands and, from there, into Charleston and Columbia. The organized resistance particularly thrived in the Old South environment of Charleston, which joined county seats like Orangeburg and Sumter as bastions of Council strength.[34]

From its inception the movement enjoyed the blessing of many of the state's power elite. The "Committee of 52," which cooperated closely with the Councils and actively participated in organizational efforts, included among its members the president of the South Carolina Farm Bureau Federation, the president of the state bar association, a leading South Carolina author, the superintendent of the South Carolina Penitentiary, a former governor, a college president, a leading South Carolina journalist, and a number of industrialists and bankers.[35] The state's leading politicians, including the two United States senators, several representatives, the governor, and the lieutenant governor, spoke at Council meetings. The Councils were not notably successful, however (at least in comparison with Mississippi, Alabama, Louisiana, and Virginia), in achieving direct state legislative influence. Generally the dominant group of legislators—those commonly associated with the "Barnwell Ring"—remained as far removed from the Councils as political considerations allowed.

In October, 1955, leaders from some thirty local Citizens' Council chapters created a state association. Unlike Mississippi, Alabama, and Louisiana, no small group of individuals became entrenched in leadership positions. Top association offices changed hands frequently. S. Emory Rogers was the association's first executive secretary and probably the most influential member during the early organizational period. Micah

---

[34] *The Citizens' Council*, June, 1956, contains the best discussion of the organization of the Council movement. "The Resistance Groups of South Carolina," 1–5; Quint, *Profile in Black and White*, 38–54; Martin, *The Deep South Says "Never"*, 62–72; and articles by William D. Workman, Jr., a member of the "Committee of 52" and a friend of the Councils, in the Charleston *News and Courier* and Bob Pierce, in *The State* are helpful on the development of the Councils.

[35] "The Resistance Groups of South Carolina," Appendix.

Jenkins, a Charleston businessman and past head of the segregationist Grass Roots League of Charleston, was the original chairman of the state group. Julian K. Stubbs of Sumter, chairman of the largest local Council in the state, was a recognized power in the movement. Farley Smith, a son of former Senator Ellison D. Smith, was a rising influence in the association who later became executive secretary. Numerous other individuals, chiefly from black-belt communities but including members from Charleston, Columbia, and even the Piedmont, held important Council positions.[36]

At their height, the South Carolina Citizens' Councils may have enrolled as many as 40,000 members.[37] Although leaders often talked of expanding the movement's influence in Piedmont areas, Council strength in South Carolina, as elsewhere, lay in the lowlands.

Choosing a name more descriptive and (for proper Virginians) less commonplace than Citizens' Councils, Virginia segregationists created the Defenders of State Sovereignty and Individual Liberties.[38] The Defenders movement was native to the Southside black belt, most of which was a part of the Fourth Congressional District. This area consistently produced the highest percentages of votes for candidates of the Byrd organization. Thus voter loyalty, combined with ideological compatibility and the skill of its politicians, gave Southside spokesmen strong voices at the top of the Byrd hierarchy and, with the advantages of malapportionment and a tradition of leadership, a pivotal position in Virginia politics.[39]

Southside leaders had already begun to exploit this position before the Defenders appeared. In June, 1954, Fourth District Representative Watkins M. Abbitt, twenty Southside state legislators, and about fifty other representatives of black-belt political power met in the historic town of Petersburg to consider a course of action. With State Senator Garland Gray presiding, the group vowed to seek a method which would allow

[36] *The Citizens' Council*, June, 1956; Charleston *News and Courier*, January 18, February 15, 1957; *The State*, August 21, 1958.

[37] See Martin, *The Deep South Says "Never"*, 67–68, and the Charleston *News and Courier*, February 15, 1957.

[38] Virginia also had several Citizens' Council chapters. In August, 1958, representatives from six local Councils formed the Virginia Association of Citizens' Councils. Although the Virginia Councils were active throughout the late 1950's, they did not succeed, as the Defenders did, in attracting a broad popular following. Richmond *Times-Dispatch*, August 12, 1958.

[39] Gates, *The Making of Massive Resistance*, 23–27; Muse, *Virginia's Massive Resistance*, 2; Muse, in Washington *Post*, January 18, 1959.

counties to maintain segregated schools. Copies of the resolution were sent to governing boards of other Virginia counties, and the legislators *en masse* called on Governor Stanley to urge resistance to integration on the state level.[40] Shortly afterward Stanley promised to "use every means at my command to continue segregated schools in Virginia."[41]

The Defenders emerged in October, 1954. During the preceding summer Prince Edward County, home of a race scare throughout the 1950's, had been the hub of considerable informal organizational activity to lay the foundations for the movement. In early October some eighty Southside whites, including both influential amateurs and established political professionals—the combination that effectively spoke for small towns of the black-belt South—formally created the Defenders of State Sovereignty and Individual Liberties. Robert B. Crawford, a dry-cleaner in Farmville, county seat of Prince Edward County, became president. Within a year, the Defenders established state headquarters in Richmond, with William E. Moxey, Jr., as executive director and Collins Denny, a Richmond attorney, as counsel and frequent spokesmen. Crawford, a man of considerable ability and integrity, remained the most authoritative voice in the organization.[42]

The Defenders never numbered more than 15,000 and, geographically, the movement was largely confined to Southside and neighboring areas, although a few chapters sprang up in the northern part of the state.[43] Yet, as the vanguard of racial extremism, the organization exercised enormous influence. In June, 1955, the Defenders made public "A Plan for Virginia," calling for legislation "to prevent the expenditure of $1.00 of public monies, state or local, in the support and maintenance of any racially mixed public school"—the first effective plea for total state resistance. Calling upon all "candidates for the General Assembly ... to state openly, frankly and fearlessly what, if anything, they have to propose, and whether they can be relied upon to give their full support to a program that will prevent integration in Virginia public schools," the Defenders successfully strove to eliminate any middle ground of

---

[40] Muse, in Washington *Post*, January 18, 1959; Gates, *The Making of Massive Resistance*, 31.

[41] As quoted in New York *Times*, June 26, 1954.

[42] Richmond *Times-Dispatch*, October 7, 8, 1954; Richmond *News Leader*, October 8, 1954; Muse, *Virginia's Massive Resistance*, 9–10.

[43] The Defenders claimed sixty chapters with 15,000 members in March, 1957. Richmond *News Leader*, March 23, 1957.

gradualism or local option, to rephrase the issue as a question of the preservation of the white race.[44]

These five states—Mississippi, Alabama, Louisiana, South Carolina, and Virginia—contained the bulk of white supremacy organizational strength. Nowhere else did the movement achieve comparable membership or political power. In several other states, however, organized white supremacists were able to exert political pressure and influence the course of events.

The Patriots of North Carolina, Inc., was organized in August, 1955. A steering committee headed by a Greensboro textile industrialist enlisted 356 prominent citizens from fifty-nine counties to sign the charter of incorporation. Although the list of signers was respectable, even impressive, it included a significant number of out-of-office politicians and no representatives from either of the state's two major political factions. The Patriot president was Wesley C. George, research professor at the University of North Carolina Medical School, and A. Allison James, a Winston-Salem druggist and a former employee of the United States Treasury Department, served as executive secretary. Piedmont textile executives were the most numerous economic group among the original slate of officers. Geographically, the Greensboro area, which supplied twenty-two of the sixty-member board of directors and five of the fifteen-member executive committee, was the center of the movement. North Carolina's black-belt whites were only marginally represented.[45]

The Patriots at first seemed active and well-financed. James served as fulltime executive secretary, and he was assisted by a four-member staff at the group's central office in Greensboro. The executive secretary and a number of other officials industriously traveled about the state striving to promote the resistance. Reportedly, the Patriots additionally employed a number of fulltime organizers to recruit new members.[46]

From the beginning, however, the Patriots had difficulty attracting a mass following. Even when local organizations such as the Durham United Political Education Council were included, white supremacy groups functioned actively in no more than a dozen (of one hundred) North

---

[44] "A Plan for Virginia," reprinted in Richmond *Times-Dispatch*, June 9, 1955.

[45] The Greensboro *Daily News*, August 23, 1955, contains the complete list of incorporators; the Richmond *News Leader*, September 19, 1955, gives the original list of officers.

[46] "Patriots of North Carolina, Inc." (unpublished Southern Regional Council field report, n.d.), pages unnumbered.

Carolina counties, these mainly in the Piedmont. The Patriots were never able to invade the eastern black belt, and this was the organization's basic weakness. Without the support of the black-belt county seat elite, no Council movement had any real hope of achieving relatively permanent influence in state politics. The North Carolina black belt, influenced by populism and traditionally a home of political insurgency, largely ignored the Patriots and offered only grudging support to the later charismatic racism of I. Beverly Lake.[47] The Patriots, lacking membership, influence within the established factions, or spokesmen at the highest echelons of the state power structure, were doomed to function on the fringe of decision-making. They were noisy, sometimes dangerous, but powerless to direct the course of state policy.

The peak of Patriot prestige came in the spring and early summer of 1956, when the organization played a major role in the defeat of two of the state's three congressmen who refused to sign the Southern Manifesto.[48] Both men were veteran House members representing Piedmont districts, and their vulnerability on the race issue sharply undermined the moderate position in North Carolina politics.

The Patriots proved unable to exploit their 1956 success and declined soon afterward. In 1958 a new state organization, the North Carolina Defenders of States' Rights, which included a number of former Patriot leaders among its directors, attempted to revive grass roots racism in the state, but the organization never achieved significance and was finally swept up into the broader, amorphous movement led by Beverly Lake.[49]

In Texas the Citizens' Councils functioned effectively as a political pressure group, but the organization, like the Patriots in North Carolina,

[47] I. Beverly Lake, a former Wake Forest College law professor, was assistant attorney general in North Carolina. In July, 1955, he made a widely publicized anti-integration speech. Reprinted in Winston-Salem *Journal*, July 27, 1955. Shortly afterward he resigned as assistant attorney general to become "North Carolina's top spokesman on segregation." Jay Jenkins, in Atlanta *Journal and Constitution*, August 21, 1955. In 1960 he ran for governor on a segregationist platform.

[48] Thurmond D. Chatham, a four-term incumbent who stated that the *Brown* decision was "the law of the land," came under attack not only for his stand on race relations but also for an allegedly high absentee record. In his unsuccessful campaign, Charles B. Deane, a highly respected five-term veteran, faced "only one issue—the Manifesto." Jay Jenkins, in Charlotte *Observer*, May 17, 1956. Representative Harold Cooley, the third nonsigner, survived the 1956 race, partly because he confused the issue by conducting a more racist and demagogic campaign than his opponent. Charlotte *Observer*, May 11, 13, 1956; Greensboro *Daily News*, May 26, 1956.

[49] The directors listed in the charter of incorporation of the Defenders are given in the Greensboro *Daily News*, November 22, 1958.

never obtained statewide membership or decisive governmental power. The first Council chapter originated during the summer of 1955 at Kilgore, in East Texas. Other groups sprang up spasmodically across the state. In November, 1955, representatives from twelve chapters created the Association of Citizens' Councils of Texas.[50] Dr. B. E. Masters, president emeritus of Kilgore Junior College and a leading organizer of the Kilgore chapter; F. Ross Carlton, a Dallas attorney and original chairman of the state executive committee; and Austin E. Burges, a Dallas author, were among the more active spokesmen for the state association. The Texas Referendum Committee, headed by Robert Cargill, a Longview oilman, later became an allied organization.

During the spring of 1956 the two groups collected more than 150,000 signatures on a petition to force a statewide vote on three segregation propositions. All three measures, one of which was an interposition resolution, received heavy approval by Texas voters in the July, 1956, primary elections and were made a part of the state Democratic Party platform.[51]

The Council had some influence with the Shivers administration, since the governor and Attorney General John Ben Shepperd were obviously sympathetic with Council aims.[52] After the Shivers forces lost a struggle for control of the state Democratic Party, a battle in which segregation shibboleths served as central rallying cries for Shivercrats, the governor did not seek reelection for a fourth term. When a new administration was inaugurated in 1957, Council-Referendum Committee influence in the executive branch declined, and the organizations turned their attention to bolstering East Texas legislators' devotion to white supremacy.[53] Although Council pressure was no doubt less authoritative than the general mood of East Texas white voters, the area's legislators, who had ignored the segregation issue in the 1956 session, showed an enthusiastic concern for anti-integration legislation in regular and special sessions during 1957.

Florida white supremacy organizations also remained on the fringes of state political power. During 1955 several local Citizens' Council chapters

[50] Dallas *Morning News*, July 23, 29, November 12, 13, 1955.

[51] Weeks, *Texas One-Party Politics in 1956*, pp. 37–38; Dallas *Morning News* (ed.), *Texas Almanac, 1958–1959* (Dallas, 1959), 455.

[52] Shepperd created his own states' rights organization, the Committee on Correspondence. *The Citizens' Council*, September, 1956; Dallas *Morning News*, June 21, 1956.

[53] See Dallas *Morning News*, October 6, 8, 1957, May 1, 1958.

appeared in the state, but none achieved a significant popular following. In June, 1956, delegates from eleven counties formed a state association, which floundered ineffectively for some nine months. In February, 1957, a larger group of Council representatives reorganized the state association, this time with professional assistance from Mississippi.[54] The Reverend George Downs, Orlando publisher of an anti-communist periodical and a "Baptist evangelist," became executive secretary. The revamped state group was more broadly based than its predecessor but still lacked wide membership and political respectability.

More formidable than the Florida Councils was the Federation for Constitutional Government, which appeared in early 1956. The federation was better financed than the Councils and encompassed several effective politicians of the rabble-rousing variety, especially Sumter Lowry, a retired army officer and 1956 gubernatorial candidate, and Prentice Pruitt, a state representative through 1956 and later a federation lobbyist in the state legislative halls.[55] Despite limited membership, the federation helped to keep the segregation question before Florida politicians and to encourage resistance to social change.

Organized white supremacists in Tennessee were ineffective. The Society to Maintain Segregation, Citizens' Council, White Citizens' Council, States' Rights Council, and Pro-Southerners were all local phenomena, based mainly on lower-class followings in Memphis and Chattanooga.[56] The Tennessee Federation for Constitutional Government was the only group pretending to possess the allegiance of a statewide membership, but even this organization had negligible grass roots support and was principally composed of a limited number of activists in Nashville and Memphis.[57] In Nashville, where the organization was most vigorous, the federation represented a Snopesean perversion of the aristocratic

---

[54] Robert Patterson, by this time executive secretary of the Citizens' Councils of America, assisted the Florida group. Miami *Herald*, February 4, 1957; Montgomery *Advertiser*, February 4, 1957. The Miami *Herald*, June 26, 1956, contains an account of the establishment of the original state association.

[55] Miami *Herald*, June 3, 1956; Price, *The Negro and Southern Politics: A Chapter of Florida History*, 109, 124. The Memphis *Commercial Appeal*, December 29, 1955, lists Florida members of the advisory board for the national Federation for Constitutional Government.

[56] Southern Regional Council, *Special Report: Pro-Segregation Groups in the South*, 10–11. The White Citizens' Council was the John Kasper organization, which had transitory chapters in Knoxville and a few hill-country communities.

[57] The federation claimed to have chapters in 14 counties and members in 230 Tennessee towns and cities. Donald Davidson, *Report of the State Chairman, Tennessee Federation for Constitutional Government* (Nashville, 1957), pages unnumbered.

agrarian tradition. Donald Davidson, a professor of English at Vanderbilt University, served as president, and a number of people associated with the cultural and artistic community in Nashville filled other offices. Since some of these individuals were men of substantial means, the organization was relatively well-financed, retaining its own legal staff to do battle for such causes as an attack on the validity of the Fourteenth Amendment.[58]

North Carolina, because of factors imbedded in its own past, did not offer fertile ground for organized white supremacy. In Texas, Florida, and Tennessee, where the twentieth century had made particularly deep intrusions, black-belt whites no longer had the power, nor, indeed, the will, to dictate the course of state politics. For relatively rational reasons, the Council movement made limited inroads in these states.

The lack of Council success in Arkansas and Georgia was a more complex phenomenon. Both of these states had broad black-belt areas which amply justified the harshest descriptive adjectives, and the whites in these regions enjoyed substantial influence in state politics. By impersonal standards the Councils should have thrived in both states. Their failure to do so again pointed to the diversity that existed even within the bedrock of southern unity.

In Arkansas white supremacy groups were active, particularly during late 1955 and the first half of 1956. White America, Inc., was the first such organization in the state, originating in Pine Bluff during early 1955. It was joined later in the year by the White Citizens' Council. Cooperating closely, the two groups for a time appeared formidable. The White Citizens' Council published its own propaganda bulletin *Arkansas Faith*, and white supremacy rallies sometimes attracted impressive crowds.[59] A number of relatively well-known—but politically unemployed—politicians were closely associated with the movement. James D. Johnson, an ambitious former state legislator and unsuccessful candidate for attorney general, was acting state director of the White Citizens' Council; Amis Guthridge, Little Rock lawyer and states' rights political figure, was executive secretary of White America. Former House Speaker Harve

---

[58] *Ibid.; A Message to the People of Tennessee from the Tennessee Federation for Constitutional Government* (n.p., 1956); Chattanooga *Times*, June 21, 1955; Nashville *Tennessean*, July 12, 1955; Memphis *Commercial Appeal*, August 11, December 29, 1955, June 26, 1956.

[59] The White Citizens' Council gave the following list of places where rallies were held and the attendance (apparently not greatly exaggerated) at each meeting: Dewitt, 500; Lake Village, 500; Hoxie-Walnut Ridge, 1,500; Dermott, 800; England "(inside on a bad night)," 350; Sheridan, 400; Forrest City, 1,000; Hamburg, 2,500; England, 2,000. *Arkansas Faith*, November, 1955, March, 1956.

B. Thorne and former Governor Ben Laney spoke at White Citizens' Council rallies.

It soon became obvious, however, that the county seat elite of the southeastern lowlands was not flocking to join the organized vanguard of segregationist extremism. Office-holding politicians from the Delta machine counties, while vigorous in their defense of segregation, were seldom seen at white supremacy meetings. At Star City, county seat of black-belt Lincoln County, white leaders refused even to allow a White Citizens' Council organizational gathering. As the county sheriff explained, "We're getting along fine without anybody stirring up trouble."[60] The Council formed chapters, but without the support of black-belt community leaders, local organizations were transitory and ineffective.

Instead, some of the southeastern lowlands' most influential spokesmen talked of local option and a flexible program designed to limit and control token social changes. Marvin E. Bird of Crittenden County, chairman of the state board of education; Richard B. McCulloch, Sr., of St. Francis County, widely regarded as the foremost legal mind in the Delta; J. L. Shaver of Cross County, a former lieutenant governor and for a time legislative secretary to Governor Faubus; and a number of East Arkansas state legislative leaders were among low-country chieftains seeking to avoid a white supremacy crusade that would force a direct confrontation with the government of the United States.[61]

By the fall of 1956, when the flagging forces of segregationist extremism united to form the Arkansas Division of the Citizens' Councils of America, the movement was primarily composed of energetic—and in some cases politically ambitious—leaders.[62] Among the few functioning chapters, the Capital Citizens' Council in Little Rock was the most active (and was to become of exceptional significance), though it too had limited membership.

The Georgia States' Rights Council suffered basically from the same disabilities that shackled bureaucratized bigotry in Arkansas. The Council originated in Augusta in December, 1954, and floundered along as a relatively powerless local organization. Its greatest accomplishment was

[60] As quoted in *Arkansas Gazette*, October 14, 1955.

[61] See, for example, Tom Davis, interview with Bird, in *ibid.*, April 1, 1956; Sam G. Harris, report of remarks by McCulloch before a meeting of the school superintendents' section of the Arkansas Education Association, in *ibid.*, August 4, 1955; Dean Duncan, report on interviews with east Arkansas educators, in *ibid.*, November 3, 1955; "Report of the Bird Committee," in *Race Relations Law Reporter*, I (August, 1956), 717–28.

[62] *Arkansas Gazette*, September 2, 1956; *Southern School News*, November, 1956.

to force cancellation of Augusta's thirteenth annual soapbox derby because two Negro boys entered the competition.[63]

Then, in the fall of 1955, the state political power structure stepped in. Roy V. Harris, whose prestige was somewhat tarnished when he backed an also-ran in the 1954 gubernatorial race, promoted a toplevel meeting of Georgia political leaders to plan anti-integration strategy and to establish a statewide white supremacy organization. Some two hundred Georgia political leaders, including Talmadge, Griffin, and most of the state's other major politicians, met in Atlanta in September, 1955, to annex the States' Rights Council. The dignitaries selected Carter Pittman, a Dalton attorney, as Council president, and among other officers chose the secretary and treasurer of the state Democratic Party as secretary and treasurer of the Council. Old Talmadge lieutenants such as James Gillis, Fred Hand, James Peters, and Roy Harris appeared on the executive committee, William T. Bodenhamer, a Baptist minister holding membership on both the state board of education and the executive committee of the Georgia Baptist Convention, became executive secretary.[64] Georgia now had the States' Rights Council in addition to the Commission on Education and the state government, all with overlapping membership and all professing as their principal *raison d'être* the promotion and protection of white supremacy.

With no pretense toward democratic organization, Georgia's political chiefs set about to recruit some Indians—preferably 100,000 to 150,000 of them "who will pay $5 a year to finance a fight to maintain segregation and remain silent about policy matters."[65] In January, 1956, Talmadge, Griffin, Harris, Lieutenant Governor S. Ernest Vandiver, Attorney General Eugene Cook, and others invaded the south Georgia county seat community of Americus to dispense inspirational oratory and to sign up the duespayers.[66] During following weeks Pittman and Bodenhamer traveled about Georgia in search of members, while top state officials sought "contributions" from state employees. The Council's Atlanta office was the center of considerable activity, publishing and distributing a variety of propaganda literature.[67]

[63] St. Louis *Post-Dispatch*, August 8, 1955.

[64] Atlanta *Constitution*, September 24, 1955; Atlanta *Journal*, September 24, October 2, November 6, 1955.

[65] Associated Press, Charleston *News and Courier*, September 25, 1955.

[66] Atlanta *Journal*, January 11, 12, 1956.

[67] Atlanta *Constitution*, May 12, 1956; Southern Regional Council, *Special Report: Pro-Segregation Groups in the South*, 4.

Despite such high-pressure salesmanship, the Council did not prosper. A considerable proportion of Georgia's political elite, while unwilling to be left outside the organization and having no objection to a sensible fund raising scheme in the interest of white supremacy, was less enthusiastic about its permanent sucess and feared the creation of a kind of Frankenstein. As if to justify their fears, the Council soon became involved in factional politics.[68] More fundamentally, however, Georgia's white citizenry did not turn out in large numbers to enlist in the organization. Middle-class whites in the black belt, the people who could have built a powerful movement with or without guidance from the state's top-level political leadership, paid little heed to the Council. White Georgians gave every evidence of being in sympathy with the state's official stance of total devotion to white supremacy, but they did not support an organized expression of this dedication.

The explanation for the movement's relative lack of success in Georgia and Arkansas rests to a considerable extent, it would appear, upon the nature of politics in these two states. The county unit system in Georgia and "pure one party politics" in Arkansas enhanced the power and influence of local leaders and county organizations.[69] Nowhere else in the South did county leaders enjoy such significance and such independence in state politics. Apparently most members of the county seat elite in Georgia and Arkansas attached their interests to the political status quo. This situation combined with an historical tradition of relative political stability. Arkansas was the only peripheral state to remain loyal to the Democratic Party in 1928, and Georgia was the only Deep South state to do so in 1948. Other factors, such as the quality of Council leadership, particularly on the local level, may also have contributed to the movement's difficulties in these states.

Like the South itself, the Citizens' Council movement varied greatly from state to state. Nevertheless, the fundamental driving force of Council militancy flowed from the black-belt South, the same area that had produced the stimuli for secession and redemption, that had provided the basic support for the defeat of populism and for the 1948 Dixiecrat campaign. The whites of the black belt were still the South's most belligerent and determined minority.

[68] For example, the Council's executive secretary ran unsuccessfully for governor in 1958. See Charles Pou, in Atlanta *Journal and Constitution*, May 7, 1961.
[69] Key, *Southern Politics*, 106–29, 183–204; Drummond "Arkansas Politics," 177–78; Bernd, *Grass Roots Politics in Georgia*, 17.

Insofar as generalizations about membership in a complex movement are possible, the Council in black-belt areas, like the Ku Klux Klan thirty years before, was a bourgeois phenomenon. Its appeal, as well as the essential nature of the movement, was to the middle class of the towns and villages. Council recruiters sought invitations to speak before small town and county seat service clubs, and from the ranks of the Lions and Kiwanis, Exchange and Rotary clubs came much of the membership of local chapters.[70] While some planters tended to regard the Councils as "townspeople stuff,"[71] farmers and plantation owners apparently joined the movement in sizable numbers, and state Farm Bureau Federations, presumably reflecting planter sentiment, were very friendly toward the organized resistance. Those rural whites at the lowest socio-economic level who wished to protect the white man's prerogatives were apt to find the Ku Klux Klan more to their liking.[72] The Councils were the instruments of the middle class.

As the organization spread into the cities, however, it tended to enlist the urban proletariat. With the exception of a few Deep South cities, most notably Jackson, Mississippi, the Citizens' Councils in urban areas appealed most strongly to the working class, as well as to white lower-income groups generally. Its attraction was least among prosperous middle- and upper-class suburbanites, although individuals in business and the professions frequently provided leadership for metropolitan white supremacy.[73]

This situation created a basic Citizens' Council dilemma: how to reconcile the profound differences between neobourbon bourgeoisie and urban proletariat. The inability to solve this perhaps insoluble problem was a fundamental failure of the movement. In the short term, during the early period of dynamic expansion, the lure of white supremacy was adequate

[70] Vander Zanden, *Race Relations in Transition*, 30–34; Vander Zanden, "The Citizens' Councils," 7; Halberstam, "The White Citizens' Councils," 293–302; Martin, *The Deep South Says "Never"*, 13–15; Carter, *The South Strikes Back*, 205–206; "The Resistance Groups of South Carolina," 17–18; *The Citizens' Council*, June, 1956. See also Matthews and Prothro, "Negro Voter Registration in the South," 135.

[71] Robert Penn Warren, *Segregation: The Inner Conflict in the South* (New York, 1956), 29, quoting a Mississippi planter.

[72] This point will be discussed in Chapter 11.

[73] Bird, in St. Louis *Post-Dispatch*, February 28, 1956; Townsend, in *Christian Science Monitor*, May 17, 1956; Popham, in New York *Times*, December 2, 1956; Bob Considine, in Charleston *Gazette*, September 19, 1957; Samuel Lubell, in Nashville *Banner*, March 2, 1960. The points made in this paragraph are discussed more fully in Chapters 14 and 16. On the attitudes of southern whites toward desegregation, see Chapter 1.

to unite the two groups in southern society most immediately concerned with race—the groups that would do most of the integrating in practice—and least concerned about the future of the public schools. But the deep economic and social incompatibility between the county seat elite and the industrial laborer, between respectability and "the ancient cry for bread and circuses," soon became apparent.[74]

Events in Alabama graphically delineated this dichotomy. During early 1956 the black-belt-based Citizens' Councils of Alabama, led by Dr. John Whitley and Sam Engelhardt, split openly with the Birmingham-centered North Alabama Citizens' Councils, headed by Asa Carter.[75] This bitterly antagonistic division in the Alabama Council ranks clearly reflected the essentially different outlooks of the membership of the two groups. The North Alabama Citizens' Councils showed open tendencies toward anti-Semitism, requiring that members "believe in the divinity of Jesus Christ," and approached a position endorsing violence as a method to prevent desegregation. In style the organization more closely resembled the Ku Klux Klan than it did the state Council Association, and, indeed, Asa Carter soon became an "advisor" to the Original Ku Klux Klan of the Confederacy as well as executive secretary of the North Alabama Citizens' Council.[76] Leaders of the Citizens' Councils of Alabama denounced their former Council compatriots to the north as "demagogic rabble-rousers," "budding bullies," and "prisoners of hate."[77] Among resistance groups appealing to the urban proletariat, these tendencies toward nativism, anti-Semitism, and, sometimes, anti-Catholicism and thinly veiled endorsements of violence were evident in several states, as was the tendency to prefer the secrecy and ritual of the Ku Klux Klan rather than the semi-respectability of the Councils.[78]

As resistance organizations, the Councils fed on racial strife and threats of social change; when lulls occurred and the resistance had nothing immediate and tangible to resist, interest, membership dues, and thus

[74] Popham, in New York *Times*, December 2, 1956.
[75] *Southern School News*, February, April, 1956. Whitley resided in the Birmingham area, but he was a middle-class druggist who was not associated with the Carter group.
[76] Birmingham *News*, November 30, 1956. These observations are based on news reports in *ibid.*, January–May, 1956, and *Southern School News*, February-June, 1956.
[77] "Statement of the Alabama Association of Citizens' Councils," reprinted in Birmingham *News*, March 11, 1956. The Alabama Association of Citizens' Councils changed its name to the Citizens' Councils of Alabama after Carter changed the name of his North Alabama Citizens' Councils to the Alabama Citizens' Councils, all of which generated considerable confusion.
[78] This point will be discussed in Chapter 11.

finances and influence lagged—particularly in areas outside the black belt. This problem, too, sorely taxed the Council leadership.

The great period for the Citizens' Council movement came during the early months of 1956. The movement's basic strength had become readily apparent; its substantial weaknesses were less clearly obvious. With local chapters mushrooming and membership leaping upward, with leading southern politicians (some of whom may not have been fully in sympathy with Council aims) hastening to endorse the resistance, with Council leaders dreaming of an organization numbering in the millions to restore and defend the privileges of the white race, the resistance clearly held the initiative in southern politics. Over the South, giant Citizens' Council rallies impressively demonstrated their growing influence.

In February, 1956, Senator James O. Eastland, the "Voice of the South," so Citizens' Council advertisements and posters proclaimed, was the featured speaker at a rally in the State Coliseum in Montgomery, Alabama. A Confederate flag waved above the speaker's platform, and the band alternated between "Dixie" and marching music. More than twelve thousand people, the largest political gathering in recent Alabama history, responded lustily to generous doses of old-school oratory. Some dropped contributions into giant barrels labeled "donations"; some signed up for Council membership at the long banquet tables where secretaries made change from cigar cash boxes; and all received literature about the Council movement. "It was a pep rally and a political convention and an old fashioned revival."[79]

The Montgomery rally was merely the largest of numerous similar outings sponsored by resistance organizations throughout the South. Governor Griffin, Attorney General Cook, and Representative James C. Davis of Georgia, Senator Thurmond of South Carolina, Representative John Bell Williams of Mississippi, and most of all, Senator Eastland, were among featured speakers. The Councils had attracted impressive crowds to previous meetings, and they would do so on future occasions. But never before or after did the movement capture the crusading elan that marked the series of public gatherings beginning with the first statewide convention of the Mississippi Citizens' Councils in Jackson in December, 1955, when Eastland lambasted the United States Supreme Court once again, and

---

[79] Based on accounts by Joe Azbell, in Montgomery *Advertiser*, February 11, 1956, and Fred Taylor, in Birmingham *News*, February 12, 1956. Azbell estimated the crowd at twelve thousand; Taylor placed it at fifteen thousand.

ending perhaps with Thurmond's speech before a large and enthusiastic crowd at the War Memorial Auditorium in Nashville in June, 1956, when the Tennessee Federation for Constitutional Government sponsored its most successful public rally.[80]

In his *The South: Old and New*, Francis B. Simkins, writing in 1947, observed: "By 1928 the Ku Klux Klan had lost most of its Southern members; yet it was more than a passing phenomenon. Its standards of social and civic morality were those of the South, and should they again be threatened, it is likely that . . . a similar group would arise."[81]

By early 1956, Simkins' prediction had been proven accurate.

---

[80] *Southern School News*, January–July, 1956. The evaluations here are my own.
[81] Francis Butler Simkins, *The South: Old and New* (2nd printing; New York, 1948), 459.

CHAPTER 7

THE POLITICAL POWER STRUCTURE

Harry Flood Byrd revered economy in government, fiscal "responsibility" and a balanced budget, states' rights and Virginia traditions, a static society and aristocratic prerogative. White supremacy in the senator's scheme of values was part of a broad and profoundly neobourbon ideology. Byrd's values had changed little during the years since he had served as governor of Virginia in the mid-1920's. He had fought for his beliefs for twenty-five years in the United States Senate, which meant opposing the ideologies of others for Harry Byrd was a negativist in the best southern tradition. He had relentlessly opposed the New Deal and the Fair Deal, and he had shared in numerous tactical victories. But the federal budget multiplied, the national debt accumulated, and the government in Washington assumed ever-increasing financial burdens at the expense of state power. Senator Richard B. Russell's ill-fated candidacy for the Democratic presidential nomination in 1952 had demonstrated the nation's anti-South bias. Now a new generation of abolitionists assaulted the southern social system and the South itself.

Byrd had welcomed General Eisenhower's victory "because he believed it represented perhaps the last opportunity for the vindication of the philosophy of conservatism in government."[1] But the Republican ad-

---

[1] William S. White, in New York *Times*, February 13, 1957. These observations on Senator Byrd are my interpretation of his speeches, statements, and activities. Helpful secondary works are Key, *Southern Politics*, 19–27; Muse, *Virginia's Massive Resistance*, 25–28, 98–102, 160–77; Gates, *The Making of Massive Resistance*, 13–19, 79–82, 117–19; and Marshall W. Fishwick, *Virginia: A New Look at the Old Dominion* (New York, 1959), 243–53. The stories by Edward T. Folliard and Benjamin Muse in the Washington *Post* and James Latimer and L. M. Wright, Jr., in the Richmond *Times-Dispatch* are also valuable.

ministration had proven both unwilling and unable to disband the federal bureaucracy and abandon national responsibilities, and it refused to turn the federal executive power to the support of white southern concepts of racial justice. Byrd spoke dejectedly of political retirement. In his apple orchard at Berryville, the senator lamented: "Another 25-year period of profligate public spending and unbelievable waste—of piling up new debts and increasing taxes—of cheapening our dollar—of continuing to destroy states' rights and concentrate greater and greater power in Washington—our country, as great as it is, can be seriously injured."[2]

The *Brown* decision cut deeply into the core of Byrd's values. The schemes of radical reformers had been endorsed by the nation's highest tribunal. The very Court assigned guardianship of the federal Constitution had overturned precedent and assaulted cherished traditions by basing its decision not on the words of the Constitution itself, but on the writings of a group of social scientists that included Negroes, a European— probably leftists all. The decision broadened the authority of the federal government, invaded the rights of states, branded as "unconstitutional" time-tested practices, and in so doing intruded "upon the personal domain of Harry Byrd."[3] The time had come, Senator Byrd decided, to speak of the rights of states and the rights of white men. A united and determined South, rededicating itself to state sovereignty, standing "firmly and courageously" on basic principles, might yet halt the expansion of federal power and reverse the trend toward "totalitarian government."[4] To accomplish such a mission, the South must be organized for "massive resistance," and Virginia must offer leadership.

In November, 1955, the Gray Commission delivered its recommendations to Governor Thomas B. Stanley. More than a year in the making, the report was a comprehensive plan for local autonomy tokenism and included among its suggestions a pupil assignment law, modification of compulsory attendance regulations, and provision for the payment of tuition grants to any student refusing to attend a school with enrollees of another race.[5] In the broadest sense the Gray Plan represented a compromise between the extreme white supremacy sentiment of black-belt

[2] As quoted in Richmond *Times-Dispatch*, May 3, 1958.
[3] Muse, *Virginia's Massive Resistance*, 26.
[4] Statement by Byrd, reprinted in Washington *Evening Star*, December 18, 1955, and account of a speech by Byrd, in Richmond *Times-Dispatch*, August 26, 1956.
[5] "Report by the Commission on Public Education," in *Race Relations Law Reporter*, I (February, 1956), 241–47.

Virginia and the more moderate attitudes evident elsewhere in the state.[6] Since the state constitution prohibited payment of public funds to private schools,[7] the report called for an amendment to legalize the tuition-grant "safety valve" provision. Stanley praised the commission's work and convened a special legislative session to submit the revision to popular will.

Even as Virginia took the first steps toward implementing the plan, strong currents were converging toward its nullification. Some of the most powerful lieutenants in the Byrd organization spoke of a more forceful commitment to segregation in Virginia. Former Governor William M. Tuck, perhaps the number-two man in the organization; Representative Watkins M. Abbitt of the Fourth Congressional District; House Speaker E. Blackburn Moore, Senator Byrd's neighbor and close friend; and Gray himself, who had conscientiously sought a plan upon which the commission could agree but who personally objected to the milder recommendations of the report that bore his name, were among those "urging more spirited leadership." The Defenders, with their own "Plan for Virginia," called for a choice, not a compromise, rejecting moderate proposals as defeatism unworthy of the Old Dominion. From the editorial pages of the Richmond *News Leader* a new—or rather very old—word was added to the vocabulary of the resistance. "Interposition" quickly became the central concept of total state opposition to school desegregation.[8]

In a statement made public in December, 1955, Senator Byrd characterized the desegregation question as "the most serious crisis that has occurred since the War between the States." He spoke of the South's continuing resistance to integration, of a long-term struggle in defense of segregated public schools, and of the possibility of "some degree of coalition between the 11 Southern states which will strengthen the position of the individual states."[9] Byrd endorsed the limited convention to amend Virginia's constitution, but, on the local option features of the Gray Plan, the senator refused to comment.

Events moved rapidly in Virginia as the organization, Defenders, and *News Leader* forces shifted the thrust of Virginia policy from local option

[6] Gates, *The Making of Massive Resistance*, 69, observes that the report was "a compromise among the various 'Virginias.' "
[7] See *Almond v. Day*, in *Race Relations Law Reporter*, I (February, 1956), 83, decided by the Virginia Supreme Court of Appeals, November 7, 1955.
[8] Richmond *News Leader*, October 24, 1955; Latimer, in Richmond *Times-Dispatch*, July 24, 1956. The concept of interposition will be discussed in Chapter 8.
[9] Statement by Byrd, reprinted in Washington *Evening Star*, December 18, 1955.

to interposition. The state's voters approved by a 2 to 1 margin the calling of a limited convention to amend the offending section of the state constitution, thus allowing payment of tuition grants and enactment of the local autonomy Gray Commission Plan. But no sooner had the election results been posted than Senator Byrd was interpreting the vote as popular espousal of segregation and the General Assembly, meeting in its regular 1956 session, was debating interposition. By the time the convention met in early March, the legislature had already passed an interposition resolution, Byrd had added the phrase "massive resistance" to the segregationist lexicon, and an all-out defense of white supremacy had become the dominant theme of Virginia politics.

Then there was quiet. The moderates had been routed, but among themselves segregationists disagreed profoundly. The Byrd-Stanley forces, correctly assessing the rightward trend in public opinion, allowed matters to drift during the spring and early summer of 1956. All sides felt the public pulse and calculated strategy.

In July, contention resumed in earnest. The Defenders took to the field with a new and more stringent legislative battle plan based squarely upon interposition. Their program called for laws withholding consent for court suits against school boards—thus making legal attacks on dual school systems state-federal clashes, placing schools involved in litigation under state control, denying funds to integrated schools, and requiring that Virginia operate only "efficient"—that is, segregated—schools. Rejecting the validity of the *Brown* decision, the Defenders demanded that Virginia entrench behind the sovereignty of the Commonwealth.[10]

Chief opposition to demands for massive resistance came from backers of the Gray Plan. In the constitutional convention referendum campaign, those segregationists who felt strongly about the issue combined against and overwhelmed those people who only favored human justice and the rule of law or who were concerned about the potential threat tuition grants might pose to the public school system. Now the issue had been rephrased, and by no means all strict segregationists wanted to join in a neobourbon crusade to reform the American federal system. Substantial leaders who had originally supported the Gray Plan continued to do so in the summer of 1956, and they were joined by those who had at first opposed the commission program as too extreme. Urban spokesmen in general; educators and friends of the schools, including a majority of the

---

[10] Richmond *News Leader*, July 6, 1956; Richmond *Times-Dispatch*, July 7, 8, 1956.

state board of education and individuals like Dr. Dabney S. Lancaster, a former state superintendent of public instruction; and numerous other leaders such as Delegates Robert Whitehead, head of the anti-organization forces, and Harry B. Davis, vice chairman of the Gray Commission, formed a powerful phalanx opposing massive resistance extremism.[11]

The Byrd organization reflected the rift among segregationists. Ex-Governor Colgate W. Darden, Jr., president of the University of Virginia, supported the Gray Plan, and ex-Governor John S. Battle, who rivaled Tuck for the second position in the organization, was noticeably absent from massive resistance ranks.[12] Attorney General J. Lindsay Almond, Jr., had already engaged in a sharp public exchange with Speaker Moore and had had differences with Governor Stanley over school strategy (although once the "nod" came down, Almond supported the policy).[13] On the other side, the senator himself, Stanley, Gray, Representatives Tuck, Abbitt, and Howard W. Smith, and most of the more powerful organization leaders in the state legislature favored a militant showdown with the Supreme Court, a statewide rejection of what Byrd called "this illegal demand."[14]

In early July, a group of the organization's mighty who associated with the massive resistance stance met in Byrd's Washington office to determine organization policy. Feeling that "hardening public sentiment over the state would now support the sterner line,"[15] the participants agreed that the governor would call a special legislative session and recommend, in addition to the nonlocal-option features of the Gray report, a bill cutting off state funds to any desegregated school. Such a law would penalize integration but would not prohibit it since a local community, by shouldering the entire cost, could shift to biracial schools. This arrangement, its advocates were speciously to argue later, was more likely to stand up in federal courts than legislation to halt all public funds to

[11] Gates, *The Making of Massive Resistance*, 168–73, 186.

[12] In 1958 Byrd announced his intention to retire from the Senate and then shortly afterward announced that he would run for reelection after all. A factor in the senator's change of mind, many felt, was the threat of a struggle between Tuck and Battle for control of the organization. Latimer, in Richmond *Times-Dispatch*, February 26, 1958.

[13] Muse, *Virginia's Massive Resistance*, 39–40; Wright, in Richmond *Times-Dispatch*, April 1, May 6, 1956.

[14] As quoted in Richmond *Times-Dispatch*, August 26, 1956. The types sketched by Gates, *The Making of Massive Resistance*, 96–98, are helpful in following the shifting trends of racial politics in Virginia.

[15] Latimer, in Richmond *Times-Dispatch*, July 24, 1956. Among a number of accounts of this meeting are Folliard, in Washington *Post*, June 17, 1957, and Muse, *Virginia's Massive Resistance*, 28.

integrating schools. It seems obvious that organization leaders would have preferred a stronger program, one more clearly based upon the interposition doctrine, but they apparently concluded that the denial-of-funds plan was the most extreme measure Virginia and the General Assembly would accept.

Governor Stanley announced his intention to convene the special session and, reversing himself once again, rejected the local-option features of the Gray report. He declared: "I cannot endorse or recommend any legislation, or action, which accepts the principle of integration of the races in the public schools."[16] The Gray Commission, now rent with internal dissension, voted 19 to 12 to reject the Gray Commission report and to endorse the Stanley withholding of funds program.

The Virginia General Assembly met during August and September, 1956. Stanley recommended thirteen anti-integration bills, the most controversial being the proposal to deny state appropriations to any "public elementary or secondary schools in which white and colored children are mixed and taught."[17] The other twelve, among them the tuition-grant and compulsory-attendance modification proposals, were part of the original Gray Plan.

The special session was a confused affair. Emotionalism and indignation over federal "encroachments" colored the atmosphere. The anti-massive resistance camp introduced a series of fourteen bills embodying the original Gray Plan. The massive resistance forces added a list of anti-NAACP bills to their demands. Both groups, as well as various legislators acting independently, offered numerous other measures, some designed as compromise proposals, some calculated to gain support for other bills, some pushed by white supremacy extremists. Debate centered around the Stanley funds-cutting measure, and the legislators were sharply divided on its wisdom and legitimacy. Eventually, organization solons, with virtually solid black-belt support, established control in both chambers, by comfortable majorities in the house but by the narrowest of margins in the senate. After winning crucial test votes on the Stanley bill, massive resistance forces pushed through the administration package, the NAACP harrassment measures, and, most important, little noticed Defenders-type bills sufficiently "massive" to gladden the heart of any resister. The result

[16] As quoted in Richmond *Times-Dispatch*, July 24, 1956.
[17] From Stanley's recommendations in his Address to the Legislature, reprinted in Richmond *News Leader*, August 27, 1956.

was twenty-three segregationist laws ranging from the relatively harmless to the fantastic.[18]

The most important law in Virginia's massive resistance program was an interpositionist measure declaring that the "Commonwealth of Virginia assumes direct responsibility for the control of any school, elementary or secondary, in the Commonwealth, to which children of both races are assigned and enrolled by any court order." Such school would immediately be closed, the measure continued, and any court suit challenging the action was permitted only against the state of Virginia, and "the Commonwealth hereby declines and refuses . . . to be subject to such a suit unless it shall be one brought by the Attorney of Virginia."[19] An accompanying statute authorized the governor to recreate "an efficient system," and, when established, to return the school to local authorities.[20] To ensure against desegregation not resulting from court orders, other legislation prohibited the expenditure of state funds for integrated schools and created a three-member state board responsible for the assignment of all students to specific schools.[21]

Senator Byrd, in late September, 1956, could announce: "Once again, Virginia offers its peaceful leadership to the South, and I believe the offer will be accepted."[22] The neobourbon rebellion was no longer confined to the Deep South.

The black belt, with its influential bloc of legislators and with the Defenders as its militant action arm, and the Byrd organization, with its prestige and its ability to influence the votes of legislators from counties outside the black belt, generated massive resistance in Virginia.[23] As Benjamin Muse has observed, "a dynamic and contagious grass-roots force joined with a power at the political summit in a combination which moderate elements in Virginia were unable effectively to resist."[24] In combining with the black belt, the area that had in the past been most consistent in voter loyalty to the organization, Senator Byrd and his lieutenants have been accused of deliberate and Machiavellian political

[18] All are reprinted in *Race Relations Law Reporter*, I (December, 1956), 1091–1113, II (October, 1957), 1015–26.

[19] *Ibid.*, I, 1104, 1106.

[20] *Ibid.*, 1107.

[21] *Ibid.*, 1109–13.

[22] Statement by Byrd, reprinted in Richmond *News Leader*, September 26, 1956.

[23] Gates, *The Making of Massive Resistance*, 184–88. See particularly his table of votes, 186.

[24] Muse, *Virginia's Massive Resistance*, 8.

calculation by seizing the racial issue as a weapon against Republicans and anti-organization Democrats.[25] As indicated earlier, upper-class organizations like the ones in Virginia and North Carolina found racism a helpful device for confusing issues and dividing opposition—no doubt, professional politicians were not oblivious to political reality. Yet such an explanation falls short of defining the phenomenon of massive resistance in Virginia. For political opportunists, organization stalwarts were at first dangerously far ahead of public opinion;[26] they risked dividing— and eventually did split—the organization itself; and, as later events would demonstrate, they battled for the principle of massive resistance far beyond the dictates of political wisdom. In general terms, the actions of both the organization leadership and black-belt spokesmen, so far as the two could be separated, were manifestations of genuine and sincere neobourbon sentiment. For years they had been more restive than Virginians as a whole, and they grasped the opportunity to act. "The attempted and illegal federal dictation is the most drastic since Reconstruction," said Harry Byrd, "and it has therefore to be resisted as drastically."[27]

The dynamics of race politics in Virginia were those of the South generally. A militant and organized black-belt bourgeoisie combined with powerful politicians who, though limited in numbers, were pervasive in influence. They received support from neobourbons and sympathizers elsewhere, including important segments of the urban press. Utilizing racial emotionalism to divide and demoralize actual and potential opposition, this coalition set about to "nullify" the *Brown* decision.

The southern mood made massive resistance possible; Citizens' Councils provided the working cadres and crusading fervor; and entrenched southern politicians contributed much of the leadership, direction, and strength. Important men in the South's political power structure, long disturbed by the trends toward change, had recognized "the threat to traditional values and to long-dominant power groups."[28] Since 1948 they had manned the barricades, and they had achieved considerable success in upholding the status quo. Now currents of southern politics

---

[25] For example, Ashmore, *An Epitaph for Dixie*, 37, and Fishwick, *Virginia: A New Look at the Old Dominion*, 252–53.

[26] See Wright, in Richmond *Times-Dispatch*, July 25, August 5, 1956.

[27] Statement by Byrd, reprinted in Richmond *News Leader*, September 26, 1956.

[28] Lewis M. Killian, "Consensus in the Changing South," *Phylon Quarterly*, XVIII (Second Quarter, 1957), 115.

ran more strongly toward reaction, and, with Council pressure from below, they seized the initiative and dragged many less enthusiastic politicians in their wake. During the winter of 1955–56 the neobourbon elite mobilized for massive resistance.

The "Southern Manifesto" was a dramatic announcement of the quickening pace of resistance politics. Signed by 19 senators and 82 representatives, or 101 of the 128 national legislators from states of the former Confederacy, the Manifesto—its formal title was "Declaration of Constitutional Principles"—was a blatant challenge to the legitimacy of *Brown v. Board of Education.* It was, as one legal scholar declared, "a calculated declaration of political war against the Court's decision."[29] Condemning "the unwarranted decision of the Supreme Court" as the substitution of "naked power for established law," the Declaration commended "the motives of these states which have declared the intention to resist forced integration by any lawful means" and appealed "to the states and people who are not directly affected by these decisions to consider the constitutional principles involved against the time when they too, on issues vital to them, may be the victims of judicial encroachment."[30]

Originally conceived as an endorsement of interposition, the Declaration was the result of weeks of backstage maneuvering. Strom Thurmond of South Carolina originated the idea and prepared three early drafts of the Manifesto. Harry Byrd promptly endorsed Thurmond's plan, and the two senators spread the proposal among southern congressmen.[31] The Declaration attracted sufficient support to coerce all but the boldest members into joining the undertaking, although the price for moderate adherence was the toning down of Thurmond's bellicose wording. A committee headed by Richard B. Russell, who had at first shown little interest in the project, rewrote the document. Several legislators, all from

[29] Alexander M. Bickel, *The Least Dangerous Branch: The Supreme Court at the Bar of Politics* (New York, 1962), 256.

[30] *Congressional Record*, 84th Cong., 2nd Sess. (March 12, 1956), 3948, 4004. Ninety-six legislators signed the Manifesto originally; five more signed later. All of the twenty-seven members from the South who did not sign the document were from the peripheral states, sixteen of them from the twenty-two members of the Texas House delegation. Three southern senators did not sign the Manifesto. Lyndon Johnson, the Senate majority leader, was not asked to sign, and Albert Gore and Estes Kefauver of Tennessee refused to do so.

[31] Strom Thurmond to M. Hayes Mizell, March 27, 1962. I am indebted to Mr. Mizell of the American Friends Service Committee for permitting me to examine the various drafts of the Manifesto and the correspondence and other documents concerning the Manifesto in his possession.

the peripheral South, refused to sign until passages specifically approving interposition and branding the Court decision as unconstitutional and illegal were deleted. Twice more the Declaration was revised. The sixth draft, written by a committee of five senators, proved generally acceptable.[32]

The Manifesto was substantially less dramatic than its original promoters intended, but it nevertheless endowed neobourbon aims and methods with the blessings of the South's most respected leaders. The proclamation tended to confuse legal and moral issues and to undermine any sense of inevitability a Supreme Court decision normally commands. The Declaration committed to the neobourbon cause politicians who did not fully agree—in some cases privately disagreed—with the document they signed.[33]

Senator Byrd seemed pleased when he explained that the Manifesto was "a part of the plan of massive resistance we've been working on and I hope and believe it will be an effective action."[34] As James F. Byrnes had added respectability, bearing, and purpose to the white supremacy reaction during the early 1950's, Byrd, with his mystical prestige in Virginia, his influence in the Senate, and his national reputation for unquestioned integrity, performed much the same function in the latter part of the decade. He originated the term "massive resistance" and played a crucial role in its evolution in his home state and in the attempt to create a South-wide effort. No man did as much to move the front lines of opposition from the Deep South to Washington, D.C., and the Potomac River.

The heartland of massive resistance remained the Deep South, however. Here Senator James O. Eastland embodied neobourbon militancy, replacing Herman Talmadge as the most garrulous champion of calloused white supremacy. Often condemned as a demagogue (a "thin-lipped and hating" man, said one critic—a man who "stands indicted of gross irresponsibility"[35]), he was nevertheless a relentless crusader who was

[32] The five senators were Thurmond, Russell, John Stennis of Mississippi, J. William Fulbright of Arkansas, and Price Daniel of Texas. Fulbright and Daniel were spokesmen for the "moderates" who demanded deletions. Elizabeth Carpenter, in *Arkansas Gazette*, March 18, 1956; Doris Fleeson, in Charleston *Gazette*, March 16, 1956; Drew Pearson, in Atlanta *Journal*, March 18, 1956; and Brooks Hays, *A Southern Moderate Speaks* (Chapel Hill, 1959), 89, are helpful accounts of the background debate.

[33] Ashmore, *An Epitaph for Dixie*, 31–33.

[34] As quoted in Richmond *News Leader*, March 12, 1956.

[35] Ashmore, *An Epitaph for Dixie*, 103–104.

never far from where decisions were being made. And he was probably
the most influential individual in shaping the direction of reaction. In a
real sense Eastland was the voice of the neobourbon South, and he
epitomized the contradictions, paranoia, and indignant belligerence of
the resistance itself.

Like Harry F. Byrd, Eastland was a simple man who found the past
far more attractive than the future. But where Byrd anguished over
extravagence in government budgets, Eastland was consumed with the
threat of communist conspiracy; and Byrd's apple orchards were in the
predominantly white Shenandoah Valley, while Eastland's manorial
cotton plantation was in Sunflower County, Mississippi, where, as one
observer wrote, a person "can easily stand in the middle of the delta's
steaming sameness and honestly believe that the world goes straight out
forever, flat all the way and overripe, and made by a God who in His
infinite wisdom gave Adam a cotton allotment."[36] In such a world white
supremacy was part of the immutable order, and segregation, said Eastland, was the way "of the Constitution, the laws of nature, and the law
of God."[37]

Racial purity was an integral part of the Americanism that Eastland
ardently defended. In the Mississippi senator's definition, Americanism
was a composite of biology, regionalism, and nationalism, the last of
rightwing Republican variety, replete with McCarthyism, Bricker Amendment, and stringent loyalty-security.[38] As chairman of the Senate Internal
Security Subcommittee, Eastland so zealously pursued "subversives" that
an Alabama journalist, covering an Internal Security Subcommittee
hearing in New Orleans in 1954, conducted a poll of all other newsmen
covering the hearing. He asked them "who in their opinion was the one
person participating in the hearing most dangerous to the American way
of life—Senator Eastland won hands down."[39]

The South—ethnologically this always meant white southerners, "the
Negroes [were only] living in their midst"—had a vital role to perform
if the sleepless communist conspiracy was to be thwarted, for "the future
greatness of America depends upon racial purity and maintenance of

36 Robert G. Sherrill, "James O. Eastland: Child of Scorn," *Nation*, CCI (October 4,
1965), 185.
37 *Congressional Record*, 83rd Cong., 2nd Sess. (May 27, 1954), 7251.
38 The Bricker Amendment, introduced into Congress by Senator John W. Bricker
(R.-Ohio), would made executive agreements unconstitutional. It was a favorite measure
of the extreme isolationists during the 1950's.
39 Bob Ingram, in Montgomery *Advertiser*, February 5, 1956.

Anglo-Saxon institutions, which still flourish in full flower in the South."[40] And so squarely did states' rights, the most important bulwark against communist subversion, rest upon a southern foundation that, "when state sovereignty falls in the South, it automatically falls elsewhere."[41] Obviously, any threat to the "southern way of life" struck at the very heart of America's national integrity.

The *Brown* decision, assaulting both Anglo-Saxon culture and states' rights, was a body blow to the Republic. For a long time the ubiquitous subversives had known that the road to Washington, D.C., led through Jackson, Mississippi, and they were joined in their attack on the South by "agitators," "racial demagogues," "meddlers," and others.[42] Ruthlessly using the Negro as a "pawn," the anti-South forces had successfully "infiltrated" the national mass media, loosing a "rising crescendo of vicious propaganda" which was largely "inspired and financed by communist front and race-minded groups" and which obscured basic issues and principles involved.[43] And now the Supreme Court had sanctified the whole plot. Eastland instinctively recognized the fact that the "Court has been indoctrinated and brainwashed by leftwing pressure groups."[44]

During the year that separated the two *Brown* decisions, the Court remained Eastland's favorite *bête noir*. On the chamber floor, the Mississippi senator stated: "Mr. President, we do not intend to permit a crowd of parasitic politicians who now sit on the Supreme Court bench, to destroy those great institutions and the great culture which are in full flower in the Southern States—the culture of the Anglo-Saxon."[45] While hardly calculated to enhance the reputation of the Supreme Court or the United States Senate, such invective was dismissed as Bilbo-style ranting and lacked general appeal outside the Deep South.

Then, in May, 1955, Eastland demanded an investigation into the extent of subversive influence behind the desegregation decision. The Court had relied upon social science studies to demonstrate the basic inequality of enforced segregation in education, and Eastland charged that some of the authorities were "to a shocking degree" connected with and had participated in "the worldwide Communist conspiracy." Among

[40] *Congressional Record*, 81st Cong., 2nd Sess. (June 22, 1950), 9043; 83rd Cong., 2nd Sess. (May 27, 1954), 7257.
[41] Statement by Eastland, reprinted in Chattanooga *Times*, October 30, 1955.
[42] *Congressional Record*, 81st Cong., 2nd Sess. (June 22, 1950), 9043.
[43] Statement by Eastland, reprinted in Chattanooga *Times*, October 30, 1955.
[44] *Congressional Record*, 83rd Cong., 2nd Sess. (May 27, 1954), 7254.
[45] *Ibid.* (July 23, 1954), 11525.

authors of works referred to by the Court, Theodore Brameld and E. Franklin Frazier "have no less than 18 citations in the files of the Committee on Un-American Activities," said Eastland, while Gunnar Myrdal, an "alien" and a socialist who blasphemed the federal Constitution as "impractical and unsuited to modern conditions," had been assisted by sixteen individuals branded with House Un-American Activities Committee citations.[46] "Mr. President," Eastland concluded in a speech introducing his resolution, "it is evident that the decision of the Supreme Court in the school segregation cases was based upon the writings and teachings of pro-communist agitators and other enemies of the American form of government."[47]

Here was an issue that transcended narrow sectionalism and camouflaged white supremacy. Here were the names and numbers that other neobourbon spokesmen, already convinced of the subversive nature of the decision, could and would cite to demonstrate the point. Within three months Eastland's office had mailed out more than 300,000 copies of the speech,[48] and for the next five years the basic points would be repeated in speeches, editorials, pamphlets, and conversations throughout the South. It was the most important speech of the resistance.

The enemies of America and their fellow travelers had chosen the South as the battleground, and, with Anglo-Saxon civilization being weighed in the balance, the South must rise to their challenge. Eastland offered a program. To oppose the propaganda campaign mounted against it, the South had to undertake its own informational offensive. Since "the average American is not a racial pervert,"[49] the South did not stand

[46] *Ibid.*, 84th Cong., 1st Sess. (May 25, 1955), 6963–64. The Court's famous footnote eleven (with all publisher's data and page citations omitted) read: "K. B. Clark, *Effect of Prejudice and Discrimination on Personality Development;* Witmer and Kotinsky, *Personality in the Making;* Deutscher and Chein, 'The Psychological Effects of Enforced Segregation: A Survey of Social Science Opinion,' 26 *J. Psychol.;* Chein, 'What are the Psychological Effects of Segregation Under Conditions of Equal Facilities?,' 3 *Int. J. Opinion and Attitude Res.;* Brameld, 'Education Costs,' in *Discrimination and National Welfare;* Frazier, *The Negro in the United States.* And see generally Myrdal, *An American Dilemma.*" Eastland attempted to discredit Frazier, Brameld, and Myrdal, all distinguished scholars, by linking them to communism; and the senator attacked the credibility of Clark, who had been employed by the NAACP and therefore, Eastland stated, was not an impartial authority.
[47] *Congressional Record*, 84th Cong., 1st Sess. (May 26, 1955), 7124. Senator Johnston joined Eastland as a sponsor of the resolution.
[48] Morris Cunningham, in Memphis *Commercial Appeal*, September 25, 1955.
[49] Speech by Eastland before the Mississippi Association of Citizens' Councils, reprinted in Jackson *Daily News*, December 1, 1955. This speech was also widely circulated by the Citizens' Councils. Association of Citizens' Councils of Mississippi, "*We've Reached Era of Judicial Tyranny*": An Address by Senator James O. Eastland of Mississippi (Winona, n.d.), hereinafter cited as *Eastland Address*.

alone; it had only to break through the propaganda barrier with truth to win allies. Many people, southern and nonsouthern, knew that the inevitable result of current trends would "be lasting economic, social and governmental effects which will go to the very foundations of the republic. Aid can be expected from these patriotic quarters."[50]

Restoration of the past required more than just the spreading of truth throughout the land; it must be spurred by a nationwide, grass roots movement, centrally coordinated, enlisting patriotic organizations and individuals from all states. In a series of speeches during the summer of 1954, Eastland sketched the nature of the movement he had in mind:

It will be a people's organization, an organization not controlled by fawning politicians who cater to organized racial pressure groups. A people's organization to fight the Court, to fight the CIO, to fight the NAACP and to fight all the conscienceless pressure groups who are attempting our destruction. We will mobilize and organize public opinion. We will attempt to pledge candidates in advance as they attempt to pledge them.

We are about to embark upon a great crusade to restore Americanism and return the control of our government to the people. In addition, our organization will carry on its banner the slogan of free enterprise and we will fight those organizations who attempt with much success to socialize industry, and the great medical profession of this country. This will give us recruits and add to our support in the North and West.

Defeat means death, the death of Southern culture and our aspirations as an Anglo-Saxon people. With strong leadership and the loyalty and fortitude of a great people, we will climb the heights. Generations of Southerners yet unborn will cherish our memory because they will realize that the fight we now wage will have preserved for them their untainted racial heritage, their culture and the institutions of the Anglo-Saxon race.[51]

The Federation for Constitutional Government was an attempt to institutionalize the Mississippi senator's program. Created formally in December, 1955, following a series of preliminary meetings, the federation was designed to fuse the southern neobourbon power structure with rising white supremacy organizations and to serve as the central agency for a broad states' rights movement, a clearing house to direct massive resistance strategy in the South and to carry the fight to the North. Coordinating efforts of the "literally hundreds of patriotic organizations" across the

---

[50] Statement by Eastland, reprinted in Richmond *Times-Dispatch*, October 30, 1955.
[51] From excerpts of a speech Eastland apparently delivered in June, 1954, reprinted in Memphis *Commercial Appeal*, December 29, 1955. Eastland made a number of speeches along this line. See *Congressional Record*, 83rd Cong., 2nd Sess. (July 23, 1954), 11522–27 and (August 5, 1954), 13375.

nation, maintaining a lobby in Washington, undertaking large-scale public relations programs, publishing a federation magazine, and conducting field organizational work were among the federation's stated aims.[52] An unstated objective, but one that was obviously on the minds of some participants, was third-party political activity.[53]

For various reasons the federation never fulfilled the ambitious role envisioned by Eastland and other promoters. Inadequate finances limited its activity. Citizens' Council leaders, some of whom were less than enthusiastic about the project, soon created their own regional agency. The federation was a leaders organization—its restricted membership list read like a who's who of neobourbonism, and this prima donna orientation boded ill for bureaucratic efficiency. For a time the federation maintained a New Orleans office, carried out limited propaganda projects, strove mightily to establish working relations with northern "patriotic" groups, and participated in a disastrous third-party campaign in 1956, after which it faded from public view. State Federations for Constitutional Government and the Virginia Defenders, which were closely associated with the federation, passed into the Citizens' Council orbit. The organization served a liaison function in molding southern opposition to desegregation, but it possessed little authority.

Establishment of the federation was nevertheless a landmark in the rise of massive resistance. In the same sense that the Southern Manifesto was a declaration of hostilities, the federation was the war council where established leaders and emerging Citizens' Council spokesmen joined in endorsing a massive resistance program, formally committing the neobourbon power structure to a militant offensive against social change. In part this represented reentry of the Dixiecrats into the fray. The federation bore a definite similarity to the old Dixiecrat National States' Rights Association, and its program was reminiscent of Dixiecrat strategy. States' Rights veteran John U. Barr was federation chairman, and Dixiecrats abounded on the one-hundred-member advisory board, although Citizens' Council, Defenders, Patriots, and state federation chieftains were most numerous and dominated the twelve-member executive committee.[54] Delegates from several nonsouthern states attended the organ-

[52] *Federation for Constitutional Government* (pamphlet published by the Federation, New Orleans, n.d.).

[53] See the report of an interview with John U. Barr, in Miami *Herald*, October 24, 1955, and James Graham Cook, *The Segregationists* (New York, 1962), 262.

[54] The Memphis *Commercial Appeal*, December 29, 1955, gives membership lists.

izational meeting (with one exception, however, they did not become members),[55] representing the first institutionalized attempt to create a national coalition.

Federation membership comprised an impressive aggregate of political influence. United States Senators Eastland and Thurmond (with Talmadge soon to become the third), Governor Marvin Griffin, and United States Representatives L. Mendel Rivers of South Carolina, John Bell Williams of Mississippi, James C. Davis of Georgia, and William M. Tuck and Watkins M. Abbitt of Virginia were among the forty-nine members holding state or federal offices.[56] Excepting some of the white supremacy organization leaders, who were nonaligned, participants broadly if imperfectly reflected state factional divisions: the neobourbon wing of the Louisiana anti-Long faction, headed by Perez, Barr, and former Governor Sam H. Jones; South Carolina members led by Senator Thurmond acceptable to the Byrnes-Dixiecrat group; Alabama Dixiecrats including 1948 Democratic Executive Committee Chairman Gessner T. McCorvey; the Old Guard-Dixiecrat Mississippi phalanx with Eastland, Wright, and Sillers; more important political leaders from the old Talmadge organization, including Talmadge, Griffin, and Roy Harris; representatives of the Byrd organization, notably Tuck and Abbitt; and rightwing Shivercrats, such as Wright Morrow, J. Evetts Haley, and former Governor Coke R. Stevenson. Few indeed were members of the Long forces or the anti-Long business conservative followers of de-Lesseps Morrison; associates of Senator Johnston and State Senator Brown of South Carolina; friends of Governor Folsom of Alabama and Governor James P. Coleman of Mississippi; former anti-Talmadgites and anti-organization Virginians; or liberal-moderate Texas opponents of Governor Shivers. Membership from Arkansas, Florida, Tennessee, and North Carolina, although containing a number of 1948 Dixiecrats and 1952 supporters of Eisenhower, was politically unimpressive and represented no identifiable factional composition.

Despite the federation's failure to become the great third force in American politics, its formation, followed by the Southern Manifesto, clearly indicated that substantial elements of the southern power structure had chosen to stand and fight. Massive resistance was taking shape.

[55] The exception was Mrs. Hallie M. Kendall of Charleston, West Virginia.
[56] James, "The South's Own Civil War," in Shoemaker (ed.), *With All Deliberate Speed*, 18.

Creation of the Citizens' Councils of America—so named to correspond
with "the expected national scope of the organization"[57]—came less than
four months after formation of the Federation for Constitutional Government. A confederated agency to coordinate activities of state associations,
Citizens' Councils of America duplicated many functions the federation
was designed to perform.

Council leaders had no intention of permitting their organization to
lose its independent identity, not while dreams of grandeur filled their
heads and *The Citizens' Council* spoke of their movement spreading "across
the United States, from the Atlantic to the Pacific and from Canada to
the Gulf."[58] Paradoxically, Council leaders, especially those of the second
echelon, were often provincial, profoundly so when compared with the
federation's political professionals. Although top men like William J.
Simmons thought in the broad perspective, the rank and file, fundamentally, just wanted to make Cottontown or Millville like it used to be.
Accomplishment of such a task required, of course, reversing the social
and political course of the nation, and Councilmen could grow enthusiastic about broad crusades aiming toward specific goals and touching
white supremacy, but they might easily be frightened by Eastland's epic
fantasies. Similarly, some questioned the wisdom of doing battle with
the CIO and all the other "conscienceless pressure groups," preferring a
strategy that concentrated on racial segregation. Devotion to the social
status quo ante, as well as the basically neobourbon nature of the movement, inevitably led to a generally reactionary outlook, and the Councils
drifted ever more deeply into the economic and political as well as the
social past. But all of this was not so obvious in the winter of 1955–56.
Furthermore, Council spokesmen frequently possessed "a curious man-in-
the-street distrust of politicians"[59] and suspected the federation, loaded
as it was with prestigious and persuasive officeholding professionals. It
seemed better, all things considered, to concentrate on spreading the
Council movement and turning back the "feds" and the "agitators" at
the state line.

---

[57] *The Citizens' Council*, May, 1956.

[58] *Ibid.*, August, 1956.

[59] Martin, *The Deep South Says "Never"*, 142. Council spokesmen reiterated that their
movement "must be an organization supported and controlled by the people and not
by any politician or political party." Association of Citizens' Councils of Mississippi,
Annual Report (1955), 2; *2nd Annual Report, August, 1956* (Greenwood, 1956), 2.

Approximately sixty-five leaders of the organized resistance movement gathered in New Orleans during April, 1956, to resolve:

That we form an organization to be named Citizens' Councils of America for the preservation of the reserved natural rights of the people of the States, including, primarily, the separation of the races in our schools and all institutions involving personal and social relations; and for the maintenance of our States' Rights to regulate public health, morals, marriages, education, peace and good order in the States, under the Constitution of the United States.[60]

Most of the major white supremacy groups in the South affiliated with the Citizens' Councils of America. Its membership eventually included the Georgia States' Rights Council, the Tennessee Federation for Constitutional Government, the Virginia Defenders, and the North Carolina Defenders of States' Rights in addition to the state Citizens' Council associations.[61] While possessing little direct authority, the regional organization served as "a co-ordinating and planning agency for the several state associations," periodically bringing together leaders of the movement for policy discussions.[62] As the largest effective coalition of white supremacy groups, the Citizens' Councils of America was the closest thing that existed to an institutionalized cockpit of massive resistance strategy.

The center of gravity shifted from the federation to the Citizens' Councils of America, and Eastland and other major leaders made the transition. It was probably no accident that the Mississippi senator's subcommittee was pursuing subversives in New Orleans at the time that the regional association was being created. But the new organization made certain that the vanguard of massive resistance—white supremacy organizations and neobourbon political professionals—would function as an alliance, rather than a single institution.

[60] *The Citizens' Council*, May, 1956.
[61] Representatives of these organizations served on the Editorial Board of the Citizens' Councils of America newspaper. Board members are listed in *The Citizens' Council*, beginning with the June, 1957, issue.
[62] *The Citizens' Council*, November, 1956.

CHAPTER 8

INTERPOSITION

The program of massive resistance flowed from the southern past. Most directly it came from the Dixiecrats, but in a broader sense it was an authentic expression of the bourbon tradition. Politicians and, in some cases, newspapers furnished direction for the resistance; Senator Eastland and the Federation for Constitutional Government along with the Byrd organization and the Richmond *News Leader* were particularly important in formulating and popularizing basic themes of neobourbon strategy. By mid-1956 the resistance had absorbed an aggressive program, and, as in the past, states' rights was a fundamental element—states' rights carried to an extreme unknown since the demise of the Confederacy.

Interposition was the theory and the battle cry of massive resistance. This obsolete and almost forgotten doctrine, now reborn, formed the central theme binding together massive state resistance to changes that threatened other obsolete but by no means forgotten beliefs, prejudices, and practices. To be sure, in the chaotic politics of the mid-twentieth century South, absurd simplifications and elaborate constitutional polemics combined with generous emotionalism to serve in lieu of a definition for interposition. Southern news media and the region's politicians spent uncounted words explaining, debating, and advocating interposition, but the overall result was more confusion than clarity. Proponents of the doctrine might have agreed with an Atlanta *Journal* writer: "In the present case 'interposition' is proposed as a basically legal and constitutional means to nullify the Supreme Court's order."[1] Simple as that. J. Evetts Haley, achieving perhaps the ultimate in constitutional distillation, explained in a radio address to fellow Texans:

[1] William Key, in Atlanta *Journal*, January 22, 1956.

If you believe in the right of contract, and everyone but a Communist does, then you believe in interposition. If you look over a menu and order ham and eggs for breakfast, you have made a contract. If Brussels sprouts and beans are brought to you instead, you, as a partner in that contract, interpose your objections, and refuse to eat and pay for them.

Interposition, in spite of all the political mumbo-jumbo, is just as ... Constitutional as ham and eggs.[2]

More often, however, advocates of interposition rested their arguments upon constitutional "mumbo-jumbo," borrowing heavily from Thomas Jefferson, John C. Calhoun, and other pre-Civil War political theorists. From the editorial pages of the Richmond *News Leader*, the pens of numerous "old school" state and county judges, and elsewhere came an elaborate defense of the compact theory of the union, a static and unchanging Constitution, a formalistic view of the role of the judiciary, and the right of interposition.

To some, during the winter of 1955–56, interposition became almost a magic panacea, an act that, like conversion, would lead inevitably to salvation. Florence Sillers Ogden, Jackson *Daily News* columnist, hallowed the passage of Mississippi's interposition resolution with: "In the years to come, a hundred years after this day, school children will read in their textbooks of this historic event in their state—and they will memorize the date, February 26, 1956."[3] Others felt that interposition would serve as a rallying point for a southern counteroffensive.[4] William M. Rainach spoke of interposition as a means of throwing "the searchlight of public opinion on the integration issue," and Sam Engelhardt said its purpose was "to serve notice on the rest of the nation that Alabama and the South will not accept integration."[5] The Richmond *News Leader* suggested that, among many other advantages, a policy based on interposition would lift the debate from sectional racism to the more defensible "higher ground" of state sovereignty.[6]

Despite ambiguities, legal gymnastics, and fantasies, interposition did rest upon a basic foundation: a commitment to use state power to oppose the *Brown* decision. By consolidating public school authority in the state

[2] Excerpts from radio address by Haley, reprinted in Dallas *Morning News*, April 12, 1956.

[3] Jackson *Daily News*, March 11, 1956.

[4] Statement by Fielding L. Wright, reprinted in *ibid.*, December 18, 1955.

[5] Rainach is quoted in New Orleans *Times-Picayune*, May 20, 1956, and Engelhardt in Memphis *Commercial Appeal*, January 20, 1956.

[6] Richmond *News Leader*, November 29, 1955.

and interposing the "sovereignty" of the state between local school officials and federal courts, neobourbon spokesmen sought not so much to avoid or evade the Court order as they did to defeat it—to achieve total victory.

Basically, neobourbons and their camp followers hoped to face down the federal courts, to force the courts to retreat by either closing affected schools (as both Virginia and Arkansas were later to do) or by militantly refusing to comply with court orders (as Louisiana officials were later to attempt). Locked public schools, resistance leaders felt, would demonstrate to the courts and to the nation that white southerners would not accept desegregation, and, just as noncompliance had led to the reversal of the Eighteenth Amendment and the Volstead Act, so the South would nullify the *Brown* decision. After all, the "southern way of life" was an abstraction more or less accepted by the American public like many another abstraction ordained by time. Furthermore, many neobourbon leaders did not believe that federal judges would find defiant governors and other state officials in contempt of court and place them behind bars, and, should the courts commit such a heresy, the resulting publicity, it was anticipated, would benefit the resistance. Eventually, the North, as it had done in the past, would grow bored with this new abolitionist crusade, thus setting the stage for a return to the principles of the past. All that the South needed to win was the courage to act.[7]

Apparently Herman Talmadge deserved credit for resurrecting the long-abandoned doctrine of interposition. As early as May, 1951, Tal-

---

[7] From the viewpoint of legal strategists associated with the resistance, interposition had the additional merit of complicating the NAACP's legal chores. The Fourteenth Amendment, by court interpretation, applied only to state action. Individuals were free to discriminate if they chose; states could not deny equal protection of the law. But the Eleventh Amendment, by court interpretation, prohibited suits by individuals against a state without the state's consent. The proponents of interposition sought to consolidate authority over the public schools in the state and to prohibit suits against the state and such state agencies as local school boards in cases concerning school operation and administration. Therefore, the NAACP would have to demonstrate that discrimination was the result of state action (under the Fourteenth Amendment) but that its clients were not suing the state (under the Eleventh Amendment). This did not prove to be a particularly difficult task. The NAACP could bring suits against individuals (such as school board chairmen) to prevent these individuals from performing unconstitutional acts (by assigning students to public schools solely on the basis of race). In the segregated South, discrimination was so overt that it was not difficult to show that an individual was using his official position, and thus state authority, to discriminate. This problem emerged most clearly in Louisiana. See Louisiana State Advisory Committee, *The New Orleans School Crisis: Report of the Louisiana State Advisory Committee to the United States Commission on Civil Rights* (New Orleans, 1961), 50–55.

madge and advisers were discussing Georgia's successful nullification of *Worcester v. Georgia* in 1832.[8] But not until 1955 did the idea begin to draw general attention. In August, 1955, William Old, a Virginia county attorney, privately published a pamphlet pleading for interposition and offering suggestions for implementing such a policy. He called upon Virginia to enact "appropriate legislation" withdrawing from school officials, "state agencies and from the Commonwealth itself all consent that they may be.sued in any matter concerning the operation of the schools."[9] During the same month, the South Carolina Committee of 52 became the first group to seek broad public support for interposition as state policy, gathering some seven thousand signatures on a petition calling upon the state legislature "to interpose the sovereignty of the State of South Carolina between Federal Courts and local school officials."[10] By October, 1955, the Jackson, Mississippi, Citizens' Council chapter was promoting interposition, and *The Citizens' Council* was discussing the doctrine in news stories.[11]

Then, on November 21, 1955, the Richmond *News Leader* proposed editorially "to recur to fundamental principles for guidance," thus beginning one of southern journalism's more successful editorial crusades. During the following weeks, editor James Jackson Kilpatrick and his associates elaborately analyzed the nature of the Union. They described a federated—almost a confederated—Union composed of sovereign states, their powers protected by a static Constitution, "unchanged by John Marshall, unchanged by the Civil War, not altered in any way since the Constitution was created in 1787," a Constitution in which the "powers delegated to the national government are painstakingly enumerated" and in which all other powers belonged to the sovereign states. The *News Leader* supplemented its editorial campaign for interposition by reprinting states' rights documents ranging chronologically from the Kentucky and Virginia Resolutions of 1798 to a series of public letters written for a Richmond newspaper in 1833.[12]

[8] New York *Times*, May 28, 1951. See also *ibid.*, January 19, 1954, and Thomas L. Stokes, in Los Angeles *Mirror*, May 19, 1954. *Worcester v. Georgia*, 6 Peters 515, concerned Georgia and the Cherokee Nation.

[9] William Old, *The Segregation Issue: Suggestions Regarding the Maintenance of State Autonomy* (privately printed, 1955), 3.

[10] Committee of 52, *Put Yourself on Record* (n.p., 1955).

[11] *The Citizens' Council*, October, 1955.

[12] Richmond *News Leader*, November 21, December 16, 26, 30, 1955. The documents and most of the interposition editorials are reprinted in Richmond *News Leader, Interposition: Editorials and Editorial Page Presentations* (Richmond, 1956).

In addition to editing some one hundred years of constitutional growth out of American history, the *News Leader* was guilty of questionable journalistic tactics. Immediately following the second *Brown* ruling, the newspaper had editorialized: "From the moment that abominable decision was handed down, two broad courses only were available to the South. One was to defy the court openly and notoriously; the other was to accept the court's decision and to combat it by legal means."[13] Choosing the latter course of action, the *News Leader* endorsed the Gray Commission report and "vigorously supported"[14] the constitutional convention referendum, devoting editorial after editorial to the merits of the tuition-grant system.[15] On January 9, 1956, Virginians approved the calling of a limited constitutional convention by a 2 to 1 majority. The *News Leader* immediately dismissed this endorsement of the Gray Plan, however, explaining that Virginia citizens had not voted for what they thought they had voted for at all but had "with a perfect, intuitive clarity" actually endorsed a policy of open and notorious opposition to the Supreme Court ruling.[16] After having meticulously described for its readers the workings of the tuition-grant system in numerous editorials during the campaign, the Richmond newspaper now pontificated: "The vast bulk of the voters knew little of 'tuition grants' and cared less."[17] The "unmistakable voice" of the electorate was a cry of protest and the duty of the General Assembly was clearly interposition.[18]

By this time interposition was being discussed in every southern state, and throughout the region white supremacy organizations were placing it at the top of their legislative programs. *The Citizens' Council* devoted most of its December issue to glorification of the doctrine, and *News Leader* editorials on interposition were printed in pamphlet form and circulated widely. One of the first acts of the Federation for Constitutional Government was to pass a resolution of support for measures "to nullify and void the court decision."[19] While neobourbons were by no means the only advocates of the policy, the basic drive for interposition was

---

[13] Richmond *News Leader*, June 1, 1955.

[14] Richmond *News Leader, Interposition: Editorials and Editorial Page Presentations*, 36. As noted earlier, the Gray Commission, while accepting the principle of desegregation, had formulated programs to limit actual desegregation to token levels.

[15] Richmond *News Leader*, December 9, 1955–January 9, 1956.

[16] *Ibid.*, January 10, 1956.

[17] *Ibid.*, February 10, 1956.

[18] *Ibid.*, January 10, 1956.

[19] Memphis *Commercial Appeal*, December 29, 1955.

neobourbon in origin. Without exception, white supremacy organizations —Citizens' Councils, Defenders, Patriots, state federations—were enthusiastic advocates, and political leaders holding membership in the Federation for Constitutional Government were particularly conspicuous in support of the doctrine. With the rising popularity of interposition as a philosophy of resistance and with an aroused neobourbon minority to provide the thrust, politicians throughout the South were soon under heavy pressure to join the crusade.

In rapid-fire order legislatures in six states, those of the Deep South and Virginia, passed resolutions of interposition. North Carolina lawmakers, meeting in special session in July, 1956, approved a resolution of protest. During the same month Texas voters decided that a statement of interposition and two other white supremacy proposals should be made a part of the platform of the state Democratic Party. Arkansas citizens by initiative petitions approved two interposition measures, a resolution and a constitutional amendment, in the November, 1956, general election. Florida legislators endorsed an interposition resolution in early 1957, and Tennessee lawmakers passed a Manifesto of Protest. Four states, Alabama, Mississippi, Georgia, and Florida, carried the doctrine to its logical conclusion and pronounced the Court's ruling null and void. By mid-1957 eight states had approved interposition measures; Texas had endorsed the doctrine; and North Carolina and Tennessee had voiced protest against the *Brown* decision.[20]

All of the legislative interposition resolutions were similar, and all in varying degrees paraphrased the Virginia document which had borrowed freely from the original Virginia Resolution of 1798. Generally statements of interposition defended the compact theory of the Union and advanced a strict interpretation of the Constitution. In creating the federal union, so the argument ran, the states had surrendered to the national government only those powers enumerated in the compact; all other powers, including control over public school policies, remained state possessions,

[20] For interposition documents, see *Race Relations Law Reporter*, I (April, 1956), 437 (Alabama); (June, 1956), 591–92, and (December, 1956), 1117–18 (Arkansas); II (June, 1957), 707–10 (Florida); I (April, 1956), 438–40 (Georgia); (August, 1956), 753–55 (Louisiana); (April, 1956), 440–43 (Mississippi); (April, 1956), 443–45 (South Carolina); II (April, 1957), 481–83 (Tennessee); I (April, 1956), 445–47 (Virginia). The Alabama legislature passed a second nullification resolution in 1957. Act 14, Legislative Acts, Alabama, 1957 Sess., in *Facts on Film*, Reel 3. The Texas statement is reprinted in Dallas *Morning News, Texas Almanac, 1958–1959*, p. 455. On the North Carolina resolution, see *Southern School News*, August, 1956.

undelegated, unimpaired, and protected by the Tenth Amendment. Ratification of the Fourteenth Amendment broadened the federal government's powers, but it in no way changed the nature of the Union nor circumscribed any state's rights to require segregated facilities. Instead, control of public school enrollment remained where it had been prior to the Civil War—a reserved function under the police powers of the state, a condition recognized by the Supreme Court in previous decisions. Therefore, *Brown v. Board of Education* was an amendment to the Constitution, not an interpretation of its intent. A state's clear duty in defense of the compact and state sovereignty—"as a matter of right" some resolutions termed it—was to resist the Supreme Court's "illegal" action until the issue was settled by constitutional amendment.

Even among neobourbons there was confusion about just what kind of constitutional amendment would be required. Some saw interposition as a means "for procuring a constitutional amendment," a method to arrest desegregation until a constitutional amendment authorizing dual school systems could be submitted to the states.[21] Interposition resolutions in Arkansas and Mississippi asserted this viewpoint. More often, however, resistance spokesmen took the Calhoun view that interposition was valid until other states approved a constitutional amendment declaring coerced racial separation in educational facilities illegal. The Alabama resolution declared "the decisions and orders of the Supreme Court of the United States relating to separation of races in the public schools are, as a matter of right, null, void, and of no effect" until ratification "of a suitable constitutional amendment that would declare, in plain and unequivocal language, that the states do surrender their power to maintain public schools and other public facilities on a basis of separation as to race."[22] As Attorney General Eugene Cook of Georgia explained: "Interposition resolutions by 13 states are an affirmative rejection under the amending power, which will uphold the position of the states that the segregation decision is null and void."[23] Most states in their interposition resolutions avoided the issue, following the lead of Virginia in merely calling for a constitutional change "designed to settle the issue of contested power here asserted."[24] In any case the problem was not an immediate one, and there was the more important task of convincing federal courts that

---

[21] Essay by Ross R. Barnett, in Jackson *Daily News*, December 21, 1955.
[22] *Race Relations Law Reporter*, I (April, 1956), 437.
[23] As quoted in Atlanta *Journal*, April 13, 1956.
[24] *Race Relations Law Reporter*, I (April, 1956), 447.

sovereign states obeyed only constitutional amendments, not unpopular Supreme Court decisions.

The drive for interposition was an expression of more than the racial fears of white men. To be sure, protection of white supremacy was paramount, and it was this emotional issue that initiated the movement; but interposition was also a genuine reaffirmation of states' rights on a broader plane. When a spokesman for the Virginia Defenders characterized the *Brown* decision "as the occasion, rather than the cause, for reasserting the sovereignty of individual states within the Union," he was voicing a widely held view.[25] A number of state interposition resolutions specifically dealt with federal "encroachments" in nonracial fields. Florida legislators declared that:

said decisions and orders of the Supreme Court of the United States denying the individual sovereign states the power to enact laws relating to espionage or subversion, criminal proceedings. the dismissal of public employees for refusal to answer questions concerning their connections with communism, "right to work" protection, and relating to separation of the races in the public institutions of a State are null, void and of no force or effect.[26]

Virginia solons lamented the growth of congressional power to regulate interstate commerce into "a power to control local enterprises remote from interstate commerce," of power to levy taxes for the general welfare into "a power to confiscate the earnings of our people for purposes unrelated to the general welfare as we conceive it," of threats to private property, and of the defense power, changed "by some Fabian alchemy, into a power to build local schoolhouses."[27] These sentiments were echoed by Mississippi and Tennessee legislators. As in the past the bourbon South chose to fight on the issue of race but, as had often happened before, the spoils of war involved matters of a wider scope.

Interposition resolutions per se were statements of policy—or in some cases protest—without direct force and certainly without constitutional sanction, as Virginia's own attorney general pointed out.[28] Yet the sound and fury surrounding interposition signified a deadly serious intent. The Richmond *News Leader* cautioned Virginia state senators just prior to the vote on interposition in that chamber:

[25] Gates, *The Making of Massive Resistance,* 138, quoting J. Barrye Wall.
[26] *Race Relations Law Reporter,* II (June, 1957), 710.
[27] *Ibid.,* I (April, 1956), 447.
[28] J. Lindsay Almond, Jr., to Delegate Robert Whitehead, February 14, 1956, in *ibid.,* I (April, 1956), 462–64.

Any member who believes the court acted constitutionally should vote against this resolution, for the resolution plainly accuses the court of unconstitutional action. Any member who is unwilling "to resist" the court's decrees in the manner described, should vote against the resolution; for resistance is a hard road and a long road, and we should not embark upon it unthinkingly.

What Virginia is setting in motion here is an earnest and honorable effort to return to government by constitutional process. We are attempting to restore to all the States that final authority over the Constitution that is their high privilege and their solemn responsibility.[29]

Having taken the step and committed themselves to such a task, legislators, as well as southern politicians in general, found it difficult to justify anything less than massive resistance.

Virginia offered leadership to the peripheral South in a program of massive resistance based upon the doctrine of interposition and, at the same time, provided states of the Deep South with a theoretical basis for opposition to desegregation. Virginia pledged resistance to "this illegal encroachment" and called upon her sister states to join in efforts "to check this and further encroachment by the Supreme Court, through judicial legislation, upon the reserved powers of the states."[30] As the movement spread throughout the region, elected officials, backed by white supremacy organizations and preponderant popular opinion, moved to transform official pronouncements into public policy.

States of the Deep South quickly acted on the doctrine. From the beginning Mississippi, Georgia, South Carolina, and Louisiana had followed such a program in practice if not in theory, and formal adoption of interposition was pretext for further bombardment of the statute books with all manner of resistance legislation—some of it dangerous to the future of federalism, more of it dangerous to the states' own citizens, and virtually all of it offensive to the American Constitution and the spirit of Anglo-Saxon jurisprudence. Mississippi legislators were most direct in their enactment of interposition in passing "an Act to give effect to the resolution of interposition." The law ordered all persons in the executive branch of government, state or local, in Mississippi "to prohibit . . . the implementation or the compliance with the Integration Decision" and to enforce segregation.[31] Normally, however, interposition received practical meaning through legislative packages conceived by segregationist strategy committees.

[29] Richmond *News Leader*, January 31, 1956.
[30] *Race Relations Law Reporter*, I (April, 1956), 447.
[31] *Ibid.*, II (April, 1957), 480.

In Louisiana the Rainach Committee bolstered interposition practices with proposals ranging from bills making the mere advocacy of integration grounds for dismissing public school teachers and even school bus drivers to a measure prohibiting "all interracial dancing, social functions, entertainments, athletic training, games, sports or contests and other such activities."[32] The key parts of the legislative program, however, were a proposed state constitutional amendment "withdrawing consent of the State to suits" against such "special agencies" as state and local school officials and a bill requiring a legislative committee to classify public schools in New Orleans, where a desegregation suit was pending, as either "white" ("for the exclusive use of children of the white race") or "Negro" ("for the exclusive use of children of the Negro race"). The bill further prohibited legal action against the resulting classification except "against the State of Louisiana with the consent of the Louisiana Legislature."[33] These measures, making the state responsible for resisting federal court orders, and other bills passed during the 1956 legislative session burdened law books already sagging under the weight of earlier segregationist legislation. Louisiana voters ratified the constitutional amendment in November, 1956.[34]

Georgia, Mississippi, and South Carolina were scenes of similar racial fanaticism, and, for the first time, Alabama joined in the war on the *Brown* decision. The Alabama legislature, called into special session to deal with other matters, evolved into a white supremacy rally, "nullifying" the desegregation rulings, passing various segregationist measures, and proposing two amendments to the state constitution that opened the way for a policy of total resistance. Most important of the constitutional amendments was a "freedom of choice" amalgam granting parents the right to choose racially segregated schools for their children, relieving the state of the requirement to provide public education, and authorizing state aid to private schools through gifts or loans of public money and the sale, lease, or donation of public property. The second amendment concerned selling, leasing, or giving away such things as public housing projects, parks, and playgrounds to prevent racial mixing. Alabama voters approved both amendments in August, 1956.[35]

---

[32] *Ibid.*, I (October, 1956), 941–45, 953–54.
[33] *Ibid.* (August, 1956), 776–77, (October, 1956), 927–28.
[34] *Southern School News*, December, 1956.
[35] *Race Relations Law Reporter*, I (April, 1956), 418, (August, 1956), 732–33; Birmingham *News*, August 29, 1956.

Yet even in the Deep South political solidarity was elusive. Race dominated politics, and the neobourbon solution was in the ascendancy; but expertise at racial demagoguery did not ensure election, and espousal of segregation did not guarantee devotion to neobourbon causes. Among Deep South governors, James P. Coleman of Mississippi, Earl K. Long of Louisiana, and James E. Folsom of Alabama, all in varying degrees, made heretical gestures, as did lesser figures in state politics. In Mississippi, for example, Coleman, whose program centered around business conservatism, avoided Negro-baiting in his successful 1955 campaign. Although a staunch defender of segregation, he also remained aloof from the Citizens' Councils and insisted upon making opposition to the *Brown* decision as orderly and dignified as possible and upon restoring stability within Mississippi following the Emmett Till murder in the summer of 1955. The governor-elect's reaction to demands for nullification was that "Any such idea . . . is foolish, ruinous and legal poppycock."[36] But the interposition forces, led by Senator Eastland, Representative John Bell Williams, and Judge Tom Brady, were too powerful to overcome, and Coleman soon tempered his opposition.[37] It was clear, however, that Coleman's participation in neobourbon projects could not be counted upon, and he was soon in a hot fight with the Citizens' Councils over political strategy in the 1956 presidential election.

The most persistent cleavage among Deep South politicians centered not around adoption of interposition—the issue had too much emotional appeal to be effectively opposed—but upon what kind of interposition measure to enact. An enormous amount of Deep South energy went into debate over whether to nullify the *Brown* decision or just to pledge opposition to the ruling. Although the two doctrines of interposition and nullification were politically similar in that they both denied the validity of the Supreme Court decision, politicians considered nullification a more profound political commitment. Governor Coleman retreated to acceptance of interposition but not to nullification, and this division was manifested in most Deep South states.[38] This fissure divided the four governors who attended a conference on interposition convened by Governor Stanley in Richmond, Virginia, during January, 1956. Stanley, Coleman, and George Bell Timmerman of South Carolina endorsed

[36] As quoted in Birmingham *News*, December 14, 1955.
[37] See the statements by Eastland, Brady, and Williams reprinted in the Jackson *Daily News*, December 12, 15, 1955.
[38] *Southern Schools News*, January, February, 1956.

interposition, but they refused Georgia Governor Griffin's invitition to join in a nullification policy. Unable to agree upon strategic details, the governors issued a broad statement recognizing the right of each state to take such measures "as it may deem advisable to protect its sovereignty and the rights of its people."[39] But both interposition and nullification served as promises of state opposition to the federal courts, and in immediate terms the differences were negligible. The states of the Deep South were committed to a massive resistance program.

The crucial struggle for southwide unity took place in the peripheral South, the area that drifted indecisively between defiance and compliance, that longed to be both southern and American. The real division in these states had at first been along lines drawn in Virginia between backers of the Gray Plan and its opponents; it was expressed in North Carolina, Florida, and Arkansas over whether or not to enact pupil assignment legislation and in Texas and Tennessee over whether to do anything at all. But the South, not the nation, asserted leadership. Virginia proffered a program and called forth the deepest loyalties and fears associated with the "South" and southern tradition—Reconstruction mythology, Yankee intervention, and states' rights—and the dangers of a profound and open-ended social upheaval.[40] The dialectic had been rephrased with the principal lines drawn between supporters of local option segregationist machinations of a Gray Plan nature and those who would enlist in the interpositionist front.

Across the upper South, interposition accelerated the pace of racial politics as the doctrine became a factor in a series of important political power struggles. The trend was toward rising racial tensions and white social reaction, but these states retained considerable heterogeneity, and politicians had some room to maneuver, some opportunity to shape the course of events.

Texas occupied a position of major importance. Although the black supremacy of petroleum was of at least equal importance to white supremacy in the social order, the two had a strong tendency to become combined, and the latter was by no means of negligible significance. With a growing Latin American population and a substantial Negro minority combined with broad and upsetting demographic and economic change,

---

[39] Reprinted in Richmond *Times-Dispatch*, January 25, 1956.
[40] George B. Tindall, "Mythology: A New Frontier in Southern History," in Frank E. Vandiver (ed.), *The Idea of the South: Pursuit of a Central Theme* (Chicago, 1964), 1–15, is suggestive in this regard.

many white Texans looked sympathetically upon a movement promising to restore and maintain a stable society based upon Protestant, Anglo-Saxon domination.[41] And the reigning power structure in Texas was more neobourbon in outlook than that of any other peripheral state, Virginia excepted.

Governor Allan Shivers had been free in his criticisms of the Supreme Court decision, but his remarks had been followed by moderate actions, and Texas had made far more progress toward desegregation than the rest of the South combined. No state legislation hampered voluntary compliance, and the state Board of Education offered consultant service to assist district school officials in "implementing locally originated plans" relating to desegregation.[42] Some eighty-four districts, all in or on the border of the predominantly white western part of the state, had desegregated by the end of 1955.[43]

The governor remained clearly unreconciled to the federal Supreme Court's infringements upon the rights of states, however, and the 1952 Democrats for Eisenhower leader retained his displeasure with liberal inclinations in the national Democratic Party. But fellow Texans seemed not to share fully the governor's antipathies. Shivers faced serious opposition for control of the Texas delegation to the national Democratic convention; settlement of the tidelands oil controversy undermined voter concern for states' rights, an issue that had served the governor well in the past; and, despite growing racial tension in East Texas, the western part of the state continued to make progress toward desegregation. Instead, criticism of the governor's administration for alleged corruption and malpractices was a mounting embarrassment.[44]

At this opportune time interposition began its spread through the South, offering an issue around which the Shivers' forces might rally. The doctrine offered the promise of reviving concern for states' rights and projecting the additional appeal of racial emotionalism. In February, 1956, Shivers called upon the state Democratic Party to conduct a referendum on interposition and, upon popular endorsement, to place the doctrine in the state party platform.[45] During early 1956 Shivers and

[41] Soukup, McCleskey, and Holloway, *Party and Factional Division in Texas*, 3–20, *passim*.
[42] *Race Relations Law Reporter*, I (February, 1956), 261–62.
[43] "Report of the Legal and Legislative Subcommittee of the Texas Advisory Committee on Segregation in the Public Schools," in *ibid*. (December, 1956), 1081.
[44] Weeks, *Texas One-Party Politics in 1956*, pp. 7–14.
[45] Dallas *Morning News*, February 24, 1956.

Attorney General John Ben Shepperd vigorously supported interposition in public pronouncements. Despite pleas from Shepperd and others for a special legislative session to act on interposition, Shivers insisted upon using the issue as a rallying cry in the struggle for control of the party. The governor's unorthodox strategy presumably stemmed from political considerations, but there was neither inconsistency nor hint of insincerity in his advocacy of the doctrine itself. Indeed, Shivers even talked of promoting a campaign to write an interposition plank into the national Democratic Party platform.[46]

The battle for command of the state party convention became increasingly bitter with the Shivers' forces making segregation and associated programs, including interposition, key issues in their campaign. But 1956 was not a Shivercrat year. An opposition moderate-loyalist-liberal coalition emerged to challenge, outmaneuver, and overwhelm the governor and his allies. United States Senate Majority Leader Lyndon B. Johnson, a master of border state, consensus politics—the art of dominating the great middle while bridging the gap and eroding the base of left and right—was the coalition's leader and favorite son candidate. Speaker of the House Sam Rayburn, a veteran of forty-three years in Congress and a devotee of Democracy with a capital "D," was the keeper of the loyalist conscience. The Democratic Advisory Committee was the organization through which labor and the liberals worked. Although its influence in state politics was limited, the Democratic Advisory Committee represented the strongest northern-type liberal movement in the South. In the face of this onrush, Shivers found his base of support ever shrinking as the consensus absorbed moderately inclined conservatives. Isolated, relying upon dyed-in-the-wool Shivercrats and Federation for Constitutional Government members like Wright Morrow and Coke Stevenson for support, Shivers watched control of the state party pass to the opposition.[47]

This Johnson-Rayburn moderation dominated the Texas Democratic convention that met in May, 1956. The assemblage scorned interposition in favor of a mild statement of states' rights, rejected an unpledged delegation in favor of party loyalty, and named Johnson the favorite son and delegation chairman. The rout of the Shivercrats did not, of course, mean elevation of liberalism to a seat of power. Instead, Democratic

[46] New Orleans *Times-Picayune*, March 6, 1956.
[47] *Southern School News*, February–June, 1956; Weeks, *Texas One-Party Politics in 1956*, pp. 18–41.

Advisory Committee supporters were soon to learn the dangers of border-state consensus. When the state convention met in its September conference, the Johnston-Rayburn forces, now allied with Democratic gubernatorial-nominee Price Daniel (a conservative but not a Shivercrat), turned on the liberals, barring them from access to the seats of party power. The middle was triumphant and, with Daniel becoming governor, any possibility that Texas would either join the interpositionist crusade or move toward a state policy of compliance with the desegregation decision was dead.

Interposition had received its first substantial check; yet the doctrine did register a token victory. Speaking in the East Texas city of Longview just after the May convention, Attorney General Shepperd suggested that a statement of interposition could yet be placed in the party platform by petition for a referendum.[48] The Texas Referendum Committee, headed by Robert Cargill, a Longview oilman, and the Association of Citizens' Councils undertook the task of circulating petitions. Within a month white supremacy organizations had more than the required number of signatures to force a vote on interposition and two other measures expressing opposition to racial intermarriage and endorsing legislation to prevent coerced integration in the public schools. Texas voters approved all three proposals by thundering majorities during July, 1956, primary elections, and all three were nominally made part of the state party platform at the September convention.[49]

The heavy vote for segregation combined with other factors to enliven concern for white supremacy among Texas politicians. Governor Shivers dramatically intervened to defend segregation at Mansfield and Texarkana; the Citizens' Councils effectively agitated for protection of dual school systems; and small-town East Texas legislators organized a segregationist bloc to promote white supremacy measures in the 1957 legislative session.[50] The catalyst for a more aggressively segregationist policy was the report of the Advisory Committee on Segregation in the Public Schools which Shivers had created earlier and had loaded with members holding ultraconservative views.[51] Instructed by Shivers to study problems related to the *Brown* decision, including interposition and methods for "the prevention of forced integration," the Advisory Committee delivered

[48] Dallas *Morning News*, May 13, 1956.
[49] *Southern School News*, August, October, 1956.
[50] *Ibid.*, October–December, 1956, January–June, 1957.
[51] Dallas *Morning News*, August 2, 1955.

in late 1956 a profoundly reactionary report of twenty-one recommendations including a proposal that the state return to a completely segregated
public school system.[52] It also recommended an interposition resolution,
a pupil placement bill, and a referendum measure prohibiting public
school desegregation unless 20 percent of the local voters had petitioned
for desegregation and a majority had approved the change in a special
election. The last measure further provided for stoppage of state funds
and withdrawal of accreditation from any district that bypassed this
method of social change through popular democracy. Governor Daniel
seemed none too enthusiastic about the report, but strong legislative
forces and, judging by the referendum vote, a substantial majority of
Texans favored efforts to protect white supremacy. When the 1957 legislature passed the assignment and referendum bills, Daniel signed both.[53]
Several interposition resolutions introduced during the session remained
interred in committee; nevertheless, the two new laws effectively halted
progress toward desegregation in Texas for the remainder of the decade.[54]
Texas had taken a long step toward, but had stopped just short of, massive
resistance.

Other upper-South states duplicated general tendencies that emerged
in Texas. Racial emotionalism failed to rally majority support for interposition as state policy, but agitation for massive resistance and hardening
public sentiment did sharply circumscribe the range of public debate.
In turning back the extremist challenge, politicians of moderate inclinations found themselves ever more aggressively defending segregation.
Throughout the region, state governments turned to a more vigorous
protection of social stability. North Carolina and Florida enacted further
barriers to all but the most nominal deviations from white supremacy,
and Arkansas and Tennessee, like Texas, adopted their first legislative
impediments to implementation of the *Brown* decision. In all of these
states, business conservatism in more or less genuine form was the
dominant political philosophy on the executive level and, to a lesser
extent, the mood of state legislators. Price Daniel of Texas, Luther H.

---

[52] *Race Relations Law Reporter*, I (December, 1956), 1077, 1086.
[53] Dallas *Morning News*, May 24, 26, 1957; *Race Relations Law Reporter*, II (June, 1957),
693–96.
[54] Two communities held successful referendums and desegregated under the referendum law. Dallas *Morning News*, January 31, 1959. This law largely accounts for
the sharp decline in the rate of desegregation during the late 1950's as compared with
the first three years after the *Brown* decision. During the earlier period, most of the desegregating districts each fall were Texas districts.

Hodges of North Carolina, and LeRoy Collins of Florida were prototypes of business conservatism. The programs of Tennessee Governor Frank G. Clement, himself more politically pragmatic, and Orval E. Faubus, a product of the Arkansas Ozark hills who never lost a distinct trace of neopopulism in style and outlook, were oriented in this direction, especially Faubus, who made creation and support of the Arkansas Industrial Development Commission a cornerstone of his administration's policy. None of these governors had been conspicuous in defense of white supremacy—indeed it was problematical whether several would privately have preferred segregation—but in the political warfare of 1956, "moderation" became a word meaningful only in the most relative sense.

In Arkansas and Florida the crucial political struggles took place in gubernatorial primaries with the incumbent governors in both states facing strong opposition from advocates of massive resistance programs. James Johnson, Arkansas White Citizens' Councils head, conducted a blisteringly racist campaign against Faubus; Sumter L. Lowry, a Federation for Constitutional Government member, campaigned on a similar platform in his effort to unseat Collins. In both states, the incumbent won an impressive first primary victory, but in both states it was the challenger who set the tone of the campaign, defined the issues (or to a large extent *the* issue), and dominated the election in spirit if not in ballots.[55] During these campaigns Collins appointed a committee to study methods for retaining segregated schools and Faubus assumed leadership of a campaign for approval of a pupil assignment law and an interposition resolution through initiative petition.[56]

In North Carolina, Governor Hodges guarded against the emergence of a major opponent of the Johnson-Lowry type by preempting the segregationist issue.[57] Containing the highest percentage of Negroes to total population of any state outside the Deep South, North Carolina was potentially one of the most volatile of upper South states, as the vulnerability of congressmen who refused to sign the Southern Manifesto had demonstrated during the 1956 primary election. Hodges protected him-

---

[55] On the Florida election, see *Southern School News*, March-June, 1956; Miami *Herald*, March 22, 25, April 22, 24, 1956; and St. Petersburg *Times*, February 8, March 14, 18, April 7, 18, May 9, 1956. On the Arkansas election, see *Southern School News*, June–September, 1956; Memphis *Commercial Appeal*, July 5, 22, August 1, 1956; and *Arkansas Gazette*, August 1–3, 1956.

[56] *Southern School News*, May, 1956; *Arkansas Gazette*, March 23, June 10, 1956.

[57] See Arthur Johnsey, in Greensboro *Daily News*, February 5, 1956; Jay Jenkins, in Atlanta *Journal and Constitution*, March 11, 1956; *Southern School News*, March–June, 1956; and Hodges, *Businessman in the Statehouse*, 154.

self on this issue by announcing his intention to call a special legislative session to enact anti-integration measures and by defending segregation almost to the point of massive resistance.

Tennessee had no major election during 1956 (Clement had won a four-year term in 1954), and free from the pressures of democracy in practice, state officials had an opportunity for more flexibility. White supremacy groups organized motorcades, originating in Memphis and Chattanooga and converging on the state capital, to carry petitions demanding interposition and mandatory statewide segregation. Governor Clement denounced these "pressure tactics" and defended local autonomy in school enrollment matters.[58] Although the governor was later to recommend anti-integration legislation, Tennessee state policy remained the most "moderate" in the South.

During 1956 and early 1957, states of the peripheral South moved solidly into opposition to compliance with the *Brown* decision. Special legislative sessions in North Carolina and Florida during 1956 and regular sessions in Arkansas, Texas, Tennessee, and Florida in 1957 enacted segregationist legislative programs that were only slightly less extreme than those being enacted in the Deep South. North Carolina provided for local option school closings; Texas achieved substantially the same result with its referendum law; and Florida lawmakers would have written "last resort" school closing legislation into the law books but for Governor Collins' veto of the measure.[59] North Carolina provided tuition grants for students attending private segregated schools;[60] Florida authorized its governor to assume extraordinary powers to deal with desegregation crises; [61] Arkansas and Florida created committees to investigate the NAACP and protect state sovereignty;[62] Tennessee approved laws hampering NAACP activites;[63] and all five states enacted pupil assignment legislation or revised previous placement measures.[64]

[58] Statement by Clement, reprinted in New York *Times*, January 24, 1956.

[59] *Race Relations Law Reporter*, I (October, 1956), 928–29, 934–37. See the "Report of the North Carolina Advisory Committee on Education," in *ibid*. (June, 1956), 581–86. Collins' veto message is reprinted in *ibid*., II (August, 1957), 843–44. See also St. Petersburg *Times*, June 7–8, 1957.

[60] *Race Relations Law Reporter*, I (October, 1956), 928–34, 938.

[61] *Ibid.*, 954–56. See also the "Report of the Special Advisory Committee," *ibid.*, 921–23.

[62] *Ibid.*, II (April, 1957), 491–94; Chapter 31498, Florida Legislative Acts, 1956 Special Sess., in *Facts on Film*, Reel 3.

[63] *Race Relations Law Reporter*, II (April, 1957), 497–501.

[64] *Ibid.*, I (June, 1956), 579–81 (Arkansas); (October, 1956) 924–27 (Florida); (October, 1956), 939–40 (North Carolina); II (February, 1957), 215–19 (Tennessee); (June, 1957), 693–95 (Texas).

But despite frenzied legislative activity, none of these states stepped over the threshold into massive resistance. Significantly, only two governors, Hodges and Faubus, endorsed interposition, and both labeled the doctrine a protest, not a statement of policy.[65] State legislatures in Arkansas and Texas did not act upon interposition;[66] and lawmakers in North Carolina and Tennessee approved manifestoes of protest rather than interposition resolutions. Only Florida's legislature seemed genuinely enthusiastic about interposition, passing a resolution despite Governor Collins' opposition and showing an obvious willingness to support extreme white supremacy legislation of a Deep South type. This deviation from the peripheral South norm was the result of malapportionment, however; even Florida's interposition resolution was opposed by senators representing a majority of the state population. Only the weighted votes of rural legislators accounted for its passage.[67]

In terms of immediate progress toward desegregation in the South, there was precious little to choose between the complex machinations of upper South states and the bellicose interposition of Virginia and the Deep South. But in terms of the future of the *Brown* decision, the difference was considerable. States of the upper South, with the exception of Virginia, accepted the validity of the Supreme Court decree and aimed to evade its consequences; Deep South states refused to accede any legitimacy to the decision. Until the American public and its national leadership chose actively to support the federal courts, this southern division was important; prior to the presidency of John F. Kennedy, it helped to keep alive the principle of *Brown v. Board of Education* in the South.

The deep fissures that rent southern homogeneity did not at first appear necessarily permanent. Political dynamics and encroaching events pressured policy throughout the South toward defense of segregation, and clearly the resistance was on the rise. In February, 1956, Harry Flood Byrd said: "If we can organize the Southern states for massive resistance to this order I think that in time the rest of the country will realize integration is not going to be accepted in the South. In interposition,

[65] Raleigh *News and Observer*, February 3, 1956; *Arkansas Gazette*, March 23, 1956, January 16, 1957.

[66] As previously noted, Texas made interposition a part of the state Democratic Party platform; Arkansas approved initiative petitions enacting an interposition resolution (supported by the Faubus administration) and a nullification amendment to the state constitution (promoted by James Johnson and the Citizens' Council forces and not a statement of administration policy).

[67] Havard and Beth, *The Politics of Mis-Representation*, 81.

"Wait a Minute, I Got Another Idea." Jim Dobbins in the Boston *Traveler*.

the South has a perfectly legal means of appeal from the Supreme Court order."[68] There were times when it appeared that the senator's hopes might become reality.

During the same month, February, 1956, a riotous mob terminated desegregation at the University of Alabama. Autherine Lucy, a young Negro woman admitted to the university by court order, was attending her third day of classes when state police, rather than controlling the mob which had sporadically dominated the campus almost from the beginning of Miss Lucy's attendance, instead removed the victim. Thus the University of Alabama remained a segregated institution. After Miss Lucy accused university officials of conspiring with the rioters, her expulsion became permanent.[69] The lesson was clear. Federal court orders could be forcibly nullified—provided that sufficient elements of the white power structure countenanced or encouraged it.

The first dramatic test of interposition came six months later. In the fall of 1956 Governor Allan Shivers intervened decisively in two Texas communities facing federal court desegregation orders. In both instances judicial authority gave way in the face of state power and community hostility. Texarkana Junior College and Mansfield High School had been ordered by federal district courts to accept Negro applicants, but in both communities there was widespread white opposition encouraged by local leaders and school authorities. When mobs formed before both schools to prevent Negro attendance, Shivers sent Texas Rangers first to Texarkana, on the Arkansas-Texas border, and then to Mansfield, a village just southeast of Fort Worth. The Ranger missions were to prevent violence, maintain order, and protect segregation in the schools. In Texarkana, Rangers allowed the crowd to turn back two Negro students; later, Attorney General Shepperd's office uncovered technicalities sufficient to disqualify the students as plaintiffs.[70] In Mansfield, where anti-Negro hysteria was particularly virulent, Negro students did not appear to face the mob. District school authorities then transferred the black pupils

---

[68] As quoted in Memphis *Commercial Appeal*, February 26, 1956.

[69] *Lucy v. Adams*, in *Race Relations Law Reporter*, I (February, 1956), 85–89, II (April, 1957), 350–58; *Southern School News*, March, 1956.

[70] On the grounds that the lawyer representing the two teenage Negro students was unknown to the students themselves and had taken legal steps beyond those authorized by the plaintiffs. The students' parents had requested assistance from the NAACP, and the organization had taken charge, conducting legal strategy apparently without close consultation with its clients. See Peltason, *Fifty-Eight Lonely Men*, 143.

back to the segregated schools. Texarkana Junior College and Mansfield High School remained segregated.[71]

During the Mansfield episode, Shivers issued a public statement proclaiming the doctrine that local hostility to desegregation took precedence over federal court orders and justified state intervention in defense of segregation. The governor instructed the Texas Rangers "to arrest anyone, white or colored, whose actions are such as to represent a threat to the peace at Mansfield" and urged Mansfield school authorities to "go ahead and transfer out of the district any scholastics, white or colored, whose attendance or attempts to attend Mansfield High School would reasonably be calculated to incite violence." Shivers went on to state:

It is not my intention to permit the use of state officers to shoot down or intimidate Texas citizens who are making orderly protest against a situation instigated and agitated by the National Association for the Advancement of Colored People. At the same time we will protect persons of all races who are not themselves contributing to the breach of peace. If this course is not satisfactory under the circumstances to the federal government, I respectfully suggest further that the Supreme Court, which is responsible for the order, be given the task of enforcing it.[72]

The executive branch of the federal government showed no apparent concern about the potential consequences of Shivers' position and actions. At a press conference approximately a week later, President Eisenhower explained that maintenance of order was primarily a state responsibility. Although expressing ignorance of the details of the Mansfield confrontation, the President stated: "Now, in the Texas case there was—the attorney for the students did report this violence and asked help, which apparently was the result of unreadiness to obey a federal court order. But before anyone could move, the Texas authorities had moved in and order was restored, so the question became unimportant."[73] Upon federal district courts, Eisenhower continued, rested the task of insuring desegregation progress, a view that seemed not to conflict with Shivers' suggestion that the Supreme Court should be responsible for enforcing desegregation orders—if it could and if it dared.

[71] Benjamin Muse, *Ten Years of Prelude: The Story of Integration Since the Supreme Court's 1954 Decision* (New York, 1964), 87–92; John Howard Griffin and Theodore Freedman, *Mansfield, Texas: A Report on the Crisis Situation Resulting from Efforts to Desegregate the School System* (New York, 1957); Peltason, *Fifty-Eight Lonely Men*, 135–46; *Southern School News*, September, October, 1956.

[72] *Race Relations Law Reporter*, I (October, 1956), 885.

[73] As quoted in New York *Times*, September 6, 1956.

Not all racial controversy resulted in victory for the resistance, of course, but the thrust of events pushed in that direction. The year-long Montgomery bus boycott, as well as the shorter but also turbulent Tallahassee boycott, ended in late 1956 with desegregated buses and a legacy of hostility and white solidarity. Clinton, a Cumberland community not far from Knoxville, desegregated under court order in August, 1956, and Frederick John Kasper, a talented and fanatical rabble-rouser, made a reputation by sparking a wave of anti-integration rioting and violence that required state police and the National Guard to subdue.[74] Segregationists had long argued that southern whites would not accept integration. Clinton almost seemed to confirm their prediction, examples of peaceful desegregation in western Texas and eastern Arkansas notwithstanding.

The illusion of southern white solidarity was immeasurably strengthened by events on the national political level, particularly the Southern Manifesto. The Manifesto did not contain the specific endorsement of interposition that its sponsors had sought, but the declaration did commend state resistance and condemn the Supreme Court decision. Southern congressional extremists individually insured that the *Congressional Record* would be sufficiently burdened with praise for interposition.[75] Even normally restrained legislators such as Representative Carl Vinson of Georgia offered "whole-hearted support" to state efforts to nullify the *Brown* decision.[76]

In July, 1956, a second congressional manifesto, "Warning of Grave Dangers," proclaimed against the civil rights bill being debated in Congress. The "Warning" was a House document drafted by Representatives William M. Tuck of Virginia, William M. Colmer of Mississippi, and Edwin E. Willis of Louisiana and signed by eighty-three southern members. It found "grave" dangers to liberty inherent in national legislative protection of civil rights.[77] White supremacy was apparently too sacred to be defended by normal methods of parliamentary procedure; it required declarations of principles and interposition.

---

[74] *Southern School News*, September, October, 1956.

[75] See, for example, *Congressional Record*, 84th Cong., 2nd Sess. (January, 1956), 1291–99.

[76] As quoted in Atlanta *Journal*, February 2, 1956.

[77] *Congressional Record*, 84th Cong., 2nd Sess. (July 13, 1956), 12761. See also *Southern School News*, August, 1956; *The State*, July 13, 1956; *Arkansas Gazette*, July 14, 1956; and Memphis *Commercial Appeal*, July 13, 1956.

By this time neobourbon leaders were broadening their assault through alliances with organizations outside the South. Since formation of the Federation for Constitutional Government, John U. Barr and his associates had sought a national coalition of "patriotic" groups, and during early 1956 the foundation for such organization was laid. Representatives of the federation and For America, a northern ultraconservative group with an estimated 30,000 members, reached agreement on political strategy and basic principles. Eleven federation members joined For America's policy board, and For America announced support of interposition as a proper and constitutionally valid method of asserting state rights.[78]

By the end of 1956 the doctrine had exploded through the South and had even gained support (distinctly minority support, of course) in the North. The Richmond *News Leader* had editorialized just after passage of the Virginia interposition resolution:

> The Southern States now joining in this effort to assert their constitutional powers are voyaging on an unmarked channel. The advocates of massive centralization, the doctrinaire Socialists who have seized positions of great influence, have done everything in their power to bloc [*sic*] the way. But it is a venture worth taking, wherever it leads us. Hopefully, prayerfully, it may bring us back to the principles of sound constitutional government and dual sovereignty, established by our fathers and abandoned in our own time.[79]

In quest of these goals, leaders in a number of southern states set about to prevent enforcement of the *Brown* decision.

And in Little Rock, Arkansas, school officials continued preparations for desegregation.

---

[78] Memphis *Commercial Appeal*, April 29, 30, 1956; "North–South Political Alliance," *Congressional Quarterly Almanac*, 84th Cong., 2nd Sess., XII (1956), 587–88; *Congressional Record*, 84th Cong., 2nd Sess. (March 28, 1956), A2717.

[79] Richmond *News Leader*, February 2, 1956.

CHAPTER 9

THIRD PARTY POLITICS IN 1956
AND THE SEARCH FOR POLITICAL UNITY

In a real sense, the South found itself politically alienated from the rest of the nation. A *Congressional Quarterly* study of roll call votes in the 1957 congressional session demonstrated that there was a "southern" position distinct from Republicans and northern Democrats.[1] On approximately 1 of every 3 recorded votes, a majority of southern Democrats parted company with the northern Democratic majority, in an intraparty sectional cleavage that transcended civil rights to encompass foreign aid, governmental domestic spending, and enlargement of federal governmental activities. On the most important substantive issues of the period, the Democratic Party was, quite literally, a house divided. Southern Democrats disagreed more frequently—approximately 50 percent of the time—with Republican majorities, but these divisions included procedural matters and lesser party issues in addition to more basic differences over foreign aid and, most fundamental of all, civil rights. On such subjects as domestic welfare spending and states' rights, however, the southerners found broad areas of agreement with the congressional Republicans.[2]

Certainly there was no "Solid South." On issues that split the Democratic Party, a minority of southerners dissented from the Dixie position more

---

[1] "How Big Is the North-South Democratic Split?," *Congressional Quarterly Almanac*, 85th Cong., 1st Sess., XIII (1957), 813–17. In this study, the *Congressional Quarterly* defined the South as thirteen states, the former Confederacy plus Kentucky and Oklahoma; the North as the remaining thirty-five states; and Republicans as all members of that party including those from southern states.

[2] Burns, *The Deadlock of Democracy*, 234–322, effectively analyzes the nature of the coalition between congressional parties across party lines. Southern political sectionalism is placed in historical perspective by Dewey W. Grantham, Jr., in his essay "The South and the Politics of Sectionalism," in Grantham (ed.), *The South and the Sectional Image: The Sectional Theme Since Reconstruction* (New York, 1967), 36–55.

often than they agreed with it.[3] Legislators in the populist tradition, such as Senators Estes Kefauver, John Sparkman, and Ralph Yarborough and Representatives Carl Elliot of Alabama and Wright Patman of Texas, independent-thinking Democrats like Senator Albert Gore and Representative Brooks Hays, and a number of other members of progressive orientation were most often found in opposition to the regional majority. Furthermore, there were numerous crosscurrents that cut across sectional voting patterns. The hard core of southern Democrats, those legislators who voted with the southern majority 80 percent or more of the time on those roll calls that sundered Democratic unity, was less than half of the total number of Democrats from former Confederate states.[4]

Yet, despite significant internal diversity and important areas of agreement with both Republicans and northern Democrats, the South during the 1950's was the nation's most politically unique region, and sectional cleavage was particularly acute within the national Democratic Party. With perverse consistency, Dixie politicians won Democratic primary elections by promising to defeat the principal measures of their own national party platform, and southern congressional Democrats established a voting pattern substantially more nativist, isolationist, and conservative than that of their nonsouthern party peers. They had written a southern platform and dramatized its most emotional element with the Southern Manifesto.

Every four years, the American political process brought southern separateness into sharp focus and intraparty dissension to the boiling point. Presidential nominating conventions freed the Democratic Party from congressional impediments—malapportionment, the committee system, seniority, the filibuster—and allowed Democratic presidential candidates, the spokesmen for religious, ethnic, and racial minorities, labor unions, liberals, patrician reformers, and the city in general, to come into their own. In 1928 Alfred E. Smith won a majority of the votes in the nation's twelve largest cities and thus freed the national Democratic Party

[3] Twenty Democrats from former Confederate states voted more frequently with the northern wing of the party. "How Big Is the North-South Democratic Split?" 815.

[4] *Ibid.* Southern politics were more regionally distinctive than were southerners generally. Various factors accounted for this phenomenon. Among them were the influence of single-member legislative districts (which magnified the influence of small majorities), malapportionment, a lower level of political participation (particularly among blue collar workers) than in other sections, and the all-pervasive influence of racism. On this point, see V. O. Key, *Public Opinion and American Democracy* (New York, 1961), 99–105.

from its southern base. History, urbanization, and both Franklin D. Roosevelt and Harry S. Truman institutionalized these changed political realities and intensified southern isolation within the party. In a surprisingly short period, the South, the homeland of Democratic loyalty, the proud possessor of a veto over party nominations, found itself the backwater of Democratic presidential politics. Though by no means impotent, it was yet powerless to command the party choice of candidates and platform.[5]

Southern traditionalists were not, of course, reconciled to the new order of things. Neobourbon spokesmen insisted that: "America today has three terrific forces operating, the Republican Party, the Democratic Party, and the NAACP, ADA and Labor Bosses, a coalition of which are exerting a terrific amount of pressure on both national parties."[6] What was needed in presidential politics was "a fourth force" to counter leftist pressure groups. On this point, southern neobourbons were in general agreement.

The question that shattered unanimity and opened a Pandora's box of alternatives was how to implement such a policy of political counterpressure. Should the "South" remain loyal to the Democratic Party and, entrenched behind committee chairmanships, attempt to oppose liberal influence with congressional seniority? Or should southern traditionalists seek haven in the Republican Party, as many had done in 1952? Or should they follow the lead of irreconcilables in their own ranks and break free of both national parties by either capturing state Democratic organizations and assigning the party emblems to electors pledged to safe southern candidates (as they had done in 1948) or by creating a new party, separate from—if perhaps not quite equal to—the established parties? Each of these alternatives found persuasive advocates.

Once again, a history of frustrated regional political development pulled against rational solutions. Neobourbon ideology led inevitably to a break with the national Democrats; yet neobourbons benefited most from attachment to the party of Hubert H. Humphrey, W. Averell Harriman, and Estes Kefauver. Only the election of northern Democratic congressmen, made possible in part by the appeal of liberal-urban presidential candidates, gave the Democrats control of Congress and the southern bourbons their chairmanships. While there was "political absurdity in the affiliation

[5] Burns, *The Deadlock of Democracy*, and Lubell, *The Future of American Politics*, especially the latter's discussion of the Smith campaign, 29–43, are both perceptive accounts of the dilemma of the Democratic Party.

[6] Interview with Farley Smith, in *The State*, November 10, 1958.

of those candidates with a national party equally determined to defeat the platform pledges of its Southern candidates and yet continuing to honor them with high positions as loyal party members," the arrangement made political rebellion profoundly difficult.[7] No other factor, with the exception of tradition itself, so hampered a political realignment in the South.[8]

Senator Richard B. Russell of Georgia epitomized the neobourbon dilemma. Entering politics in the 1920's, when the Democratic party was still the party of William Jennings Bryan and Woodrow Wilson in substance as well as spirit, Russell followed the well-worn path of conservatives generally. He supported the New Deal during the early Roosevelt years, when the government focused its attention on the problems of businessmen and landowners and when economic crisis and Roosevelt's popularity made opposition both irresponsible and politically dangerous. He shifted into opposition as reformers, ever multiplying within the New Deal agencies, directed increasing attention to sharecroppers, labor unions, minimum wages, and the like at the very time that returning prosperity seemed, some thought, to lessen the need for governmental action. Such programs not only threatened the South's exploitative and therefore competitive wage scales but dared even to tamper with the region's social system.[9] The rise of the antisegregation crusade—and the inauguration of Harry Truman to lead it—intensified the northern-urban assault on southern rights and rural values and revealed the fundamentally anti-South bias of misguided Yankee reformism, or so it seemed to Senator Russell.

"We submit," he said, "that the white people of the South, though widely misunderstood and oft maligned, have some few rights as American citizens." Surely, he continued, "we are entitled to better treatment at the hands of our fellow Americans than to be kicked as a political football

---

[7] Savage, *Seeds of Time*, 269.

[8] Even the irreconcilables in the South were deeply conscious of congressional seniority. For example, when Mississippi segregationists gathered to organize a third party movement, a segregationist speaker said that southern congressmen, instead of supporting the third party effort, should "vote the straight Democratic ticket even if Thurgood Marshall were running so as not to lose their positions in the Congress." As quoted in *Chattanooga Times*, August 22, 1956. The speaker's point was a persistent theme in the politics of the decade.

[9] James T. Patterson, "A Conservative Coalition Forms in Congress, 1933-1939," *Journal of American History*, LII (March, 1966), 757-72; and William E. Leuchtenburg, *Franklin D. Roosevelt and the New Deal, 1932-1940* (New York, 1963), 252-74, are capable discussions of congressional politics and the New Deal. See also Frank Freidel, *F.D.R. and the South* (Baton Rouge, 1965).

in every election year, and to have our good name constantly bartered by political auctioneers in bidding for votes."[10] The southern states were being treated as "provinces," and southern Democrats in the Senate were "so threatened with legislative riders of all kinds" that they found it difficult "to function as senators."[11]

Russell launched his most intensive effort to restore southern influence and reverse the course of the Democratic Party in 1952 when he actively campaigned for the Democratic presidential nomination. Although carrying his search for national support to the point of endorsing repeal of the Taft-Hartley Act, Russell remained the candidate of a past Democratic Party, the proponent of "the spiritual life and the simple faith and fullness which sustained our forefathers," the opponent of "new adventures that could lead this country down the road to socialism."[12] He attracted only a sectional following and was swamped by the "draft Stevenson" movement.[13] The northern reformers had triumphed once again. Russell took little part in Stevenson's campaign.

Republican occupancy of the White House modified but did not substantially change the Democrat's intraparty feud. Presidential Democrats created the Democratic Advisory Committee to keep alive their versions of proper party policy; Russell established himself as leader of Washington's Dixie Democrats and the heart of the "southern position." "Statistically and intellectually," concluded the *Congressional Quarterly*, "Russell has become the leading spokesman for Southern Democrats in Congress."[14] The weight of northern-southern, liberal-conservative, urban-rural dissension strained against the bonds of party unity as before.

At times Senator Russell hinted that the "South" might find it necessary to abandon the party to northern reformers:

[10] From a national radio address by Russell, March 23, 1948, reprinted in *Congressional Record*, 80th Cong., 2nd Sess., A1864–65.

[11] *Congressional Record*, 80th Cong., 2nd Sess. (May 10, 1948), 5494 and (May 26, 1948), 6459.

[12] From a radio address by Russell, June 27, 1952, reprinted in *ibid.*, 82nd Cong., 2nd Sess., A4131–32. The full sentence from which the latter quotation is taken reads: "I do not think this dangerous period is the time to strike out on new adventures that could lead this country down the road to socialism." The speech, carried on a nationwide radio network, was a campaign address delivered in Denver, Colorado. The Taft-Hartley Act was, of course, the bill passed over Truman's veto that, among other things, permitted a state to enact open shop legislation.

[13] On the convention and Russell's candidacy, see David, Moos, and Goldman (eds.), *The National Story*, 38–39, 62, 108, 151–54.

[14] "How Big is the North-South Democratic Split?," 814.

I'm very frank to say that I'm apprehensive about the growing strength and domination in the party of the extreme left wing group—Reuther, Clark, Humphrey, Douglas and Williams—whose stock in trade is abuse of the South. They have said the Democratic Party would be better off without us.

If that group ever dominates the party, we might be driven out of the political house of our fathers. But we would carry with us the ark of the covenant—the Constitution.[15]

But powerful forces pulled against this alternative. Studies have demonstrated the tenacity of party identification.[16] For men like Senator Russell, himself a lifelong Democrat, the son of a Georgia supreme court justice who was also a lifelong Democrat, the Democratic Party was a career as well as a symbol; it was " the political house of our fathers," a thing not to be discarded lightly or perhaps at all. Compounding this emotional attraction was, of course, political expediency, the attachment of a senator to a constituency which had voted for none but Democrats since Reconstruction. And there was yet a further institutional aspect—Russell was, above all else, a senator, a member of an often ineffective chamber which, though buffeted by Truman's civil rights program and soiled by McCarthyism, nevertheless maintained its customs, its continuity, its position as the most powerful independent legislative body in the world. Within this body, Russell was more than just a leader of bourbon southerners; he was a power within the congressional Democratic Party, a spokesman for all those senators who found, or whose constituents found, the values of the past more attractive than those proposed for the future, a part of the inner circle which helped to manipulate the complex and shifting system of alliances and compromises that expressed the will of the United States Congress. "This institutional interest of legislators can express itself in complex ways," wrote one perceptive observer, "especially in the Senate where its adherents have almost transformed it into a mystique."[17] And for Russell, a part of that mystique was the Democratic Party, the reservoir in which he had deposited years of seniority and from which he drew the chairmanship of the Senate Armed Forces Committee and much of his personal influence. There were bonds not easily loosened.

[15] Interview with Russell by Harold Davis, in Atlanta *Journal*, July 28, 1957. Russell was referring to Walter Reuther, president of the United Automobile Workers; Senator Joseph S. Clark of Pennsylvania; Senator Hubert H. Humphrey of Minnesota; Senator Paul H. Douglas of Illinois; and Governor G. Mennen Williams of Michigan.

[16] Donald B. Matthews and James W. Prothro, "Southern Images of Political Parties: An Analysis of White and Negro Attitudes," *Journal of Politics*, XXVI (February, 1964), 82–111.

[17] Murphy, *Congress and the Court*, 258.

"I have never scratched the Democratic ticket," said Russell, "and I hope I will never have to."[18]

In varying degrees, other members of the southern political power structure found their own vested interests bound up with at least nominal party loyalty. Officeholders on the national level, state leaders who aspired to such offices or who benefited from personal alliances with such office-holders, state party leaders who feared further undermining of one party arrangements in state elections—all were imprisoned by the system. Thus those same neobourbon political leaders who had instigated the Southern Manifesto, who had leaped to the front ranks of massive resistance, who had felt threatened and ideologically isolated from national politics, found themselves an impediment to the "fourth force" many so badly wanted. Such were the ironies of history and southern politics.

In 1956 the neobourbon dilemma was further complicated by national political equations. Of all years, 1956 seemed about the least propitious for political adventure. Theoretically, third party action aimed to dead-lock the electoral college, placing the selection of a president in the hands of Congress. Since neobourbons could not hope to do much better than they had done in 1948, their stated strategy was logically applicable only when a close national election—preferably with the Democratic candidate a slight favorite—was expected. Then, by denying the Democratic candi-date part of his normal southern electoral vote, neobourbons could realistically savor the possibility of preventing an electoral college major-ity. In 1956 none of these factors existed. Eisenhower was the favored candidate, and a southern revolt could only contribute to his prospects. Well aware of this situation, pragmatic professionals in the national Democratic Party recognized that without the southern electoral vote as a foundation the Democratic cause had little hope. Reciprocally, more sophisticated southern politicians, already mindful of the futility of the 1948 Dixiecrat experiment, "were under no illusions about the price that they would pay if the Democratic candidate were beaten through a third party split."[19] And even if substantial elements of the neobourbon elite had opted for political secession, a successful southern bolt from the Democratic Party would by no means have been assured. Many other southern Democratic leaders, those of different political persuasions, favored party loyalty.

[18] Interview with Russell by Harold Davis, in Atlanta *Journal*, July 28, 1957.
[19] Anderson, *Eisenhower, Brownell, and the Congress*, 112.

Against this background, with many of their leaders and particularly the more astute ones anchored to the political status quo while other influential politicians pressured for party harmony, southern neobourbons endeavored to extend massive resistance to national politics. *Brown v. Board of Education* and the South's response, while creating an apparently auspicious climate for a political revolt, served as a pretext for third party activity rather than as a cause. The demands for a revival of Dixiecratism that followed hard upon the Court ruling came from those same sources that had in previous years sought escape from "Eastern machine politicos and labor czars."[20] Again, as in 1948, agitation centered in South Carolina and Mississippi.

The first crucial test of Dixiecrat strength came in South Carolina, where James F. Byrnes, Senator Thurmond, Governor Timmerman, and lesser leaders had been hinting at a *coup d'etat*.[21] When the state Democratic Party convention met in March, 1956, the first such convention in the South, Timmerman delivered a fighting speech calling for a recess convention and a mobilization of southern strength to "take the offensive" in national politics.[22] The convention was divided. Senator Olin Johnston, State Senator Edgar A. Brown, keynote speaker Jeff B. Bates—the loyalist wing of the state party generally—opposed moves that seemed designed to force an open break with the national party and secured approval of a resolution which, while bitingly critical of the presidential Democrats, did endorse party loyalty. Nevertheless, the Dixiecrats set the tone of the convention. South Carolina Democrats voted to reconvene following the national Democratic convention to decide what course the state party would pursue, and they named Timmerman chairman of a steering committee to promote a united southern front.[23] Governor Timmerman was soon writing to southern senators, representatives, governors, and national committeemen seeking a solid-South movement within the Democratic Party.

Party infighting spread to other southern state parties, but, outside South Carolina, the Dixiecrat revival quickly lost momentum. Defeat of the Shivercrats in Texas in May, 1956, deflated the whole movement,

---

[20] Tom Ethridge, in Jackson *Daily News*, December 18, 1955.
[21] Charleston *News and Courier*, August 27, 1955; Charlotte *Observer*, March 4, 1956; Washington *Evening Star*, March 12, 1956.
[22] As quoted by S. L. Latimer, Jr., in Atlanta *Journal and Constitution*, March 25, 1956.
[23] *Southern School News*, April, 1956; *The State*, March 22, 1956; Charleston *News and Courier*, March 22, 1956.

and most other southern states largely ignored the issue at their state conventions. Alabama, which chose delegates by direct election rather than by convention, was an exception. There, former Representative Laurie C. Battle, who called for an all-southern preliminary convention and harshly criticized the national party, received Citizens' Council support and finished first in delegate-at-large balloting, running ahead of Senator Sparkman, Stevenson's 1952 running mate and loyalist leader. The Alabama delegation ignored tradition, however, and chose Sparkman as chairman.[24] Even in Mississippi the Dixiecrat revival failed. In May, 1956, the state Association of Citizens' Councils drew the lines of intra-party battle, sending to county Democratic organizations a resolution demanding that the Mississippi delegation be instructed to accept nothing short of a national party presidential candidate who endorsed the principles of interposition. The resolution called for a recess convention and the selection of Mississippi electors who "unequivocally" and "positively" supported interposition and "who, in turn, will cast their votes in the Electoral College only for candidates for President and Vice President who have positively taken a stand which is in concurrence" with the doctrine.[25] Governor Coleman and William J. Tubb, chairman of the state Democratic executive committee, took charge of the Mississippi loyalist forces. Tubb attacked the Citizens' Councils for meddling in "the realm of partisan politics."[26] And Coleman insisted upon an unpledged delegation. Supported by the state administration and by Senator John Stennis, party regulars routed the Councils, and the state convention chose the "un-fettered and un-bound" delegation that loyalists demanded.[27]

In the meantime, Governor Timmerman pushed ahead with his letter writing campaign to create a southern front at the national convention. The governor's penmanship provoked a decidedly restrained response from major southern politicians and served mainly to enliven loyalist countermeasures. The two interstate meetings of southern Democratic Party officials that resulted from Timmerman's appeals, rather than laying a foundation for a southern confrontation with the national Democrats, instead confirmed the collapse of the Dixiecrat revival. The first conference, held in Atlanta in July, attracted state party chairmen from seven states.

---

[24] *Southern School News*, June-August, 1956; Montgomery *Advertiser*, July 25, 1956.
[25] Association of Citizens' Councils of Mississippi, *Resolution* (n.p., 1956).
[26] As quoted in Jackson *Daily News*, May 30, 1956.
[27] *Ibid.*, July 16, 1956, quoting Senator Stennis. See also Carter, *The South Strikes Back*, 68–69, and *Southern School News*, June-August, 1956.

Participants at this meeting released a statement supporting party loyalty and opposing "any bolts, walkouts or third parties."[28] The party chairmen did encourage southern cooperation at the Democratic convention, however, and suggested a larger meeting of state leaders to discuss anti-civil rights tactics.[29]

All eleven southern states dispatched representatives, including several governors and senators, to the second conference, held in Atlanta during early August of 1956. Again, advocates of conciliation dominated the discussions. Governor Coleman advanced the basic doctrine that was to guide southern convention strategy. In keeping with his "friendly persuasion" policy in Mississippi, Coleman insisted that southern spokesmen, negotiating from a position of dignity and restraint, should concentrate upon finding an acceptable compromise on the basic civil rights-school desegregation question within the privacy of convention committees and avoid inflammatory statements and public quarrels that would force delegates, northern and southern alike, into rigid and inflexible positions. Correctly predicting that political reality would encourage a conciliatory attitude among northern party leaders, Coleman argued that the South could win concessions outside the glare of television cameras and, if northern liberals chose to initiate a floor fight over civil rights, then they would be responsible for the results. Senator Sparkman, a persuasive proponent of party loyalty and a key figure at the conference, was named chairman of a liaison committee designed to coordinate southern tactical maneuvers and to improve communications between northern and southern Democrats at the convention.[30] The Atlanta conference achieved a substantial measure of southern cooperation, but it was of an entirely different type from the cooperation that Governor Timmerman had had in mind. As a Charleston *News and Courier* journalist later summarized the results of the governor's endeavors: "It was one of Timmerman's keenest disappointments in public life that he could awaken no genuine or sincere cooperation among Southern Democrats in presenting a solid front in national political affairs."[31]

---

[28] Reprinted in Chattanooga *Times*, July 15, 1956.

[29] *Southern School News*, August, 1956.

[30] This account is based upon Patrick Earl McCauley, "Political Implications in Alabama of the School Segregation Decisions" (M.A. thesis, Vanderbilt University, 1957), 55ff. McCauley, a Southern Education Reporting Service staff member, interviewed a number of the participants shortly after the conference.

[31] W. D. Workman, Jr., in Charleston *News and Courier*, July 26, 1959.

Although held in the year of interposition and the maturing of massive resistance, the national Democratic convention was, paradoxically, the most harmonious in more than a decade. "Friendly persuasion" predominated in southern councils, while national party leaders guarded against any disruption of Democratic unity. The call inviting state delegations to the convention included a mild loyalty pledge and a provision requiring state parties sending delegations to agree that the convention candidates would be placed on the ticket under "the Democratic Party label and designation."[32] While southern dissidents did not seem to take these provisions seriously, the call did prevent a recurrence of the bitter loyalty oath controversy that had sundered the 1952 convention. In addition, Governor Clement of Tennessee served as temporary convention chairman and keynoter; Sam Rayburn of Texas was permanent chairman.[33] A majority of the northern members on the platform committee were anxious to reach an accommodation on the vital civil rights issue, and this plank was a study in compromise. It recognized that "Recent decisions of the Supreme Court of the United States relating to segregation in publicly supported schools and elsewhere have brought consequences of vast importance to our Nation . . . " and, buried in another paragraph, that Supreme Court decisions "are part of the law of the land." The plank also met basic southern demands by omitting direct endorsement of the *Brown* decision and specifically rejecting "all proposals for the use of force to interfere with the orderly determination of these matters by the courts."[34] Northern liberals were able to collect only fourteen signatures on a civil rights minority report—from the 108-member platform committee—and their efforts to force a floor fight on the issue collapsed at the rap of Rayburn's gavel.[35]

[32] Ruth Aull and Daniel M. Ogden, Jr. (eds.), *Official Report of the Proceedings of the Democratic National Convention* (Richmond, 1956), 4.

[33] Estes Kefauver was chosen as nominee for Vice President, but southern conservatives hardly considered this as a concession by the liberals.

[34] Aull and Ogden (eds.), *Official Report of the Proceedings of the Democratic National Convention*, 322. See also Hays, *A Southern Moderate Speaks*, 105–11. Hays was one of the five southern members on the civil rights plank subcommittee.

[35] Aull and Ogden (eds.), *Official Report of the Proceedings of the Democratic National Convention*, 323–32. There were, to be sure, tense moments during the convention. Specifically, there was the threat that Averell Harriman and the sectionalist-liberals might provoke an open civil rights struggle as a part of their campaign for the presidential nomination, and there was an injudicious remark made by Stevenson, who was the moderate candidate favored by many southern delegates, stating a preference for a stronger civil rights plank, a comment that angered his southern supporters and momentarily gave southern dissidents an issue.

Southern intransigents had to content themselves with a last-ditch and relatively harmless strategy. By nominating favorite son candidates, massive resistance spokesmen like Marvin Griffin could at least take advantage of the national television and radio coverage to explain why "the unbridled license of the Supreme Court must be curbed."[36]

Only South Carolina Democrats, having previously recessed their state convention, held a postmortem on the national assembly. Although major state leaders—Timmerman, Thurmond, Gressette, and others—continued to direct sharp criticism at the national party, its candidates, and its platform,[37] South Carolina now found itself effectively isolated and had little choice but to endorse the Stevenson-Kefauver ticket. When the state party reconvened later in August, even Timmerman was ready to strike the colors and endorsed party loyalty in a speech before the convention. Nevertheless, the delegates were closely divided, and in a tumultuous session the state party pledged its electors to Stevenson and Kefauver rather than to an independent ticket by a narrow $167-152\frac{1}{2}$ margin.[38] The Democratic Party remained, at least temporarily, in the hands of Democrats.

Despite these defeats, proponents of uncompromising resistance in Mississippi and South Carolina were by no means willing to capitulate. Instead they prepared to battle on yet another front. By the time of the second South Carolina convention, the foundations for independent political activity outside the two major parties were already being established. Virtually all of the higher echelon neobourbon leaders lapsed into inactivity, or supported—often grudgingly—the Democratic candidates, or, in several notable cases, turned again to presidential Republicanism. Lower-level activists, however, pushed forward a program to revive the fire of political rebellion throughout the South and the nation.

The independent movement originated with the formation of the Mississippians for States Rights in May, 1956. Among its creators were Circuit Judge M. M. McGowan, a longtime spokesman for ultraconservative causes; W. B. Fontaine, administrative assistant to former governor

---

[36] *Ibid.*, 359. At least on the part of Georgia, this was a preconceived strategy originated apparently by Roy Harris. See Atlanta *Constitution*, May 25, 1956. Georgia, South Carolina, and Virginia nominated favorite son candidates, and Texas placed Lyndon B. Johnson's name in the race.

[37] *The State*, August 21, 1956; Atlanta *Journal and Constitution*, August 26, 1956; *Southern School News*, September, 1956.

[38] John N. Popham, in Chattanooga *Times*, August 28, 1956; Quint, *Profile in Black and White*, 134-36.

and Dixiecrat vice-presidential nominee Fielding Wright (who had died on May 4, just days before the founding meeting); and a number of state legislators and other prominent public figures, most of whom were associated with the Citizens' Councils.[39] Mississippians for States Rights at first followed a dual course. The organization made preparations to field its own slate of electors; at the same time, by working within the Democratic Party and then by threatening to revolt from it, they attempted to win nomination of independent electors on the Democratic Party label. Defeated at the state convention, states' righters pushed ahead with their own program and formally chose uncommitted electors at a public rally in Jackson.[40]

South Carolina dissidents followed a similar pattern. During June, Micah Jenkins, state director of the Federation for Constitutional Government and chairman of the state Association of Citizens' Councils, circulated petitions to place unpledged electors on the state ballot for "protecting the rights and wishes of South Carolinians in event the National Democratic Convention adopts a program distasteful to South Carolina and the South."[41] Citizens' Council leaders and a number of state legislators were early associated with the drive, but not until their defeat at the state Democratic convention did they create a formal organization. At a public rally in Columbia, irreconcilables formed the South Carolinians for Independent Electors, with Farley Smith as chairman.[42] A slate of unpledged electors qualified soon afterward.

Recruits from other states promptly enlisted in the movement. In Tennessee, the State Federation for Constitutional Government, later joined by emissaries from the Society to Maintain Segregation and the States' Rights Council of Tennessee, created a third party movement. The Tennessee organization called itself "Democrats for State Rights" in Democratic middle and western Tennessee and "States Rights in Tennessee" in the Republican eastern hill country.[43] Constitution parties emerged in Texas, Georgia, and Arkansas; Louisiana and Virginia spawned States' Rights parties; and in Alabama an independent electors movement developed. In virtually all of these states spokesmen associated with the

[39] Jackson *Daily News*, May 1–31, 1956; *Delta Democrat-Times*, May 1–31, 1956.
[40] Jackson *Daily News*, August 11, 12, 19, 20, 1956; Chattanooga *Times*, August 22, 1956.
[41] Charleston *News and Courier*, June 5, 1956, quoting Jenkins.
[42] *Ibid.*, August 28, 1956. Smith was an early Citizens' Council organizer and later became executive secretary of the state association.
[43] Chattanooga *Times*, September 28, 1956.

Citizens' Council movement were conspicuous in top leadership positions.[44]

During the same period states' rights activists aggresively promoted grandiose plans for a broader and more coordinated movement. Preparations for an independent campaign had been under way since formation of the Federation for Constitutional Government in December, 1955. In August, 1956, representatives from seven states met in Jackson to make arrangements for a "general conference of states."[45] The aim was to activate the great design of combining the many independent "patriotic" groups behind a general declaration of principles and an independent political movement.

Delegates from twenty-five states attended the National States' Rights Conference held in Memphis in mid-September. The participants represented a hodgepodge of splinter and radical-right organizations and parties ranging from the White Circle League of America to the Pro-Southerners of Memphis. Robert G. Chandler, a Louisiana Citizens' Council leader and longtime states' rights activist, was chosen temporary chairman; Earl Evans, Jr., president pro tempore of the Mississippi senate and the possessor of equally impressive states' rights credentials, was made permanent chairman; and Clarence E. Manion, co-chairman of the For America group, delivered the keynote address, calling for a third party on the "political and moral right."[46] John U. Barr, chairman of the regional Federation, and Sims Crownover, a Tennessee state Federation spokesman, were leading organizers of the conference. Second echelon members of the Federation for Constitutional Government, the For America spokesmen, state white supremacy organization leaders, and politically influential individuals such as Evans generally dominated the meeting.[47]

On only one point was there open discord. Various northern delegates demanded creation of a formal third party; southern participants successfully insisted upon "a federation of independent State parties."[48] The conference approved a sixteen-point "Declaration of Principles" and adopted the name "National Conservative Movement." Most of the participating organizations "endorsed" T. Coleman Andrews, former

[44] See *Southern School News*, September-December, 1956.
[45] Jackson *Daily News*, August 23–24, 1956; Montgomery *Advertiser*, August 24, 1956.
[46] As quoted in Memphis *Commercial Appeal*, September 16, 1956.
[47] *Ibid.*, September 15, 16, 1956; John N. Popham, in Chattanooga *Times*, September 15, 16, 1956; Birmingham *News*, September 16, 1956; and Washington *Evening Star*, September 16, 1956.
[48] Memphis *Commercial Appeal*, September 16, 1956.

director of Internal Revenue and later charter member of the John Birch
Society, for President and Thomas H. Werdel, former Republican
congressman from California, for Vice President.[49]

The Andrews-Werdel campaign won support from numerous rightist
malcontents. Representative were Vivien Kellums, organizer of the
anti-income tax Liberty Belles; Lieutenant General George E. Strate-
meyer, USAF-ret., onetime chairman of a pressure group to fight the
censure of Senator Joe McCarthy; and Dan Smoot, moderator of Facts
Forum.[50] The For America organization; those members of the Federation
for Constitutional Government that Barr could carry with him; and
various state groups provided the chief organized support for the ticket.

In October, Andrews-Werdel backers held a convention of sorts in
Richmond and formally nominated the two candidates to run on an
"Independent States' Rights" ticket with an eight-point platform. The
platform firmly supported states' rights, the Bricker Amendment, and
"creation of permanent, overwhelming American air superiority, supported by adequate modern surface forces." It opposed the income tax, the
"dangerous trend toward socialism," communism, and the "Atlantic
union and world government."[51] In the background a church choir sang
"Our Flag of Stars," which contained such lines as:

> Let no thoughtless court decree
> What our way of life shall be.
>
> Every star with equal light,
> Not one state a satellite.[52]

Despite considerable enthusiasm among its supporters, the Independent
States' Rights movement failed to develop into a viable political alternative.
Andrews inspired little popular response; he drew embarrassingly small
crowds at public rallies.[53] No political leaders of significance endorsed the
movement, and campaign workers often failed to materialize on the state
level. The Andrews-Werdel ticket appeared on the ballots of only six
states, all but one in the South,[54] and in only three of these, Louisiana,

[49] *Ibid.* The "Declaration of Principles" is reprinted in the Birmingham *News*, September 16, 1956.

[50] Robert E. Baker, in Washington *Post*, October 15, 1956.

[51] Reprinted in Richmond *Times-Dispatch*, October 7, 1956.

[52] As quoted by Charles E. Egan, in Atlanta *Constitution*, October 16, 1956.

[53] Andrews, for example, attracted only three hundred people when he brought his
campaign to Montgomery, Alabama. Montgomery *Advertiser*, November 4, 1956.

[54] The states were Arkansas, Louisiana, Tennessee, Texas, Virginia, and Wisconsin.
In Alabama, Independent electors remained unpledged.

Tennessee, and Virginia, were more than nominal campaigns undertaken.

The Independents gained respectability only in Mississippi and South Carolina, but there states' rights leaders rejected Andrews and eventually endorsed Senator Harry Flood Byrd for President and Representative John Bell Williams for Vice President. In these two states, the irreconcilables, having raised adequate finances and conducted aggressive campaigns, won support from influential newspapers and a few major political leaders, notably James F. Byrnes and John Bell Williams.[55]

The Independents failed to win a plurality in a single state in the 1956 election, but their campaign represented a genuine effort to extend massive resistance into national politics. The concept of a national political party based on state sovereignty, on "a federation of independent State parties," was a logical application of the principle of interposition to politics. The states' rights campaign sought to win northern allies as did the southern propaganda offensive. Like massive resistance, sheer reaction characterized the Independents' campaign. It represented the reaction of men unreconciled to prevailing trends and unwilling to compromise further. Provincialism, nativism, and economic conservatism were basic items of the Independent platform in every state where their candidates appeared on the ballot. A Mississippian for States Rights leader summed up the movement's fundamental ethos: "You can't settle principles by manipulation. You have to stand on them."[56]

Generally, individuals within or closely associated with southern white supremacy organizations provided the nucleus of leadership for the states' rights campaign. The Citizens' Councils, as organizations, remained officially neutral, and the 1956 campaign by no means represented a united effort on the part of Council enthusiasts. Nevertheless, most activists who publicly supported the Independents were identified with the Council movement.[57] The campaign may have attracted some support

[55] On the South Carolina campaign, see Quint, *Profile in Black and White*, 137–44; on the Mississippi campaign, see Jackson *Daily News*, *Delta Democrat-Times*, and Memphis *Commercial Appeal* during August–November, 1956. Byrnes's statewide radio and television speech endorsing the Independent candidates is reprinted in Charleston *News and Courier*, October 27, 1956; a similar statewide address by Williams in Mississippi is summarized in Memphis *Commercial Appeal*, October 23, 1956.

[56] *Delta Democrat-Times*, May 31, 1956, quoting M. M. McGowan.

[57] In most states, white supremacy organization leaders who occupied institutional positions in the movement (such as William Simmons, Robert Patterson, and William Rainach) did not openly back the third party campaign. In South Carolina and Tennessee, however, numerous top leaders of the largest white supremacy groups in both states were openly active in the states' rights campaign. And Citizens' Council leaders generally made no secret of their preference for the Independents.

in Mississippi and South Carolina from local politicians who preferred
to "run only against the Negro, who is in a very safe minority as a voter,
and . . . also against every other government policy about which the
voter may be unhappy,"[58] but, on the whole, officeholding politicians
remained outside the states' rights movement. Together, white supremacy
organizations and the political power structure had provided the thrust
for the interposition crusade and for massive resistance. When activists
attempted to expand this same program into national politics, however,
the alliance broke apart. The power structure refused to participate, and
white supremacy organizations failed to mobilize their strength effectively.

The Independent movement proved abortive, and the result was a
splintered effort on the part of neobourbon southerners. Top echelon
conservatives who did choose to revolt against the national Democratic
Party found presidential Republicanism the most enticing avenue of
rebellion. Allan Shivers and his associates in Texas and former Governors
Robert Kennon and Sam Jones in Louisiana once again, as in 1952, led
the Eisenhower forces in those two states.[59] For the most part, however,
massive resistance stalwarts followed the course of Senator Eastland in
nominally endorsing the Democratic candidates, or of Senators Byrd and
Russell in remaining aloof from the election altogether.[60] The states'
rights movement, failing to establish itself as a viable political force,
largely served to drain hard-core neobourbon activists away from the
more meaningful two party competition.

The Byrd-Williams ticket won 29.4 percent of the vote in South
Carolina and 17.3 percent in Mississippi. In these two states, the only
ones to give states' righters more than 10 percent of the vote, the Independents were squarely in the mainstream of political protest. Their
campaign fared best in counties that were high in relative Negro population, had voted heavily Dixiecrat in 1948, and had shown a major shift
to Republicanism in 1952. In South Carolina, the Republicans in 1952

---

[58] Smith, *Congressman from Mississippi*, 116. Smith was referring here to the 1960
election in Mississippi.

[59] Weeks, *Texas One-Party Politics in 1956*, p. 43; Steamer, "Southern Disaffection with
the National Democratic Party," 161–66.

[60] For Eastland's position, see Birmingham *News*, September 16, 1956; for Byrd's
position, see William S. White, in New York *Times*, October 11, 1956; and for Russell's
position, see Harold Davis, in Atlanta *Journal*, July 28, 1957. Although Byrd stated that
he was not a candidate for the presidency, his name nevertheless headed the Independent
ticket in Mississippi and South Carolina.

won 49.3 percent of the votes; in 1956 they took 25.2 percent. In Mississippi, the 1952 Republican vote of 39.6 percent dropped to 24.5 in 1956. The differences between these figures in each state represented the bulk of the states' rights vote. Often, the shift from Republicanism to the Independents was startling. In the South Carolina low-country counties of Clarendon and Williamsburg, voters favored the 1952 Republicans by landslides of 68.5 and 66.1 percent of the vote, respectively; in 1956 these same counties gave the same Republican candidates 8.4 and 8.8 percent— a massive shift of approximately 70 percent of their ballots to the Byrd-Williams ticket. A similar though less striking shift occurred in the cities. Charleston County's 66.9 percent and Richland County's (Columbia) 64.4 percent for the Republicans shrank to 29.9 and 30.0 percent, respectively, as both cities favored the Independents.[61] A similar situation existed in Mississippi. The Byrd-Williams appeal was strongest in the western half of the state, particularly in the lower Delta and the southwest, and was weakest in the northeastern hills and along the Gulf Coast. The ticket carried pluralities in seven counties, all with above 50 percent Negro population, five of the seven had been in the Dixiecrat top quartile, and six of the seven had been in the Republican top quartile in 1952. Fourteen of the twenty top-quartile Republican counties in 1952 were also in the Byrd-Williams highest quartile.[62] Throughout the state, Republican losses correlated closely with the Independent vote, sagging sharply in the areas of Byrd-Williams strength; the Democratic vote, however, remained relatively consistent in both the 1952 and the 1956 elections.

In both states, the Independents apparently appealed most strongly to upper-income voters. In a study of ward returns in Jackson and Charleston, Professor Donald S. Strong found that upper-income areas in both cities were the most enthusiastic for the Independents. This was particularly true in Charleston, where "the venerable city's silk-stocking wards" favored states' rights politics by a 70 percent majority.[63] On the whole, of course, the Byrd-Williams ticket did best in rural, black-belt counties.

---

[61] Charleston voters cast a majority of their ballots for Byrd and Williams; Columbians, a plurality. Voting statistics are from Scammon (ed.), *America Votes: A Handbook of Contemporary Election Statistics*, I, II.

[62] The chief exceptions were counties containing smaller cities (Greenville, Vicksburg, Columbia, Greenwood) where voters were somewhat more hesitant to abandon the Republicans.

[63] Donald S. Strong, *Urban Republicanism in the South* (University, Ala., 1960), 20.

In no other state did the Independent movement gain general respectability nor offer a realistic alternative to the major party candidates.[64]
Perhaps for this reason, voting patterns in Alabama, Arkansas, Louisiana,
Tennessee, Texas, and Virginia were more erratic than in Mississippi and
South Carolina. The shift from 1952 Republicanism to the Independents
in 1956 was less pronounced. In Louisiana the reverse seems to have been
the case: Democrats of 1952 provided the bulk of the 1956 states' rights
vote. In Virginia, the states' rights ticket apparently drew from both
parties about equally. Furthermore, in none of these states was there a
noticeable correlation between states' rights voter appeal and voter
income.[65] Throughout the South the Independents did, however, appeal
most strongly to white voters in black-belt counties.

Republicans were the chief beneficiaries of southern voter dissatisfaction with the national Democrats. The GOP improved its 1952
showing, winning five southern states and a plurality of popular votes in
the South. Eisenhower again won Florida, Tennessee, Texas, and Virginia
and added the Louisiana electoral votes to his national majority. As in
1952, the Republican ticket ran well in the cities and upper-South hill
country, but the states' rights electors took a substantial toll from the 1952
high-quartile, black-belt Republican counties. Particularly significant
shifts of GOP strength occurred in Texas and Louisiana, the two states
where top echelon Democratic politicians provided leadership for white
protest. In the aftermath of the Mansfield and Texarkana incidents, the
Republicans for the first time made major inroads into the East Texas
piney wood, and in Louisiana the GOP invaded the traditionally Democratic (and pro-Long) hill-country parishes.[66]

Southern neobourbons failed to achieve political unity in presidential
politics, and they also failed to solidify the southern states behind a uni-
form massive resistance strategy. The 1954 Richmond conference of state
officials from all the southern states ended without having established a

[64] The vote received by states' rights electors ranged from 0.7 percent in Texas to
7.2 percent in Louisiana.
[65] Strong, *Urban Republicanism in the South*, 9–29.
[66] An even more notable indication of disaffection with the Democratic ticket was the
decrease in the number of votes cast in the Louisiana election. Louisiana Democrats
remained away from the polls in droves. While Republicans were moderately improving
their 1952 showing (by about 20,000 votes), the Democratic vote fell by more than
100,000. The approximately 44,000 votes won by the Andrews-Werdel ticket accounted
for part of this loss, but apparently large numbers of Democrats simply refused to participate. Trends in Louisiana politics are analyzed in William C. Havard, Rudolf Herberle,
and Perry H. Howard, *The Louisiana Elections of 1960* (Baton Rouge, 1963), 61ff.

general southern policy.[67] Later in that year, an attempt to create a regional coalition at the Southern Governors Conference collapsed when Governors Frank Clement of Tennessee and Francis Cherry of Arkansas and Governors-elect James Folsom of Alabama and LeRoy Collins of Florida refused to participate.[68] Other efforts by state officials to achieve a united front met similar fates.[69] The Citizens' Councils of America sought, in part successfully, to fill this void. The four-point "blueprint for victory" drafted by Council representatives in October, 1956, came closest to serving as a massive resistance platform. The plan called for interposition, a national propaganda campaign, a "sharp counterattack" on the NAACP and other integrationist groups, and the organization of southern white people in defense of white supremacy.[70] The Councils were never strong enough, however, to translate programs into South-wide policy. States of the Deep South and Virginia continued to follow generally similar policies. Resistance leaders, sharing a community of interests and goals, no doubt established considerable informal cooperation through telephone conversations, correspondence, and the like. But the inability of neobourbons to make massive resistance a South-wide crusade was a fundamental flaw of the movement.

[67] New York *Times*, June 11, 1954.

[68] *Ibid.*, November 14, 1954; *Southern School News*, December, 1954, January, 1955. Collins did not attend the conference but announced that he would not support such a move.

[69] One example of these efforts would be the Richmond conference on interposition mentioned in Chapter 8.

[70] *The Citizens' Council*, November, 1956.

CHAPTER 10

PROPAGANDA

Neobourbon southerners tended to view the civil rights movement as the result of conspiracy and political manipulation. The NAACP and its allies—among them the CIO, the Urban League, and other organized expressions of key minority political influence—were deemed responsible for this attack on the "South." Well-financed and highly organized, these groups had effectively spread "the socialist-collectivist concept from its spawning ground in the revolutionary hotbeds of Eastern Europe."[1] They had utilized the techniques of infiltration, propaganda, and bloc voting to transform many northern politicians into "pawns," to control the national news media, to infiltrate the northern academic community, and to indoctrinate the Supreme Court.[2]

S. Emory Rogers, one of the attorneys for Clarendon County, South Carolina, in the *Briggs v. Elliott* litigation, returned from the judicial wars convinced that "sound" constitutional principles could not get a fair hearing until there was an alteration of public sentiment. While helping to organize the South Carolina Citizens' Council movement, he explained: "Our only hope, at present, lies not in the carrying on of the battle in the courts by the presentation of legal defense, but in taking the battle to the people and using the same psychological and sociological warfare that has been so successfully carried on against us, i. e., the prin-

---

[1] Judge M. M. McGowan, "Rationale of Resistance," in Jackson *Daily News*, March 4–6, 1959. The quotation is from part three of the three-part essay.

[2] Paul Anthony, "An Analysis of the Hate Literature of Resistance Groups of the South" (unpublished Southern Regional Council memorandum, 1956), and Denison, "A Rhetorical Analysis of Speeches by Segregationists in the Deep South," are helpful both on the neobourbon outlook and on the southern propaganda offensive. I. A. Newby, *Jim Crow's Defense: Anti-Negro Thought in America, 1900–1930* (Baton Rouge, 1965), is a good study of the historical background of these same points.

ciples of mass psychology expressed through organized public opinion."[3]

Interposition was the first line of defense, but the long-range interests of the "South" additionally demanded not only a political "fourth force" but also an informational program to counter NAACP activities. "We must," as the executive secretary of the Georgia States' Rights Council said, "unbrainwash the people who believe that integration is right."[4] Success lay in solidifying the South and awaking the northern majority, now immobilized by the "paper curtain" of anti-South propaganda.

The most aggressive advocate of a southern informational offensive was James O. Eastland. The Mississippi senator called for a southern commission, lavishly financed through state appropriations and authorized to undertake a vast national public relations program. Eastland said, "We must take the offense. We must carry the message to every section of the United States. Our position is righteous. The great majority of the rank and file of the people of the North believe exactly as we do. The law of nature is on our side. After all, the average American is not a racial pervert. We must place our case at the bar of public opinion."[5] A centrally directed campaign of mass persuasion fueled by the taxes of Negro and white alike would endeavor to impose black-belt ideology not only upon the South but upon the entire nation as well. During the winter of 1955–56, Eastland popularized the idea in speeches throughout the South.[6]

Citizens' Council audiences received the senator's plan with apparent enthusiasm, but despite wide discussion, the commission proposal never succeeded, as did interposition, in capturing the southern imagination. The most serious effort to activate the scheme—a $500,000 appropriation by the Florida legislature to be available for a northern campaign when matched by five other southern states—terminated abruptly with Governor Collins' veto of the measure.[7]

Both the Federation for Constitutional Government and the Citizens' Councils sought to accomplish Eastland's purpose under private auspices. Leaders dreamed grandiose dreams: "When the Citizens' Councils are in a position to operate on a budget of $2,000,000 a year and field a force of 400 or 500 employees, skilled in the many-sided undertaking of

[3] Statement by Rogers, reprinted in Charleston *News and Courier*, August 23, 1955.
[4] Atlanta *Journal*, January 12, 1956, quoting William T. Bodenhamer.
[5] *Eastland Address*, 10.
[6] *Southern School News*, January-July, 1956.
[7] Miami *Herald*, June 18, 1959.

influencing public opinion, on that day you will see the tide begin to turn."[8]

As a step toward this goal, state Council associations in Mississippi and South Carolina chartered Educational Funds modeled after the NAACP Legal Defense and Educational Fund. Although the Council Funds were designed to qualify for tax-exempt contributions and thus to "be attractive to large contributors,"[9] difficulties establishing the exemptions and a disappointing public response limited their achievements. The Mississippi Educational Fund of the Citizens' Councils remained active, but its finance chairman admitted in 1958 that "we have had only two individuals who have contributed $1,000 or more."[10] The grand design envisioned by Eastland was not to be realized.

Instead, the propaganda offensive accompanying massive resistance emerged haphazardly. White supremacy organizations, newspapers, politicians, private citizens, and, increasingly, state governments participated in the quest for public support. In some cases this was a deliberate part of massive resistance strategy, in some cases merely from the yearning to be understood or the desire to defend the southern homeland from outside attack. For various reasons—lack of funds, provincialism, the realization that the South itself needed constant attention—southern publicists concentrated their advertising on the home market as had their ideological ancestors one hundred years before. The accumulated mass of words, printed and spoken, was impressive.

Citizens' Councils and similar groups distributed an enormous amount of literature promoting segregation and associated causes. Several organizations published their own newspapers, and virtually all distributed an infinite number of pamphlets and handouts. Among periodicals, *The Citizens' Council*, official voice of the Mississippi Association and the Citizens' Councils of America, was the largest and most influential. Competently edited by William J. Simmons and featuring articles and essays by prominent southern journalists, the monthly publication circulated regionally and even registered sales in a few northern cities. The bulk of its readership, however, was in the Deep South.[11] Pamphlet

---

[8] *The Citizens' Council*, January, 1957.

[9] Association of Citizens' Council of Mississippi, *4th Annual Report* (Greenwood, 1958), 4.

[10] *Ibid.* See also *The Citizens' Council*, December, 1956, January, 1957; Association of Citizens' Councils of Mississippi, *The Educational Fund of the Citizens' Councils* (Greenwood, n.d.); and Charleston *News and Courier*, January 6, 1957.

[11] *The Citizens' Council*, November, 1956, stated that the paper's "average national circulation" was 40,000. Martin, in *The Deep South Says "Never"*, credited the paper with 60,000 subscribers in 1957, and Carter, in *The South Strikes Back*, uses the figure 65,000.

literature advertising the virtues of segregation, states' rights, and a considerable number of other causes was legion. In early 1958 Simmons stated that Council offices in Mississippi had distributed more than seven million literary tracts and that his Jackson office answered from three to seven hundred letters weekly.[12] White supremacy organizations in half a dozen other states circulated similar literature on a large scale.[13] Pamphlets, often handsomely printed, included reproductions of speeches by leading neobourbon politicians as well as addresses and essays by lawyers, religious spokesmen, educators, and journalists.

By 1958 the Councils were distributing radio and television programs to local stations throughout the South. "Citizens' Councils Forum," a fifteen-minute weekly television show produced by Simmons and his growing staff, first appeared in early 1957 on a Jackson, Mississippi, television station. Simmons reported in early 1958 that a rating agency placed the Forum's weekly audience at 125,000.[14] After the spring of 1958 Council publicists filmed and taped radio and television shows in Washington, D.C., where southern congressmen gave Simmons and his aides access to government studios and equipment. The federally subsidized programs were "designed to present the Southern point of view on important issues of the day, and to counteract the propaganda barrage leveled at the South by most national media."[15] In mid-1958, Mississippi Association spokesmen reported that at least seventeen stations in nine southern states carried the television forum and that more than one hundred southern radio stations broadcast the Councils' radio forum.[16]

More active state organizations maintained speakers' bureaus and promoted a variety of other public relations projects. A Council favorite was encouraging southern segregationists to write to "friends and personal acquaintances" outside the region explaining the "South's" position on racial issues.[17]

---

[12] Educational Fund of the Citizens' Councils, *The Mid-West Hears the South's Story: An Address by William J. Simmons before the Oakland Farmers-Merchants Annual Banquet, Oakland, Iowa, Feb. 3, 1958* (Greenwood, n.d.), 13–14, hereinafter cited as *Simmons Address*.

[13] The libraries of the Southern Regional Council and the Southern Education Reporting Service contain fairly extensive samplings of this type of material.

[14] *Simmons Address*, 15.

[15] W. J. Simmons, *Citizens' Council Forum* (Jackson, 1958), 2. Reportedly, Representative John Bell Williams served as the Councils' Washington liaison. See Elizabeth Carpenter, in the *Arkansas Gazette*, May 12, 1959.

[16] Association of Citizens' Councils of Mississippi, *4th Annual Report* (1958), 2.

[17] *The Citizens' Council*, June, 1956; Montgomery *Advertiser*, March 28, 1956.

The Councils also employed far less ethical means to influence what was and what was not said on the southern home front. In Mississippi they offered well-paying "spare time" positions to reporters on some of the state's major newspapers as writers of Citizens' Councils publicity literature, a move that many observers viewed as a deliberate effort to influence the reporting of racial news events.[18] On several occasions, the Councils organized or participated in boycotts against newspapers deemed inadequately segregationist in policy. The Greenville, Mississippi, *Delta Democrat-Times* and the Little Rock *Arkansas Gazette* were the best-known newspapers subjected to organized advertising and circulation strikes, but a number of smaller publications suffered similar consequences. In some cases economic pressure directed toward dissident editors was supplemented by physical violence or threats of violence, usually emanating from Ku Klux Klan groups.[19]

But for the most part the Councils had few quarrels with the southern press. In addition to the numerous county newspapers whose small-town southern values were the same as those that motivated the resistance generally, most urban dailies were vigorous advocates of the "southern way of life." During the peak years of massive resistance, no more than one-third of the top thirty southern newspapers (in terms of circulation) could have been classified as being anything other than adamantly hostile to desegregation.[20] One survey of fifty-three southern newspapers found forty-two "openly opposed" to the *Brown* decision. Of the remaining eleven journals, seven took no stand at all and only four "more or less accepted the decision."[21] Some city dailies, led by the Jackson *Daily News* and the Charleston *News and Courier*, both highly influential in their home states, were as profoundly neobourbon as any Citizens' Council executive committee meeting. Frederick Sullens, editor of the *Daily News*, thundered in page one editorials:

These leaders (in the fight against misegenation [*sic*], mixed marriages, mongrelization and wholesale bastardy) are our governor, our two Senators, our six

---

[18] Jay Milner, in *Delta Democrat-Times*, March 11, 1956.

[19] For examples, see Reed Sarratt, *The Ordeal of Desegregation: The First Decade* (New York, 1966), 256–59; Peters, *The Southern Temper*, 30–31, 115–30; Carter, *The South Strikes Back*, 154–58; Homer Bigart, in St. Petersburg *Times*, September 22, 1955; and Montgomery *Advertiser*, February 18, 1956.

[20] Weldon James, "The South's Own Civil War: Battle for the Schools," in Shoemaker (ed.), *With All Deliberate Speed*, 34; Oliver Allen and Chester S. Williams, *Report on the Robert P. Patterson Memorial Conference: One Nation Indivisible* (New York, 1958), 17.

[21] Hero, *The Southerner and World Affairs*, 395.

members of Congress, our Citizens Councils, and substantial citizens, both men and women, everywhere. It is to their voices we should listen, and not the twaddle being talked by wishy-washy people who prat [*sic*] about "academic freedom," and "freedom of thought and of speech," and similar nonsense.

Puny parsons who prattle imbecilic propaganda in pulpits about obedience to the Supreme Court desegregation decision being a "manifestation of the Christian spirit" ought to have their pulpits kicked from under them and their tongues silenced. Christianity has nothing whatever to do with it. This is a fight for sane existence, for perpetuation of the purity of the white race.[22]

Somewhat more restrained, in keeping with its historic role as defender of South Carolina's aristocracy (or upper class, if one prefers), the Charleston *News and Courier* was equally committed to the cause. Editor Thomas R. Waring vigorously endorsed Citizens' Council efforts to spark "new life into time-honored principles of the Republic—principles that have been neglected and even besmirched in recent years."[23] Most other major dailies, while not openly endorsing the Councils, were in agreement with their basic aim of protecting the southern way of life and halting federal expansion—unless, of course, federal expansion meant homestate defense spending or other vitally necessary measures.

There were numerous exceptions, notably in North Carolina, where all the major dailies took relatively "moderate" editorial positions. Furthermore, southern newspapers generally did an adequate job of reporting the news. In the age of national news wire services, even those newspapers most devoted to white supremacy largely confined their views to headlines, local feature stories, and the editorial pages.[24] But southern editors, like their peers elsewhere, tended to give the headlines to the sensational, and the thrust of southern journalism was in keeping with the tone of the resistance.[25]

[22] Jackson *Daily News*, February 21, 1956. Sullens died in late 1957. His departure had no noticeable effect upon *Daily News* editorial policy as it related to racial issues.

[23] Part three of a three-part series on the Citizens' Council movement by Waring in the Charleston *News and Courier*, September 15–17, 1955.

[24] Walter Spearman and Sylvan Meyer, *Racial Crisis and the Press* (Atlanta, 1960).

[25] For evaluations of the southern press, see *ibid.;* Hugh Davis Graham, *Crisis in Print: Desegregation and the Press in Tennessee* (Nashville, 1967); Matthews and Prothro, *Negroes and the New Southern Politics*, 239–48; Roy E. Carter, Jr., "Segregation and the News: A Regional Content Study," *Journalism Quarterly*, XXXIV (Winter, 1957), 3–18; Roy E. Carter, Jr., "Racial Identification Effects upon the News Story Writer," *Journalism Quarterly*, XXXVI (Summer, 1959), 284–90; Quint, *Profile in Black and White*, vi–vii; Ashmore, *An Epitaph for Dixie*, 164; Silver, *Mississippi: The Closed Society*, 28–35; James, "The South's Own Civil War," 33–35; Muse, *Virginia's Massive Resistance*, 94–96; Louisiana State Advisory Committee, *The New Orleans School Crisis*, 31–37; Havard and Beth, *The Politics of Mis-Representation*, 228–29; Sarratt, *The Ordeal of Desegregation*, 247–63; and Peters, *The Southern Temper*, 115–30.

Whether seeking to feature racial themes or merely to cover the news, newspapers rarely lacked subject matter for stories concerning race relations. Southern politicians kept up a drumfire of manifestos, speeches, resolutions, statements, legislation, ad infinitum. On the national level perhaps the most successful propaganda ploy, with the possible exception of the Southern Manifesto itself, was the special investigation of conditions in the Washington, D.C., school system. Whatever were the conditions in Washington's schools, the House District of Columbia subcommittee probe had all the makings of a propaganda exploration. The investigation was touched off by John Bell Williams, a subcommittee member.[26] The subcommittee chairman was James C. Davis of Georgia, who, one month before the investigators delivered their report, advised a Georgia States' Rights Council audience not to concern itself "about what is said by the Communists, the pinkos, the radicals, the NAACP, the ADA, the one-worlders, and all that motley group of crackpots who are clamoring for desegregation and mongrelization."[27] Subcommittee counsel was William E. Gerber who was later to insist that the investigation proved "conclusively" that Negroes were intellectually inferior to whites.[28] Four of the six subcommittee members were southerners. Neither the hearings, held in September, 1956, nor the subcommittee report, released in December, 1956, hinted at a quest for objectivity. The investigators concluded "that the integrated school system in the District of Columbia cannot be copied by those who seek an orderly and successful school operation."[29] The four southerners added a majority report recommending "that racially separate public schools be reestablished...."[30] While the investigation seemed to indicate that integration had not solved Washington's public school problems, it was doubtful that it justified such emotion-charged "Findings and Conclusions." Nevertheless, the subcommittee report, like Eastland's "the Court was Communist in-

[26] Jeanne Rogers, "Nation's Showcase?: The Washington Experience," in Shoemaker (ed.), *With All Deliberate Speed*, 156–61.

[27] Georgia Commission on Education, *Congressman James C. Davis Speaks to the States' Rights Council* (Atlanta, 1956), 9–10.

[28] As quoted in *Arkansas Gazette*, September 24, 1958.

[29] U.S. House of Representatives, 84th Cong., 2nd Sess., *Investigation of Public School Conditions: Report of the Subcommittee to Investigate Public School Standards and Conditions and Juvenile Delinquency in the District of Columbia of the Committee on the District of Columbia* (Washington, 1957), 46.

[30] *Ibid.*, 47.

fluenced" speech, gave an "official" sanction to what many southerners had long been arguing.[31]

Segregationist activity by southern politicians naturally made its principal impact on the home press, and politicians, like newspaper editors and Council publicists, contributed primarily to maintenance of domestic morale. But the desire to win northern toleration of—or, as many neobourbons wanted, northern conversion to—southern social concepts remained. During 1956, as the nation began to take notice of the unusually deviant behavior of its regional stepchild, growing national interest gave southern publicists greater access to national audiences. In *Harper's Magazine*, Thomas R. Waring gave "The Southern Case Against Desegregation"; in *U.S. News and World Report*, James F. Byrnes explained why "The Supreme Court Must Be Curbed" and why "Guns and Bayonets Cannot Promote Education"; and in the *Atlantic Monthly*, Herbert R. Sass, a South Carolina Committee of 52 member and a literary figure, described the relationship between "Mixed Schools and Mixed Blood."[32] And the Montgomery *Advertiser* initiated a series of editorials entitled "Publish It Not in the Streets of Askelon."

Grover C. Hall, Jr., editor of the *Advertiser*, was perturbed by the influx of journalists from "Up Nawth" that poured into his city—"The 1st, Best and Next Capital of the Confederacy"—to cover the Montgomery bus boycott.[33] To Hall, the cause of racial discord was simple: "The truth is, of course, that race disharmony follows wherever the Negro settles in significant numbers. This is a sorrowful but evident fact."[34] Negroes also lived in the North, and Yankee journalists should

[31] The Councils publicized widely the investigation's results. See Educational Fund of the Citizens' Councils, *Congressional Committee Report of What Happened When Schools Were Integrated in Washington, D.C.* (Greenwood, n.d.), and Citizens' Councils of Alabama, *What Integration Has Done to Your Nation's Capital* (Montgomery, n.d.).

[32] Thomas R. Waring, "The Southern Case Against Desegregation," *Harper's Magazine*, CCXII (January, 1956), 39–45; James F. Byrnes, "The Supreme Court Must be Curbed," *U.S. News and World Report*, XL (May 18, 1956), 50–58, and "Guns and Bayonets Cannot Promote Education," *ibid.*, XLI (October 5, 1956), 100–104; and Herbert Ravenel Sass, "Mixed Schools and Mixed Blood," *Atlantic Monthly*, CXCVIII (November, 1956), 45–49. These were the most important of a rash of articles by southern publicists defending—or promoting—the southern position that appeared in national media during 1956. Such articles as Ralph McGill, "The Angry South," *Atlantic Monthly*, CXCVII (April, 1956), 31–34, and C. A. McKnight, "The Troubled South," *Collier's*, CXXXVII (June 22, 1956), 25–31, were serious efforts to interpret southern behavior and were in a different category (although even these were written from a southern point of view and suggested the importance of gradualism and toleration for white southern attitudes).

[33] Montgomery *Advertiser*, February 8, 1956.

[34] *Ibid.*, March 11, 1956.

spend their time and energy reporting their own domestic racial strife. Instead, Hall contended, northern media (and northern politicians), with few exceptions, smugly trumpeted southern problems while ignoring their own. The North's refusal to recognize its social difficulties was like the biblical passage from II Samuel: "Tell it not in Gath, publish it not in the streets of Askelon; lest the daughters of the Philistines rejoice, lest the daughters of the uncircumcised triumph." With so many northern reporters covering Alabama's racial problems, Hall launched a campaign to "fill their vacuum" by uncovering incidents of racial ill-will and violence in the North.[35] From searching the northern press, by exchanging "reciprocal" interviews with visiting reporters operating from *Advertiser* offices, and, after the campaign began, through letters from "Askelon" residents, the editorial staff got leads to stories that were verified and detailed directly by telephone, telegraph, or by a national wire service acting at the *Advertiser*'s request.[36]

Researchers found what they sought, of course, and for four and a half months, from March 10, 1956, until late July, the newspaper documented the existence of nonsouthern racial disharmony and double-standard reporting. The obvious conclusion, as Hall later explained to the 478 editors and publishers of the Inland Daily Press Association, was that "Until New York, Chicago, Detroit, and Philadelphia can quell their own state of guerilla warfare between the races and crush the reign of rape and knife on schoolhouse staircases, their politicians and editorial Jingoes should have the graceful forebearance to take sabbatical leave from their aggressions against the South."[37]

There was nothing startling in the *Advertiser*'s "Askelon" series, except the naked amoral pusillanimity of the editorials themselves. It was no secret that northern whites possessed an abundance of bigotry and hypocrisy. Northern Negroes hardly needed reminding that their opportunities of appearing on the New York *Times* society pages,[38] finding a house outside a ghetto, or even moving into a community like Dearborn, Michigan, whose mayor said: "I am for complete segregation, one million per cent, on all levels,"[39] were considerably less than meager. That northern publishers had traditionally found "Race disharmony in Dixie . . . more picturesque" than local troubles (with some justice, since

---

[35] *Ibid.*
[36] *Ibid.*, March 25-April 5, 1956.
[37] Reprinted in *ibid.*, February 25, 1958.
[38] *Ibid.*, March 29, 1956.
[39] As quoted in *ibid.*, March 26, 1956.

Autherine Lucy, the first Negro ever enrolled at the University of Alabama. Two days of violent demonstrations began when she met her first classes.   (WIDE WORLD)

A white student jumps on the roof of a Negro's car on the University of Alabama campus during demonstrations protesting the enrollment of Autherine Lucy.　(WIDE WORLD)

Singing "Dixie" and waving the Confederate flag, University of Alabama students stage a protest demonstration in downtown Tuscaloosa. Townspeople joined the crowd. (WIDE WORLD)

One of the two 25-ton tanks sent to quell rioting in and near Clinton, Tennessee, resulting from the desegregation of the town's high school. (WIDE WORLD)

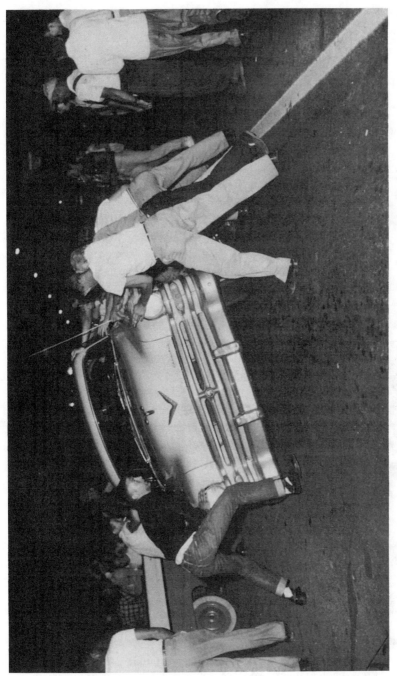

An unruly mob stopped and threatened to overturn this carload of Negroes passing through Clinton, Tennessee, in August, 1956. (WIDE WORLD)

"First Day at School, Little Rock." Jack Jenkins, a United Press photographer, won the tenth annual George Polk Memorial Award in 1957 for this picture of a Negro girl as she passed through a jeering crowd of students and adults on her way to her first classes at Little Rock's Central High School. (UPI)

National Guard troops, ordered here by Governor Orval E.
Faubus, form a protective ring around Little Rock's Central
High School. (WIDE WORLD)

Four weeks after Central High School was first integrated,
it was still necessary for National Guardsmen to escort the
Negro students to their classes. White students look on from
the windows and the doorway. (UPI)

A small crowd gathers outside the Governor's Mansion in Atlanta to protest school integration. Ku Klux Klan spokesmen had predicted a crowd of 15,000 taking part in this 1959 demonstration. (WIDE WORLD)

A Negro first-grader peers wide-eyed over the shoulder of the deputy U.S. marshal who escorted her to school in New Orleans on the first day of integrated schools. The city started desegregation by direction of the federal courts but in defiance of the Louisiana Legislature. (WIDE WORLD)

only in the South was prejudice required by law) was generally known.[40] None of this was new; southern publicists, including the *Advertiser*, had long been calling attention to all of these things.

But the timing, concentration, and biblical title of the "Askelon" campaign captured public attention. By July 29, 1956, when Hall terminated the series, the *Advertiser* had already run a parallel series, "Published in Askelon," listing examples of a blossoming concern by Yankee media for nonsouthern social discord.[41] "What *The Advertiser* has tried to show," the newspaper editorialized, "is the folly of rash demands on the South, which still harbors two-thirds of the Negro."[42] The "Askelon" campaign was very likely the most successful of all deliberative southern efforts to influence northern opinion.[43]

Another significant attempt to transmit southern conservative viewpoints outside the South was the work of the "Putnam Letter Committee." Carleton Putnam, a retired airlines executive and a southern resident who had been born and educated in the North, came to public attention in the fall of 1958 when his well-articulated defense of segregation, in the form of an open letter to President Eisenhower, was printed in a number of southern newspapers. A group of Alabama resistance leaders that included Lieutenant Governor Albert Boutwell and former Governor Frank Dixon formed a committee to raise funds for publishing the letter as an advertisement in northern newspapers. The "Putnam Letter" appeared in the New York *Times* on January 5, 1959, and in other newspapers during following months. Each advertisement included a plea for contributions, and the funds thus obtained were used to purchase further advertising space. In early 1959, Putnam wrote a lengthy open letter to Attorney General William P. Rogers taking issue with the social science authorities cited by the Supreme Court in the *Brown* decision. This "Second Putnam Letter" was also widely reprinted in the southern press and was circulated outside the region.[44]

---

[40] *Ibid.*, March 11, 1956.

[41] The "Published in Askelon" series ran irregularly during May and June, 1956.

[42] Montgomery *Advertiser*, July 29, 1956. The "Askelon" editorials are reprinted in the Montgomery *Advertiser* pamphet, *Publish It Not in the Streets of Askelon* (Montgomery, 1956).

[43] The "Askelon" series attracted national attention. See the examples in the "Published in Askelon" series.

[44] Carleton Putnam, *Race and Reason: A Yankee View* (Washington, 1961), 1–33; I. A. Newby, *Challenge to the Court: Social Scientists and the Defense of Segregation, 1954–1966* (Baton Rouge, 1967), 146–57. The Putnam Letters are reprinted in *Race and Reason*, 5–9, 21–29.

State governments, however, sponsored the most intensive and persistent efforts to reach national audiences. Many state political figures showed a concern for public relations that went well beyond personal political considerations. The resolutions and memorials condemning the Supreme Court and begging for a return to states' rights that poured from southern legislatures were crude and impulsive efforts to shape public thinking. Even interposition had publicity as well as strategic purposes. But not until creation of the Mississippi State Sovereignty Commission in early 1956 was the model established for a more broadly conceived public propaganda program.

The State Sovereignty Commission was Governor James Coleman's conception of what was needed to implement his policy of "friendly persuasion." The governor called for an agency with extraordinary authority to pacify racial hysteria in the state, thus removing Mississippi's racial incidents from national attention and opening the way for a sedate program to improve the state's image and alleviate national pressure. The commission would forcibly curb the NAACP and prevent future "provocations" such as the barrages of desegregation petitions that had stirred white social fears in the summer of 1955. Simultaneously the commission would dispel the atmosphere that energized the Citizens' Councils. Coleman said on one occasion that, "when the urgency passes, I feel that the Citizens' Councils will pass along with it."[45] And the governor felt that the Sovereignty Commission would be able to perform just such a mission. Neobourbon legislators who participated in molding the commission's enactment legislation took a significantly different view; they visualized it as an instrument for agressively cementing racial orthodoxy at home and cooperating with Citizens' Council propaganda efforts abroad.[46] The result was an enormously powerful state agency capable of performing both tasks.

Endowed with virtually blank-check authority "to do and perform any and all acts and things deemed necessary and proper to protect the sovereignty of the State of Mississippi, and her sister states," the commission was granted almost unlimited powers of investigation and was authorized to cooperate with private groups striving for maintenance of states' rights. Membership on the commission, like that of the Legal Education Advisory Commission which it had replaced, included the

[45] As quoted in Memphis *Commercial Appeal*, October 8, 1956.
[46] Carter, *The South Strikes Back*, 62–77.

state's executive and legislative leadership. An appropriation of $250,000 provided initial operating capital.[47]

During Coleman's governorship, the commission, despite occasional flare-ups of internal dissension, remained oriented toward "friendly persuasion." With Mississippi journalist and friend of the governor Hal Decell as publicity director, the commission strove to improve Mississippi's image. It distributed to national media such pamphlets as *All Mississippi Asks Is Fairness and a Chance to Present Its Side of the Case*, which pictured Mississippi as a much-maligned and long-suffering state that only wanted equal treatment in news reporting.[48] The commission offered invitations to newspaper executives outside the South to visit Mississippi at the state's expense for a firsthand inspection of social conditions. Eighteen New England editors and publishers, mostly from small weekly newspapers, accepted the invitation, and their week-long tour of the state in the fall of 1956 was the commission's most publicized promotional endeavor. The New Englanders' published accounts of their observations were largely sympathetic toward Mississippi's problems.[49] By the end of 1957, the commission had spent only some $65,000 of its appropriation, most of it for propaganda projects.[50] Its level of activity did not noticeably increase during the following two years.

The inauguration of Ross R. Barnett as governor in 1960 marked a fundamental reorientation of commission policy toward the neobourbon goal of a positive assertion of southern orthodoxy at home and abroad. Among numerous projects during the early 1960's, the commission made monthly contributions to the Citizens' Councils, reportedly donating some $200,000 to finance Citizens' Council propaganda activity;[51] granted similar sums to a Washington lobby opposing civil rights legislation;[52] dispatched orators to carry "The Message from Mississippi" throughout the nation, an expanded and more handsomely financed version of what the Citizens' Councils had been doing in the past; and vigorously pro-

[47] *Race Relations Law Reporter*, I (June, 1956), 592–95.

[48] Mississippi State Sovereignty Commission, *All Mississippi Asks Is Fairness and a Chance to Present Its Side of the Case* (Jackson, n.d.).

[49] Mississippi State Sovereignty Commission, *Report to the People: A Summary of Articles Written by New England Editors after their Tour of Mississippi* (Jackson, n.d.).

[50] *Delta Democrat-Times*, December 3, 1957.

[51] *Atlanta Journal and Constitution*, January 31, 1965.

[52] Through 1963 the commission had contributed $120,000 to the Coordinating Committee for Fundamental American Freedoms. Silver, *Mississippi: The Closed Society*, 8.

moted an undeviating devotion to white supremacy at home.[53] The Mississippi Sovereignty Commission during Barnett's governorship came closest to fulfilling the function that Eastland and other neobourbon leaders had hoped for on a South-wide basis.

Eastland's appeals for a public propaganda program and the example being set in Mississippi stimulated similar activity in other states. In Georgia Attorney General Eugene Cook, soon joined by Roy Harris and others, took up the cry for a state campaign to counter NAACP-integrationist public relations work. The Georgia Education Commission's 1957 legislative recommendations included proposals vastly broadening the commission's powers and authorizing expenditures of state money for public information purposes. The legislature promptly approved these proposals, and the Education Commission, with authority almost as great as that of the Mississippi Sovereignty Commission and with a vigorous new executive secretary, T. V. Williams, launched a campaign to sell the "Georgia way of life."[54]

The program was barely under way when the agency scored its greatest *coup*. A commission agent "made contact and infiltrated"[55] a public meeting at the Highlander Folk School, a radical (home-grown rural-southern type, not subversive or Communist) center for labor and civil rights activity in the South, in Monteagle, Tennessee.[56] The agent snapped pictures of civil rights activists and integrated social functions, listened to the folk singing, and observed workshop sessions discussing methods for broadening civil rights in the South. The commission was soon distributing nationally a pamphlet entitled "Communist Training School" that purported to prove a direct connection between subversive activities and integration.[57]

[53] "The Message from Mississippi" was the standard speech delivered by Mississippi orators before service clubs and other groups outside the South. It is reprinted in Denison, "A Rhetorical Analysis of Speeches by Segregationists in the Deep South," Appendix. The commission also imported out-of-state segregationists for speeches in Mississippi. See Chapter 12 for a discussion of more forceful efforts to maintain domestic orthodoxy.

[54] *Race Relations Law Reporter*, II (April, 1957), 454–55; Margaret Shannon, in Atlanta *Journal and Constitution*, June 30, 1957.

[55] As quoted by Charles Pou, in Atlanta *Journal*, October 4, 1957. Either Williams, who made the statement, or Ed Friend, the agent, had been reading too many mystery stories. Friend "made contact and infiltrated" the school by walking in like everyone else, since the meeting was public and visitors and the press were welcome.

[56] On the Highlander Folk School, see H. Glyn Thomas, "The Highlander Folk School: The Depression Years," *Tennessee Historical Quarterly*, XXIII (December, 1964), 358–71.

[57] Georgia Commission on Education, *Highlander Folk School: Communist Training School, Monteagle, Tenn.* (Atlanta, n.d.).

For a time the Georgia Education Commission was the most active of all southern public propaganda centers. Williams and his growing staff—nine fulltime members by the end of 1957—engaged in a variety of projects and mailed substantial amounts of segregationist literature on a nationwide basis.[58] But, increasingly, the project that captured Williams' interest was Georgia's 1958 gubernatorial primary and the candidacy of William T. Bodenhamer, past executive secretary of the States' Rights Council. In July, 1958, the commission's assistant executive secretary resigned, publicly charging that Williams was transforming the agency into a publicity center for Bodenhamer's campaign and even distributing forged photographs smearing the candidate's chief opponent.[59] Williams resigned under fire, and the Georgia Education Commission went into permanent eclipse. It was later replaced by the Governor's Commission on Constitutional Government, also empowered to advertise the "southern way of life," but the new agency never became publicly active.[60]

State Sovereignty Commissions or similar agencies also emerged in Florida, Arkansas, and Virginia (and later, in the early 1960's, in Louisiana and Alabama). The Rainach Committee in Louisiana also engaged in sporadic public relations ventures, notably the running of a full-page advertisement in a New York City newspaper pleading for segregation and understanding of the white South.[61] Among latecomers to the public propaganda field, the Virginia Commission on Constitutional Government, with *News Leader* editor James Jackson Kilpatrick as Publications Committee chairman, was most consistently energetic in propaganda and lobbying activity during the massive resistance phase of southern race politics.[62]

[58] By the end of 1957, the commission had mailed more than 500,000 segregationist tracts and was busily compiling a mailing list of 2 million national public opinion leaders for future and more ambitious distributions. See William M. Bates, in Atlanta *Journal and Constitution*, December 25, 1957.

[59] The charges, denials, and countercharges surrounding the agency's political activities were covered in detail by both the Atlanta *Constitution* and the Atlanta *Journal*, July 22–31, 1958.

[60] Atlanta *Journal*, June 2, 1959.

[61] New York *Herald-Tribune*, February 17, 1958.

[62] The Virginia commission, among other projects, published an impressive series of "For Your Reference Library" pamphlets on such subjects as *Report of the Conference of Chief Justices at Pasadena, August, 1958* (Richmond, 1959); *The Kentucky-Virginia Resolutions of 1798 and Madison's Report of 1799* (Richmond, 1960); *The Fort Hill Address of John C. Calhoun* (Richmond, 1960); and *Equality v. Liberty: The Eternal Conflict, An Essay by R. Carter Pittman (of the Georgia Bar)* (Richmond, 1960). The publicity work of the Virginia Commission is summarized by Kilpatrick in the Richmond *News Leader*, January 26, 1966.

Generally, in their defense of past values, southern propagandists relied primarily upon endless repetition of three basic—and largely spurious—propositions. One was, of course, the constitutional guarantees of the rights of states and the consequent "unconstitutionality" of *Brown v. Board of Education*. States' rights agitation centered around the same arguments that had been used to justify interposition; when aimed toward nonsouthern audiences, however, constitutional polemics often sought to broaden sectional fears into national concern by stressing the threat that growing federal power and Supreme Court intervention posed for all states. Exemplifying this appeal, William Simmons told guests at a Farmers-Merchants banquet in Oakland, Iowa:

> May I say to you that when any court takes leave of the law and starts rendering edicts based on sociology, it is high time for all Americans to wake up. . . . If any court can tell the people of Mississippi or Louisiana that they shall run their public schools according to the theories of certain social revolutionaries, then the Court can tell the people of Iowa or Nebraska that they shall run *their* schools according to notions equally as radical. If our States' Rights are usurped with impunity, are yours safe?[63]

Similarly, there was the inevitable refrain that race relations and social customs were local affairs which could only be dealt with on the state level without outside interference.

The asserted biological or sociological inferiority of Negroes was the second point. Southern publicists trumpeted the inherent supremacy of white men, reiterating the dangers of biological race mixing and offering racial interpretations of history. Several "scientific racists," a few of whom possessed impressive academic credentials and not all of whom were southern, utilized intelligence and achievement tests to "demonstrate" the limited learning capacity of Negroes.[64] Other segregationist propaganda substituted sociology for biology, thus permitting a more re-

---

[63] *Simmons Address*, 6.

[64] Newby, *Challenge to the Court*, is an excellent discussion of the revival of "scientific racism" in the late 1950's and early 1960's. Among the proponents of massive resistance, the most influential exponent of innate Negro inferiority was Wesley C. George of the University of North Carolina School of Medicine. See his *The Race Problem from the Standpoint of One Who Is Concerned About the Evils of Miscegenation* (Birmingham, 1955); *Race Heredity and Civilization* (Norfolk, Va., n.d.); and *Human Progress and the Race Problem* (Atlanta, n.d.). Also important were Audrey M. Shuey, *The Testing of Negro Intelligence* (Lynchburg, Va., 1958); Frank C. J. McGurk, "A Scientist's Report on Race Differences," *U.S. News and World Report*, XLI (September 21, 1956), 92–96; and Henry E. Garrett, "Professor Cites Fallacies of Integration Arguments," in *The Citizens Council*, October, 1956.

spectable factual foundation while still (like the Black Codes of yore) drawing the division squarely along caste lines.[65] White supremacy propagandists insisted that Negroes had not only made their greatest gains under segregation but that the system was essential to further Negro progress; that Negroes preferred the "separate but equal" system; that racial tension unfailingly accompanied the presence of Negroes and whites in the same community (unless muted by segregationist practices); and that changes in the mutually beneficial Jim Crow system could only bring discord and violence.[66] Both of these basic propositions—the constitutional rights of states and the fundamental inferiority of Negroes —were, of course, tired and ancient arguments that have seemed to leap forth spontaneously whenever some peculiar southern institution has come under attack.

The third basic premise was of somewhat more recent origin, and in many ways it was most startling of all. Southern publicists blatantly asserted that the quest for social justice and human dignity was nothing more than a foreign plot, a conspiracy dominated and directed by "Communist" subversives. To be sure, the assumption that unwelcome ideologies were by nature alien and immoral represented a traditional southern reaction, and the "Communist-dominated" labor unions of the 1930's were forerunners of "Communist-controlled" civil rights activists of the 1950's. Nevertheless, the attempt to associate social change with foreign subversion and conspiracy represented the greatest deviation from past justifications of white supremacy.

The pseudo-nationalist campaign to discredit the civil rights movement generally and the NAACP in particular was both a propaganda ploy and a part of broader massive resistance strategy aimed at crushing the NAACP. Georgia Attorney General Eugene Cook, whose speech on "The Ugly Truth About the NAACP" became a classic among segregationists, relentlessly propagated the theme that: "Either knowingly or unwittingly, it [NAACP] has allowed itself to become part and parcel of the Communist conspiracy to overthrow the democratic governments of this nation and its sovereign states."[67] Cook revealed that his staff and those

[65] Perhaps the best statement of this view was Waring, "The Southern Case Against Desegregation."

[66] Books like Brady, *Black Monday*, and Talmadge, *You and Segregation*, included most of these standard shibboleths.

[67] Educational Fund of the Citizens' Councils, *The Ugly Truth About the NAACP: An Address by Attorney General Eugene Cook of Georgia Before the 55th Annual Convention of the Peace Officers Association of Georgia* (Greenwood, n.d.), 10.

of Representative James Davis and Senator Eastland had spent "many weeks of intensive investigation" assembling "facts" about "the subversive designs behind the current crusade of the misnamed National Association for the Advancement of Colored People and its fellow-traveling fronts."[68] The NAACP and its allies were unconcerned with the welfare of Negro citizens, Cook asserted. They had simply seized the racial issue "as a convenient front for their more nefarious activities and as one with which they could dupe naive do-gooders, fuzzy-minded intellectuals, misguided clergymen and radical journalists to be their pawns."[69] The attorney general concluded that the NAACP was pursuing aims that could contribute only toward "delivering this nation into the hands of international Communism."[70] The *Brown* decision, said James Eastland, was the result of communist manipulation; the civil rights movement, said Cook, was inspired by the same subversive influences.

Southern publicists endlessly reiterated these paranoiac aspersions. Representative Ezekiel C. Gathings of Arkansas filled forty pages of the *Congressional Record* with charges against the NAACP, asserting that 89 of its 193 officeholders during 1954 had been cited by the House Committee on Un-American Activities.[71] *The Citizens' Council* explained (in a story beneath the headline "Anti-White Plot Hatched in Moscow") that the integration movement "is the offshoot of a diabolical plot first hatched in Soviet Russia by Communists nearly three decades ago."[72] Eastland, Talmadge, Thurmond, James F. Byrnes, former House Committee on Un-American Activities Chairman Martin Dies—indeed virtually the unanimous voice of the neobourbon South—supported these efforts to smear the NAACP and social change as being substantially foreign, un-American, immoral, and communist.[73]

---

[68] *Ibid.*, 1.

[69] *Ibid.*, 2.

[70] *Ibid.*, 10.

[71] *Congressional Record*, 84th Cong., 2nd Sess. (February 23, 1956), 3215-59.

[72] *The Citizens Council*, April, 1956.

[73] This is not to say that all neobourbons charged that the NAACP was a Communist-front organization or that all of them said that civil rights activity was a direct part of the "Communist conspiracy." Instead, neobourbon spokesmen often avoided such direct statements. Martin Dies, for example (in a speech before the Mississippi Councils), said only: "The NAACP grew out of the National Negro Congress, a Communist organization created to carry out the Moscow program. I won't say the NAACP is a Communist group but the leaders of the Negro Congress had a great influence on the NAACP after the Negro Congress dissolved." As quoted in *Delta Democrat-Times*, November 5, 1957. Or as James Byrnes stated in an address before the Texas Bar Association: "Because of

Southern legislatures soon joined this witch-hunting crusade. In March, 1957, Louisiana's Rainach Committee conducted hearings on the causes of racial unrest in the South. Relying overwhelmingly upon the testimony of imported, professional witnesses, the committee, the radio-television audience, and officials from other southern states who attended as observers heard such people as Manning Johnson, a longtime House Un-American Activities Committee "expert" witness, explain that the NAACP "is nothing more than a vehicle of the Communist Party, in which the Communists are colonizing for the purpose of inciting racial rebellion in the South, with the ultimate object, in the insane confusion, to seize power and take over the reins of government in the United States."[74] Rainach and his committee promptly determined that desegregation activity was a part of the communist conspiracy and that the NAACP was a communist-front organization.[75] The hearings, said Representative John S. Garrett, a committee member and Citizens' Council spokesman, "proved that communism and integration are inseparable."[76]

Although the Louisiana hearing was the first and most publicized legislative effort to defame the civil rights movement by calling it subversive, legislative committees in Florida, Mississippi, and Arkansas staged similar productions. The Arkansas Legislative Council's Special Education Committee, with firebrand segregationist Attorney General Bruce Bennett as general counsel, investigated the causes of the Little Rock school desegregation crisis. Again, a parade of professional, non-southern witnesses—including the same Manning Johnson—gave "expert" testimony before the committee and television cameras in Little Rock. Not unpredictably, the Arkansas Committee found the NAACP knowingly or unknowingly to be an instrument of communist subversion.[77] In Arkansas, Mississippi, and Florida, a major witness before the legislative committees was J. B. Matthews, former chief investigator for the House Un-American Activities Committee and a professional witness who once made a name for himself by labeling seven thousand

the secrecy of their methods, it is difficult to secure positive proof of their acts, but circumstantial evidence convinces me the recent lunch counter demonstrations were inspired and directed by Soviet Russia." Speech reprinted in *The State*, July 5, 1960.

[74] Testimony by Manning Johnson, March 8, 1957, in Louisiana Joint Legislative Committee, *Subversion in Racial Unrest* (Baton Rouge, 1957), Pt. II, 206.

[75] *Ibid.*, 250ff.

[76] As quoted in Jackson *Daily News*, June 10, 1958.

[77] *Arkansas Gazette*, January 17, 1959; *Southern School News*, January, February, 1959.

Protestant ministers pro-Communist.[78] Before the Mississippi General Legislative Investigating Committee Matthews made such observations as: "Considering the general run of infiltrated organizations, I know of no other in the United States that has been so heavily infiltrated as the NAACP, infiltrated with Communists and the Communist influences."[79] Neither the Mississippi nor Florida investigating committees directly cited the NAACP as being subversive, but they both came very close to doing so.[80]

Conveniently, both national sovereignty commissions chose this period for major forays against the South's hardpressed "subversives." Senator Eastland's Internal Security Subcommittee conducted hearings on "Communism in the Mid-South" in Memphis during October, 1957, and a House Committee on Un-American Activities subcommittee headed by Edwin Willis of Louisiana probed "Communist Infiltration and Activities in the South" in Atlanta during the summer of 1958.[81] Although neither subcommittee directly attacked desegregation, their activity did contribute to a general atmosphere that linked patriotism with the status quo.

Against this background, the Georgia Education Commission's "Communist Training School" report on the Highlander Folk School became something of a *cause celebre*. The existence of a school teaching what T. V. Williams chose to term "methods and tactics of precipitating racial strife and disturbances"[82] hinted of manipulation and conspiracy, particularly since some participants at the meeting had indeed been cited or had belonged to organizations cited by one of the national sovereignty commissions. "The meeting of such a large group of specialists in inter-

[78] Matthews reportedly received $960 for his "expert" testimony before the Arkansas Committee. *Arkansas Gazette*, December 19, 1958.

[79] Testimony by J. B. Matthews, November 18, 1959, in General Legislative Investigating Committee, *Report to the 1962 Regular Session, Mississippi State Legislature on the Investigation of Un-American Activities in the State of Mississippi* (Jackson, 1962), 153.

[80] *Ibid.*, i–iii; Georgia Commission on Education, *Communism and the NAACP* (2 vols.; Atlanta, n.d.). The latter is a report of the public hearings of Florida's Legislative Investigation Committee.

[81] U.S. House of Representatives, 85th Cong., 2nd Sess., *Hearings Before the Committee on Un-American Activities: Communist Infiltration and Activities in the South, July 29, 30, and 31, 1958* (Washington, 1958); U.S. Senate, 85th Cong., 1st Sess., *Hearings Before the Sub-Committee to Investigate the Administration of the Internal Security Act and Other Internal Laws of the Committee on the Judiciary, United States Senate: Communism in the Mid-South, October 28 and 29, 1957* (Washington, 1957). There were in addition two less publicized hearings of a similar type in North Carolina and Louisiana in 1956.

[82] As quoted in Atlanta *Journal*, October 4, 1957.

racial strife under the auspices of a Communist Training School, and in the company of many known Communists," the commission report stated, "is the typical method whereby leadership training and tactics are furnished to the agitators."[83] On the basis of the Georgia report, a Birmingham *News* writer devoted a six-part feature series to answering in the affirmative the question "Is there a master plan, Soviet-inspired, behind the racial incidents so widespread in America today?"[84] And a Tennessee legislative committee was soon conducting an investigation that eventually forced Highlander's closing.

The total effect of all the sound and fury surrounding the southern propaganda offensive would be difficult to evaluate. Certainly it must have done something to harden white southern sentiment and may have won some converts outside the region. The campaign went hand-in-hand with interposition and with neobourbon efforts to oppose progressive policies on the national political level. It sought to associate human rights with communism and insisted "that the attempt to abolish segregation in the South is fostered and directed by the Communist party."[85] By these tactics, the propaganda barrage undermined the validity of the right of dissent and became a part of a general effort to stamp out the expression of unorthodox thought in the South. And, most of all perhaps, it undermined Negro confidence in the basic commitment to justice by white men.

[83] Georgia Commission on Education, *Highlander Folk School: Communist Training School, Monteagle, Tenn.*, 1.

[84] Edwin Strickland, in Birmingham *News*, October 6–11, 1957.

[85] Citizens' Councils of Alabama, *The Undeniable Facts About the NAACP* (Montgomery, n.d.).

CHAPTER 11

THE QUEST FOR CONFORMITY
PART I

The advocates of massive resistance envisioned a solid South united behind a program of states' rights and white supremacy. Such a vision left little place for tolerance, and efforts to silence internal dissent were a part of the quest for solidarity. Sociologists have long known that a social group threatened with unwanted outside intervention tends to become more cohesive, and the rise of a sense of beleaguered solidarity among white southerners in the 1950's was further evidence of this general social tendency. Capitalizing on the atmosphere thus created, massive resistance proponents sought, as Samuel Lubell put it, to hammer "southern opinion into an embattled, unified state of feeling which will brook no compromise."[1] Southern propagandists contributed substantially to this goal and often equated nonconformity with foreign ideologies and sectional disloyalty. Beyond this, the resistance attempted to systematize southern society by stamping out dissent and organizing the entire regional community in defense of the "southern way of life."

The Citizens' Councils were the cutting edge of the drive for regimented orthodoxy. "There are 40 million white Southerners and only 300 thousand members of the NAACP in the entire Nation," executive secretary Robert Patterson stated in the Mississippi association's second *Annual Report*. "Forty million white Southerners, or a fraction thereof, if properly organized, can be a power in this Nation," he wrote, "but they must be thoroughly organized from the town and county level up."[2]

---

[1] Lubell, *Revolt of the Moderates*, 197. See also Frank E. Vandiver, "The Southerner as Extremist," in Vandiver (ed.), *The Idea of the South*, 43–55.

[2] Association of Citizens' Councils of Mississippi, *2nd Annual Report* (1956), 2. See also Citizens' Councils of America, *The Citizens' Council* (Greenwood, n.d.), and Citizens' Councils of Alabama, *The Citizens' Council: The South's Only Answer* (Montgomery, n.d.).

Senator James O. Eastland advised a Council audience: "There is only one prescription for victory. As we prepare to fight this is basic: Organization."[3] Council administrator William J. Simmons demanded "organization" and *"more* organization," even "some degree of military discipline."[4] From the beginning, Council spokesmen had conceived of their movement's providing "solid and unified backing of circuit clerks, sheriffs, and local and state officials in the proper discharge of the sworn duties."[5] But the Councils' goal of organized southern unity went well beyond the political field. The ineffectiveness of state government "in the battle in the fields of Education and Religion," Simmons stated, was a prime reason for the existence of a citizens' movement.[6] "The Citizens' Councils think and plan as a group," a Mississippi association *Annual Report* explained, "and then they are able to act as individuals within their various churches, schools and any other organization to which they may belong."[7] The maintenance of white supremacy required not only the efforts of political leaders but also a united public led by the Citizens' Councils.

In pursuit of this objective the Councils developed substantial statewide organizational structures. Council chapters normally established four basic committees to deal with particularly significant areas of interest. Information and Education Committees endeavored to reinforce devotion to the status quo both by distributing state Council literature in the local community and by carrying out their own grass roots propaganda campaigns. Political and Elections Committees institutionalized the Councils' role as political pressure groups by investigating and publishing the racial views of political candidates. These committees also concerned themselves with countering Negro voting influence and discouraging Negro voter registration. Membership and Finance Committees dealt with those perennial problems faced by many another organization. Ultimately, the Councils' hopes of being the vanguard of a solid South rested heavily upon the success of their recruiting, and much of the Councils' energy was absorbed in the omnipresent struggle to win and retain dues paying members. Finally, model Council chapters included Legal Advisory

[3] *Eastland Address*, 7.
[4] As quoted in Silver, *Mississippi: The Closed Society*, 41, and Carter, *The South Strikes Back*, 163.
[5] Association of Citizens' Councils of Mississippi, *Annual Report* (1955), 1.
[6] As quoted in Carter, *The South Strikes Back*, 163.
[7] Association of Citizens' Councils of Mississippi, *2nd Annual Report* (1956), 2.

Committees to keep abreast of general legal developments, anticipate the activities of "agitators," and suggest segregationist countermeasures. Above the local groups, which represented counties, school districts, towns, urban neighborhoods or precincts, or some other limited geographical area, were district associations usually composed of representatives from local Councils in congressional districts, judicial circuits, or urban or metropolitan areas. Next in the hierarchy, state associations coordinated intercouncil affairs, directed membership drives, acted as propaganda centers, plotted general strategy, and undertook other projects of a broader nature. Finally, the regional Citizens' Councils of America performed a planning and liaison function among state groups.[8]

Roy V. Harris, then president of the Citizens' Councils of America, was harshly specific in outlining a six-point program for translating this penchant for organization into specific policy. Addressing a Citizens' Council rally in Orlando, Florida, Harris called for distilling the issues in southern political campaigns to one question: "Who's the strongest for segregation?" He proposed organizing boycotts against all businessmen who were not members of white supremacy organizations or who did not support Citizens' Council aims and "straightening out . . . clergymen who preach the brotherhood of man." Harris further recommended driving Ralph McGill, publisher of the Atlanta *Constitution*, "clean out of the state of Georgia"; waging a determined war against the national mass media; and totally opposing "by every means and at every cost" court decisions that favored racial integration. "We are engaged in the greatest cause and the greatest crusade in the history of mankind," Harris told the Florida audience, and in this great struggle there was no middle ground: "If you're a white man, then it's time to stand up with us, or black your face and get on the other side."[9] Harris was probably the most incautious proponent of segregation among top Council leaders, and his recommendations may have overstated the movement's aims. Yet, despite exaggeration, the Georgian had summarized the essence of the Councils' approach to questions of conformity and dissent in the South. A militant movement based on an either-for-us-or-against-us

---

[8] *The Citizens' Council*, November, 1955, June, 1956; Citizens' Councils of America, *The Citizens' Council;* Citizens' Councils of Alabama, *The Citizens' Council;* Association of Citizens' Councils of Mississippi, *2nd Annual Report* (1956), *4th Annual Report* (1958); James, "The South's Own Civil War," 18–19; Carter, *The South Strikes Back*, 199; W. D. Workman, in Charleston *News and Courier*, July 1, 1956; Chattanooga *Times*, March 12, 1956; Quint, *Profile in Black and White*, 48–50.
[9] As quoted in Chattanooga *Times*, September 22, 1958.

psychology could only encourage the intolerance, reprisal, and coercion that Harris openly advocated.

Although Council spokesmen were fond of picturing the Councils as examples of "town meeting" democracy, in practice they more closely resembled vigilante committees. The primary function of local organizations was to serve as guardians of community orthodoxy, and they often performed this role by ferreting out and crushing deviant behavior. At first, Council leaders endorsed economic intimidation as a proper instrument of retribution, advising that local Councils authorize their Legal Advisory Committees to recommend economic sanctions against "troublemakers." An Alabama spokesman bluntly stated: "The white population in this county controls the money and this is an advantage that the Council will use in a fight to legally maintain complete segregation of the races." Continuing, he explained that "We intend to make it difficult, if not impossible, for any Negro who advocates desegregation to find and hold a job, get credit or renew a mortgage."[10] Herman Talmadge advised a Citizens' Council group in the same state: "Anyone who sells the South down the river, don't let him eat at your table, don't let him trade at your filling station and don't let him trade at your store."[11]

When NAACP chapters in the South sponsored petitions asking for school desegregation in the summer of 1955, the Councils played a prominent role in determining the reaction of Deep South whites. In communities such as Yazoo City, Mississippi, and Orangeburg, South Carolina, local Councils published the names of Negroes who signed petitions. Although suggesting no specific action but merely listing the names of signers, a wave of firings and cancellations of credit quickly followed. More often, however, a Negro who signed a petition or who simply sought to register as a voter was visited by a prominent white citizen who suggested that such behavior was not proper for a "colored person" wishing "to stay here in peace." Similar visits to the employer, creditors, landlord, or anyone else the Negro deviate did business with followed when necessary. Not infrequently, segregationist partisans also dealt summarily with white citizens whose pronouncements or actions dissented from the prevailing view of what constituted racial orthodoxy.[12]

[10] Nashville *Tennessean*, November 28, 1954, quoting Alston Keith of Dallas County.
[11] As quoted by Fred Taylor, in Birmingham *News*, June 23, 1955.
[12] On the Citizens' Councils and economic intimidation, see Carter, *The South Strikes Back*, 17–33; Martin, *The Deep South Says "Never"*, 4–31; Cook, *The Segregationists*, 53; Quint, *Profile in Black and White*, 32; Dan Wakefield, *Revolt in the South* (New York, 1960), 45; "Resistance Groups of South Carolina," 20–22; Bem Price, in Montgomery *Advertiser*,

Incidents of economic retaliation against nonconformists were widespread
in the South, but organized, sustained pressure of the type described
above was largely confined to areas of Citizens' Council strength in the
Deep South. The results demonstrated the method's effectiveness. In
counties in Mississippi, Alabama, and South Carolina, numerous Negro
petitioners withdrew their names, and the petitions were not followed
with further requests or court cases.[13] The Councils were, of course, by
no means alone responsible for the truculence of white society in the
Deep South. As John Dollard, in his study of a southern community, had
long before observed, "Southerntown is a veritable Cheka in its vigilance
on caste matters."[14] The Councils did, however, serve as the nucleus,
the cementing force, that gave direction to white reaction.

For various reasons, Council spokesmen soon disavowed—or at least
qualified their endorsement of—the open, aggressive use of economic
intimidation as an instrument of policy. The discovery that such coercion,
despite its success, was also a substantial liability was in part responsible
for this tactical shift. The wide employment of economic reprisal during
the summer of 1955 coincided with the murders of Emmett Till and three
Negro civil rights activists in Mississippi to create what the NAACP
termed a "state of fury" in the South.[15] The result was a great amount
of national publicity critical of the South and the Councils. Economic
coercion—the critics called it an economic lynch law—also proved a
two-edged sword. Negro counterboycotts, especially in Orangeburg,
South Carolina, demonstrated the dangers of this type warfare in black-
belt counties where Negroes were an important part of the consumer
public. The spread of economic strife threatened to get even farther out
of hand when Mississippi segregationists launched boycotts against three

August 22, 1955; *Southern School News*, January, 1955; Atlanta *Journal*, September 8,
1955; and Jackson *Daily News*, December 11, 1955. For the fate of white residents of
Providence Farm, Holmes County, Mississippi, and Koinonia Farm, Sumter County,
Georgia, see *Southern School News*, October, November, 1955, and Atlanta *Journal*, April
14–22, 1957. And see additionally Peters, *The Southern Temper*, 21–56; and Southeastern
Office of the American Friends Service Committee, Department of Racial and Cultural
Relations of the National Council of Churches of Christ in the United States of America,
and the Southern Regional Council, *Intimidation, Reprisal, and Violence in the South's Racial
Crisis* (Atlanta, 1959), 9–14, hereinafter cited by title only.

[13] *Southern School News*, September-December, 1955; Martin, *The Deep South Says
"Never"*, 30–31.

[14] John Dollard, *Caste and Class in a Southern Town* (New Haven, 1937), 48.

[15] Memphis *Commercial Appeal*, September 8, 1955, quoting an NAACP spokesman.
See, for example, the full-page NAACP advertisement, "Help End Racial Tyranny in
Mississippi," which combines a lengthy list of incidents of violence and reprisal with
an effective plea for financial support. New York *Times*, October 3, 1955.

national manufacturing firms.[16] The small-town businessmen and property owners flocking to the Councils' standard no doubt sensed the dangers to normal property and business relationships inherent in such activity. More fundamentally, however, as the Councils emerged as a powerful force in the South and as white reaction to social change stiffened, the need for such crude tactics declined. Over wide areas of the South, particularly those areas that supported the Council movement, "public opinion itself," as Ralph McGill has observed, "became a sort of mob which terrorized or silenced any who might dare oppose it."[17] The cities, even in the Deep South, offered more challenges to defenders of the segregationist faith, but urban impersonality and ghettos circumscribed the effectiveness of tactics developed in and suited to a town and village environment.

Council leaders, with the exception of a few ultra-extremists such as Roy Harris, responded to the changing situation with a compromise policy that formally disavowed economic reprisal while at the same time leaving local chapters free to adopt whatever measures they wished. "We do not recommend economic pressure," Patterson explained. "That's false propaganda from the press. But of course we don't denounce 'freedom of choice' in business arrangements. If employers fire their help, that's their business."[18] Thus, when more than half of the Negro signers of a desegregation petition lost their jobs in Selma, Alabama, a Council spokesman (the same spokesman who, one year before, had been so direct in his advocacy of the uses of economics) announced that the Councils deserved neither "credit or censure" for this "spontaneous reaction" by white employers.[19] The economic prospects for dissidents who advocated integration remained perilous in the rural, small-town South.[20] And

---

[16] *Southern School News*, September-December, 1955; Cook, *The Segregationists*, 58–59.

[17] Ralph McGill, *The South and the Southerner* (Boston, 1963), 252.

[18] As quoted in Wakefield, *Revolt in the South*, 45. As an unnamed observer summarized the transition: "The original Council people were astonished. They didn't realize they were doing anything controversial. They lived by the old ethos—the Negro is dependent and if he gets out of line you put the squeeze on him. All at once this was wrong So they backed off. Now they disavow economic pressure. But they've continued to use it, surreptitiously." Martin, *The Deep South Says "Never"*, 26.

[19] As quoted in Louisville *Courier-Journal*, September 9, 1955.

[20] Indeed, a second wave of reprisals swept through the Deep South in the mid-1960's, claiming the occupational livelihoods of a larger number of people than the economic retaliations of the mid-1950's. Compare *Intimidation, Reprisal, and Violence in the South's Racial Crisis* with Southern Regional Council and the American Jewish Committee Institute of Human Relations, *The Continuing Crisis: An Assessment of New Racial Tensions in the South* (Atlanta, 1966).

Negroes continued on occasion to use economic pressure against white segregationists.[21] But, by the end of 1955, Council leaders were directing their attention to other programs, and the economic purge as an open and organized policy fell into disuse for the remainder of the decade.

Economic intimidation, while clearly serving as a warning to the Negro community as a whole, was nominally aimed at "agitators" who sought to disrupt the normally tranquil state of southern race relations. Like segregationists generally, Council spokesmen failed to perceive the depth of Negro discontent with the system,[22] and, like the politicians who thought Negro leaders would accept "voluntary" plans of segregation, the Councils initiated early experiments in interracial cooperation. In South Carolina some local Councils added a Race Relations Committee designed to encourage acceptance of the status quo among Negro leaders ("other than those belonging to the NAACP or other integration groups," of course).[23] Mississippi segregationists actually fostered the formation of a Negro Citizens' Council, the existence of which, needless to add, was transitory.[24] These efforts proved abortive; on the whole, white supremacy groups demonstrated both more enthusiasm and more effectiveness in programs that worked on, rather than with, the Negro minority.

Council strategists were only too well aware that urban diversity was a central flaw in their vision of a solid southern society. While generally relying upon malapportionment and emotionalism to check the stirrings of urban moderation, the Councils also turned again to organization as the vehicle for transferring small-town unity into the cities. Ambitious Council chapters in urban areas of Mississippi, Alabama, and Louisiana undertook door-to-door canvasses—"freedom of choice" surveys they were sometimes called—to promote both Council membership and white solidarity. In Jackson, Mississippi, where the segregationist census was pushed most aggressively, the Council dispatched throughout the city volunteers armed with questionnaires designed "to determine the expected conduct of our citizens when and if an attempt is made to integrate

[21] Notable examples were a buying strike in Tuskegee, Alabama, and the bus boycotts in Montgomery and Tallahassee. *Southern School News*, January-December, 1956, August-October, 1957.

[22] See Matthews and Prothro, "Southern Racial Attitudes: Conflict, Awareness and Political Change," 108–21.

[23] *The Citizens' Council*, June, 1956.

[24] *Ibid.*, February, 1956; *Delta Democrat-Times*, July 24, 1955.

our public schools."[25] Among the dozen questions posed to Jackson's white citizens were inquiries concerning whether parents would refuse to send their children to integrated schools, whether residents agreed with Council aims, whether they would cooperate with the Council leadership in an "emergency," and whether they were or would like to become members of the Citizens' Council. The results of the poll revealed that white Jacksonians were virtually unanimous in answering yes to the first three questions (at least when responding to recorded inquiries by representatives of the Council). The project also apparently netted the chapter a substantial number of new members.[26] Surveys of a similar nature were launched, sometimes with considerable fanfare, in such cities as New Orleans and Montgomery, but only in a few Mississippi communities—notably Jackson, McComb, and Greenwood—were the Councils able to inspire an adequate number of pollsters with sufficient zeal to come anywhere close to completing such a Herculean project.[27] The block-to-block census proved workable only in those cities where the white population was already substantially solid in its commitment to the resistance.

But most of all, the Councils conceived of southern solidarity in political terms. Increasingly, they concentrated their organizational talents on this field. From the beginning, of course, they had functioned as political pressure groups. The Councils were "non-partisan in nature," editorialized *The Citizens' Council*. "But there is a vast difference between being non-partisan and being non-political."[28] This tendency became more pronounced following the tactical shift away from economic coercion and the rise of a massive resistance program. State Council leaders urged local chapter members and white people generally to study political candidates carefully and "elect men to public office who are courageous, intelligent, patriotic and who have conservative beliefs regarding the application of constitutional government."[29]

A favorite tactic in several states was the political questionnaire. The

[25] The Council questionnaire is reprinted in the Jackson *Daily News*, April 25, 1958.

[26] *Delta Democrat-Times*, June 3, 1958; Silver, *Mississippi: The Closed Society*, 41.

[27] *Delta Democrat-Times*, June 3, 1958; Smith, *Congressman from Mississippi*, 272; New Orleans *Times-Picayune*, January 27, 1956; Birmingham *News*, October 2, 1958. The Greater New Orleans Citizens' Council held a mass rally to inaugurate their block-to-block drive in search of 50,000 members. Anthony, "Resistance!," 5.

[28] *The Citizens' Council*, September, 1960.

[29] Association of Citizens' Councils of Mississippi to local chapters, July, 1955, mimeographed memorandum, Southern Regional Council files.

Councils sought to pledge public officials to orthodoxy by sending standard questions to all candidates for major offices. The answers were then passed on to local chapters and made available to the state news media. Local chapters sometimes followed this same procedure toward candidates for local offices. William Rainach and his Council associates in Louisiana devised the first such segregationist questionnaire used in a statewide election, offering five questions for each gubernatorial candidate in the 1956 primary contest. The inquiries concerned general attitudes about devotion to segregation, opposition to Negro voting, and, more specifically, the candidate's willingness to close the public schools to avoid desegregation. All major candidates answered with affirmative, though in some cases qualified, responses.[30] Similar questionnaires were soon being used in Alabama, South Carolina, and elsewhere. The effectiveness of these tactics is difficult to gauge. In South Carolina, where the Councils showed taste and finesse in devising and distributing the questionnaires, virtually all serious candidates responded with prosegregation answers.[31] In Alabama, where the questions were brusquely phrased and required that candidates' signatures be notarized, only 51 of 104 candidates queried returned the documents. Nevertheless, the questionnaires did gain a certain prestige in the 1956 Alabama elections. Governor James Folsom and a number of candidates associated with and sometimes endorsed by him ignored the Council forms, but Folsom's opponents for national committeeman and a number of other candidates who were highly critical of the governor's policies returned the forms with the responses that the questions were designed to elicit. The election results were a disaster for Folsom and his closest allies. While there was no evidence that the questionnaires per se had any significant effect on the balloting, the Councils did offer effective support to the governor's chief opponent and claimed that they "could take some credit" for the outcome.[32] The impact of the Alabama election was heightened by the North Carolina Patriots' role in the defeat of the two representatives who failed to sign the Southern Manifesto. In states of lesser resistance strength, such as Tennessee, the white supremacy questionnaires were considerably

[30] New Orleans *Times-Picayune*, December 9, 1955, January 4, 1956.

[31] "Resistance Groups of South Carolina," 12–13; Charleston *News and Courier*, May 27, 1956.

[32] Birmingham *News*, May 11, 1956, quoting John H. Whitley. See also Fred Taylor, in *ibid.*, March 25, April 15, May 2, 8, 1956; Bob Ingram, in Montgomery *Advertiser*, April 29, 1956; *Southern School News*, May, June, 1956; and Anthony, "A Survey of the Resistance Groups of Alabama," 14.

less intimidating.[33] Overall, the Councils' campaign activities combined with other pressures in each state to give a politician one more reason for perceiving that the safest course in racial matters was to the right of the path he might have taken.

The Councils also employed other tactics familiar to pressure groups generally. Their propaganda activity, while rarely directed toward a specific candidate or faction, helped to color the political atmosphere. With few exceptions, white supremacy groups actively lobbied in state legislatures, and, like other special interest groups with small-town ties, they often received a sympathetic hearing. This was particularly true in Mississippi, Louisiana, Alabama, and Virginia, where important legislators were closely associated with the Council movement. Segregationist lobbies also functioned with some apparent success in Texas, Florida, Tennessee, and South Carolina.[34] The Councils strove to counter political pressure activities of moderate and integrationist groups and to rally support behind segregationist public officials. Thus, when 179 New Orleans citizens signed a petition urging the Orleans Parish school board to comply with the *Brown* decision, the Greater New Orleans Citizens' Council answered within two weeks with a petition containing almost 15,000 signatures demanding a continuation of segregation.[35] Not infrequently, individual Council leaders attempted to use their popular images as crusading segregationists for their own political advancement. The campaigns of William Rainach of Louisiana, James D. Johnson of Arkansas, Sumter Lowery of Florida, I. Beverly Lake of North Carolina, William Bodenhamer of Georgia, and Sam Engelhardt of Alabama were among the more obvious examples of leaders of the Council movement who ran for major statewide offices. Although usually unsuccessful (all the aspirants just mentioned met defeat), such candidacies tended further to color the southern political atmosphere. Through these tactics, the Councils were able to make a significant direct impact on southern politics and to orient the governmental process more sharply toward social reaction.[36]

[33] See Nashville *Banner*, July 11, 25–29, 1956. Only about one-third of the candidates in Tennessee responded to the Tennessee Federation for Constitutional Government questionnaires.

[34] See Chapter 6.

[35] Anthony, "Resistance!," 5; New Orleans *Times-Picayune*, September 27, 1955.

[36] The Councils' growing concern with politics did not mean that the movement's leaders had lost their fear of, or their contempt for, professional politicians. Instead, Council leaders hoped to make the politicians dependent on the Councils, to demonstrate

The Council leadership's attention to political matters accompanied the rise of interposition and greater emphasis on "legal" methods of resistance. Segregationist spokesmen talked loosely of the maintenance of segregation by "legal" means, but, like other resistance catchphrases, the term had more specific implications. When applied broadly to the desegregation controversy, "legal" opposition was merely a denial of the constitutional validity of the *Brown* decision and thus a part of the general interposition argument. When applied to homestate matters, the slogan was acutely pertinent to the question of conformity and dissent in the South. Here, it referred to the enforcement of social orthodoxy through the exercise of the coercive power of the state; "legal" methods of resistance meant violation of the law through properly constituted authority. Professor Oscar Handlin has observed that "The Councils . . . offered a means of protest to men of substance who did not wish violence or disorder, but who somehow hoped to subvert the law while still clinging to its forms and procedures."[37] "Legal" opposition was the practical application of this attitude to public policy. "The law is on our side," State Senator Walter Givhan told an Alabama Council audience, "because you are the jury."[38] If the *Brown* decision was "unconstitutional," state segregation laws remained valid, and state and local officials were duty bound to enforce them. As a former United States senator from Alabama explained: "We'll have no violence, no night riding, no arson, no intimidation, but a solid stand that the people back up our state law."[39]

A notable example of the Councils' employment of "legal" means to protect white supremacy was in the field of voter registration. Particularly in Louisiana, Council activists undertook to enforce voter qualification requirements and to purge "unqualified" voters from the rolls. The Louisiana constitution contained a literacy and understanding clause, and the Rainach Committee encouraged its strict application by conducting classes for voter registrars throughout the state. The state constitution also permitted any two registered voters to challenge the

---

that "we're bigger than they are." See Martin, *The Deep South Says "Never"*, 142. As Mississippi Association spokesmen explained: "Politicians don't lead, they follow. They find out which way the people are going and then they get in front of them so that they can lead them there." *2nd Annual Report* (1956), 3.

[37] Oscar Handlin, *Fire-Bell in the Night: The Crisis in Civil Rights* (Boston, 1964), 40.

[38] As quoted in New York *Times*, February 7, 1956.

[39] *Ibid.*, quoting J. Robin Swift, chairman of the Escambia County Citizens' Council chapter.

qualifications of any other registrant. On the basis of this provision, Council members in thirteen parishes succeeded in removing some eleven thousand Negroes from the voter lists during the winter of 1956–57, and other purges followed during the late 1950's. As a Louisiana Council spokesman explained, "The problem of Negro registration will be solved in a legal way."[40]

Private pressure from the Citizens' Councils, public pressure from state governments, and the general demand for conformity generated by the prevailing atmosphere among the white population all took their toll on the right of dissent. And there was yet another intimidating factor that was less oriented toward "legal" methods of coercion. The Ku Klux Klan exercised an influence that could easily be underrated. In the dynamics of the drive for southern solidarity, the hooded defenders of Anglo-Saxon supremacy found a definite role, and they performed it in the face of enormous obstacles. The Klan lacked political power, organization, and respectability. Yet it served as the crucible where those of violent inclination could meet with others of violent inclination in an atmosphere of hooded secrecy that lent itself to violence. This everpresent threat of physical retribution was a significant factor in encouraging those who would dissent to hold their peace.

Politically, the Ku Klux Klan was a relatively minor force during the 1950's. Only in Alabama did it win respect from state-level politicians. Governor Folsom chose his words rather carefully when commenting on the Klan. In 1957 the governor was quoted as saying that "I have a lot of good friends in the Klan. . . ." Although Folsom specifically refused to endorse the order, he added that it "could be a good, genuine fraternal organization."[41] Folsom's statement was as near as the Klan came, during the 1950's, to receiving the endorsement of a major southern politician. Similarly, John Patterson, in his successful bid to become Folsom's successor as governor, came closer to openly seeking Klan support than any other important officeholder. Patterson solicited the backing of individuals associated with the Klan, and in some cases Klan officers—notably Robert M. Shelton, leader of the largest sheeted frater-

---

[40] As quoted in *Pro-Segregation Groups in the South*, 7, which also reprints the pertinent part of the Louisiana Constitution. See Price, *The Negro and the Ballot in the South*, 15–20; Kenneth N. Vines, "A Louisiana Parish: Wholesale Purge," in Price, *The Negro and the Ballot in the South*, 34–46; United States Commission on Civil Rights, *Report, 1959* (Washington, 1959), 101–106; and Association of Citizens' Councils of Louisiana, Inc., *Voter Qualification Laws in Louisiana: The Key to Victory in the Segregation Struggle* (n.p., 1958).

[41] As quoted by Bob Ingram, in Montgomery *Advertiser*, September 11, 1957.

nity in the state—actively campaigned for Patterson.[42] Elsewhere, the Klan sometimes had influence on the local level, but, even then, it was rare indeed to find a politician who would speak before or associate himself with the secret order.[43]

The Klan's organizational network could only be described as chaotic. From 1915 to 1944 the Klan had maintained a basic unity, with all Klansmen at least nominally recognizing the suzerainty of one Imperial Wizard. But in 1944 pressure from the Internal Revenue Service for payment of back taxes led to dissolution of the Invisible Empire, Knights of the Ku Klux Klan, which by this time bore faint resemblance to the powerful organization it had been twenty years before. Its place was filled by the Association of Georgia Klans, an unincorporated alliance headed by Dr. Samuel Green of Atlanta as Grand Dragon (a title of lesser rank than Imperial Wizard). After two years of relative inactivity, the Klan symbolically announced its post-World War II revival in 1946 with an initiation ceremony at Stone Mountain, Georgia, birthplace of the second Ku Klux Klan. In 1949, Green became Imperial Wizard in an attempt to reunite the forces of the Invisible Empire. Green's death just afterward thwarted the effort, however, and the struggle for succession that followed gave impetus to centrifugal tendencies which had long existed within the Klan. By the end of 1949, almost a dozen independent organizations had emerged.[44]

The Klan drifted through the early 1950's, burdened by bickering, rivalry, and a shortage of new recruits, until the *Brown* decision gave the hooded segregationists a mission. In 1955 the U.S. Klans, Knights of the Ku Klux Klan, Inc., received a Georgia charter and called for the allegiance of all knights of the order. Growing out of the Association of Georgia Klans, this group claimed to be the legitimate successor of the Invisible Empire, and its leader, Eldon L. Edwards, an Atlanta paint sprayer, bore the title Imperial Wizard.[45] The U.S. Klans, Knights

[42] *Ibid.*, May 15, 24, 1958, January 3, May 3, August 16, 1959, January 27, 1960; Birmingham *News*, May 15, 1958, October 11, 1959, January 28, 1960.

[43] To my knowledge, State Senator Albert Davis of Aliceville, Pickens County, Alabama, was the only officeholding politician in the South who habitually spoke before Ku Klux Klan rallies. See Montgomery *Advertiser*, May 19, 1957, December 11, 1958; Chattanooga *Times*, August 27, 1956.

[44] Arnold S. Rice, *The Ku Klux Klan in American Politics* (Washington, 1962), 108–18; David M. Chalmers, *Hooded Americanism: The First Century of the Ku Klux Klan, 1865–1965* (New York, 1965), 319–42.

[45] "U.S. Knights of the Ku Klux Klan" (unpublished Southern Regional Council field report, n.d. [1956]); Robert S. Bird, in New York *Herald-Tribune*, April 23, 1957;

of the Ku Klux Klan, Inc., established active organizations in Georgia, Alabama, South Carolina, and Florida, and less vigorous groups emerged in North Carolina, Louisiana, Tennessee, and Arkansas.

The revival of interstate organization did not, however, mean a return to Klan unity. Quite the reverse. Edwards and his sheeted associates were hounded by competing Imperial Wizards and Grand Dragons by the score. In Alabama there were at least six independent organizations in addition to the U.S. Klans, Knights of the Ku Klux Klan.[46] In South Carolina the Edwards group had at least six rivals,[47] and in Florida at least four.[48] Even in Georgia, the U.S. Klans faced competition.[49] Not infrequently, Edwards' competitors were former lieutenants who severed relations with the home office and established their own empires or who created what Edwards called "outlaw splinter groups" after having been fired by the Imperial Wizard "for treason, or what have you."[50] Often in states where the Klan was active, local Klaverns emerged as small independent Klans unassociated with any larger group.[51]

Furthermore, there were numerous fringe organizations which did not include Ku Klux Klan in their titles. Frederick John Kasper's Seaboard White Citizens' Councils (earlier called White Citizens' Councils), Asa Carter's Alabama Citizens' Councils (earlier called North Alabama

---

his series on the Ku Klux Klan in the *Herald-Tribune*, April 14–28, 1957, is an able journalistic study.

[46] These included Dixie Ku Klux Klan; Original Ku Klux Klan of the Confederacy; Gulf Coast Ku Klux Klan; Alabama Ku Klux Klan; Alabama Knights of the Ku Klux Klan; and Knights of the Ku Klux Klan of the Confederacy. Harrison E. Salisbury, New York *Times*, April 13, 1960; Birmingham *News*, June 14, July 24, 1957; Alabama Council on Human Relations, Inc., "Pro-Segregation Group Trends," 2–3.

[47] These included South Carolina Klans; Knights of the Ku Klux Klans; National Klan of South Carolina; South Carolina Knights of the Ku Klux Klan; Association of South Carolina Klans; York County Klan; and Greenville County Klan. Charlotte *Observer*, January 26, 1958; Bird, in New York *Herald-Tribune*, April 23, 1957.

[48] These included Florida Klans; Knights of the Ku Klux Klan; Southern Knights of the Ku Klux Klan; U.S. Klans; and Association of Florida Klans. Bird, in New York *Herald-Tribune*, April 24, 1957; Miami *Herald*, August 11, 1955.

[49] From such groups as the U.S. Klans, Inc., of Atlanta and the Christian Knights of the Ku Klux Klan. Arkansas *Gazette*, June 7, 1957; Atlanta *Journal*, February 29, 1960.

[50] As quoted by Douglas Kiker, in Atlanta *Journal*, February 29, 1960.

[51] This chaotic situation was further complicated by the tendency of Klan leaders to reorganize their "outfits" under new names. Thus Bill Hendrix, Grand Dragon of the Southern Knights of the Ku Klux Klan of Florida, abrogated this fraternity and formed the Knights of the White Camellia. During the same period he also tried to revive an older group called the American Confederate Army and attempted to consolidate a number of independent Klans into a multi-state Knights of the Ku Klux Klan. Miami *Herald*, January 24, 1957; Charleston *News and Courier*, April 23, 1957; "U.S. Knights of the Ku Klux Klan."

Citizens' Councils), and what one writer termed "the unaffiliated bigot group" that revolved around Rear Admiral (ret.) John G. Crommelin of Alabama were among the better known.[52] Such factions tended to gravitate toward the Ku Klux Klan. Kasper became a featured speaker on the Klan circuit, and Carter became the head of his own Klan, the Original Ku Klux Klan of the Confederacy.[53]

The U.S. Klans failed to establish institutional unity within the order, and various efforts by the other Klan and fringe groups were even less successful. Formation of the Knights of the Ku Klux Klan, organized by Bill Hendrix of Florida; the Knights of the Ku Klux Klan, Inc., with a former officer in Edwards' group as Imperial Wizard; and the National States' Rights Party, which included representatives of Klans and the Nazi Party, were among several attempts to consolidate the numerous smaller organizations.[54] None of these unity movements accomplished its objectives, although the National States' Rights Party lived on as a small but highly active fringe group. "By 1958," Professor Arnold S. Rice has observed, "there were so many different splinter groups that the tabulation of them is unreliable."[55]

The Ku Klux Klan seemed incapable of promoting competent leaders, and this failure was to a large extent the result of institutional factors. Generally, the Klan's membership, which was drawn almost exclusively from lower socio-economic groups in southern white society, simply lacked the education and sophistication to hold its leaders accountable for their actions.[56] Furthermore, the Klan, unlike the Citizens' Councils, failed to attract support from established elements of the southern power structure and thus could not rely upon accustomed authority to provide leadership and stability. The secrecy, the excessive concern for status, and the thinly veiled propensity for violence that permeated Klan organizations exaggerated this unstructured situation. Klan leaders tended to

[52] Wakefield, *Revolt in the South*, 63.
[53] *Southern School News*, October, 1956, February-April, 1957; Chalmers, *Hooded Americanism*, 344–47.
[54] Charleston *News and Courier*, April 23, 1956; Nashville *Tennessean*, December 3, 1958; Atlanta *Journal*, February 29, 1960.
[55] Rice, *The Ku Klux Klan in American Politics*, 122.
[56] James W. Vander Zanden, "The Klan Revival," *American Journal of Sociology*, LXV (March, 1960), 456–62; Vander Zanden, "A Note on the Theory of Social Movements," 6; Bird, in New York *Herald-Tribune*, April 16, 1957; David M. Chalmers, "The Ku Klux Klan and the Radical Right," in *The Radical Right: Proceedings of the Sixth Annual Intergroup Relations Conference at the University of Houston, Houston, Texas, March 27, 1965* (n.p., n.d.), 4.

emerge in a haphazard fashion, Elmer Gantry-like—relying heavily upon sheer gall and often motivated by status-psychological factors and by the desire for money, or power, or both. Often they were men of highly questionable backgrounds, which not infrequently included police records.[57] Few demonstrated any noticeable talent for organization or even for effective rabble-rousing. Many regarded the order as a vehicle for personal gain, and, more often than not, the catalyst for splits within the Klan was nothing more than quarrels over the division of funds received from membership dues and sale of Klan regalia.[58] Spokesmen spent a substantial amount of time and energy denouncing each other and thus undermining the prestige of the whole order.

With its organizational defects and its ineffective leadership, the Klan stumbled along from one disaster to the next. The most famous such catastrophe occurred in North Carolina when James W. "Catfish" Cole and his North Carolina Knights of the Ku Klux Klan, the largest Klan organization in the state, decided to teach an Indian tribe in Robeson County to have a proper respect for white supremacy. After burning a cross and undertaking other advance publicity, the Klan held its big rally in a field near the town of Maxton. None of the local people showed up for the rally, except for the thousand or so gun-toting Indians, some of them wearing warpaint, who surrounded the Klan meeting place. Encouraged perhaps by the bullets being fired into the air by the encroaching ring of redskins, the Klansmen reached a quick consensus that discretion was surely the better alternative, and white-sheeted people were soon fleeing panic-stricken in all directions.[59] The whole affair became a nationally publicized embarrassment for the Klan.

And then there was the case of John Kasper, a fiery public speaker

[57] As a somewhat extreme example, the most successful North Carolina organizer was James W. "Catfish" Cole. The Raleigh *News and Observer*, January 21, 1958, outlined his experiences with the law: 1940, charged with assault; 1941, charged with reckless driving and fined for driving without a license; charged with perjury for false statements made to obtain a driver's license, fined, and license revoked; 1943, charged with assault and resisting arrest and fined; 1951, charged with drunken driving; charged with assault with a deadly weapon. Cole had been, among other things, a circus pitchman and a self-styled Baptist minister.

[58] See Bird's discussion of Klan leaders in the New York *Herald-Tribune*, April 16, 1957, and the sketches of Klan leaders in Chalmers, *Hooded Americanism*, 335–74. That there were also status-psychological factors involved in Klan factionalism is made clear by Vander Zanden, "The Klan Revival," 459–60.

[59] Since the Klan security guard at the meeting was also armed, the confrontation was a deadly serious encounter. No one, however, was seriously hurt. The incident is recounted in numerous sources. The most perceptive account is probably that of Wayne Phillips, in New York *Times*, January 26, 1958.

whom, as historian David M. Chalmers put it, "the hooded knights took . . . to their hearts as one of their own."[60] When a Florida investigating committee called Kasper to testify, the Miami *Herald* disclosed that Kasper had dated a Negro girl and participated in integrated social functions while running a book store in New York. Kasper admitted before the committee that the "charges" were true, and he was denounced by a number of red-faced Klansmen.[61] In Alabama, the leader of the state's most active sheeted defenders of morals and virtue, a 45-year-old widower with six children, became involved in a highly publicized scandal when he married a 15-year-old girl under circumstances so unusual that only the young lady's pregnancy prevented her parents from having the marriage annulled.[62] And there were also recurring incidents like the "giant," four-state rally of Klansmen at Columbus, Georgia, in late 1956. The city government denied the Klan use of the baseball park, and, after many trials and tribulations, the giant four-state rally culminated with three Klansmen obligingly burning a cross for the benefit of a few newspaper reporters and policemen.[63]

Throughout most of the South, politicians, news media, and community leaders kept up a running attack on the Invisible Empire.[64] As in Columbus, government officials often denied use of public facilities for Klan meetings. State officials sometimes refused to grant charters to Klan organizations, and two states investigated the order.[65] Although government authorities normally showed considerably less enthusiasm for measures designed to harass the Klan than they did for projects to hinder the NAACP, the hooded order clearly found the weight of governmental authority in hostile hands.

Yet, despite popular disapproval and the bumbling performance of its leaders, "the robe-and-hooded tradition," as Robert S. Bird has

---

[60] Chalmers, *Hooded Americanism*, 346.

[61] *Ibid.*, 346–47; John Boyles, in Miami *Herald*, March 12, 31, 1957.

[62] Chattanooga *Times*, June 10, 1957; Birmingham *News*, June 10, 1957.

[63] Atlanta *Journal*, November 26, 1956; *Christian Science Monitor*, December 3, 1956.

[64] There was an element of psychological and tactical expediency in the public attack on the Klan. Neobourbons could assault the "extremists," including both the NAACP and the Ku Klux Klan, and thus strengthen their conservative position. See, for example, William D. Workman, *The Case for the South* (New York, 1960), vii. White moderates, on the other hand, could ease their consciences by lambasting the Ku Klux Klan, which was a bit less formidable than the Citizens' Councils or the moral issue of segregation.

[65] In addition to the Florida investigation mentioned above, Attorney General Cook's office in Georgia probed Klan activities. See Macon *Telegraph*, August 26, 1955. On the general subject of relations between the Klan and government, see Rice, *Ku Klux Klan in American Politics*, 111–14.

observed, "has a prevailing power of its own even without 'organization' and 'leadership.' "[66] The Klan filled a psychological void felt by many of its recruits. It appealed most strongly to unskilled and semi-skilled workers, particularly those with a rural background who found themselves isolated and rootless in the city; to members of the lower-middle class, especially those in low-status occupations or marginal entrepreneurial enterprises who felt threatened and fearful of the future; and to lower-class rural whites, particularly those who lived in counties adjacent to burgeoning cities and who sensed the encroaching urban invasion of rural values.[67] The Klan offered an outlet for frustration and status insecurity, and it provided a sense of hell-of-a-fellow adventure to people who were likely to think more in terms of action than abstracts. As James W. Vander Zanden summarized the order's appeal: "The Klan gives such individuals a 'cause,' a sacred 'mission' with meaningfulness and purposiveness. . . . Frequently they cling to the Klan with blind devotion and religiosity, finding in it the source of virtue and strength. The secret attire and rituals serve to cement the 'in-group' bonds, to develop rapport and a sense of 'belonging.' "[68]

Klan recruiting efforts were almost entirely confined to the six states of Alabama, Florida, Georgia, North Carolina, South Carolina, and Tennessee. Membership figures were secret, of course, and estimates varied enormously. Three informed and competent observers who appraised the order's numerical strength during the late 1950's came up with the figures 10,000, 50,000, and more than 100,000.[69] At any rate, the Klan often attracted impressive crowds to its public rallies (just as it staged impressive flops, as noted earlier).[70] Klan motorcades were not uncommon in rural counties in several southeastern states.

But the strength of the Klan lay not in its numbers but in its capacity

[66] Bird, in New York *Herald-Tribune*, April 23, 1957.

[67] See *ibid.*, April 14–28, 1957, and Vander Zanden, "The Klan Revival." Bird concentrated his investigation on the Klan in rural communities; Vander Zanden emphasizes the Klan's appeal to urban dwellers.

[68] Vander Zanden, "A Note on the Theory of Social Movements," 6.

[69] Respectively, Vander Zanden, "The Klan Revival," 457; Bird, in New York *Herald-Tribune*, April 16, 1957; Rice, *The Ku Klux Klan in American Politics*, 118. In 1958, the Anti-Defamation League estimated Klan membership at between twenty-five and thirty thousand. *Intimidation, Reprisal, and Violence in the South's Racial Crisis*, 2.

[70] Klan rallies drawing more than a thousand spectators were not at all unusual. Less frequent were such rallies as those held in South Carolina by the U.S. Klans, Knights of the Ku Klux Klan, which attracted an estimated four thousand at Spartanburg, some forty-five hundred in Florence County, and reportedly above ten thousand in Union County. *The State*, October 8, 1956; Charleston *News and Courier*, March 4, 1956; Quint, *Profile in Black and White*, 39.

for violence. While "respectable" proponents of massive resistance championed "legal" means to maintain segregation, the Klan was not "respectable," and it was oriented toward a different standard of values. Its members, as Bird explained, "are extremists, defiant in the face of the Klan's general disrepute. Their ignorance is of the most arrogant kind, and is supported by a Klan ideology that offers specific hate targets. The capacity of these people for perverting the Gospel to fit their particular, private prejudices is chilling to hear. They are not a fraternal organization on a picnic. They are a dangerously misguided group, led by opportunists who deal in hate."[71] The Klan's tradition was one of direct action and physical violence, and, in fulfilling its traditional role, the order represented a powerful force in southern society.

The significance of the Ku Klux Klan was a raid by more than a hundred sheeted men into the black section of Maplesville, Alabama, that left six Negroes injured.[72] It was the castration of a Negro handyman in Birmingham, Alabama, as part of a Klan ceremony.[73] It was the flogging of a white school teacher in Camden, South Carolina, because he had allegedly made a favorable reference to desegregation.[74] It was an attempt to blow up a Negro school as a Klan publicity stunt in Charlotte, North Carolina.[75] It was the shotgun displayed by a robed Klansman as a motorcade of some one hundred cars drove through a Negro residential section in Summerville, Georgia.[76] It was the dynamiting of a white physician's home in Gaffney, South Carolina, because the physician's wife had written an article favoring racial justice.[77] It was the Negro woman who withdrew her suit against a North Carolina school board after receiving threats that her children would never return if they attended the white school.[78] It was anti-Negro violence in a north Florida county where the sheriff was an officer in the Ku Klux Klan.[79] It was the flogging of a white sawmill worker in Stanton, Alabama, because he was accused of "associating too freely with Negroes."[80] It was bombed houses

[71] Bird, in New York *Herald-Tribune*, April 15, 1957.
[72] Birmingham *News*, August 13, 1957.
[73] New York *Times*, September 5, November 8, 1957.
[74] *Southern School News*, January, 1957.
[75] Charlotte *Observer*, February 17, 21, 1958.
[76] Atlanta *Journal*, November 20, 1956.
[77] Charlotte *Observer*, December 7, 1957. She had been a contributor to *South Carolinians Speak: A Moderate Approach to Race Relations* (compiled by Ralph E. Cousins and others and privately printed in 1957).
[78] Winston-Salem *Journal*, October 13, 1955.
[79] Chattanooga *Times*, June 26, 1958.
[80] Montgomery *Advertiser*, August 27, 1957.

belonging to NAACP members, burned crosses before the homes of those who deviated or were deemed to have deviated from white supremacy, and Negroes who were beaten and flogged for no apparent purpose other than for the psychological gratification of the Klansmen.

BACK TO SCHOOL

"Back to School." Jim Dobbins in the Boston *Traveler*.

All of this is not to imply that there was a reign of terror in the South. Yet violence was more than an occasional phenomenon. It was a real and ever-present threat to anyone who became publicly identified with dissident behavior or thought. Throughout most of the South in the 1950's, a person who publicly deviated on social issues was fortunate if he was harrassed only by threatening telephone calls.[81]

Certainly the Klan was not alone responsible for the violent reaction of a minority of southern segregationists. Historical factors, a society that hesitated to convict white men for crimes against Negroes, and a massive resistance atmosphere all contributed. Yet it was the Klan which provided the institutional framework for violence and helped to make dissent not only unpopular but also dangerous.

---

[81] This statement is by no means an exaggeration. See, for example, *Intimidation, Reprisal, and Violence in the South's Racial Crisis*. The files of the Southern Education Reporting Service and those of the Southern Regional Council bulge with instances of "intimidation, reprisal, and violence" against people who questioned the orthodox. My own discussions with field workers in the Southern Regional Council and the American Friends Service Committee have convinced me that this discussion probably minimizes the influence of sheer terrorism in the South.

CHAPTER 12

THE QUEST FOR CONFORMITY
PART II

The Klan's willingness to resort to violence, the Councils' use of economic and other sanctions, and the chilling winds of social ostracism visited upon dissenters by southern white society—all these promoted conformity. The primary responsibility for enforcing orthodoxy, however, rested with governmental officials. The Councils demanded protection of white supremacy by "legal" means, and many southern officeholders responded promptly, showing considerable ingenuity in finding "legal" methods to discourage dissent. Both public authority and private pressure insisted upon an undeviating conformity that posed a serious danger to civil liberty in the South.

Predictably, Mississippi practiced this policy most wholeheartedly. There dissent was literally made illegal. A 1956 statute declared it "unlawful for any person or persons ... to incite a riot, or breach of the peace, or public disturbance, or disorderly assembly, by soliciting, or advocating, or urging, or encouraging disobedience to any law of the State of Mississippi, and nonconformance with the established traditions, customs, and usages of the State of Mississippi."[1] The Mississippi legislature had already gone so far as to pass a bill making it a crime for any person to violate Mississippi's segregation laws even when acting "under color of any law, statute, ordinance, regulation or custom of any other state or of the United States."[2] This one, however, was vetoed by the governor.[3]

---

[1] *Race Relations Law Reporter*, I (April, 1956), 450.
[2] *Ibid.*, 448–49.
[3] *Southern School News*, March, 1956.

In Mississippi actual attempts to comply with the law of the land as enunciated in the *Brown* decision brought arrest on criminal charges. When Clennon King, formerly a faculty member of a Negro college, tried to enroll at the University of Mississippi in June, 1958, the state highway patrol arrested him on the Ole Miss campus and whisked him away to the state capital. King was first jailed and then committed to the state mental hospital, where he was held ten days before being certified as sane and released. An NAACP spokesman duly observed that "no other state has ruled that a man was crazy because he wanted an education."[4] Governor James P. Coleman countered with the statement that if King "were not a lunatic," he would realize that there would be no integration in Mississippi.[5] After threatening to enroll his daughter in an all-white public school in Gulfport, King left the state. More tragic was the case of Clyde Kennard, who sought admission to segregated Mississippi Southern College. After being refused admission in the fall of 1959, Kennard was immediately arrested for speeding and then charged with illegal possession of alcohol (although he did not drink). While fighting these charges in state courts, Kennard was next convicted of theft and sentenced to seven years in prison in a case where "much of the evidence," as Professor James W. Silver put it, "points to the conclusion that Clyde Kennard was 'framed' into Parchman penitentiary."[6] Kennard developed cancer while imprisoned and died in 1963.

Mississippi was by no means alone in its use of law and public authority to coerce conformity. In varying degrees, all the southern states employed state power to hinder, harass, or crush dissent. The weight of governmental authority fell with particular force upon the NAACP. It was easily the most effective voice for integration in the South; in most states the NAACP was virtually the only public proponent of integration. It was also involved in most desegregation lawsuits. Since few Negroes in the South possessed sufficient means to bring lengthy suits for school

[4] As quoted in *Delta Democrat-Times*, June 10, 1958. On the whole episode see *ibid.*, June 6, 9, 10, 1958; Jackson *Daily News*, May 4, June 5, July 11, 1958; New York *Times*, June 15, 1958; Memphis *Commercial Appeal*, July 15, 1958.

[5] As quoted in New Orleans *Times-Picayune*, August 31, 1958. In keeping with his "friendly persuasion" policy, Coleman sought to avoid a riot situation such as the University of Alabama had witnessed; therefore, he used state officers to prevent Negro enrollment at the state universities. Similarly, Coleman consistently sought to avoid forcing a direct confrontation with the federal executive branch; thus his veto of the bill mentioned above was predictable.

[6] Silver, *Mississippi: The Closed Society*, 93–94. See Jackson *Daily News*, September 12, 15, 16, 1959, and St. Louis *Post-Dispatch*, October 1, 1959.

admission (even had the legal task not been opposed by both hostile state legislation and the best legal talent southern state treasuries could retain), the burden fell to the NAACP. Thus destruction of it would be both a long step toward silencing internal dissent (and particularly effective expression of internal dissent) and a significant contribution to massive resistance. Furthermore, the NAACP was politically vulnerable. Although potent in the law courts, the organization was largely powerless in southern politics. Attacking the NAACP in the South was politically analogous to assaulting the Communist Party in the rest of the nation. It afforded politicians—especially rural politicians—free and easy publicity with little political risk. Few state legislators cared openly to oppose an anti-NAACP bill.[7] Most of all, ambitious attorneys general found in NAACP-baiting a convenient path to popularity. Attorney General Cook of Georgia became the South's most vociferous critic of the organization. Alabama Attorney General John Patterson's long and highly publicized campaign against the association was a distinct asset in his successful 1958 gubernatorial campaign. Bruce Bennett of Arkansas and John Ben Shepperd of Texas tried unsuccessfully to employ the same gambit. Bennett attempted literally to turn the attack on the NAACP into a crusade. The Arkansas attorney general promoted a "Southern Plan for Peace," which called for the use of criminal prosecution, economic pressure, and other tactics against the association's membership. As Bennett put it: "No NAACP, no NAACP-inspired law suits, no federal court integration orders, no more Little Rocks."[8] The war on the NAACP represented the gravest overt threat to basic civil liberties during the 1950's.

The assault began in 1956 and continued through the remainder of the decade. It was pushed on a variety of fronts. Investigating committees probed the organization for traces of communist infiltration. Other committees searched for evidence of criminal law violations or tax evasions. Numerous statutes designed to prevent the NAACP from supporting desegregation suits poured out of state legislatures. Existing laws regulating foreign corporations and governing taxes and tax exemptions were applied harshly in the case of the association. State employees were

[7] A majority of North Carolina's state senators were exceptions. They defeated an anti-NAACP bill on the senate floor in 1957. *Southern School News*, July, 1957. Often, of course, legislators cooperated with a state administration to bottle up unwanted segregationist legislation within committees.

[8] As quoted in *Arkansas Gazette*, October 3, 1958.

required to list membership in organizations, and some states made membership in the NAACP grounds for dismissal from state employment. Governors were granted emergency powers to halt organizational activity. State government officials demanded NAACP membership lists. The intimidating effect of making names of the organization's members available for public inspection and known to local law enforcement officials and school boards was obvious. It was a method used both to expose local "troublemakers" and to cripple the association. The NAACP consistently, but not always successfully, refused to surrender its rolls, thus giving attorneys general cause to seek state court injunctions prohibiting the organization from functioning within state boundaries.[9]

Five states passed laws requiring the NAACP to register and to provide membership lists or the names of all contributors (including dues paying members) or both. The Virginia legislature initiated this approach and passed two such laws in its 1956 massive resistance session. The Virginia acts required organizations collecting money to finance litigation or engaging in activities to further racial causes to provide the state with complete data including names and addresses of contributors. The Tennessee legislature adopted almost identical legislation in 1957. The Texas legislature authorized county judges to require various information, including membership lists, from "certain organizations engaged in activities designed to hinder, harass, and interfere with" state control of the public schools. Arkansas lawmakers, in addition to enacting other similar legislation, borrowed the Texas statute almost intact. South Carolina was the fifth state to attack the NAACP in this method.[10] The association eventually evaded all of these laws, however. In 1958, a three-judge federal district court in a split decision declared the two Virginia acts unconstitutional, and the United States Supreme Court ruled that the Fourteenth

---

[9] See Walter F. Murphy, "The South Counterattacks: The Anti-NAACP Laws," *Western Political Quarterly*, XII (June, 1959), 371–90; American Jewish Congress, *Assault Upon Freedom of Association: A Study of the Southern Attack on the National Association for the Advancement of Colored People* (New York, 1957), hereinafter cited by shortened title only; Joseph B. Robinson, "Protection of Associations from Compulsory Disclosure of Membership," *Columbia Law Review*, LVIII (May, 1958), 614–49; Robert B. McKay, "The Repression of Civil Rights as an Aftermath of the School Segregation Cases," *Howard Law Journal*, IV (January, 1958), 9–35; and Vanderbilt University School of Law, "Freedom of Association," *Race Relations Law Reporter*, IV (Spring, 1959), 207–36.

[10] For Virginia, see *Race Relations Law Reporter*, II (October, 1957), 1015–16, 1021–23; for Tennessee, see *ibid.* (April, 1957), 497–501; for Texas, see *ibid.*, III (February, 1958), 90–91; for Arkansas, see *ibid.* (October, 1958), 1054–57, II (April, 1957), 495–96; and for South Carolina, see *ibid.*, IV (Spring, 1959), 235.

Amendment protected NAACP members from compulsory disclosure.[11]

Louisiana was more successful. Attorney General Jack P. F. Gremillion
and the Rainach Committee demanded that the NAACP comply with
a 1924 statute originally aimed at the Ku Klux Klan. The law, which
had slumbered unused for more than three decades, required a wide
range of organizations to submit membership lists to the state.[12] The
NAACP's refusal to comply brought an involved series of legal maneuvers
which led the attorney general to confess that he was "confused, just like
everybody else."[13] Louisiana won a state court injunction in 1956 prohibiting operation of the NAACP until it conformed to the registration
requirements. Several urban chapters then surrendered lists of their
members and renewed operations; however, white economic reprisals,
a high resignation rate, and continued harassment by the state hampered
their activities.[14] Outside the cities, the organization ceased to function
for the remainder of the decade.

Alabama, Texas, and Arkansas put the NAACP completely out of
business for temporary periods. In the spring of 1956, Attorney General
Patterson of Alabama brought suit against the association for failing to
register as a foreign corporation, for supporting the "illegal" Montgomery
bus boycott, and for other activities. State Circuit Judge Walter B. Jones,
who was well known for his writings in defense of segregation, issued a
temporary restraining order prohibiting NAACP activity in the state.[15]
Patterson then asked that the court direct the organization to "produce
certain books, documents and papers (including membership lists)." This
information, Patterson contended, would allow the state to determine

[11] *NAACP v. Patty*, in *ibid.*, III (April, 1958), 274–311; *NAACP v. Alabama ex rel.
Patterson*, in *ibid.* (August, 1958), 611–18. But see also *Gibson v. Florida Legislative Investigation Committee*, in *ibid.*, IV (Summer, 1959), 253.

[12] *Race Relations Law Reporter*, IV (Spring, 1959), 234.

[13] As quoted in *Assault Upon Freedom of Association*, 18. See also *Louisiana ex rel. LeBlanc
v. Lewis*, in *Race Relations Law Reporter*, I (June, 1956), 571–76; *Lewis v. Louisiana ex rel.
LeBlanc*, in *ibid.*, 576–77; *Louisiana ex rel. Gremillion v. NAACP*, in *ibid.*, II (February,
1957), 185–89.

[14] *Race Relations Law Reporter*, I (June, 1956), 571–76; Robinson, "Protection of
Association from Compulsory Disclosure of Membership," 617; *Southern School News*,
March, 1960. The law was eventually declared unconstitutional in 1960. The Louisiana
legislature continued to harass the association with a law prohibiting any foreign corporation "affiliated with" an out-of-state organization which included among its officers
"members of Communist, Communist front or subversive organizations from operating
in the state." *Race Relations Law Reporter*, V (Summer, 1960), 530–31.

[15] Peltason, *Fifty-Eight Lonely Men*, 65; *Alabama ex rel. Patterson v. NAACP*, in *Race
Relations Law Reporter*, I (July, 1956), 707–709.

whether a permanent injunction should be sought. Jones issued the order. When NAACP officials refused to comply, he held the association in contempt and imposed a $100,000 fine.[16] By 1958, two years after the restraining order had been issued, the NAACP had appealed the case to the United States Supreme Court. In a unanimous opinion, the Court reversed the state court's contempt citation and vacated the $100,000 fine. The Supreme Court justices stated:

We hold that the immunity from state scrutiny of membership lists which the Association claims on behalf of its members is here so related to the right of the members to pursue their lawful private interests privately and to associate freely with others in so doing as to come within the protection of the Fourteenth Amendment. And we conclude that Alabama has fallen short of showing a controlling justification for the deterrent effect on the free enjoyment of the right to associate which disclosure of membership lists is likely to have.[17]

The federal court did not overrule the state court injunction but instead remanded the case to the Alabama supreme court. The latter body, after long delay, ruled that the NAACP was still in contempt because of actions other than those dealt with by the United States Court. The temporary restraining order remained effective. More litigation followed, but at the end of the decade, the NAACP was still unable to conduct business in the sovereign state of Alabama.[18]

Attorney General Shepperd of Texas hauled the association into state court in 1956 on a medley of charges, including those of being a profit-making organization (while claiming nonprofit status), failing to pay taxes, and engaging in unlawful political activity. A state district court issued first a temporary restraining order and then a temporary injunction against the organization.[19] Shepperd, assisted by the Texas Rangers, gathered evidence for his case by searching NAACP offices in major Texas cities. Nevertheless, some ten months later, the state judge modified his decree and permitted the NAACP to resume business under certain penalties and restraints.[20] In Georgia, the Revenue Commission also acted against the NAACP for failure to pay taxes. Revenue Commission agents raided the association's main offices, won a court order jailing

---

[16] *Race Relations Law Reporter*, I (September, 1956), 917–18.

[17] *NAACP v. Alabama ex rel. Patterson*, in *ibid.*, III (August, 1958), 618.

[18] *Race Relations Law Reporter*, IV (Spring, 1959), 227. For details and documentation, see Peltason, *Fifty-Eight Lonely Men*, 65–70.

[19] *Texas v. NAACP*, in *Race Relations Law Reporter*, I (February, 1956), 1068–73.

[20] *Assault on Freedom of Association*, 26; *Texas v. NAACP*, in *Race Relations Law Reporter*, II (June, 1957), 678–81.

the Atlanta chapter president and fining the Association $25,000, and determined that the NAACP owed $17,000 in back taxes.[21] Arkansas eventually disbanded the organization by executive fiat. Governor Orval Faubus issued a proclamation declaring the NAACP delinquent in tax payments and "to have forfeited all rights to do business in this State and to be dissolved or withdrawn as the case may be."[22]

With so little attractive employment open to educated Negroes, public school teaching was a disproportionately desirable position for the same middle-class Negroes who were most likely to be NAACP supporters. Local school boards, virtually all of which were entirely white and all of which were white dominated, thus held a powerful club over the heads of Negro malcontents. This situation explains one of the motivations behind state drives to acquire NAACP membership lists, and a number of southern states promptly brought the point home by repealing or modifying teacher tenure provisions. More directly, Arkansas, Georgia, Louisiana, Mississippi, and South Carolina enacted laws striking openly at the association's state-employed members.

Louisiana's laws prohibiting teachers and various other state employees from advocating or in any way promoting school desegregation in public institutions have already been mentioned. The Louisiana legislature also authorized the dismissal of teachers and other public employees who held membership in or contributed to "any group, organization, movement or corporation that is by law or injunction prohibited from operating in the State of Louisiana."[23] The NAACP was prohibited from operating in Louisiana at the time the statutes were enacted. Both South Carolina and Arkansas specifically banned the public employment of NAACP members.

South Carolina provided a particularly revealing example of the difficulties faced by individual dissenters who attempted to defy the massed power of the state. In March, 1956, South Carolina's lawmakers decreed that NAACP members were no longer eligible for state employment. Explaining that NAACP membership was "wholly incompatible with the peace, tranquility and progress that all citizens have the right to enjoy," the South Carolina law directed government agencies to

---

[21] *Williams v. NAACP*, in *Race Relations Law Reporter*, II (February, 1957), 181–85; *Assault on Freedom of Association*, 15–16; Murphy, "The South Counterattacks: The Anti-NAACP Laws," 378.

[22] *Race Relations Law Reporter*, III (April, 1958), 361–62.

[23] *Ibid.*, I (October, 1956), 941–45.

refrain from hiring members of the association and to purge all such individuals already on the public payroll. State officials who failed to fulfill the statute's intent were themselves subject to punishment.[24] In Orangeburg County twenty-four Negro teachers refused to execute an oath of nonmembership, and their contracts were not renewed for the 1956–57 school year. Seventeen of these teachers (represented by the NAACP) then brought suit attacking the law as a violation of freedoms guaranteed by the Fourteenth Amendment. After failing to obtain relief in federal district court, the plaintiffs on April 22, 1957, appealed to the United States Supreme Court.[25] On the following day, the South Carolina legislature repealed the law and substituted a new statute that directed state employees to provide complete information "as to active or honorary membership in or affiliation with all membership associations and organizations."[26] The Supreme Court then dismissed the original case as moot.[27] The new law requiring revelation of membership left NAACP members open to reprisal throughout the state.

In 1958 Arkansas enacted legislation requiring state personnel to list organizations to which they belonged and then, in 1959, prohibited the hiring of NAACP members by state and local governmental agencies. Similarly, Mississippi legislators required school employees to reveal organizations with which they had been in any way associated during the previous five years.[28] When combined with other Mississippi legislation, the intent of this law was obvious.

The most controversial attempt to drive integrationists from the classrooms took place in Georgia. Well before the *Brown* decision, Georgia officials had taken formidable precautions to protect the state from "subversive" teachers. In 1935 the legislature had adopted a "Teachers' Oath" requiring instructional personnel to vow that they would:

Uphold, support, and defend the Constitution and laws of this State and of the United States, and will refrain from directly or indirectly subscribing to or teaching any theory of government or economics or of social relations which is

---

[24] *Ibid.* (August, 1956), 751–53.

[25] *Bryan v. Austin*, in *ibid.*, II (April, 1957), 378–94.

[26] *Race Relations Law Reporter*, II (August, 1957), 853.

[27] *Bryan v. Austin*, in *ibid.*, 777. On these events generally, see Henry Lesesne, in *Christian Science Monitor*, June 22, 1957, and *Assault Upon Freedom of Association*, 21–23.

[28] *Race Relations Law Reporter*, III (October, 1958), 1049–51, IV (Summer, 1959), 460–61, I (April, 1956), 425–26. On harassment of state employees generally, see Arthur Garfield Hays Memorial Fund, "Racial Integration and Academic Freedom, Part I," *New York University Law Review*, XXXIV (April, 1959), 725–52.

inconsistent with the fundamental principles of patriotism and high ideals of Americanism.[29]

In 1949 Georgia supplemented this declaration with a second anti-subversive oath that applied to all state employees. Finally, after 1953, Georgia required job applicants to complete a "Security Questionnaire" which included a listing of "all groups, societies, or organizations of which you are, or have been a member."[30] The Georgia Board of Education did not consider these safeguards adequate, however, and, during the summer of 1955, the board formulated a more positive policy. Board members approved a resolution revoking "forever" the license and salary of "any teacher who supports, encourages, condones, offers to or agrees to teach in a mixed grade."[31] Attorney General Cook criticized the resolution as being a trifle vague, so the agency approved a second resolution broadening and strengthening the first. By this time, church groups, newspapers, and citizens' organizations had been aroused. The board's actions came under attack for being too extreme. When assured by the attorney general that the resolutions were unnecessary anyway, the board, its members apparently somewhat surprised at all the outcry, rescinded both declarations. Cook explained that Georgia law required segregation, and the "Teachers' Oath" offered sufficient grounds for state and local authorities to deal with integrationists and NAACP members.[32]

Six states attempted to curtail NAACP access to the courts. Arkansas, Georgia, Mississippi, South Carolina, Tennessee, and Virginia enacted legislation providing criminal penalties for "the offense of stirring up litigation."[33] A Mississippi statute, to take a somewhat extreme example, made it unlawful to give or receive aid in a lawsuit and required that

[29] See *Georgia Conference of the American Association of University Professors v. Board of Regents*, 246 F. Supp. 553 (1965). The quotation is a reproduction of the oath as it appeared on the contracts of Georgia teachers prior to the 1966–67 school year. The case just cited declared it unconstitutional.

[30] See *Georgia Conference v. Board of Regents*, 246 F. Supp. 553. The quotation is from a copy of the questionnaire in the author's possession. It also included the inquiry: "Is any member of your immediate family . . . a present or past member of any of the organizations enumerated. . . ."

[31] As reprinted in Macon *Telegraph*, July 12, 1955.

[32] *New South*, July, August, 1955; *Southern School News*, August, September, 1955; New York *Times*, August 16, 1955.

[33] These were laws defining and prohibiting barratry, champerty, and maintenance. For discussion of the laws and documentation, see Vanderbilt University School of Law, "Inciting Litigation," *Race Relations Law Reporter*, III (December, 1958), 1257–77, and Murphy, "The South Counterattacks: The Anti-NAACP Laws," 374ff.

anyone initiating legal proceedings must take an oath stating that he had received no aid in bringing the suit.[34]

The legislatures of Florida, Georgia, and South Carolina placed extraordinary and potentially dangerous powers in the hands of their governors. The South Carolina law authorized the chief executive to assume emergency powers that included calling out the state militia, discontinuing any public facility, enjoining activity or planned activity, and taking control of any situation threatening the peace and good order of the state. The Florida and Georgia statutes were no less inclusive.[35]

State authorities declared open season on active integrationists, and local officials often zealously joined in the pursuit. Several states enacted laws authorizing local anti-NAACP campaigns. Texas and Arkansas empowered county judges to demand membership lists and other information from the NAACP or any other organization attempting "to hinder, harass, and interfere" with state control of the public schools. Arkansas additionally authorized its attorney general to cooperate with local law enforcement officials in uncovering tax violations by "certain organizations" which had "interfered with the peace and proper administration of the public schools."[36] Legislatures in Alabama and South Carolina passed special acts granting specified counties extraordinary authority to suppress unpopular organizations or individuals. The first legislation of this type was an Alabama law enacted in 1955 over Governor Folsom's veto. It assessed almost prohibitive licensing fees on organizations soliciting members in rural Wilcox County. The bill's sponsor in the Alabama legislature explained that "Without such a proposal it would be very easy for the NAACP to slip into Wilcox County and teach the Negroes undesirable ideas."[37] Another law applying to Marengo County required membership-soliciting organizations—religious, governmental, charitable, and a few other such groups excepted—to register with the county probate court and place on public record names and addresses of all contributors within the county.[38] Other statutes allowed the Marengo and Macon county boards of education to fire teachers "at any time" and specifically denied affected teachers the right of appeal

---

[34] *Race Relations Law Reporter*, I (April, 1956), 451–53.
[35] *Ibid.*, II (August, 1957), 855–56; I (October, 1956), 954–56; and II (April, 1957), 505–506.
[36] *Ibid.*, III (February, 1958), 90–91, (October, 1958), 1055–56.
[37] As quoted in *Southern School News*, September, 1955.
[38] *Ibid.*, April, 1956.

to the boards, the courts, or elsewhere.[39] In South Carolina special acts applying to four counties required individuals soliciting membership for dues paying organizations first to obtain a permit from the county.[40]

Local governmental agencies, frequently inspired and applauded by state officials, enacted their own anti-NAACP programs. The "Little Rock Ordinance" was the model for many of these measures. Drafted and popularized by Attorney General Bennett, this ordinance permitted city officials to require lists of contributors and dues paying members from organizations doing business in the city. The Little Rock Council enacted the proposal in October, 1957, and promptly demanded that the NAACP and various other groups comply with its requirements.[41] At least twelve other Arkansas communities adopted similar ordinances, and the plan, which was part of Bennett's general campaign to restore "peaceful harmony between the white and Negro races," soon spread to other states.[42] In Georgia, Attorney General Cook circulated copies of the Little Rock enactment, and local government agencies in Georgia as well as Texas, Virginia, and probably elsewhere adopted such proposals.[43]

The most extreme governmental harassment of dissenters in general and NAACP members in particular resulted from the activities of investigating committees. Most southern states created commissions of one sort or another to probe those organizations which, as the Florida law creating a legislative investigating committee put it, "would be inimical to the well being and orderly pursuit of their personal and business activities by the majority of the citizens of this state."[44] Like so many similar agencies on the state and national level, these committees frequently did not allow themselves to be hampered by such impediments as due process of law. After all, as a member of the Florida committee shouted at a recalcitrant witness during an NAACP hearing: "Anyone

[39] *Ibid.*, February, 1956. The legislature extended this act to three other counties in 1961.

[40] *Ibid.*, May–July, 1957.

[41] *Race Relations Law Reporter*, II (December, 1957), 1158–59. See also *Bates v. Little Rock*, in *ibid.*, III (Spring, 1958), 136–41, V (Spring, 1960), 35–41.

[42] As quoted in *Arkansas Gazette*, October 3, 1958.

[43] *Southern School News*, March, December, 1957, March, 1958; *Race Relations Law Reporter*, I (October, 1956), 958–59, III (February, 1958), 128–31. The constitutional— or rather the unconstitutional—aspects of these measures are discussed in Robinson, "Protection of Association from Compulsory Disclosure of Membership," and Murphy, "The South Counterattacks: The Anti-NAACP Laws," 386ff.

[44] Chapter 31498, Florida Legislative Acts, 1956 Special Sess., in *Facts on Film*, Reel 3.

refusing to answer questions of this committee which is attempting to improve conditions in this state . . . is not fit to be a citizen of Florida."[45]

Legislative committees in Florida, Louisiana, South Carolina, Virginia, Georgia, Mississippi, and Arkansas; state sovereignty commissions in Arkansas and Mississippi; and the Georgia Education Commission all had broad powers to conduct investigations, hold hearings, issue subpoenas, and perform other activities.[46] As noted previously, some of these committees concerned themselves with searching for communists in the integration movement. Some, such as the two hyperactive Virginia committees, probed for evidence of litigation offenses, particularly by organizations "which seek to influence, encourage or promote litigation relating to racial activities."[47] A few, like the Florida joint legislative committee, investigated the NAACP on both counts.[48] Without exception, the association was pronounced guilty of whatever wrongs the committees investigated. In some cases state officials attempted to intimidate plaintiffs and lawyers involved in desegregation suits.[49] In Florida and Virginia, committees demanded NAACP membership lists and won court orders directing the organization to comply.[50] At one hearing the Florida committee cited fourteen witnesses for contempt for refusal to answer questions. But more important than the authority to seek contempt convictions was the power of a committee to discredit individuals and organizations by associating them with unpopular and illegal or subversive activities. A white NAACP official in Florida, after being subpoenaed and questioned about the alleged influence of Communism within the NAACP, remarked simply: "I wonder if the damage hasn't already been done."[51]

These committees maintained their own staffs and sometimes hired investigators and obtained information from paid informers. The Florida agency had four full-time investigators (plus two secretaries and an attorney) on its staff and was originally headed by a former secret service agent imported from New York.[52] Mississippi's State Sovereignty Com-

[45] As quoted by John B. McDermott, in Miami *Herald*, February 28, 1958.
[46] See the discussion and references in Vanderbilt University School of Law, "Freedom of Association," 228ff.
[47] From the Virginia legislative act creating the Committee on Law Reform and Racial Activities. *Race Relations Law Reporter*, II (October, 1957), 1023.
[48] See Miami *Herald*, February 5–26, 1957, February 8–28, 1958.
[49] See Peltason, *Fifty-Eight Lonely Men*, 61–63.
[50] *Race Relations Law Reporter*, IV (Spring, 1959), 229–33.
[51] Miami *Herald*, February 28, March 1, 1958.
[52] St. Petersburg *Times*, November 13, 1956, September 2, 1962.

mission was authorized to hire secret investigators, who, Governor Coleman explained, would be "the eyes and ears" for segregation and would maintain a file on potential troublemakers. In 1956 the agency employed a former state highway patrol chief to head this section.[53] When no desegregation suits or other major internal threat to segregation materialized in Mississippi during the 1950's, the commission turned its attention to publicity work and apparently made little use of secret agents. Later, after Barnett became governor, the commission took fuller advantage of its secret investigating authority.[54]

The Georgia Education Commission and T. V. Williams, Jr., its ambitious executive secretary, carried on antisubversive activity not only in Georgia but in two neighboring states. The commission created an investigation subcommittee, worked with the state Bureau of Investigation, conducted its own undercover activities which included watching over Georgia colleges, and, in addition, "infiltrated" the Highlander Folk School in Tennessee and dispatched a "confidential" agent for six months of undercover work in Florida.[55] In the last episode, the commission borrowed $4,500 from the Georgia States' Rights Council to pay Meyers Lowman, head of the right-wing Circuit Riders and an Ohio resident, to investigate the NAACP in Florida. When the affair was later made public by the Atlanta *Journal and Constitution*, Roy Harris, a member of the Georgia Commission's investigation subcommittee, explained that "We were trying to get those folks active and give them something to do."[56] Governor Griffin, also a subcommittee member, added that Louisiana segregation leaders had recommended Lowman, and he "did an excellent job for us."[57] On another occasion, Williams obtained the governor's approval for the purchase of several thousand dollars worth

[53] Chattanooga *Times*, May 16, 1956; Memphis *Commercial Appeal*, May 16, 1956; Carter, *The South Strikes Back*, 63–64.

[54] Silver, *Mississippi: The Closed Society*, 8.

[55] Atlanta *Journal and Constitution*, June 24, 1958; Atlanta *Journal*, August 1, 1958; St. Petersburg *Times*, June 25, 1958; Jack Nelson and Gene Roberts, Jr., *The Censors and the Schools* (Boston, 1963), 151–55.

[56] As quoted in St. Petersburg *Times*, June 25, 1958. Harris was, of course, an influential member of both the States' Rights Council and the Commission on Education. The Council actually loaned the commission $2,000 and endorsed a bank loan to the commission for the other $2,500. The whole affair became public when the Council asked for repayment of the loan. See Charles Pou, in Atlanta *Journal*, August 1, 1958. The commission borrowed the money, according to Harris, because the investigation "was a confidential proposition," and state expenditures would have been more likely to become public. See St. Petersburg *Times*, June 25, 1958.

[57] As quoted in Nelson and Roberts, *The Censors and the Schools*, 154.

of wiretapping equipment and refused to divulge the proposed use of these devices. After the Atlanta press publicized this action, Lieutenant Governor Ernest Vandiver warned against allowing the agency to become "a state gestapo where intrigue and dangerous tactics are substituted for sincerity, sound thinking and legal procedure."[58] Other individuals and organizations joined in the attack. These rebukes were a considerable embarrassment to the commission and demonstrated that southern investigating committees were by no means beyond criticism. Nevertheless, they possessed broad powers, substantial finances, and a public image as defenders of segregation, and they often became formidable institutions in their own right. William C. Havard and Robert F. Steamer, commenting on the Louisiana Joint Committee to Maintain Segregation, observed that "This committee has the necessary funds and the authority to act as roving investigator of any event, person or group even remotely connected with the issue, and it has made maximum use of its potential power."[59] This statement was applicable to several similar agencies in the South during the 1950's.

Most of this activity—the state and local laws and the investigations —was directed at the NAACP, but it also applied to numerous other organizations and individuals. State officials sometimes interpreted laws and committee members in some cases construed their legislative mandates to include such groups as Councils on Human Relations, American Civil Liberties Union chapters, the Urban League, labor unions, and even several prosegregation groups.[60] All in all, the assault on the NAACP posed a profound threat to basic freedoms of association and dissent in the South.

The quest for conformity in the South led to other serious invasions of academic freedom and in some cases to outright censorship. Neobourbons not only attempted to curtail the NAACP and other organizations deemed subversive to the southern way of life, but they sought generally to purge the South of liberal social teachings. Dr. W. M. Caskey, a Mississippi College political science professor and a frequent speaker before Citizens'

[58] As quoted by Bruce Galphin, in Atlanta *Constitution*, November 1, 1957. See Pou, in Atlanta *Journal*, October 30, 1957; Atlanta *Constitution*, October 31, 1957.

[59] William C. Havard and Robert F. Steamer, "Louisiana Secedes: Collapse of a Compromise," *Massachusetts Review*, I (October, 1959), 141.

[60] *Southern School News*, January, 1958; New York *Times*, November 14, 1957; *Staubs v. Baxley*, 355 U.S. 313 (1958); St. Petersburg *Times*, September 2, 1962; *Race Relations Law Reporter*, II (December, 1957), 1159–71, III (August, 1958), 781, IV (Spring, 1959), 232.

Council meetings, explained that "we of the South are in a desperate fight for survival of our Anglo-Saxon people" and, to win the struggle, it was essential to "rescue our priceless jewels—our finest young men and women—from harmful indoctrination by left-wing teachers in our colleges." That this mission might endanger the intellectual independence and integrity of the schools was of little concern to the more extreme segregationists. After all, as William M. Shaw, executive secretary of the Louisiana Citizens' Councils and counsel for the Rainach Committee, pointed out, cries like "destroyers of academic freedom" were "a song familiar to anyone who had studied the Aesopian language of Communism."[61]

Segregationists sometimes sought positively to promote the teaching of white supremacy in the public schools. The Mississippi Association of Citizens' Councils was most active in this regard. The association printed several versions of "A Manual for Southerners" and made them available to the state's schools. Each edition of the work was designed for a specific age group. The "Manual" for third and fourth grade classes (also recommended for "many adults who might benefit from a review of these fundamental truths") presented such "truths" as: "Do you know that some people in our country want the Negroes to live with the white people? These people want us to be unhappy. They say we must go to school together. They say we must swim together and use the bathroom together. We do not want to do these things."[62] Some Mississippi schools actually used this literature for classroom teaching.[63]

In addition to promoting its "Manuals," the Mississippi Councils provided prosegregation books for public school libraries and encouraged students to read them by sponsoring county and state student essay contests on such subjects as "Why I believe in Social Separation of the Races of Mankind," "Why the Preservation of States' Rights is Important to Every American," and "Subversion of Racial Unrest."[64] Directing the essay contests was Mrs. Sara McCorkle, who served on the Councils' staff as director of women's activities and who also conducted school chapel programs throughout the state. Concerned that "Women don't

[61] Caskey is quoted in Jackson *Daily News*, December 14, 1955; and Shaw in *ibid.*, June 10, 1958.

[62] "A Manual for Southerners," as partially reprinted in *The Citizens' Council*, February, 1957.

[63] Smith, *Congressman from Mississippi*, 270.

[64] *Delta Democrat-Times*, October 9, 1958.

realize just how far communism and racial integration is infiltering [*sic*] into our school system,"[65] Mrs. McCorkle sought to encourage adults to teach children "the dangers of integration" and to make students aware of "what has happened to nations that have experienced racial amalgamation."[66] Within four months after the Councils began this service to Mississippi education in January, 1958, Mrs. McCorkle had presented some sixty public school chapel programs.[67] Outside of Mississippi, projects to convert the public schools into instruments for the furtherance of white supremacy dogma were far less frequent.[68]

Normally segregationists did not so much demand that the schools teach white supremacy as that they refrain from teaching anything that conflicted with white supremacy. Apparently neobourbon southerners assumed that, with the exception of a few "left-wingers" found mainly on college faculties and among NAACP members, school instructional personnel were already teaching a viewpoint sympathetic to segregation. Therefore, segregationists usually directed their attention toward insuring that this minority of integrationists did not corrupt southern youth. Florida county officials fired a white health officer because she had lunch with a Negro nurse while discussing business and then asked for the resignation of two educators who had voiced objections to her summary dismissal.[69] The Georgia Board of Education stopped the pay of a Gwinnett County teacher who told high school students that she would teach in an integrated classroom if their school accepted Negro pupils.[70] A South Carolina school board dismissed three Negro teachers whose relatives had signed a desegregation petition.[71] A Virginia county school board dropped the contracts of two white grade school teachers who had been, as one of the victims explained, "falsely accused" of favoring integration.[72] Some fifty teachers in the Little Rock area were fired

[65] As quoted in Jackson *Daily News*, January 3, 1958.
[66] As quoted by Cliff Sessions, in *ibid.*, April 24, 1958.
[67] *Ibid.*
[68] Among groups outside Mississippi that promoted programs of this type were the Citizens' Councils of Alabama, which were the first to organize student segregationist essay contests. See Montgomery *Advertiser*, May 18, 1956.
[69] As the matter worked out, only one of the two objectors was actually fired. See *Southern School News*, November, December, 1956.
[70] While still under investigation, the teacher resigned because of pregnancy. *Southern School News*, November, December, 1956.
[71] Charlotte *Observer*, August 25, 1955.
[72] *Southern School News*, June, 1956.

during the desegregation controversy in that city.[73] The Georgia Board of Regents even fired a former educator, depriving the past head of a state college of his title as president emeritus because of his liberal racial views.[74] While incidents of this sort were relatively uncommon, they were sufficiently numerous to keep teachers reminded of the professional perils of dissent.[75]

Southern colleges and universities were subjected to similar pressures. In a few cases dissent from racial orthodoxy by faculty members or students resulted in blatant violations of academic freedom. At Alabama Polytechnic Institute in Auburn, Alabama, a faculty member was dismissed for writing a letter to the campus newspaper. In February, 1957, the college newspaper, *The Plainsman*, published an editorial entitled "New York City Forces Integration," which criticized the New York City Commission on Integration's efforts to promote desegregation through bussing arrangements. Bud R. Hutchinson, assistant professor of economics, answered the criticisms with a letter to the editor that appeared in the newspaper's next edition. Hutchinson observed that "Your editorial in last week's *Plainsman* . . . deals but superficially with an extremely complex social problem" and defended the commission's bussing efforts and integration generally. These comments sparked some controversy in the letters-to-the-editor section of the college newspaper and then passed from campus attention. The incident was by no means forgotten, however, by a member of the Board of Trustees, who insisted on taking the issue up when the institute's governing body met in March, 1957. In executive session, the board voted not to rehire Hutchinson and ordered the institution's president to carry out its edict. Hutchinson was dropped from the faculty at the end of the 1957–58 school year. President Ralph B. Draughon said in a public statement that the professor's views "are not in keeping with the viewpoint of the Alabama Polytechnic Institute on the question of segregation" and "that

[73] Forty-four of these teachers were fired by the Little Rock School board in a single session. This "purge" touched off a major political contest in the city that resulted in the voiding of all forty-four dismissals. See *Southern School News*, June, July, 1959. Several Negro teachers who lost their jobs during the controversy were not so fortunate. See *Intimidation, Reprisal, and Violence in the South's Racial Crisis*, 11.

[74] *Southern School News*, April, 1956.

[75] On this point see National Comission on Professional Rights and Responsibilities of the National Education Association of the United States, *Report of an Investigation, Florida: A Study of Political Atmosphere as It Affects Public Education* (Washington, 1966), 64, *passim*.

Mr. Hutchinson could not expect to advance his career at this institution."[76]

At the University of South Carolina, Dr. Chester C. Travelstead, dean of the School of Education, wrote to Governor Timmerman in April, 1955, expressing disagreement with the governor's segregationist public statements. Shortly afterward, Travelstead stated in a speech that segregation was a dead institution and should be abandoned. His dismissal "in the best interest of the university" followed almost immediately. In 1958, the contract of another faculty member, Dr. Joseph Margolis, was not renewed by the same university because of Margolis' public criticism of segregation.[77]

In Louisiana the state legislature and Louisiana State University carried on what sometimes seemed a cold war. When the Rainach Committee drafted a new package of racist legislation in 1958, the Louisiana chapter of the American Civil Liberties Union responded by circulating petitions on state college campuses opposing the bills. The petitions were a reasoned nine-point criticism of the legislative program, and the points were reinforced by two Louisiana State University faculty members who testified against the proposed legislation at committee hearings. The reaction was instantaneous. At Northwestern Louisiana State College, a faculty member who had disseminated petitions was released for "insubordination." The Louisiana Legislature enacted all the Rainach Committee measures and then voted to investigate subversion on the LSU main campus in Baton Rouge. The university received support from its Alumni Council and from neighboring Tulane University, and the legislative investigation was relatively perfunctory. After President Troy Middleton assured investigating committee members that there was no subversive teaching on his campus, the legislators dropped plans to call the sixty-six LSU faculty members who had signed petitions.[78] They did, however, elicit from the nonconforming faculty members questionnaire responses involving such subjects as their personal attitudes toward segregation, their membership in organizations, and whether they taught integrationist views in their classrooms. An unqualified affirmative

[76] Quotations in this paragraph are from Birmingham *News*, May 15, 1957, which reprints all the pertinent documents. American Association of University Professors, "Alabama Polytechnic Institute," *AAUP Bulletin*, XLIV (Spring, 1958), 158–69, provides a detailed account of these events.

[77] *New South*, January, 1956; *Southern School News*, October, 1958.

[78] New Orleans *Times-Picayune*, June 2, 10–12, 1958; Sarratt, *The Ordeal of Desegregation*, 141.

on the last question would have been admission of an illegal act under Louisiana law, and no teacher returned such an answer.[79]

The Citizens' Councils continued to attack the university and particularly its desegregated New Orleans branch, and they threatened to send segregationist questionnaires to all state-employed faculty members.[80] Then, in 1960, an LSU professor of English, Waldo F. McNeir, who was also head of the Louisiana Civil Liberties Union, wrote to leading segregationist legislators attacking their white supremacy activities. The letters touched off another legislative storm. The lawmakers again voted to investigate LSU, and the university was vigorously condemned on the floors of both houses. Legislators debated a number of bills designed to curb dissent on the campus. This new tempest subsided after McNeir offered and the university administration eagerly accepted his resignation. Academic freedom remained intact at LSU, but, as the Louisiana Commission on Civil Rights stated, "the faculty has been timid about taking a public stand for open schools [during the New Orleans school desegregation crisis] since the legislature has shown itself quite willing to punish the university."[81]

Nowhere was academic freedom at white colleges in more peril than in Mississippi. Both the state legislature and the Citizens' Councils maintained a constant vigil over the academic community. An elaborate screening process insured that unorthodox speakers would have no opportunity to mislead students at state institutions.[82] When this process failed to exclude an Episcopal minister who, so it was learned at the last moment, had contributed to the NAACP, his speaking invitation was summarily retracted.[83] The Citizens' Councils maintained a record of the social views of Mississippi professors (particularly at the state university and at Millsaps College), placed spies at suspected faculty-student gatherings, circulated among legislators an edited document purporting to show

[79] *Race Relations Law Reporter*, III (August, 1958), 781.

[80] New Orleans *Times-Picayune*, September 14, November 27, 1958, March 11, 1960.

[81] Baton Rouge *State-Times*, December 16, 17, 21, 1960; New Orleans *Times-Picayune*, January 5, 8, 1961. A resolution calling upon state college administrations to screen applicants for faculty positions to insure their dedication to segregation received legislative approval. See the discussion in Louisiana Advisory Committee, *The New Orleans School Crisis*, 26–28.

[82] Jay Milner, in *Delta Democrat-Times*, February 9, 1956; Silver, *Mississippi: The Closed Society*, 108.

[83] This widely publicized incident prompted all other speakers invited to the university's Religious Emphasis Week to return their invitations, and an embarrassed University of Mississippi held its Religious Emphasis Week without the participation of ministers. See *Delta Democrat-Times*, November 9, 1955–February 21, 1956.

that the dean of the University of Mississippi Law School had urged compliance with the *Brown* decision, and generally carried on a running war against free inquiry.[84] At Ole Miss the Director of Religious Life committed the atrocity of playing ping-pong with a Negro guest and was harassed from the campus.[85] Given the atmosphere in Mississippi, there was a basis for the closing sentence in a Mississippi State College faculty member's letter of resignation: "Before the law is passed which might make the expression of these sentiments a criminal act, I wish to submit my resignation."[86]

Worst of all was the plight of Negro institutions. State officials, particularly in South Carolina, betrayed no indication that they acknowledged the existence of academic freedom at Negro colleges. On three different occasions South Carolina state leaders successfully demanded that Negro campuses be purged of "subversive" influences.

South Carolina State College was the first victim. The state's only public institution of higher learning for Negroes, the college in Orangeburg, incurred the wrath of white legislators when many students and faculty members supported the Negro boycott against white merchants who were active in the Citizens' Council. The South Carolina legislature voted in March, 1956, to investigate the extent of NAACP activity at the college. The resolution creating the nine-member investigating committee instructed its members to determine whether NAACP involvement on the campus was "detrimental to the welfare of the college and its students" and "whether or not the faculty and students are serving to mislead the Negro citizens and foment and nurture ill feeling and misunderstanding...."[87] A South Carolina State student-faculty group answered with its own resolution defending the NAACP and condemning legislative efforts to intimidate the college community. Governor Timmerman then ordered state police to maintain surveillance over the campus. In protest against the proposed investigation, police scrutiny, and the activities of the college administration during the Orangeburg boycott, students initiated a class-attendance strike in April, 1956. At this point, the college administration acted. School authorities expelled the student

[84] Silver, *Mississippi: The Closed Society*, 36; Peters, *The Southern Temper*, 136; *Delta Democrat-Times*, June 25, July 15, 1957; Jackson *Daily News*, March 9, 1958.

[85] Personal interview with the former director, February, 1966.

[86] Reprinted in New York *Times*, February 11, 1956. On the state of academic freedom in Mississippi generally, see Silver, *Mississippi: The Closed Society*.

[87] *Race Relations Law Reporter*, I (June, 1956), 600.

body president and informed some twenty-five other student leaders that they would not be permitted to register for the next school year. Five faculty members were notified that their contracts would not be renewed, and several others resigned. By these tactics the administration broke the student strike and curbed what Timmerman had referred to as "subversive elements" on the campus.[88] By the time the investigating committee met in the summer of 1956, the college president was able to assure its members that the situation at South Carolina State was well in hand. The committee held a brief one-day hearing on the campus and terminated the investigation.

Allen University in Columbia was the next South Carolina institution for Negroes to fall into political disfavor. A private institution supported largely by the African Methodist Episcopal Church, Allen replaced South Carolina State as something of a focal point for protest against state segregationist policies. Allen students challenged local Jim Crow seating arrangements on busses, and, in September, 1957, a white Hungarian refugee enrolled at the university, thus making it the only desegregated educational institution in the state.[89] By the summer of 1957, talk of Communist influence on the Allen campus was becoming more frequent. Governor Timmerman's office informally advised the Allen administration to dismiss three faculty members who were known to be openly opposed to segregation. The university president promptly demanded letters of resignation from the three offending professors. All three refused to comply with the request, however, and the Allen Board of Trustees came to the defense of academic freedom and repudiated the president's demands. Infuriated, South Carolina state leaders immediately lashed out at the university's intransigence. In executive session the State Board of Education, of which Governor Timmerman was an ex officio member, adopted a resolution declaring that "The approval of Allen University for teacher training is withheld . . . and the State Department of Education is directed to withhold certification of its graduates until approval is granted."[90] Again, the college president stated that capitulation to the

[88] As quoted in *Assault on Freedom of Association*, 24. On this episode generally, see *The State*, March 15–July 30, 1956; *Assault on Freedom of Association*, 23–24; and Quint, *Profile in Black and White*, 53–54.

[89] Desegregated faculties at Negro colleges were not at all uncommon at schools with all-Negro enrollments. Indeed, five of the six faculty members who were the centers of the controversy that will be discussed in the following paragraphs were white.

[90] Reprinted in American Association of University Professors, "Academic Freedom and Tenure: Allen University and Benedict College," *AAUP Bulletin*, XLVI (Spring, 1960), 91.

white power structure was in the university's best interests; again, the Board of Trustees, joined this time by the Commission on Education of the African Methodist Episcopal Church, stood by the professors.

Several months of sparring between the state and the university followed. Then, on January 15, 1958, Timmerman devoted a considerable portion of his annual address to the state legislature to "Communist activities" at Allen University. The governor said that three professors were following the Communist "party-line" and were engaged in "typical CP projects and campaigns." On the same day, a group of Allen students appeared on the campus of the University of South Carolina, also in Columbia, asking for admission to the white state university. Shortly afterward, several students from Benedict College, a private Negro school in Columbia which had ties with the American Baptist Convention, attempted to register at the state university. Timmerman dispatched another message to the legislature on January 29, 1958, again directing the lawmakers' attention to "Communist activities and influence" at Allen University and adding three Benedict faculty members to the growing list of subversives in South Carolina Negro colleges.[91]

During the early months of 1958, political pressure mounted against both schools. Allen remained in limbo, with its graduates being denied teacher certification, and Benedict was overtly threatened with the same fate. In the spring, resistance at both schools collapsed. The Allen Board of Trustees gave up the fight and voted to dismiss the three professors, who were paid for the remainder of the year and immediately released. At Benedict the executive committee of the Board of Trustees also voted to fire that institution's branded professors. The State Board of Education restored accreditation to Allen, and talk of reprisals against Benedict faded away.[92]

South Carolina had no monopoly on outrages against academic freedom in Negro colleges. In June, 1960, Governor John Patterson of Alabama, angered by sit-in demonstrations emanating from Alabama State College, accused one of that institution's faculty members of being a "known agitator" and linked his name to communism. Patterson convened a meeting of the State Board of Education, which promptly directed the college president to fire the professor "before sundown today." The

[91] Quotations are from *ibid.*, 95–96.
[92] This account is based on *ibid.*, 87–104, and Quint, *Profile in Black and White*, 116–25.

Alabama State College administration carried out the edict, sans due process and fair play. In Mississippi, the Alcorn A. and M. College Board of Trustees retaliated against student protests by dismissing both the college president and the student council president. In Florida, the legislative committee investigating the NAACP extended its inquiry to the Florida A. and M. University campus. Testifying before the committee, university President George W. Gore, Jr., explained that he had urged faculty personnel not to become involved in the Tallahassee bus boycott. When several members of the teaching staff, acting as individuals, participated anyway, Gore talked to each professor personally and pointed out that he could not protect any faculty member who antagonized state leaders.[93] Gore's predicament was not unlike that of most other Negro college presidents in the South.

Aside from overt violations of academic freedom, the general political atmosphere engendered by massive resistance was perhaps equally damaging to the cause of free inquiry in the South. The Mississippi legislature passed a resolution commending state college administrative officials for their "actions in safeguarding our culture and traditions from vicious attacks and influences contrary to the beliefs of the people of Mississippi and the South." The resolution directed that "Every effort be made by those in charge of our Institutions of Higher Learning to prevent subversive influences from infiltrating into our institutions." Similarly, the Alabama legislature commended the University of Alabama Board of Trustees for expelling Autherine Lucy.[94] In Florida the state university system board of control directed college administrations to dismiss students "who stir up trouble."[95]

Too much could, of course, be made of these restrictions on academic freedom. As the examples above indicate, overt violations of academic liberty were largely—though certainly not entirely—confined to the Deep South. Furthermore, the maintenance of an atmosphere of free inquiry was by no means a peculiarly southern problem; it was, however, more acute in the South during the late 1950's than in any other area of the

[93] Patterson is quoted in Montgomery *Advertiser*, June 15, 1960; the Alcorn dismissals are discussed in Sarratt, *The Ordeal of Desegregation*, 138; Gore's testimony is summarized in St. Petersburg *Times*, February 19, 1957.

[94] *Race Relations Law Reporter*, I (April, 1956), 422–23. The Mississippi resolution referred specifically to the cancellation of a speaking invitation sent to an Episcopal minister by University of Mississippi officials.

[95] As quoted in Sarratt, *The Ordeal of Desegregation*, 138. See also *Southern School News*, March, 1957.

nation.[96] Even in the Deep South, freedom of discussion in classrooms was the rule; students and faculty members risked their positions only by carrying unorthodox viewpoints outside the lecture halls. Nevertheless, the massive resistance drive for conformity left its mark on the state of higher learning in the South. Political pressure, the omnipresence of the race problem, the consequent hesitancy of universities to become involved in controversial issues, relatively low pay scales, and other factors hampered the development of academic excellence. When combined with the severe pressures exerted against free discussion in the elementary and secondary schools, the total impact was a formidable blow to public education in the South.

The dynamics of the drive for conformity that led to the onslaught against the NAACP and the attack on academic freedom spilled over into demands for censorship of reading materials. Sometimes these efforts were almost comical. In Alabama, a black-belt state senator carried on a ferocious quixotic tilt against a children's book about two rabbits, one of which was white and the other black.[97] In Florida, a new edition of "Three Little Pigs" came under heavy attack, since one pig was black, one white, and the other somewhat in between. "The book follows the same old brainwashing routine," said a segregationist leader. "It shows a white pig and a mulatto pig who are destroyed and the black pig survives."[98] More often, censorship endeavors had an air of tragedy. In Louisiana, there was the Bossier High School librarian who had to remove 1,300 copies of *Life* magazine dating back to 1935 from the library shelves because the school boards of Claiborne and Bossier parishes ordered all copies of *Time, Life,* and *Look* removed from school premises. And there was the dilemma of the Mississippi library commission. In its 1954 appropriations, the Mississippi legislature specifically set aside $5,000 of its library appropriations for the purchase of "books dealing with the subject of ethnology." When the library commission asked just what the legislature had in mind, the sponsor of this provision explained that it referred to works on white supremacy. The library commission searched diligently, rounded up forty-seven copies of Herman Talmadge's *You and*

---

[96] On the state of academic freedom in the nation generally, see Willis Moore, "Causal Factors in the Current Attack on Education," *AAUP Bulletin,* XLI (Winter, 1955), 621–28.

[97] Birmingham *News,* May 22, 23, 1959; Montgomery *Advertiser,* May 23, 24, August 13, 1959.

[98] As quoted in St. Petersburg *Times,* June 2, 1959.

Segregation and a few similar books, and finally invested most of the badly needed $5,000 in technical works on ethnology and anthropology which were not needed.[99]

Most of all, book censorship represented another serious threat to the achievement of an open society in the South. Citizens' Councils, "patriotic" groups of various sorts, and numerous southern politicians demanded the screening of public school textbooks and library books. As J. Evetts Haley, a member of the Federation for Constitutional Government and a leader of Texans for America, explained: "The stressing of both sides of a controversy only confuses the young and encourages them to make snap judgments based on insufficient evidence. Until they are old enough to understand both sides of a question, they should be taught only the American side. . . ."[100] In addition to battling subversion at Southern Methodist University and West Texas College, Haley and his Texans for America associates successfully demanded a more rigid screening process for Texas public school textbooks. Mississippi also adopted further safeguards against subversive school texts. The Georgia Board of Education banned several works from Georgia schools because they were deemed not "in accord with the Southern way of life." The South Carolina legislature instructed the State Library Board to insure that books "inimical and antagonistic" to the "customs and traditions" of that state were not placed on the book shelves.[101] While white supremacy figured prominently in their arguments, the proponents of censorship in the South were in many ways a part of a national drive by "patriotic" citizens and groups to purge "alien" doctrines from the school books. This was particularly true of Haley's Texans for America, which was basically a western movement. The drive, nevertheless, fitted easily into the general demand for orthodoxy in the South.

Yet even these actions failed to exhaust the "legal" methods of maintaining white supremacy employed by southern segregationists. While attempting to crush opposition to segregation, public officials in the Deep South also sought to institutionalize the system still further, to establish even more barriers against any activities that might conceivably facilitate moderate accommodation to the principle of the *Brown* decision. Louisiana

[99] Birmingham *World*, May 8, 1956; New Orleans *Times-Picayune*, March 4, 1956; Jackson *Daily News*, March 13, 1956.

[100] As quoted in Nelson and Roberts, *The Censors and the Schools*, 121.

[101] *Ibid.*, 90–96, 114–20; Atlanta *Journal*, May 3, 1955; Charleston *News and Courier*, May 27, 1956.

legislators enacted a law prohibiting "all interracial dancing, social functions, entertainments, athletic training, games, sports or contests and other such activities. . . ."[102] Attorney General Cook of Georgia, in an official opinion declaring that state law prohibited Negro teams from playing a football game on a white field, pontificated: "For segregation to remain an integral part of Georgia's social customs and traditions, it must and will be practiced twenty-four hours a day, seven days a week, and three hundred and sixty-five days a year."[103] The Georgia Board of Education returned to the fray in 1957 with a resolution prohibiting all student organizations in the state's public schools from planning or participating in any integrated activity.[104]

On the local level government authorities enacted such things as Montgomery Ordinance No. 15–57, which made it "unlawful for white and colored persons to play together . . . in any game of cards, dice, dominoes, checkers, pool, billiards, softball, basketball, baseball, football, golf, track, and at swimming pools, beaches, lakes or ponds, or any other games."[105] And to make certain that no law enforcement official missed an opportunity to maintain segregation by "legal" means, Georgia legislators passed a law to deprive peace officers of retirement and disability benefits for failure or refusal to enforce racial statutes.[106]

Overall, massive resistance leaders achieved a surprising degree of success in sharply limiting the range of dissent in the South. They had set about to bureaucratize the South in defense of white supremacy and to lead a unified South into war against the *Brown* decision and some of the major trends of mid-twentieth century America. Their activities severely threatened basic civil liberty in the region.

[102] *Race Relations Law Reporter*, I (October, 1956), 953.
[103] *Ibid.*, II (February, 1957), 267.
[104] *Ibid.* (June, 1957), 715. On another occasion, the Georgia Board of Education adopted a resolution urging the state legislature to repeal compulsory attendance laws. Atlanta *Constitution*, January 14, 1958.
[105] *Race Relations Law Reporter*, II (June, 1957), 714.
[106] *Ibid.*, I (April, 1956), 450–51.

CHAPTER 13

THE RATIONALE
OF MASSIVE RESISTANCE

Southern neobourbons capitalized on a growing white reaction to social change and gained the initiative in southern politics. They advanced a broad program of massive resistance, which included interposition, propaganda, political insurgency, and coerced conformity as its essential elements. In the simplest sense, perhaps, southern segregationists merely sought to put society back together in its accustomed pattern, rejecting and suppressing the social and ideological aspects of change. But the ideology that underlay massive resistance was more complex, and its basic tenets found effective expression in the resistance program.

White supremacy was, of course, central to the neobourbon rationale. Southern conservatism, more so than in other areas, has traditionally stressed the organic and hierarchical nature of society, placing high value upon order and status as the natural way of things. To the chief justice of the Florida supreme court, the fact that "fish in the sea segregate in schools of their kind" was so logically applicable to human society that it properly belonged in a legal opinion as a justification for segregation.[1] To the patriarchal, or feudalistic, mind, the well-known southern dual standard of justice was completely rational. Law should fit the person, not the crime; a person had the same status before a jury that he enjoyed in society. The Negro's place—by tradition, by nature, by law—was at the bottom of the social order. Segregation was a part of the traditional social system, and it corresponded to the fixed natural order of things.[2]

---

[1] *Southern School News*, November, 1955, quoting Senior Justice Glenn Terrell.

[2] Among numerous revealing works on southern conservatism are Carter, *Southern Legacy*; Shannon, *Toward a New Politics in the South;* James McBride Dabbs, *The Southern Heritage,* and *Who Speaks for the South?* (New York, 1964); Cash, *The Mind of the South;* Francis Butler Simkins, *The Everlasting South* (Baton Rouge, 1963); and Keith F. McKeon, *Cross Currents in the South* (Denver, 1960).

But an even more fundamental foundation for white supremacy was the naked fact that southern neobourbons in particular and a great many white southerners generally did not deem Negroes worthy of white society. Negroes were inferior; they were either the product of a separate and less complete evolutionary process or simply inferior by nature. Given this assumption, the possibility of racial intermarriage was frightening. Herman Talmadge stated, "The ultimate aim and goal of NAACP leaders in the present segregation fight is the complete intermingling of the races in housing, schools, churches, public parks, public swimming pools and even in marriage. It is so evident that even White apologists for this organization must now admit it."[3] To Talmadge and to a great many other white southerners (and northerners, too, for that matter) the mere idea of a fully integrated society was enough to discredit the NAACP and its "White apologists." Negroes were inferior, or at least "different," a word that itself carried the connotation of inferiority, and southern whites just "instinctively" rebelled against integration. "The break-down of segregation in any of its aspects," as sociologist James W. Vander Zanden summarized a key point in the white supremacy argument, "will inevitably lead to racial amalgamation, resulting in a host of disastrous consequences."[4] The sanctity of white blood and Anglo-Saxon civilization rested on segregation.

That modern bourbons (more so than the original redeemers) added a harsh—even cruel—Jim Crow tinge to their white supremacy largely resulted from historical developments. These included the decline of the paternalistic tradition, the arrival of the Snopeses as dominant defenders of bourbon ideals, and the legacy of half a century of racial demagoguery in politics and Social Darwinism in the world of thought.[5]

Southern neobourbons evidenced a distinct distrust of democracy. In part, their opposition to mass political participation stemmed from practical considerations. The court house-merchant clique—indeed, the county and small-town bourgeoisie generally—was suspicious of any suffrage modifications that might alter the status quo. Established politicians whose political careers were structured on the most restricted franchise in the

---

[3] Herman Talmadge, *You and Segregation*, 42.

[4] James W. Vander Zanden, "The Ideology of White Supremacy," *Journal of the History of Ideas*, XX (June-September, 1959), 386. And see Vander Zanden, *American Minority Relations*, 136–63.

[5] See C. Vann Woodward, *The Strange Career of Jim Crow* (2nd rev. ed.; New York, 1966).

nation were naturally dubious about suffrage upheavals in their own bailiwicks. Practical considerations were particularly current in the 1950's, when spokesmen for the burgeoning urban population were demanding a more equitable voice in the state legislatures. A strong undercurrent of southern politics during the 1950's was the rural and small-town battle to prevent legislative reapportionment.[6]

But this distrust of popular democracy was also ideological, resting on assumptions that have been endorsed by many nonsouthern conservatives. Southern neobourbons rejected the equality of man, accepted a Spencerian view of human nature, held a Sumnerian attitude toward reform, and visualized a hierarchical society—all of which went hand-in-hand with the concept of oligarchical rule. So distasteful was the idea of equalitarian democracy that some neobourbon leaders came precariously close to equating democracy with communism.[7]

From white supremacy, distrust of democracy, and other assumptions came a decided preference for an organic and closed society. It was this attitude, rather than abstract theories about federalism, that accounted for the logical contradictions in the neobourbon position on nationalism, sectionalism, states' rights, and local government. Southern traditionalists endorsed that governmental theory which seemed most likely to deter the erosion of small-town, southern values. They most frequently stood on the rights of states, of course, but, in truth, they were nationalists, sectionalists, states' righters, and devotees of local government, depending on the issues involved. To draw attention to this fact is not to accuse neobourbons of duplicity; an ideology need not be logically consistent to be accepted. And indeed, this position was not so irrational as it might first appear. From their patriarchal viewpoint, local communities made up an organic state which blended into a homogeneous region that possessed blood ties and common customs. The region, neobourbons believed, was a part of a yet larger and more varied national entity held together by emotional symbols like Old Glory, emotional words like Americanism,

---

[6] Havard and Beth's *The Politics of Mis-Representation* is the best study of the dynamics and complexities of the resistance to reapportionment.

[7] For example, Talmadge, *You and Segregation*, 15–16, and *"Great Masses of People Leaderless: Confused by Slogans of Highly Organized Minorities,"* Address by Hon. Herman E. Talmadge at Washington, D.C., April 21, 1959 (Atlanta, n.d.); and R. Carter Pittman, "Equality Versus Liberty: The Eternal Conflict," *American Bar Association Journal,* XLVI (August, 1960), 873–80, and Pittman, *The Supreme Court, the Broken Constitution, and the Shattered Bill of Rights* (Atlanta, n.d.). See Jasper Shannon's perceptive discussion of southern, small-town values in *Toward a New Politics in the South,* 41ff.

and a mutual acceptance of such catchwords as individualism and free enterprise.

Thus Senator Eastland could speak grandly of a "return to the genius of the American system of government, which is local government, by the people of the communities."[8] He then condemned those chief executives who sought to promote local democracy: "I'm ashamed that we have three Southern governors who howl that it is a local matter and feel no obligation to the people of their states."[9] Neobourbons could repeatedly insist that racial problems could only be solved on the local level and then agree with the sentiments expressed by Representative William Tuck of Virginia: "We cannot allow Norfolk or Arlington to integrate. If they won't stand with us, I say make them."[10] Neobourbons defended the right of local communities to uphold orthodox values and customs, but in matters pertaining to home rule or local deviation from white supremacy, neobourbons favored centralizing power in the state capital.

Similarly, proponents of this ideology were nationalists, usually in a belligerently isolationist sense of the word. They summarily rejected any suggestion that America's role as an international power was being hampered by racial injustice at home, asserting that domestic practices in the United States were of no concern to foreign nations and that foreign opinion should have no influence upon internal policies.[11] Instead, Senator Eastland explained, "Patriotism demands that our leaders unify the American people rather than divide them in the face of a common menace."[12] At the same time neobourbons emphasized regional differences within the republic, Eastland opposed the nomination of John M. Harlan as a Supreme Court justice on the grounds "that Judge Harlan is from the State of New York, and the people of this great State possess views and philosophies which are different from those entertained by the rest of the country."[13] Neobourbons called for sectional unity and frequently talked

[8] *Congressional Record*, 83rd Cong., 2nd Sess. (August 5, 1954), 13375.

[9] As quoted in Jackson *Daily News*, October 5, 1955.

[10] As quoted in Richmond *Times-Dispatch*, November 15, 1958.

[11] For example, Talmadge, *You and Segregation*, vi–vii, and Association of Citizens' Councils of Mississippi, *Annual Report* (1955), 3–4. On the connection between isolationism and nationalism in America, see Selig Adler, *The Isolationist Impulse: Its Twentieth Century Reaction* (New York, 1961).

[12] As quoted in New Orleans *Times-Picayune*, August 21, 1958.

[13] *Congressional Record*, 84th Cong., 1st Sess. (March 16, 1955), 3013. For a discussion of some of these same points from a different point of view, see Marian D. Irish, "Political Thought and Political Behavior in the South," 406–20.

of the South and the southern way of life as if it were a civilization distinct from the rest of the nation.

Most of all neobourbons championed the rights of states. They made state sovereignty, carried to the point of interposition, the foundation for their program of massive resistance. States' rights served as a cloak for white supremacy and economic favoritism and an instrument for blunting the threat of an open society, but, again, neobourbons did not necessarily extol this doctrine insincerely. After all, it, too, was a part of southern tradition. John C. Calhoun himself a century earlier had carefully defined the role of the state as the protector of minority superiority. States' rights or, synonymously, constitutional government was accepted, at least in certain areas, as a part of the ordained order. The constitutional polemics that went into the defense of interposition were sincerely expressed, but their purpose was the promotion of social and ideological orthodoxy and rural and small-town values.

Like the Ku Klux Klan in the 1920's, massive resistance was "a prosperity period protest against change and the erosion of the small town, old-stock, Protestant image of America."[14] Southern neobourbons associated the threat to white supremacy with the decline of economic individualism, respect for private property, limited government, the influence of religion, family solidarity, traditional sexual norms, and patriotism.[15] All of these were basic neobourbon values, as, indeed, they were basic values of American conservatives generally. And like a past generation of bourbons horrified by the changes wrought by Reconstruction, southern bourbons of the 1950's sought to restore conventional values. As William J. Simmons explained,

I consider the Citizens' Council movement the beginnings of a fundamental conservative revolt throughout the country. Much more is involved than the school segregation issue. Many of our membership is [sic] concerned also about the trend toward the welfare state, the drift toward totalitarianism, the dangers of the United Nations.

The integration issue is merely an entering wedge. The movement to integrate schools is part of the liberal trend that should be stopped.[16]

---

[14] Chalmers, "The Ku Klux Klan and the Radical Right," 3. Chalmers was describing the Ku Klux Klan in the 1920's.

[15] See Victor C. Ferkiss, "Political and Intellectual Origins of Americanism, Right and Left," *Annals of the American Academy of Political and Social Science*, CCCXLIV (November, 1962), 1–12.

[16] As quoted in Jackson *Daily News*, July 23, 1955. See also Simmons' comments to Associated Press correspondent Bem Price in *The State*, August 26, 1955.

The Citizens' Council, in a front-page editorial advocating interposition, stated that the *Brown* decision

is but the most appalling of a series of usurpations.

The Interstate Commerce clause of our Constitution has been tortured into a regulation to control enterprise and to coerce racial mixing.

Confiscatory income taxes are levied to place crushing financial power in bureaucratic hands. Private property rights have been trampled upon.[17]

In Tennessee the Federation for Constitutional Government, in its questionnaires to political candidates, included not only queries relating to the candidates' stands on segregation and states' rights but also attitudes toward the Bricker Amendment, federal aid to education, and federal taxing policies.[18] The Virginia Defenders at their 1957 statewide convention adopted a "Declaration of Convictions" that opposed "the further depletion of our economic resources in the continuation of the so-called aid to foreign nations," liberalization of immigration restrictions, the United Nations, high federal taxation, and federal aid to education as well as any weakening of segregationist resolution.[19] The Mississippi Association of Citizens' Councils distributed *The NAACP Legislative Scoreboard*, which graded congressmen on whether they "voted favorably to NAACP" or "unfavorably to NAACP" on such issues as public housing, social security, statehood for Hawaii and Alaska, minimum wage legislation, and civil rights.[20] The *Brown* decision was but one of several problems that attracted the interest of Council leaders.

Neobourbon values were essentially rural values, and neobourbons betrayed a distrust of cities and vigorously opposed reapportionment. Yet they embraced New South economic doctrines and generally favored programs for the promotion of material progress. In this regard they differed substantially from an older generation of political demagogues, such as Coleman Blease of South Carolina, Eugene Talmadge of Georgia, W. Lee O'Daniel of Texas, and Thomas Heflin of Alabama. Their concept of progress, however, was entirely materialistic and Snopesean. Because of their ideology and, not infrequently, their own economic

[17] *The Citizens' Council*, January, 1956.

[18] Reprinted in Nashville *Banner*, July 11, 1956.

[19] Reprinted in Richmond *Times-Dispatch*, March 24, 1957. See also the broader statement of principles adopted by the Defenders in 1960 and reprinted in *ibid.*, December 4, 1960.

[20] Association of Citizens' Councils, *The NAACP Legislative Scoreboard: The Civil Rights Crisis and the 84th Congress* (Greenwood, n.d.); *Delta Democrat-Times*, July 14, 1957.

activities, neobourbons—while upholding rural values—showed sympathy and even admiration for large-scale capitalist enterprise. The result was, of course, a blend of the less progressive features of farm and factory.

Neobourbons could usually be counted upon to prefer taxes of a non-progressive variety (income, property, and severance taxes were despicable but sales taxes were somewhat more tolerable) and economy in government (which meant limiting or eliminating social services by the state). They normally favored bestowing all manner of favoritism upon manufacturers through tax exemptions and such programs as Mississippi's "Balance Agriculture with Industry," which Professor James W. Silver has appropriately described as "a colossal program of state socialism."[21] Neobourbons were, of course, avidly anti-union. Open-shop legislation protected the liberty of the laboring man, while an absence of governmental regulation of business did the same for the capitalist. Not infrequently, massive resistance leaders had also been active in the drive for right-to-work legislation in the late 1940's and early 1950's.[22] Their concept of progress often led neobourbons to consider schools and highways as worthy recipients of public aid. They normally insisted, however, that such aid fall generally within the confines of sound fiscal policy and economy in government; that school appropriations go primarily into minimum foundation programs, which meant draining funds from the cities to pay rural school expenses; and that road expenditures favor the counties rather than the cities. But neobourbon support for progressive measures even on this minimal level could be easily exaggerated. White supremacy clearly took precedence over public education, and, indeed, as William H. Nicholls has pointed out, "far too much of the South's conservative socio-political leadership, particularly that important segment rooted in the rural Black Belt, has remained indifferent or even antagonistic to the whole idea of universal public-school education right up to the present day."[23] On the national level the federal farm program, which lavished governmental benevolence upon the planter while provid-

---

[21] Silver, *Mississippi: The Closed Society*, 21.

[22] Harry L. Mitchell, "On the Rise of the White Citizens' Council and Its Ties with Anti-Labor Forces in the South" (confidential AFL-CIO report, Southern Regional Council files, January, 1956), and Mitchell, "The White Citizens Councils vs. Southern Trade Unions" (confidential AFL-CIO report, Southern Regional Council files, March, 1956). For example, six of the ten Louisiana members on the Advisory Committee of the Federation for Constitutional Government had been active in the Louisiana right-to-work movement.

[23] Nicholls, *Southern Tradition and Regional Progress*, 110–11.

ing little aid to the small farmer, approached the ideal.[24] Taking changed conditions into account, there was little that a nineteenth century bourbon, who favored crop lien laws and the convict-lease system while opposing child labor legislation, would have found objectionable.

Almost inevitably these programs became entwined with white supremacy. Howard H. Quint observed in reference to South Carolina politics: "The race question is applied to nearly every political issue, either openly or covertly, and all-out attempts have been—and to be sure, still are— made to discredit any proposal or policy that would alter the *status quo*."[25] Neobourbons, for example, customarily denounced labor unions by linking organized labor with integration and the NAACP. Alabama columnist John Temple Graves wrote: "A package deal that won't pack is integration and unionization—now planned for the South by the CIO-AFL [*sic*]."[26] Lieutenant Governor Ernest F. Hollings of South Carolina stated: "We are not going to have labor unions, the NAACP and New England politicians blemish the Southern way of life."[27] This tendency to associate race and conservative economic policies was a general one. Massive resistance involved far more than white supremacy, but the battle lines in the South were most often drawn on the issue of color.

Like their ideological ancestors, southern neobourbons saw neither the desirability nor the legitimacy of social change. That demands for Negro equality might ultimately rest on a moral foundation, or might even contain a moral component, was repugnant to the whole system of neobourbon values. Reflecting this blurred moral focus, some neobourbons with apparent sincerity advocated spreading Negro citizens evenly throughout the Union. Richard B. Russell introduced a Senate bill "to reduce and eliminate racial tensions and improve the economic status of the American people by equitably distributing throughout the several states those citizens belonging to the two largest racial groups included in the population of the United States who of their own

[24] On neobourbon policies generally, see Shannon, *Toward a New Politics in the South,* 41ff; Havard and Beth, *The Politics of Mis-Representation,* 111ff; Silver, *Mississippi: The Closed Society,* 20ff; Smith, *Congressman from Mississippi,* 120ff; and Irish, "Political Thought and Political Behavior in the South," 406–20.

[25] Quint, *Profile in Black and White,* 7.

[26] Birmingham *Post-Herald,* March 23, 1956.

[27] As quoted in Charleston *News and Courier,* May 18, 1956. See also Talmadge, *You and Segregation,* 18; Workman, *The Case for the South,* 76, 91; and *The Citizens' Council,* November, 1959.

volition desire to change their place of residence."[28] Georgia segregationists incorporated the American Resettlement Foundation to resettle Negroes in white neighborhoods in the North, particularly in areas where white integrationist politicians resided.[29] To be sure, neobourbons realized, as did the chief justice of the Alabama supreme court, that there were some "fantastic ideas going around about the brotherhood of man and so forth."[30] Such notions, however, were no more than testimonials to the success of integrationist propaganda.[31]

Neobourbons viewed segregation as a natural form of social organization, and they denied the validity of social change and the moral aspects of human equality. Basic changes in the patterns of white-Negro relations, they felt, would produce racial strife and social disorganization. Consequently, southern traditionalists had difficulty understanding the motives of civil rights advocates, those who would "question or attack values which have been set . . . in the hard concrete of custom."[32] If both Negroes and whites benefited from the established system, the civil rights movement was an essentially malicious perpetration that could only be explained as the result of conspiracy or political manipulation by agitators or subversives. As Professor Silver described the Mississippi reaction to Negro civil rights efforts, "this slowly accelerating historic change is seen not as a legitimate outcome of classic American values but as a criminal conspiracy against sanctified institutions."[33] These attitudes, combined with political opportunism, gave rise to the McCarthyism which permitted integrationists to be denounced as communists and dissenters to be summarily silenced.

To defend these values, neobourbonism offered a program of massive resistance. Interposition was its fundamental element—the means whereby the South would halt the shift away from conventional values and restore the Compromise of 1877. This doctrine formed the base upon which other projects were structured. Neobourbons rested the defense of white suprem-

[28]*Congressional Record*, 81st Cong., 1st Sess. (January 27, 1949), 569.

[29] Atlanta *Constitution*, October 5, 17, November 2, 5, 1957; Atlanta *Journal*, November 5, 1957, January 14, 1958.

[30] Birmingham *News*, March 5, 1959, quoting Chief Justice J. Edwin Livingston.

[31] See, for example, Workman, *The Case for the South*, 121; Talmadge, *You and Segregation*, 12–16; *Delta Democrat-Times*, August 15, 1957, quoting Ross R. Barnett; Jackson *Daily News*, October 28, 1955, quoting Tom Brady; and Nashville *Tennessean*, February 18, 1956, quoting Walter Givhan.

[32] On this point see Matthews and Prothro, *Negroes and the New Southern Politics*, 435–38. The quotation is from Shannon, *Toward a New Politics in the South*, 51.

[33] Silver, *Mississippi: The Closed Society*, 6.

acy on a foundation of state sovereignty, and they attempted to insure that the "southern people" (meaning the whites among them) would support undeviating resistance to the *Brown* decision. A formidable propaganda offensive sought to maintain home-front morale, while state governments and private organizations often dealt brutally with domestic nonconformists. Seeing the struggle as a political one, segregationists searched for national political leverage. They exported their propaganda nationwide, and the extreme neobourbons turned to third party activity and sought a political alliance with ultraconservatives of the North. Interposition, propaganda, third party activity, and the quest for a closed society thus formed the platform of massive resistance.

Not all neobourbons, and certainly not all segregationists, endorsed this this program in its entirety nor held all the views associated with the neobourbon rationale. A Michigan Survey Research Center team has convincingly demonstrated that less than 3 percent of American citizens in the 1950's could be credited with a political ideology, while only another 9 percent had enough political sophistication to be placed in a generously defined "near-ideology" category.[34] Since a great many southerners with sufficient education to be considered "ideologues" held other views, neobourbonism, as a conscious ideology, was limited to a small fraction of the southern white population. Yet the activists, the political leaders and Citizens' Council spokesmen who provided guidance for the resistance, did generally accept the neobourbon ideology and program in a more or less undiluted form. And they defended many conventional values and established social patterns and customs that great numbers of inarticulate white southerners accepted as correct modes of behavior. Most of all, neobourbons enjoyed the political advantage of defending racial injustice.

They came to the defense of segregation and insisted that there was no middle ground. "Moderation means gradualism," declared Roy Harris, "and gradualism means race mixing."[35] A southern moderate was a southern burglar who "comes into your house and tells you that if you give him just a FEW of your valuables, he'll go away," Ross Barnett stated. "Just sort of a 'token burglary,' you might call it."[36] Or, as Represen-

---

[34] Angus Campbell, Philip E. Converse, Warren E. Miller, and Donald E. Stokes, *The American Voter* (New York, 1960), 249.

[35] As quoted in Montgomery *Advertiser*, June 8, 1956.

[36] Ross R. Barnett, "Address to Statewide Citizens' Council Banquet, Columbia, South Carolina, January 29, 1960" (press release copy, Southern Regional Council files), 4.

tative John Bell Williams explained, "The self-styled moderates are simply saying they believe in a little bit of pregnancy."[37] Senator Richard Russell agreed: "There can be no such thing as token integration. This is merely a device of the race mixers to obtain total and complete integration."[38] The proponents of massive resistance drew the line sharply and insisted that there could be no "fence-straddling." Roy Harris phrased it crudely and accurately: "If you're a white man, then it's time to stand up with us, or black your face and get on the other side."[39]

Southern neobourbons asserted that only through the rigid maintenance of separate schools could the South avoid violence and anarchy. Robert Patterson said that with integration "we'll have violence and you know it."[40] This sentiment was repeated almost endlessly. The Citizens' Councils pictured themselves as practitioners of "legal" resistance and as defenders of order and stability. "An outstanding accomplishment of the Citizens' Council movement that has become increasingly acknowledged," the Mississippi Association's *Annual Report* for 1956 stated, "is the channelling of popular resistance to integration into lawful, coherent and proper modes, and the prevention of violence or racial tension."[41] But the opposite was more nearly true. The Councils fed on disruption and racial disharmony. They existed as a resistance group, and only by constantly discovering threats to white supremacy could they sustain an atmosphere of emotionalism and command a following. The Councils were a juggernaut that fed on the fears and anxieties of white men, and, therefore, they incessantly discovered or manufactured new objects of fear and anxiety. The massive resistance program rather than token desegregation threatened to commit the region to anarchy. The intolerance and extremism of the resistance posed a severe threat to democracy, federalism, and the health of American as well as southern politics.

The Councils demanded absolute fidelity to segregation, and they talked of "legal" means to maintain it, but these aims were difficult to reconcile. Council leaders were no doubt sincere in their advocacy of nonviolent resistance, but the whole thrust of their movement was in another direction. As a speaker at a Citizens' Council meeting in Alabama said: "We intend to maintain segregation and do so without violence. But

[37] As quoted in *Delta Democrat-Times*, February 29, 1956.
[38] As quoted in Charles J. Bloch, *We Need Not Integrate to Educate* (Atlanta, n.d.), 11.
[39] As quoted in Chattanooga *Times*, September 22, 1958.
[40] As quoted in *The State*, October 30, 1954.
[41] Association of Citizens' Councils of Mississippi, *2nd Annual Report* (1956), 2.

I know the first time a Negro tries to enter Parrish High School at Selma, or any other white school, blood will be spilled on the campus."[42]

In a courageous speech before the West Alabama Citizens' Council shortly after the Autherine Lucy riots, Buford Boone, publisher of the Tuscaloosa *News*, asked the assembled segregationists what they intended to do when a federal court again ordered the state university to accept a Negro student.[43] The no-quarter position taken by massive resistance advocates ultimately meant closure of the public schools and, beyond that, force and violence.

Many neobourbons considered a temporary sacrifice of school children an eminently acceptable alternative to desegregation. Indeed, W. Scott Wilkinson, a Louisiana Citizens' Council leader, contended that southern whites "would prefer that our youth grow up in ignorance than to permit them to attend integrated schools."[44] As Professor William H. Nicholls concluded from his study of the southern tradition, "many of the angry voices proposing the abolition of public schools as a 'solution' to this problem never considered public schools important even before desegregation became a political issue."[45] Sims Crownover of the Tennessee Federation for Constitutional Government said: "I don't agree that they [the public schools] are essential. Let the people educate their own children."[46] In a few cases segregationists visualized destruction of the public schools as a constructive step toward a better society. R. Carter Pittman, past head of the Georgia States' Rights Council, argued that a shift from public to private schools "would contribute 20 years to the advancement of education in this state." Not only would money be used more wisely in private schools, Pittman declared, but through the free enterprise system in education "we could get Karl Marx and John Dewey out of our schools."[47] But, generally, southern neobourbons agreed that destruction of the public schools would be an "inconvenience," an unfortunate necessity required by the Supreme Court's "unconstitutional" decision. It was an unavoidable exigency, and one that had to be faced. "I can't help but feel sorry for anybody, minister or not," stated a Georgia

[42] *The State*, December 8, 1954, quoting McClain Pitts.
[43] Montgomery *Advertiser*, January 5, 1957.
[44] As quoted in Jackson *Daily News*, May 1, 1959.
[45] Nicholls, *Southern Tradition and Regional Progress*, 114.
[46] As quoted in Chattanooga *Times*, February 27, 1956.
[47] As quoted in Atlanta *Constitution*, January 9, 1959. Such views were not confined to the South. See David Lawrence's column in the Washington *Evening Star*, October 4, 1958.

states' rights leader," who thinks that the closing of the public schools is an extremity that must be avoided at *any* cost."[48]

While prepared to take whatever action was necessary, most neobourbon leaders did not at first envision complete obliteration of the public school systems in the South. They thought in terms of closing only those specific schools forced to desegregate (and in some cases the Negro schools from which Negro students transferred). Then through private school schemes, provisions for leasing public school property to private groups, and tuition-grant arrangements, the closed public schools could promptly be reopened under the guise of private, segregated institutions. On the basis of these tactics, proponents of massive resistance could correctly point out that public school closures would only be an inconvenience. Such machinations would be difficult to justify in the courtrooms, of course, but neobourbon leaders hoped that by militantly refusing to comply with the *Brown* decision, they would force the federal courts to temporize, retreat, and ultimately abandon the whole principle.

But, the federal courts, while they did temporize, did not abandon the principle of the *Brown* decision. Instead, they denied a state the right to close some but not all of its schools and refused to accept the subterfuge of publicly subsidized private schools. When Virginia closed only those nine public schools that desegregated, a federal court in January, 1959, held this action contrary to the Fourteenth Amendment's mandate that no state can deny any person equal protection of the law. Virginia was bound to deny all its young people a public education or none of them, said the court. "A state that directly or indirectly operates a school system cannot close one public school or grade to avoid the effect of the law."[49] Shortly before this, in September, 1958, the United States Supreme Court ruled out the various private school plans. In *Cooper v. Aaron* the Court declared that a state cannot "bar children on racial grounds from attending schools where there is state participation through any arrangement, management, funds or property."[50] The Supreme Court upheld the Alabama pupil assignment law,[51] thus permitting state government to comply with the *Brown* decision while drastically limiting the amount of actual desegregation, but the federal courts insisted that the principle

---

[48] Bloch, *We Need Not Integrate to Educate*, 5.
[49] *James v. Almond*, 170 F. Supp. 331.
[50] *Cooper v. Aaron*, 358 U.S. 4.
[51] *Shuttlesworth v. Birmingham Board of Education*, in *Race Relations Law Reporter*, III (June, 1958), 425.

could not be avoided "through evasive schemes for segregation."[52] Southern states were left with the alternative of totally abolishing their public school systems and relying upon extralegal means to protect white supremacy or of admitting at least nominal numbers of Negro students to white schools.

Neobourbons thus found themselves trapped in a painful dilemma; they were "caught between the industrial and agrarian mores."[53] They had to choose between devotion to segregation and old-time values on the one hand and dedication to progress and pecuniary pursuits on the other. They had to close the schools and suffer the inevitable economic consequences—as well as facing the potential political dangers of such a drastic step; or they had to retreat from massive resistance. Eventually, the dilemma became acute; the conflict between tradition and economic progress became irreconcilable. The years 1957 and 1958 set in motion a chain of events that finally brought the southern dilemma to a head.

[52] *Cooper v. Aaron*, 358 U.S. 19.
[53] Nicholls, *Southern Tradition and Regional Progress*, analyzes this conflict. The quotation is from Shannon, *Toward a New Politics in the South*, 48.

CHAPTER 14

LITTLE ROCK
AND THE TEST OF A DOCTRINE

Virginia offered leadership to the South, by advancing a program of massive resistance structured on the theory of interposition.[1] Surprisingly, however, the great test for this resurrected doctrine came in Little Rock, Arkansas. Of all southern cities, Little Rock was among the least likely scenes for a dramatic confrontation between state and federal power. This comparatively progressive upper-South capital city had been among the first communities below the Potomac to make preparations for compliance with the *Brown* decision. The percentage of Negro students in Little Rock public schools was less than that of Wilmington, Louisville, Washington, Baltimore, or St. Louis—all of which had previously abandoned Jim Crow educational facilities. The Little Rock school system also contained relatively fewer Negroes than did those of Nashville, Charlotte, Greensboro, or Winston-Salem—the southern cities that joined Little Rock in desegregating in the fall of 1957.[2]

Although segregation remained the rule (and the vast majority of Little Rock's white citizenry preferred it that way), the community had no record of political extremism on the race question. Little Rock had already made inroads on caste inequities in several fringe areas, which included the seating arrangements on city busses. In November, 1956, almost half of Little Rock's voters opposed a White Citizens' Council-sponsored constitutional amendment "nullifying" the *Brown* decision.[3] When white supremacy advocates directly challenged the city's token

---

[1] This chapter is a revision of Numan V. Bartley, "Looking Back at Little Rock," *Arkansas Historical Quarterly*, XXV (Summer, 1966), 101–16.

[2] *Southern School News*, January, 1958.

[3] Corinne Silverman, *The Little Rock Story*, 36.

desegregation plan in school board elections held in March, 1957, the
extremists were soundly defeated by moderate candidates.[4]

Yet in the fall of 1957 Little Rock became the epitome of state resistance.
The upheaval in this city sharply and directly questioned the sanctity
of the federal court system and the validity of the Supreme Court's
desegregation ruling. It threw down the gauntlet before the bench and
demanded that federal judges retreat from the principle of the *Brown*
decision. It challenged the executive branch of the federal government
either to come to the rescue of the courts or to permit a fundamental
deviation from the course of American federalism. And still more significant, it was the first really fundamental test of the national resolve
to enforce Negro rights in the face of southern defiance. The Little Rock
controversy sharpened political antagonisms in the South, and ultimately,
it graphically illustrated the economic costs of total resistance to social
change. Little Rock was the most decisive test of the decade.[5]

Ironically, this crisis resulted not from massive resistance strategy but
from an accumulation of failures by well-meaning leaders in Little Rock.
A breakdown in community leadership, compounded by the refusal of
both state and federal governments to accept responsibility for desegregation in the city, created a vacuum that invited political demagoguery
and mob action. The city school board failed to provide constructive
guidance toward desegregation, and school administrative officials led
unwisely. Both Little Rock's "civic elite" and the city government sought
to avoid involvement or responsibility for the shift away from wholly
segregated schools.[6] In the end, Governor Orval E. Faubus reluctantly
filled the leadership void by coming to the defense of segregation and
thereby created a major constitutional crisis. This explanation differs
from a number of other published accounts which have pictured the
Little Rock debacle as the result of a deliberate conspiracy originating
either when Deep South racists persuaded Governor Faubus to thwart
the creeping advance of integration or when Faubus himself decided to

---

[4] *Ibid.; Arkansas Gazette*, March 10, 17, 1957.

[5] For thoughtful evaluations of the broad significance of Little Rock, see Lubell,
White and Black: Test of a Nation, and Bickel, *The Least Dangerous Branch*.

[6] There was a broad similarity between the crisis in Little Rock and the later crisis
in New Orleans. A study of the failure of desegregation efforts in New Orleans concluded
that the "crisis arose from a general failure of community leadership, resulting in a
breakdown of social control over the masses. The school board, the mayor, and the civic
elite all shied away from taking action." These same observations apply to Little Rock.
See Robert L. Crain and Morton Inger, *School Desegregation in New Orleans: A Comparative
Study of the Failure of Social Control* (Chicago, 1966), 97.

manufacture a racial crisis for political gain.[7] Because of this fact and also because of the importance of Little Rock to the course of massive resistance, the origins of that conflict merit reexamination.

One day after the May 17, 1954, school desegregation decision, the Little Rock school board instructed Superintendent of Schools Virgil T. Blossom to draw up a plan for compliance.[8] Although not enthusiastic about the change, neither Blossom nor any board member suggested defiance of the High Court ruling. Later in May, 1954, school authorities made public their decision and announced that planning would begin immediately.[9]

During the following year Blossom formulated and reformulated desegregation arrangements. Originally conceived as a plan for substantial integration beginning at the grade school level, the Little Rock Phase Program that emerged in May, 1955, provided for token desegregation starting in September, 1957, at one senior high school. The second phase would extend tokenism to junior high schools by 1960, with the final step of desegregation on the elementary level, tentatively scheduled for the fall of 1963.[10] A transfer provision would permit students to escape from districts where their race was in the minority, thus assuring that the heavily Negro Horace Mann High School zone would remain segregated. A rigid screening process eliminated most of those remaining Negro students who were eligible and who wanted to attend the formerly white high school.[11]

Although devoting enormous time and energy to the creation and promotion of the Phase Program, Blossom showed questionable wisdom in his approach to the problems of desegregation. The plan contained a central flaw. Desegregation was delayed until 1957 specifically to allow time for construction of Hall High School, Little Rock's third center of secondary education. With the exception of limited facilities for technical training, Little Rock had traditionally operated two senior high schools —one for Negroes and one for whites. Upon completion, Hall, located

---

[7] On the former interpretation, see Oscar Handlin, *Fire-Bell in the Night*, 44–45, and Bickel, *The Least Dangerous Branch*, 266. The latter interpretation is well developed in J. W. Peltason, *Fifty-Eight Lonely Men*, 155–65.

[8] Virgil T. Blossom, *It Has Happened Here* (New York, 1959), 10.

[9] *Race Relations Law Reporter*, I (October, 1956), 853.

[10] *Ibid.*, 854–55.

[11] Blossom, *It Has Happened Here*, defends the plan; George C. Iggers, "An Arkansas Professor: The NAACP and the Grass Roots," in Record and Record (eds.), *Little Rock U.S.A.*, 283–91, offers sharp criticism.

in the western part of the city, enrolled students from the Pulaski Heights region, the status residential area and home of Little Rock's most influential people. Central, the old white high school and the one to be desegregated, was left with pupils drawn primarily from the city's lower and middle classes. Thus the Phase Program insured that much of Little Rock's civic leadership was effectively isolated while those white citizens most likely to hold strong racial prejudices were immediately involved. This arrangement added an element of class conflict to the racial controversy and allowed segregationist spokesmen to charge that integrationists were sacrificing the common citizen while protecting the wealthy. More important, it removed the center of white moderation from direct involvement.[12]

In addition to creating this Achilles' heel, Blossom and the school board did little to construct a solid foundation of public support. Compared to some southern cities, Little Rock had a relatively flourishing moderate community, whose sentiments were given voice by institutions such as the *Arkansas Gazette*, the Greater Little Rock Ministerial Alliance, and the Good Government Committee and by individuals such as Winthrop Rockefeller, Sidney McMath, and Brooks Hays. Furthermore, substantial parts of Little Rock's business conservative-oriented civic leadership were actively involved in city affairs and had successfully promoted a drive to reform the city government in 1956; the Good Government Committee, a group of 165 prominent citizens who had spearheaded the drive, was still active in local politics.[13] Yet Blossom made no visible effort to enlist affirmative support from these sources. When, for example, the Ministerial Alliance offered to publicly endorse desegregation plans, Blossom successfully opposed the action.[14] Similarly, school authorities encouraged city news media to play down events concerning the Phase Program, although both daily newspapers—the *Gazette* and the *Arkansas Democrat*—supported the plan.[15]

Blossom did, of course, undertake a program of community education.

---

[12] The tendency for Little Rock citizens to divide along class as well as racial lines on racial questions is amply demonstrated by voting statistics. See the tables in Silverman, *The Little Rock Story*, 36–38.

[13] *Arkansas Gazette*, November 10, 1957; Walter Lister, Jr., in New York *Herald-Tribune*, November 3–6, 1957.

[14] Colbert S. Cartwright, "Lesson from Little Rock," *The Christian Century*, LXXIV (October 9, 1957), 1194.

[15] Comments by William T. Shelton, city editor of the *Arkansas Gazette*, in a letter to the author, October 5, 1965.

He delivered some two hundred speeches, addressing any group that would provide a rostrum. In these talks, the superintendent often pointed out his own and the board's disapproval of integration, explaining that there was no alternative to some desegregation and that the Phase Program would insure gradual change. Many Negro observers were soon "convinced that Superintendent Blossom was more interested in appeasing the segregationists by advocating that only a limited number of Negroes be admitted than in complying with the Supreme Court decision."[16]

Basically, school authorities, as well as community leaders generally, regarded desegregation as a problem in school administration, and from this assumption flowed a negative approach. Early in the planning stage, Blossom and his staff sampled public opinion and concluded that prevailing sentiment was to respect the law while delaying social change as much as possible. They also discovered that white parents with small children seemed more committed to segregation than those with children in high school.[17] As a practical administrator dependent upon public support, Blossom devised a functional plan tailored precisely to these findings and went about explaining it to the community. Since many of his speeches were delivered before service clubs, businessmen's groups, and church organizations, he spent a disproportionate amount of time among people of higher socio-economic standing—many of whom could send their children to Hall High School anyway—and thus he encountered little hostility. With everything going smoothly, the superintendent apparently saw no reason to muddy the waters with a more vigorous program of community preparation.

When opposition to desegregation developed during the summer of 1957, the school administration had no reservoir of public support. The moderate position was based on acceptance of the inevitable rather than on commitment, making it psychologically easy for many of the city's more responsible citizens to ignore the school board's growing dilemma. Little Rock's civic elite watched from the sideline, accepting school desegregation as an administrative question properly to be dealt with by school authorities. Upper-class citizens exerted their influence to ensure that Hall High School was not included in Blossom's desegregation plans and to prepare for the campaign of "good government" candidates for

---

[16] Daisy Bates, *The Long Shadow of Little Rock: A Memoir* (New York, 1962), 51–52. See also Iggers, "The NAACP and the Grass Roots," 284.

[17] Blossom, *It Has Happened Here*, 14.

city offices in the November, 1957, election.[18] Furthermore, Blossom and his staff sacrificed to community sentiment an educator's plan to begin desegregation on the grade school level where problems of scholastic inequality and developed race consciousness were minimal, and then they failed to prepare teachers and students for the problems of adjustment to a biracial student body. Finally, by choosing a single school serving those citizens least tolerant of social change, they not only gave segregationists a ready-made class issue but also allowed them to focus all their attention on a single place. Compared to Louisville or St. Louis, Little Rock was singularly unprepared for integration.

Contributing substantially to Little Rock's headaches was the discredited and lame duck status of the city government. Mayor Woodrow Wilson Mann headed an unsuccessful administration that had been effectively repudiated at the polls in November, 1956, when voters chose to replace the mayor-alderman system with a city-manager form of government. Mann's tenure did not end, however, until after the election of city directors in November, 1957. For all practical purposes Mann, like everyone else, turned desegregation arrangements over to Blossom to deal with as another educational problem. City officials took virtually no advance precautions. Little Rock police faced near-riot conditions without benefit of mob control training, although concerned citizens had suggested this step well in advance.[19] Apparently not until August, 1957, did city officials formulate even a meager and—considering the circumstances—inadequate concrete plan for maintaining order in the Central High School area.[20] Given the mayor's lack of confidence in Chief of Police Marvin H. Potts, this negligence was particularly surprising.[21] Similarly, during the weeks prior to school opening, when a forceful statement warning that the city would not tolerate disorder was obviously needed, the mayor issued no policy statement at all.

Well before the first jeering crowd appeared, the Capital Citizens' Council—later assisted by the League of Central High School Mothers—

[18] See Ernest Q. Campbell and Thomas F. Pettigrew, *Christians in Racial Crisis: A Study of Little Rock's Ministry* (Washington, 1959), 179–80.

[19] Cartwright, "Lesson from Little Rock," 1194. A Little Rock minister at the time of the crisis, Cartwright offers perceptive observations. See also his "The Improbable Demagogue of Little Rock, Ark.," *Reporter*, XVII (October 17, 1957), 23–25, and Robert R. Brown, *Bigger Than Little Rock* (Greenwich, Conn., 1958).

[20] Silverman, *The Little Rock Story*, 6.

[21] Woodrow Wilson Mann, in New York *Herald-Tribune*, January 29, 1958. Mann's account of the crisis was serialized in the *Herald-Tribune*, January 19–31, 1958.

was aggressively promoting public opposition to desegregation. Although a member of the Arkansas Association of Citizens' Councils, the Capital chapter was a local movement which drew its greatest popular support from working-class districts; but it also enjoyed sympathy from substantial numbers of other white citizens, particularly those in lower-class neighborhoods and in lower-status, middle-class areas. Ministers, lawyers, and occasional independent businessmen were most prominent among the organization's leadership. Ministers, mainly of the Missionary Baptist faith, were probably the most active single group.[22] Robert E. Brown, publicity director for a Little Rock radio-television station, was chapter president during 1957, but most observers believed Amis Guthridge, an attorney and states' rights political figure, to be the Council's *de facto* head.

Neither the Capital Citizens' Council nor the Mothers' League, which was created only two weeks before the National Guard intervened at Central High School, enjoyed large membership, and neither succeeded in enlisting support from Little Rock's traditional civic leadership. Nevertheless, segregationist influence easily could be underestimated. With the civic elite neither being invited nor volunteering to participate in preparing the community for desegregation and with the city government taking no action, the Capital Citizens' Council partially filled the vacuum and became a real voice in racial affairs. As a local political party, organized segregationists polled 35 percent of the city vote in March, 1957, and almost 50 percent in November of the same year.[23]

In the spring of 1957 the Capital Citizens' Council launched an intensive propaganda campaign, disseminating leaflets and sponsoring advertisements attacking integration, holding rallies (three times with out-of-state speakers), initiating letter writing campaigns aimed at Governor Faubus, spreading—perhaps originating—rumors about impending violence, and organizing crowds to disrupt public meetings of the school board. Above all, segregationists demanded that Faubus intervene to prevent violence and preserve dual school systems in the state capital.[24]

---

[22] Campbell and Pettigrew, *Christians in Racial Crisis*, 41–62, provides an able analysis of the segregationist activity of "sect" ministers.

[23] Silverman, *The Little Rock Story*, 36–38.

[24] *Arkansas Gazette*, May 1, July 9, 17, 21, 1957; *Southern School News*, August, September, 1957; Blossom, *It Has Happened Here*, 35–47; Campbell and Pettigrew, *Christians in Racial Crisis*, 45; Brown, *Bigger than Little Rock*, 16–17.

The appearance of Governor Marvin Griffin and Roy Harris of Georgia at a Council dinner on August 22 was one of the more publicized events in the summer-long war of nerves. Assuring listeners that Georgia would not allow school integration, the two featured speakers called upon Arkansas to join in the defense of segregation.[25] That night Griffin and Harris stayed at the executive mansion, and on the following morning they breakfasted with Faubus. Reportedly the breakfast conversation concerned topics other than segregation. As Harris explained, "We thought he was so far on the other side that we didn't even speak about it."[26] Although much has been made of this visit, no valid evidence has yet contradicted this version of the affair. After all, Griffin and Harris were frequent orators on the Citizens' Council circuit throughout the South. Little Rock segregationists were seeking big-name speakers to lure patrons to a fund-raising banquet, and, in Griffin's words, "they knew me and Roy would attract a crowd."[27] It was logical that the Capital Citizens' Council should consider the two well-known racists, and it was equally logical that Griffin and Harris, when invited, should offer their support to white supremacy in Little Rock. On August 20, two days prior to the dinner, Faubus had telephoned Griffin to request that he refrain from advocating violent action while in Arkansas. When Griffin gave assurances, the Arkansas governor invited the visiting Georgia governor to stay overnight in the executive mansion.[28] The Georgians' visit proved to be one of several effective Capital Citizens' Council propaganda strokes. "People are coming to me," Faubus testified shortly afterward, "and saying if Georgia doesn't have integration, why does Arkansas have it."[29]

None of these factors—lack of preparation, absence of city leadership, rise of a militant opposition—was in itself fatal to desegregation. Little Rock remained basically a moderate community, and most citizens assumed that preparations for token integration were proceeding on schedule.

[25] *Arkansas Gazette*, August 23, 1957.

[26] As quoted in New York *Times*, September 9, 1957. "Georgia: Rallying Point of Defiance," *Look*, XXI (November 12, 1957), 34, provides an account of the visit by Griffin and Harris. "Text of TV Interview with Governor Faubus," in Memphis *Commercial Appeal*, September 9, 1957, gives Faubus' account. All are in agreement.

[27] As quoted in "Georgia: Rallying Point of Defiance," 34.

[28] Fletcher Knebel, "The Real Little Rock Story," *Look*, XXI (November 12, 1957), 32.

[29] As quoted in *Southern School News*, September, 1957.

The situation did have a vital effect on the actions of the school administration, however. "The integration of Central High School," Blossom wrote in his memoirs, "was no longer a local, school administrative problem."[30] Fearing difficulties and perhaps becoming aware of their exposed position, school authorities began a desperate search for support. During the summer of 1957, Blossom conferred frequently with Chief of Police Potts. Although promising to maintain law and order, Potts, who was opposed to desegregation, showed little enthusiasm and was apparently hesitant to make concrete commitments.[31] The superintendent and School Board President William G. Cooper, Jr., decided to seek assistance elsewhere.[32] Blossom appealed to Federal District Judge John E. Miller asking for a public pronouncement pointing out to potential troublemakers the consequences of obstructing the court-approved desegregation plans. The judge refused.[33]

Blossom then turned to Governor Faubus. The superintendent sought from the governor a public statement promising to maintain order and to permit no obstruction to integration, thus making the state responsible for peaceful desegregation in Little Rock. Faubus steadfastly refused. Beginning in early August, 1957, Blossom, accompanied twice by School Board Secretary Wayne Upton and three times by the entire school board, tirelessly pressed the governor for a commitment. Anxious to justify their request, school spokesmen probably exaggerated the dangers of public disorder by reiterating fears that outside agitators might converge on Little Rock to disrupt desegregation. On at least three occasions Blossom related to Faubus threats of impending violence—once, for example, retelling a story about the existence of a secret society that intended to halt desegregation by armed terror.[34] "The more the tension mounted late in August," Blossom wrote later, "the more anxious the

[30] Blossom, *It Has Happened Here*, 48.
[31] "Statement Made by Blossom to FBI," September 7, 1957, reprinted in *Arkansas Gazette*, June 18, 1958; Peltason, *Fifty-Eight Lonely Men*, 162; *Arkansas Gazette*, August 30, 1957.
[32] Blossom, *It Has Happened Here*, 49.
[33] *Ibid.*, 50. The district court upheld the Phase Program in *Aaron v. Cooper*, in *Race Relations Law Reporter*, I (October, 1956), 851–60.
[34] "Statement Made by Blossom to FBI," September 7, 1957. Blossom comments more fully on the discussions in *It Has Happened Here*, 40–75. Other accounts shedding light on these conferences include "School Board Statement," reprinted in *Arkansas Gazette*, June 18, 1958; Dale and L'Moore Alford, *The Case of the Sleeping People* (Little Rock, 1959), 8; Wayne Upton, in New Orleans *Times-Picayune*, January 29, 1959; Mann, in New York *Herald-Tribune*, January 21, 22, 1958; and "The Story of Little Rock—as Governor Faubus Tells It," *U.S. News and World Report*, XLIV (June 20, 1958), 101–106.

school board was to persuade Governor Faubus to issue a formal statement."[35] Little Rock insisted upon making Faubus part of its troubles.

Prior to his intervention in Little Rock, Faubus had sought more or
less consistently to avoid involvement in the school desegregation question,
holding that it was a local problem best solved on the community level.
Raised in the isolated hill country of Madison County where the number
of Negroes in the population is negligible, Faubus was not a racist by
personal conviction. After being elected governor in 1954, he oversaw
the integration of Negro members into the state Democratic Party
machinery and the dropping of racial barriers on the undergraduate
level at state colleges.[36] During his early period as chief executive, he
rarely commented on school desegregation. Even when the northern
Arkansas community of Hoxie became involved in a much-publicized
integration controversy that offered the governor an ideal opportunity
to come to the defense of white supremacy, he ignored the event.

Segregation was a topic too fraught with emotional appeal to remain
buried, and Faubus was too much a politician not to shift with the
political winds. The publicity resulting from Hoxie's desegregation
difficulties in the summer of 1955, effective agitation by white supremacy
organizations, and the growing mood of social reaction spreading across
the South made social issues too immediate to be ignored. In January,
1956, Faubus released the results of a public opinion poll which showed
a large majority of Arkansas citizens opposed to integration.[37] At the
same time, the governor made his first detailed statement on racial issues
during his thirteen-month tenure in office. He declared: "I cannot be
a party to any attempt to force acceptance of a change to which the
people are so overwhelmingly opposed." Faubus encouraged local communities "to work out a definite plan of action in accordance with the
needs of the district and the demands of its patrons" and promised "that
the force of the executive office would be used to defend the decisions of
the individual school districts of our state."[38] Shortly afterward he en-

[35] Blossom, *It Has Happened Here*, 58.

[36] Drummond, "Arkansas Politics: A Study of a One-Party System," 91; *Southern
School News*, October, 1955.

[37] New York *Times*, January 29, 1956; *Arkansas Gazette*, January 29, 1956. The poll
showed 85 percent opposed to integration and 15 percent favoring integration, but these
figures excluded the 18 percent who had no opinion. The pollsters also admitted that it
was difficult to correlate the answers of Negroes, most of whom were apparently relegated
to the 18 percent "no opinion" category.

[38] These comments were in the form of written answers to questions submitted by
Damon Stetson, in New York *Times*, January 29, 1956.

dorsed the work of an unofficial committee studying problems posed by the Supreme Court ruling. The committee, composed entirely of East Arkansas spokesmen, recommended two proposals: a locally administered pupil assignment measure and a protest interposition resolution. With Faubus' backing both measures became law by initiative petition.[39]

Then came the 1956 gubernatorial primary. The governor's chief opponent, White Citizens' Council organizer James D. Johnson, rested his appeal to Arkansas voters on racial demagoguery and thus set the tone of the campaign. Since the race developed no other issue, Faubus turned to a more positive defense of segregation. At the same time he was denouncing Johnson and another stanchly segregationist candidate as "hate preachers," Faubus repeatedly promised that "there will be NO forced integration of public schools as long as I am governor."[40] In light of Faubus' future actions in Little Rock, the 1956 gubernatorial primary results are interesting. Whatever else the election demonstrated, it did not provide a basis for convincing Faubus and his advisers that the route to political success in Arkansas lay along the path of racial extremism. Faubus handily won in the first primary by polling more votes than his four opponents combined. Johnson carried only seven counties, all but one of which were contiguous "friends-and-neighbors" counties grouped around Johnson's home. Faubus ran well everywhere else in the state. He continued to be the favorite of the Ozark hill country, and he ran strongly in the cities and in the heavily Negro populated Mississippi Delta area.[41] The election results seemed to indicate that the governor's "common man" approach and racial "moderation" were pleasing to a solid majority of Arkansas' citizens.

When the state legislature met in its 1957 regular session, Faubus devoted most of his second inaugural address to the need for increased taxes and expanded state services. Commenting briefly on race relations, he restated his opposition "to any forcible integration of our public schools. These matters," he continued, "must be left to the will of the people in the various districts. The people must decide on the basis of what is best as a whole for each particular area." The governor went on

[39] "Report of the Bird Committee," in *Race Relations Law Reporter*, I (August, 1956), 717–28. The two bills are reprinted in *ibid.* (June, 1956), 579–81, 591–92. *Southern School News*, December, 1956, gives election results.

[40] The quotation is from a Faubus campaign ad published in *Arkansas Gazette*, July 27, 1956. See also *Southern School News*, June-August, 1956.

[41] *Arkansas Gazette*, August 1, 2, 1956. See also Pettigrew and Campbell, "Faubus and Segregation: An Analysis of Arkansas Voting," 436–47.

to praise Arkansas' pupil assignment law and to insist that better schools
for all citizens would go far toward alleviating the school desegregation
problem.[42] When faced with pressure from East Arkansas lawmakers
demanding further protection for segregation, however, Faubus supported and signed four additional anti-integration bills.[43]

Through all of these maneuvers Faubus continued to insist that desegregation "is a local problem which can best be solved on the local
level."[44] During his campaign, he had pledged that "no school board
will be forced to mix the races in schools while I am governor."[45] Yet,
when asked about his support of segregationist legislation at a press
conference on July 17, 1957, Faubus responded that "everyone knows . . .
state laws can't supersede federal laws," adding that he would not attempt
to nullify federal authority with state legislation.[46]

A thread of logical consistency marked the governor's tortured path.
All administration-sponsored racial legislation was written by a member
of the governor's advisory committee and carried out a basic strategy
designed to block desegregation in communities where white race feeling
ran high and to limit it within the bounds of community acceptance
elsewhere. The program centered around the pupil placement act, which
delegated to district school authorities the task of assigning pupils to
schools according to certain criteria. Among various other legal stratagems
were some irresponsible and potentially dangerous laws to intimidate
the NAACP. None of these measures penalized integration, and the
governor and his advisers consistently rejected nullification theories. This
approach allowed Faubus to uphold local autonomy while promising to
prevent forced integration. In practice, the state followed a laissez-faire
policy prior to the autumn of 1957, leaving each district to work out its
own racial problems. Under this arrangement, five Arkansas communities desegregated, and five more were planning to do so in 1957.
One of these, Van Buren, was acting under court order.[47]

[42] "Text of Governor Faubus' Second Inaugural Address," reprinted in *Arkansas
Gazette*, January 16, 1957.
[43] *Race Relations Law Reporter*, II (April, 1957), 453, 456, 491–96. The legislature also
passed the governor's tax program, and there may well have been a connection between
Faubus' support for segregationist legislation and substantial East Arkansas support for
his tax program.
[44] As quoted in New York *Times*, March 25, 1956.
[45] As quoted in *Arkansas Gazette*, June 10, 1956.
[46] As quoted in New York *Times*, July 18, 1957.
[47] *Southern School News*, September, 1957.

Little Rock, however, interrupted the state's policy of drift. Here, school authorities and organized segregationists—the effective voices of both the proponents and the enemies of desegregation—insisted that the governor take action to preserve order. Faubus found himself in a dilemma. He had promised not to force integration upon an unwilling community, a pledge which the Mothers' League reminded him of in a petition late in August,[48] and he had indicated an intention not to subvert federal law with state action. Although political expediency eventually overrode executive responsibility, Faubus, rather than being a conniving politician coolly manufacturing a crisis, was more correctly a much-worried man fearful of being pushed to the unpopular side of a major racial controversy. During the last days of August, 1957, as time ran out for laissez faire, Orval E. Faubus maneuvered to avoid taking a stand at Little Rock.

The governor first invited the Eisenhower administration to accept the burden. The Justice Department responded to Faubus' telephone inquiry by sending Arthur B. Caldwell, head of the civil rights section, to Arkansas on the twenty-eighth of August. Faubus, expressing fear of violence, questioned the Justice Department representative about federal assistance in the event of trouble. Caldwell could only explain that the Eisenhower administration did not wish to get involved and would assume no advance responsibility for maintaining order.[49] Even at this late date, the national government had no plans for dealing with opposition to desegregation. With massive resistance reaching its crest and with the University of Alabama and Mansfield, Texas, incidents a part of the immediate past, such lack of forethought bordered on the incredible. The indecisiveness of national leadership was to become clear during following weeks. But, in the meantime, the Eisenhower administration compounded Faubus' problems by allowing a report on the confidential conversation with Caldwell to leak to the press. The 1950's was not a period when consorting with the federal government on racial issues was regarded as politically advantageous in the South, and Faubus reacted angrily when reporters asked about the talks. The federal government, the governor said, was "cramming integration down our throats"

---

[48] *Ibid.*
[49] Warren Olney III, "A Government Lawyer Looks at Little Rock," *Congressional Record*, 85th Cong., 2nd Sess. (March 24, 1958), 5090–92; New York *Times*, August 31, September 1, 1957.

and then demanding that we "protect ourselves while we're carrying out their orders."[50]

After the conference with Caldwell, the governor next attempted a legal gambit to free himself from the perils of social change in Little Rock. He helped initiate and testified in support of a Mothers' League petition asking an Arkansas chancery court to enjoin school authorities from carrying out planned desegregation. Faubus informed the court that violence was likely if immediate integration were attempted in the tense city. Relying heavily upon the governor's testimony, the chancery court judge issued the injunction on August 29; on the next day a federal district court injunction voided the chancery court order.[51]

With the school opening date fast approaching, Faubus had to choose. Given the assumptions from which the governor viewed the problem, his decision was perhaps predictable. He feared that a leaderless city was slipping into violence. He felt that political considerations and past commitments prevented him from underwriting peaceful desegregation. There remained only one choice, even this was not an enviable one for a cautious politician who had never shown a desire either to fan racial discord or to alienate Negro voters. On September 1, 1957, the governor announced publicly that he had no plans concerning Little Rock and privately indicated that he intended to let city officials deal with the problem.[52] That night he had a long talk with Superintendent Blossom, who again impressed upon Faubus the necessity for state support. When the governor remarked during the discussion that desegregation could likely be accomplished by local officials, Blossom answered: "We will succeed if only you will issue a statement that you will not tolerate defiance of the law."[53] Faubus refused to make the commitment, hinting instead that he might intervene to block the school board's plans.[54] The governor did act on the next day, by ordering the National Guard, which had been alerted earlier, to prevent desegregation in Little Rock.[55] Appearing on television that night, he explained that the mission of the

---

[50] As quoted in *Arkansas Gazette*, August 31, September 1, 1957. See also New York *Times*, August 31, September 1, 1957.

[51] *Arkansas Gazette*, August 30, 1957; *Southern School News*, September, 1957; *Race Relations Law Reporter*, II (October, 1957), 931–34.

[52] Memphis *Commercial Appeal*, September 2, 1957; Knebel, "The Real Little Rock Story," 31–32.

[53] Blossom, *It Has Happened Here*, 66.

[54] *Ibid.*

[55] *Race Relations Law Reporter*, II (October, 1957), 960.

soldiers was "to maintain or restore order and to protect the lives and property of citizens."[56] During the emotion-packed weeks that followed, Faubus insisted that he was not interposing nor attempting to defy any court order. He reiterated that he was neither opposing integration nor defending segregation. In fact, he often pointed to Arkansas' progress toward racial equality and bragged that "my only child . . . is now attending classes in a state-supported integrated college."[57] He stated repeatedly that he acted only to prevent violence. Having committed himself nevertheless to a segregationist course of action—and finding that he rode a wave of popularity—Faubus found his range of political maneuvering sharply narrowed. He became increasingly demagogic and irresponsible.

Governor Faubus dispatched the National Guard to Central High School on Monday, September 2. That evening, Blossom and the school board released a public statement asking the nine Negro children scheduled to begin classes with their approximately 1,900 white schoolmates on the next morning to remain at home until the legal issues involved had been settled.[58] The Guard contented itself with turning back the Negro employees at Central High School, while the board, now trapped between national and state power, appealed to the federal district court in Little Rock for instructions. Judge Ronald Davies ordered the board to carry out its desegregation plan.[59] On September 4, the nine Negro pupils braved the mob surrounding the high school only to be refused admittance by armed Guardsmen. School officials returned to court the next day; this time they petitioned Judge Davies for a temporary suspension of desegregation. The board called attention to developing tension and antagonism which, it felt, would disrupt education at the school.[60] Hearings on this request were held September 7, and on that same day Judge Davies rejected the board's plea. He stated that "the testimony and arguments this morning were, in my judgment, as anemic as the petition itself."[61] Two days later, Davies ordered the United States Attorney General to "file immediately a petition" for an injunction against Faubus and two officers of the Arkansas Guard. The Justice Department

---

[56] As quoted in *Arkansas Gazette*, September 3, 1957.
[57] As quoted in *ibid.*, September 27, 1957.
[58] *Ibid.*, September 3, 1957.
[59] *Race Relations Law Reporter*, II (October, 1957), 938–39.
[60] *Ibid.*, 939.
[61] *Ibid.*, 940–41.

filed the petition on September 10, and Davies set the hearing for ten days hence.[62]

During this period, between September 2 and September 20, the Eisenhower administration watched indecisively as National Guard troops maintained segregation at Central High School in defiance of federal authority. On the morning after Faubus called out the guard, President Eisenhower said at a press conference: "You cannot change people's hearts merely by laws. Laws . . . presumably express the conscience of a nation and its determination or will to do something. But the laws here are to be executed gradually." Eisenhower noted the "very strong emotions" on the segregationist side but offered no comments about the immediate problems of Little Rock.[63] Not until the fifth of September did the President make a firm statement that "the federal Constitution will be upheld by me by every legal means at my command."[64] But this pronouncement was qualified on the following day, when an administration spokesman assured reporters that Eisenhower still opposed the use of federal troops to enforce court orders.[65] Most of all, the Eisenhower administration allowed the Little Rock dispute to fester for three weeks without taking the simple expedient of federalizing the National Guard and changing its orders.[66] Later, after Faubus removed the Guard on September 20, Little Rock officials begged for assistance from federal marshals, and their plea was denied by the Justice Department.[67] The administration did eventually take action, but only after opportunities for preventing or minimizing the crisis had been rejected.

Meanwhile, the National Guard lazed around Central High School watching the curious crowds which in turn had gathered to watch them. Faubus, in a telegram to Eisenhower, stated his suspicions that federal agents were not only tapping his telephone lines but were "discussing plans to take into custody, by force, the head of a sovereign state."[68] The governor dramatically surrounded the executive mansion with

---

[62] *Ibid.*, 941–43.

[63] As quoted in New York *Times*, September 4, 1957.

[64] As quoted in *Southern School News*, October, 1957.

[65] Chattanooga *Times*, September 7, 1957.

[66] This step was frequently discussed and rejected within the administration. See New York *Herald-Tribune*, September 4, 1957; *Arkansas Democrat*, September 7, 1957; and Hays, *A Southern Moderate Speaks*, 160.

[67] Hays, *A Southern Moderate Speaks*, 169–71; Blossom, *It Has Happened Here*, 101.

[68] As quoted in *Southern School News*, October, 1957.

Guardsmen. Representative Brooks Hays sought a negotiated settlement of the impasse and arranged a meeting between Eisenhower and Faubus which ended inconclusively.[69] Race relations deteriorated, and sentiment hardened on all sides.

On Friday, September 20, the federal district court began hearings on the Justice Department's petition for an injunction against Governor Faubus and the National Guard commanders. The governor's attorneys immediately presented arguments that the district court had no right to question a chief executive's judgment in relation to "the performance of his constitutional duties" and that Davies should disqualify himself for lack of impartiality. When the judge dismissed the motion, Faubus' attorneys demanded and received permission to depart.[70] The hearings continued despite the absence of the defense. Later in the day Davies issued the petition enjoining Faubus, the National Guard commanders, or any of their agents from further obstructing desegregation in Little Rock.[71] Faubus promptly removed the Guard and departed for a southern governors' conference. He predicted that violence would result if desegregation were attempted.[72]

The governor's precipitous removal of the soldiers left Little Rock to rely upon its own resources in dealing with what had now become a dangerously tense situation. The city had the weekend of September 21–22 to prepare for the beginning of desegregation on Monday, the twenty-third of September. During this period Mayor Mann attempted to support the school administration. He released a statement calling for peaceful acceptance of integration and warning that peace officers would deal sternly with illegal interference.[73] But by this time Mann's authority had collapsed. He proved unable to control his own administration, and not a single Little Rock civic club or any other element of civic leadership offered support to the beleaguered mayor. The police department agreed to maintain order but refused to escort Negro children to Central High School.[74] The city then appealed to both Judge Davies and the Justice Department for federal marshals to escort the Negro students. Both refused.[75] The fire department balked at providing hose equipment, al-

[69] Hays, *A Southern Moderate Speaks*, 136–53; Adams, *Firsthand Report*, 345–51.
[70] New York *Times*, September 21, 1957.
[71] *Race Relations Law Reporter*, II (October, 1957), 958–63.
[72] *Arkansas Gazette*, September 22, 1957.
[73] Reprinted in *ibid*.
[74] Hays, *A Southern Moderate Speaks*, 166, 170.
[75] *Ibid.*, 169–71; Blossom, *It Has Happened Here*, 101.

though, Mann later noted, "police officials had made it clear that success in mob control depended largely on the supplementary use of water."[76] A leaderless city was slipping into violence.

Desegregation began under the protection of city police and a limited number of state troopers on Monday morning. The Negro students entered Central High School, but by lunchtime the mob outside had become so large and so belligerent that the Negro children were removed.[77] That afternoon Mann asked the Eisenhower administration for federal troops to restore order. Eisenhower issued a proclamation commanding "all persons engaged in such obstruction of justice to cease and desist therefrom, and to disperse forthwith."[78] Although the Negro students did not appear at Central High School on the next day (September 24), a crowd, though smaller and less violent than the one the day before, reformed. The situation in Little Rock remained explosive. Mann, after several telephone conversations with Justice Department officials, sent a telegram to Eisenhower officially asking for federal intervention.[79] Later the same morning, the President issued a second proclamation which provided "Assistance for the Removal of an Obstruction of Justice Within the State of Arkansas."[80] He federalized the National Guard, and that evening units of the 101st Airborne Division arrived in Little Rock. The following morning federal troops escorted Negro students to Central High School and cleared the mobs from the school area.[81]

By this time Little Rock had become the hub of southern resistance to racial desegregation. The city became a mecca to be visited by segregationist speakers from throughout the South. Race relations worsened, and the Capital Citizens' Council assumed a major voice in urban affairs. Central High School took on the appearance of an armed camp, and the nine Negro students faced an organized campaign of harassment.[82] Governor Faubus demonstrated a growing talent for demagoguery, filling the air and the newspapers with accusations such as the charge that soldiers were entering the girls' physical-education dressing rooms at the high school.[83] In July, 1958, Faubus won an almost unprecedented

[76] Mann, in New York *Herald-Tribune*, January 27, 1958.
[77] *Southern School News*, October, 1957.
[78] *Race Relations Law Reporter*, II (October, 1957), 964.
[79] Blossom, *It Has Happened Here*, 113–14; Silverman, *The Little Rock Story*, 15.
[80] *Race Relations Law Reporter*, II (October, 1957), 964–65.
[81] *Southern School News*, October, 1957; Silverman, *The Little Rock Story*, 14–16.
[82] Blossom, *It Has Happened Here*, 131.
[83] *Southern School News*, November, 1957.

third term by such a sweeping majority that the *Arkansas Gazette* editorial-ized: "The moderate position formerly espoused by many Southern political leaders, and by this newspaper as a matter of principle, has been rejected by the mass of voters in this upper Southern state and is now clearly untenable for any man in public life anywhere in the region."[84]

Little Rock reestablished the front lines of massive resistance in the upper South and became an integral part of the course of massive resistance, but not because Arkansas' "commoner in the statehouse" de-liberately planned it that way. Unconcerned with state sovereignty con-cepts, massive resistance strategy, or even the sanctity of segregation, Orval E. Faubus threw up sudden, crude barricades against national law and created a major constitutional crisis. Three governments—local, state, and federal—failed to avert a debacle that reasonable planning and a modicum of responsible leadership could have halted at any of several stages in its development.

[84] *Arkansas Gazette*, July 31, 1958.

CHAPTER 15

THE CLIMAX
OF MASSIVE RESISTANCE

The Little Rock crisis checked the trend toward "moderation" in the upper South. During the 1954–57 period, token desegregation had spread to several districts in Texas and Arkansas and to one community in Tennessee. In the fall of 1957, three North Carolina cities and the state capitals of Tennessee and Arkansas were in the process of enrolling Negro students in formerly white schools. But state intervention in Little Rock broadened the massive resistance front as Arkansas joined Virginia in openly defying the federal courts in the upper South. Events in these two states did much to determine the fate of massive resistance as the movement reached high tide during 1957 and 1958.

In the backlash of Little Rock, Virginia voters endorsed massive resistance candidates by about the same 2 to 1 majority with which they had approved the Gray Plan almost two years previously. Byrd organization leaders sought to make the November, 1957, state elections a plebiscite on massive resistance. They worked for an overwhelming victory that would both crush the threat of a revitalized Republican party in Virginia and demonstrate to the federal courts and to the nation that the Old Dominion would not accept the *Brown* decision. Virginia Democrats made the issues of states' rights and public schools the first two planks of their platform and stated: "Let there be no misunderstanding, no weasel words, on this point: We dedicate our every capacity to preserve segregation in the schools."[1] The Republican ticket, headed

---

[1] "Virginia Democratic Platform," in *News From the Democratic Campaign Headquarters* (Richmond, 1957). See James Latimer, in Richmond *Times-Dispatch*, October 6, November 7, 1957, January 5, 1958; Edward T. Folliard, in Washington *Post*, June 9, 19, 1957; Muse, *Virginia's Massive Resistance*, 44–45.

by Theodore R. Dalton, sought to arouse Virginia moderates. Dalton, who had made a strong bid for the governorship in 1953, denounced massive resistance as a "massive myth" and called for a program of gradual, controlled social change reminiscent of the original Gray Plan. The Republican candidate talked of "an intelligent approach that will meet the situation in our schools by keeping the white schools as white as possible under law and order—but by all means to keep the public schools open."[2] To Senator Byrd, the Democratic and Republican positions meant that "the issue has been clearly defined . . . as between integration and segregation."[3]

The Democratic gubernatorial nominee was J. Lindsay Almond. As attorney general under Governor Stanley, Almond had defended white supremacy in the federal courts and was popularly identified with resistance to integration. During the campaign he championed segregation eloquently and often. "I will fight as long as I have breath in my body," Almond declared, "to preserve and defend the right to govern the state's internal affairs in response to the will of the people and not in response to the wishes of an alien organization born in New York."[4] Against Dalton he received all-out support from Byrd and the organization. As one observer viewed the gubernatorial contest, "The way to victory in Virginia in 1957 appears to be on the far, right-hand side of the road, and as usual that's where the Byrd machine is traveling, its throttle wide open."[5]

But Almond, the massive resistance candidate, gave recurrent indications that he was somewhat skeptical about the program of which he had become the champion. Prior to the 1957 campaign, Almond, while following organization policy, had never been identified with the massive resistance camp. He had stated in an official opinion as attorney general that interposition had no legal validity.[6] He had engaged in a heated exchange with E. Blackburn Moore, speaker of the house of delegates and hiking companion of Senator Byrd, when Moore had suggested a deviation from the Gray proposals. He had pushed for enactment of the Gray Plan and publicly differed with Governor Stanley at

[2] As quoted by Robert E. Baker, in Washington *Post*, March 24, 1957.
[3] As quoted in Washington *Evening Star*, October 8, 1957.
[4] As quoted in Richmond *Times-Dispatch*, April 19, 1957.
[5] Folliard, in Washington *Post*, June 19, 1957.
[6] Almond to Delegate Robert Whitehead, February 14, 1956, in *Race Relations Law Reporter*, I (April, 1956), 462–64.

the very time the organization was shifting away from the program. During the 1956 general election, Almond had worked for the national Democratic ticket while Senator Byrd remained neutral.[7] The attorney general was a political veteran, however, and he commanded a substantial following in Virginia. After he announced for governor in late 1956, organization leaders concluded that he could not be stopped. Without much enthusiasm, they endorsed his candidacy.[8]

Almond campaigned vigorously on the party's massive resistance platform, yet one month prior to the election he expressed doubts about the validity of his own campaign promises. Appearing on a television program in Washington, D.C., Almond said: "No doubt there will be some in some areas—enforced integration under the mandate of Federal Courts. It will be our purpose to mitigate it as much as possible."[9] For the first time since the summer of 1956, a high ranking member of the organization had acknowledged the possibility of desegregation—a heresy that sent Senator Byrd rushing to Richmond to reaffirm that the governor's race was a choice between "whether to accept integration in our public schools or to oppose integration with all the powers in our command."[10]

Almond's deviant remark did not change the tenor of the campaign, and the Democratic ticket swept to the overwhelming victory which Byrd had wanted. The senator hailed the election as one that "will be recognized through the South and the nation as showing Virginia's determination to resist integration." Almond seemed to view it as a mandate "to stand firm against the unwarranted abrogation of power" by the federal government.[11] Shortly afterward he restated his belief that the election was a mandate "to defend and preserve the inherent powers of Virginia's sovereign statehood." In his inaugural address, the new governor gave unqualified endorsement to a program of total opposition to the *Brown* decision. "Against massive attacks," he stated, "we must marshall massive resistance," and he added that "integration anywhere means destruction everywhere."[12] Almond recommended and

[7] L. M. Wright, Jr., in Richmond *Times-Dispatch*, April 1, May 6, 1956; Washington *Evening Star*, June 4, 1956; *Southern School News*, November, December, 1956.

[8] Benjamin Muse, in Washington *Post*, January 19, 1958; Latimer, in Richmond *Times-Dispatch*, November 18, 1956; New York *Times*, December 9, 1956.

[9] "Transcript of Interview with Almond by Joseph F. McCaffrey," reprinted in Washington *Post*, October 10, 1957.

[10] As quoted in Washington *Evening Star*, October 12, 1957.

[11] As quoted by Latimer, in Richmond *Times-Dispatch*, November 7, 1957.

[12] From "Text of Governor Almond's Inaugural Address," reprinted in Richmond *Times-Dispatch*, January 12, 1958.

the 1958 legislative session promptly passed additional segregationist legislation that further consolidated state control of pupil assignment and strengthened school-closing authority.[13] In the summer of 1958, with desegregation suits against five Virginia school boards pending in the federal courts, Governor Almond made clear that "there will be no enforced integration in Virginia."[14]

Concurrently, Arkansas moved toward a similar confrontation with federal authority. Governor Faubus declared in January, 1958, that "the Supreme Court decision is not the law of the land"—the first time that he had questioned the validity of the *Brown* decision.[15] In his quest for the Democratic gubernatorial renomination, Faubus campaigned against the federal government, outsiders in general, the NAACP, and the *Arkansas Gazette* as well as against two moderate opponents and a number of prominent politicians supporting them. Faubus reiterated his statement that the *Brown* decision was no more than the opinion of nine men, and he stated that once before "I called out the guard. And I'll do it again if they push me."[16] Although the incumbent's opponents conducted energetic campaigns and received support from three former governors, they discovered, as did Dalton in Virginia, that the silent vote for moderation was difficult to arouse. Faubus won almost 70 percent of the ballots and carried every county in the state. In the same July, 1958, election, former Citizens' Council president James Johnson won nomination for a seat on the Arkansas supreme court, and, in November, Dale Alford, an extreme segregationist on the Little Rock school board, completed the rout of the moderates by beating incumbent Brooks Hays for a seat in Congress.[17] The people, Faubus said of the primary election, "have expressed their approval of my efforts to retain the rights of a sovereign state as set out in the federal constitution." He added that he had new plans for continuing the struggle with federal authority.[18]

Events moved rapidly in Arkansas during late August and September, 1958. On August 19, Faubus released a statement which called upon

[13] *Race Relations Law Reporter*, III (April, 1958), 340–45. *Adkins v. School Board of Newport News*, in *ibid.*, II (February, 1957), 46–49, declared the original Virginia placement act passed by the 1956 massive resistance session unconstitutional. The 1958 assignment measure refilled this gap in Virginia's defenses.

[14] As quoted in Richmond *Times-Dispatch*, August 22, 1958.

[15] As quoted in *Arkansas Gazette*, January 18, 1958.

[16] As quoted in Memphis *Commercial Appeal*, July 5, 1958.

[17] *Southern School News*, June–August, December, 1958; *Arkansas Gazette*, July 1, 5, 26, September 7, 1958.

[18] As quoted in *Arkansas Gazette*, July 30, 31, 1958.

the Little Rock school board either to come up with a plan to avoid integration or to resign and allow a more courageous board to do it. President Eisenhower indicated on the following day that he would insure enforcement of court decisions pertaining to Little Rock's schools. Faubus answered with: "I must say that my position of last fall is unchanged."[19] Shortly afterward the governor called a special session of the legislature and recommended measures to strengthen the state's authority over the public school system. The most important of these recommendations was a bill authorizing the Arkansas chief executive to close any school by proclamation. Attorney General Bruce Bennett supplemented the governor's requests by offering his own legislative package for the lawmakers' consideration. Convening on August 26 in a crisis atmosphere, the legislators promptly approved all the bills recommended. The special session added fourteen new laws to Arkansas' legislative arsenal. However, Faubus delayed signing them until the United States Supreme Court refused an opportunity to retreat from the principle of the *Brown* decision.[20]

Earlier the Little Rock school board had petitioned the federal courts for permission to return temporarily to segregation at Central High School. The board argued that actions by the state government, community hostility, and the turmoil of the 1957–58 school year had made orderly education on a desegregated basis impossible. Fundamentally, the board asked the federal courts to abandon the *Brown* decision and to accept community hostility to integration as grounds for the maintenance of segregation. In August the United States Supreme Court agreed to hold a special session to consider the question. The school board therefore delayed school opening while both the Arkansas legislature and the Supreme Court met in extraordinary sessions to decide the fate of desegregation in Little Rock. On September 12, 1958, the High Court denied the stay and ordered the school board to proceed with its gradual integration program.[21] Governor Faubus immediately signed the fourteen bills and released a proclamation closing all four Little Rock high schools.[22]

[19] As quoted in New York *Times*, August 20, 21, 1958.

[20] *Race Relations Law Reporter*, III (October, 1958), 1043–52; *Southern School News*, September, October, 1958; New York *Times*, September 13, 14, 1958.

[21] This was the preliminary decision in *Cooper v. Aaron*, in *Race Relations Law Reporter*, III (August, 1958), 619. The rather intricate legal maneuvering preceding this judgment is lucidly reviewed in Silverman, *The Little Rock Story*, 17–28.

[22] *Arkansas Gazette*, September 13, 1958; *Race Relations Law Reporter*, III (October, 1958), 869.

On the same day, September 12, 1958, Governor Almond removed Warren County High School from Virginia's public school system and ordered it closed. One week later he closed two schools in Charlottesville and, later in the month, the six white high schools in Norfolk. All nine of these schools were under federal court orders to admit Negro students. Unlike Faubus, who shut down all of Little Rock's secondary schools, including the Negro one, Almond closed only those schools actually threatened with desegregation. On September 27, the date that Almond intervened in Norfolk, Little Rock citizens voted by a better than 70 percent majority against reopening their high schools on an integrated basis.[23]

These momentous occurrences made Virginia and Arkansas the front lines of massive resistance as the movement surged to a climax during 1957–58. Throughout the South, state governments strengthened barriers to desegregation and intensified the attack on the NAACP.[24] The aggressive thrust of the resistance was exemplified most clearly, perhaps, by the shift of emphasis away from segregationist strategy committees (the planning agencies common during the earlier 1950's) toward state sovereignty commissions (action bodies designed to carry out resistance programs).

Events in Tennessee demonstrated the momentum that massive resistance had accumulated. In 1955 Governor Frank Clement vetoed local pupil assignment bills applicable to four small Tennessee counties partly on the grounds that these measures represented "an attempt to circumvent the efficacy of the recent opinion handed down by the Supreme Court of the United States."[25] In early 1957 Clement recommended to the Tennessee legislature a five-point anti-integration package which included a much broader locally administered pupil assignment measure applicable throughout the state. The 1957 session passed these five proposals, the Tennessee manifesto of protest, and three additional segregationist measures. Clement signed all eight bills and supported the manifesto, which did not require the governor's signature.[26] Yet Clement

[23] *Southern School News*, October, 1958. The fact that Governor Faubus and the segregationists assured the voters that private segregated schools would promptly replace the public schools prevented this vote from being a true referendum on school closing.

[24] North Carolina was the only state that failed to enact segregationist legislation during the 1957–58 period.

[25] From Clement's veto message, reprinted in Nashville *Tennessean*, March 15, 1955.

[26] *Southern School News*, February, April, 1957; *Race Relations Law Reporter*, II (February, 1957), 215–22, (April, 1957), 455.

retained his moderate image. In his address to the legislature he declared that "we must not overlook the fact that the Negro is equal to the white in the eyes of the law and in the sight of God."[27] He helped to defeat an interposition resolution introduced in the legislature and vetoed a bill repealing Tennessee's compulsory attendance law.[28] Given the rightward swing in southern politics, Clement's 1957 stance was relatively no less moderate than his 1955 position. "Moderation" had come to signify anything short of massive resistance.

Insofar as massive resistance was a struggle for men's minds, the movement reached its crest in the summer and fall of 1957. During this period, polls conducted by the American Institute of Public Opinion showed significant shifts away from desegregation in the attitudes of both southerners and Americans generally. In August, 1957, for the first time pollsters recorded a decline in national approval of the *Brown* decision. Prior to this, public opinion samples had shown a steadily growing national trend in favor of the correctness of the Supreme Court desegregation decision. In July, 1954, a Gallup poll had found 54 percent of American citizens expressing approval of the Court decision. This percentage had increased to 56 percent in early 1955, 57 percent in early 1956, and 63 percent in January, 1957. The August, 1957, survey, however, recorded 58 percent of Americans responding favorably to queries about the desegregation decision, a drop of 5 percentage points. Ominously, a September, 1957, poll discovered a continuation of the trend away from support for the *Brown* decision. This poll, undertaken prior to the Little Rock controversy, found only 56 percent of United States citizens responding favorably, with 38 percent answering in the negative.

These same popular tendencies were evident in the South. In May, 1955, the Gallup poll found that only 20 percent of the citizens below the Potomac viewed the *Brown* decision favorably. This percentage increased to 22 percent in early 1956 and to a high of 27 percent in January, 1957. But the August, 1957, survey reported a drop back to 20 percent and the September, 1957, poll marked an all-time low of only 16 percent of southerners favoring the *Brown* decision. Even more significant, perhaps, was a decline in popular acceptance of the inevitability of desegregation. In February, 1956, 55 percent of southern whites foresaw the day when southern "whites and Negroes will be going to the same schools, eating

[27] As quoted in Chattanooga *Times,* January 10, 1957.
[28] *Southern School News,* April, 1957.

in the same restaurants and generally sharing the same public accommodations." By August, 1957, the percentage of southern whites visualizing such a day had declined to 43 percent. Among southerners generally the August, 1957, survey found 45 percent perceiving an eventual desegregated society, and, among Americans generally, 54 percent predicting the eventual demise of Jim Crow in the South.[29] Finally, in the summer of 1957, Gallup found a significant drop in national esteem for the United States Supreme Court.

The Little Rock crisis, with its white mobs and federal intervention, had a decisive impact on public attitude. A Gallup poll conducted in early October, 1957, indicated a sharp reversal of the trends evident earlier in the year. The October, 1957, survey found 59 percent of all Americans and 23 percent of southerners expressing approval of the *Brown* decision, jumps of 3 and 7 percent respectively. Furthermore, the next survey querying southerners about the future prospects for integration in the South, which was conducted in October, 1958, found a shift back toward the inevitability of desegregation. The poll reported that 52 percent of southern whites and 53 percent of all southerners perceived a day when the South would abandon the caste system. These trends continued for the remainder of the decade.[30]

The political climax of massive resistance came after the Little Rock crisis. Governor Faubus' intervention with the National Guard to block desegregation and the Eisenhower administration's use of federal troops to clear away the obstruction reverberated throughout the South. Senator Herman Talmadge compared "the spectacle of the President of the United States using tanks and troops in the streets of Little Rock to destroy the sovereignty of the state of Arkansas" with "the destruction of the sovereignty of Hungary by Russian tanks and troops in the streets of Budapest." Governor George Bell Timmerman dramatically resigned his commission as a naval reserve officer, stating that his military position was "no longer compatible with my duties as Governor of South

[29] Southern Negroes approved the *Brown* decision by a growing majority and were more optimistic about the future of integration than were whites. In February, 1956, 53 percent of southern Negroes approved the *Brown* decision, and in December, 1957, 69 percent registered approval. In 1956, 70 percent of southern Negroes foresaw the eventual passing of the caste system.

[30] A convenient source for a number of the more important polls concerning race relations is Hazel Gaudet Erskine, "The Polls: Race Relations," *Public Opinion Quarterly*, XXVI (Spring, 1962), 137–48; for broader discussions of opinion trends, see Hyman and Sheatsley, "Attitudes Toward Desegregation," and Sheatsley, "White Attitudes Toward the Negro."

Carolina." Governor Price Daniel of Texas sent a telegram to President Eisenhower demanding to know: "Does this mean you will occupy with troops every nonintegrated school in the South."[31] Three state legislatures passed resolutions condemning the President for, as the Georgia declaration put it, "this deliberate and palpable executive encroachment on the Constitution and laws."[32]

The Little Rock controversy quickened the pace of race politics and shifted the political spectrum further to the right, but no other upper-South state joined Arkansas and Virginia in overt defiance of the Supreme Court. Florida, North Carolina, Tennessee, and Texas continued to follow the same broad policies that they had established during 1956. In these states the forces of massive resistance commanded insufficient backing to dictate the course of events. Governors of the peripheral-South and their legislative allies were able to maintain general control over state policy.

Florida was one of the two states that held special legislative sessions in the wake of the Little Rock crisis. Governor Collins convened the special session in October, 1957, to deal with reapportionment, but the lawmakers promptly turned their attention to white supremacy and Little Rock. Leading members of the legislature had long been at odds with the governor over both reapportionment and matters pertaining to segregation. Favoring a "moderate" course in race relations, Collins insisted that "Supreme Court decisions are the law of the land" and that "We should frankly . . . put the true label of demagoguery on any doctrine of nullification."[33] A substantial number of Florida legislators, while considering equitable apportionment to be an anathema, consistently favored massive resistance measures. In 1956, when under sharp attack by Sumter Lowry in the gubernatorial primary, Collins had appointed a Special Advisory Committee to recommend legislation for mitigating the effects of the *Brown* decision. The committee report, delivered in July, 1956, made a refined local pupil assignment measure and proposals granting the governor extraordinary powers "to prevent or suppress disorder" its chief recommendations. A special legislative

[31] Talmadge is quoted in New Orleans *Times-Picayune*, September 25, 1957; Timmerman is quoted in *The State*, September 29, 1957; and Daniel's query is reprinted in Dallas *Morning News*, September 25, 1957.
[32] *Race Relations Law Reporter*, III (April, 1958), 357. The other two states were Florida and Texas.
[33] From "Text of Governor Collins' Inaugural Address" (1957), reprinted in St. Petersburg *Times*, January 9, 1957.

session passed and Collins signed bills enacting the program later in the year.[34] Attorney General Richard W. Ervin, Federation for Constitutional Government spokesmen, and legislative extremists criticized these measures as being inadequate and demanded stronger legislation. When the legislature convened in its 1957 regular session, its members passed an interposition resolution and a local option school closing bill. Collins retaliated by vetoing the school closing measure and criticizing the nullification declaration, which as a resolution was not subject to veto.[35] The struggle promptly resumed when the special legislative session on reapportionment met in the fall of 1957. Legislators again took up extreme anti-integration proposals, and the Collins administration lobbied against them and vainly tried to direct attention to rectifying malapportionment. The legislature passed a resolution calling upon Congress to "enact an appropriate measure censuring the President . . . for his deliberate interference with the constitutioral guarantees of the citizens of Little Rock, Arkansas" and a bill providing for "the automatic closing and suspension of operation of any public school in the state upon the employ of Federal troops in the vicinity of said school."[36] Collins allowed this school closing bill to become law.

In the Deep South opponents of massive resistance faced a much more difficult task. Governor James E. Folsom of Alabama and Governor Earl K. Long of Louisiana, both rural liberals in the Populist tradition, sought to orient politics away from white supremacy toward bread-and-butter issues. Folsom called for better roads (particularly farm to market roads), higher old-age pensions, increased expenditures on education, tax increases, and legislative reapportionment—a program similar to the one endorsed by Long.[37] Both governors considered white supremacy a

[34] *Southern School News*, August, 1956; *Race Relations Law Reporter*, I (October, 1956), 921–27, 940–41, 954–56.

[35] *Southern School News*, June-August, 1957; *Race Relations Law Reporter*, II (August, 1957), 843–44.

[36] *Race Relations Law Reporter*, II (December, 1957), 1173, 1149. Texas was the other state to hold a special legislative session in late 1957. Texas legislators, like those in Florida, passed legislation to provide for closing any school that could not be operated "without resort to military occupation" and other segregationist measures. *Ibid.*, III (February, 1958), 87–97.

[37] Folsom's program is summarized by Fred Taylor in the Birmingham *News*, April 10, 1955. On Folsom generally, see Havens, *City Versus Farm?;* Twitty, *Y'All Come;* McCauley, "Political Implications in Alabama of the School Segregation Decision"; and Charles Morgan, Jr., *A Time To Speak* (New York, 1964), 28–37. On Earl Long, see Opotowsky, *The Longs of Louisiana;* Sindler, *Huey Long's Louisiana;* Thomas Martin, *Dynasty: The Longs of Louisiana* (New York, 1960); T. Harry Williams, *Romance and Realism in Southern*

spurious issue that diverted attention away from these more meaningful matters. "When politicians start hollering 'whip the nigger,' " Folsom told a reporter, "then you know damn well they are trying to cover up dirty tracks." And Long spoke of the "fakers trying to make themselves politically by using that issue to befuddle the people."[38] Both were oriented toward the camp meeting-style of democracy, favoring expanded suffrage and rivaling Andrew Jackson in "common man" inaugurations. Stan Opotowsky, in his *The Longs of Louisiana*, has described the 1948 Long inauguration held in the football stadium of Louisiana State University as being an extravaganza at which the guests consumed "16,000 gallons of buttermilk plus 240,000 bottles of soda pop, 200,000 hot dogs" and viewed a two-hour parade that included 140 high school bands. Although more subdued than Long's, Folsom held two big inaugurations in 1954—one for whites and one for Negroes.[39] Both tended to view society in the Populist mold, in terms of producers and nonproducers rather than black and white. Agrarian and anti-interest in style and program, they directed their appeals toward the common man and held that common men were not necessarily white skinned. They sometimes seemed incredulous at the extremes to which segregationists carried anti-Negro hysteria. Referring to Alabama Negroes and the attitudes of black-belt legislators, Folsom said: "If they had been making a living for me like they have for the Black Belt, I'd be proud of them instead of cussing and kicking them all the time."[40] Although friendly to Negro aspirations, neither, of course, was an integrationist. "All I can say is what I told the good colored people of this state during my campaign," Folsom said, "that they wouldn't have to go to school with us white folks."[41] Both

---

Politics (Athens, 1961), 82–84; and Liebling, *The Earl of Louisiana*. On the liberal tradition in the South generally, see Grantham, *The Democratic South*.

[38] Folsom is quoted by Homer Bigart, in St. Louis *Post-Dispatch*, September 21, 1955; Long is quoted by Jay Hall, in New Orleans *Times-Picayune*, May 4, 1956.

[39] Opotowsky, *The Longs of Louisiana*, 149. Both Folsom and Long encouraged Negro voter registration, a point that perhaps betrayed an element of political expediency— politicians appealing to the dispossessed would not be expected to approve barriers to the same people's access to the polls. Allan P. Sindler has observed that Earl Long encouraged Negro registration in New Orleans, but, when these same voters supported deLesseps S. Morrison over his candidate for mayor, Long supported a purge of the registration rolls. See Sindler, *Huey Long's Louisiana*, 259. But devotion to political democracy by Long and Folsom went well beyond considerations of political gain. The almost heroic efforts of Folsom and Long forces to extend Negro voting rights during the heyday of massive resistance were more akin to political suicide than expediency.

[40] As quoted in Birmingham *World*, June 1, 1955.

[41] As quoted in Huntsville *Times*, October 14, 1954. Long used almost exactly the same words to describe his attitude toward segregation. See Williams, *Romance and Realism in Southern Politics*, 82.

governors were spoils politicians who were accused of extravagance and favoritism in the granting of state contracts.[42] This tendency also carried over into racial issues. As an Alabama state senator representing black-belt Macon and Bullock counties complained to reporters, Folsom threatened to "register every damn nigger in Macon county if I did not support his road program."[43] Both Folsom and Long were rough-and-tumble campaigners whom their opponents called demagogues. Yet, during the 1950's, they appealed for reason in the face of racial fanaticism. "Here was a Long," as a student of Louisiana politics put it, "trying desperately to talk reason to a people captivated by the cries of the demagogues."[44]

While similar in outlook and program, Folsom and Long differed on strategy. The Louisiana governor followed the traditional Long policy of politically evading the race issue. He tried to avoid being maneuvered into an integrationist position and took care not to oppose segregationist measures. Long recommended no white supremacy legislation and cautioned against "a lot of segregation bills—even though I would favor them—when the Supreme Court probably would knock them out anyway," but he signed whatever anti-integration legislation the Louisiana lawmakers passed.[45]

Folsom faced the issue squarely and staked his political future on racial moderation. He insisted that the Supreme Court decision was the law and that the whole problem could be resolved "on local levels the way local people want it to work out." He called for racial "cooperation rather than coercion" and explained: "All I want is for everyone to get along together without trouble."[46] When segregationist legislators demanded a private school plan to stave off integration, Folsom denounced the program on the grounds that "if we deed our schools to private individuals, they could make apartment houses out of them; if strings

[42] Hugh Sparrow, columnist for the Birmingham *News*, was a persistent critic of the Folsom administration and filled many of his columns with accounts of governmental irregularities. See, for example, his column of November 20, 1955, and see also the "Analysis of Mansion and Emergency Funds," reprinted in Montgomery *Advertiser*, January 20, 1957. On Long, see Sindler, *Huey Long's Louisiana*, 144–262.

[43] Bob Ingram, in Montgomery *Advertiser*, February 13, 1955, quoting Sam Engelhardt. Folsom refused to deny the statement, but he did get his road program through the legislature.

[44] Opotowsky, *The Longs of Louisiana*, 169.

[45] As quoted in New Orleans *Times-Picayune*, May 13, 1956.

[46] As quoted by Homer Bigart, in St. Louis *Post-Dispatch*, September 21, 1955; by Rex Thomas, in Huntsville *Times*, September 26, 1954; and in Montgomery *Advertiser*, September 27, 1957.

are attached, the maneuver won't hold up in the courts."[47] In his battle against the proponents of massive resistance, Folsom received aid in the state legislature from his hill-country followers who were, themselves, under increasing pressure from constituents demanding a white supremacy *Götterdämmerung*. Urban members, often hostile to the administration on economic and governmental matters, were also willing to collaborate in a generally moderate approach to race relations. This support represented a legislative minority and, being based on the politically indefensible position of elementary racial justice, tended to melt away in crisis votes. Thus, when Folsom vetoed an anti-NAACP bill, urban legislators, the bulk of whom had voted against the measure originally, shifted to support passage of the bill over the governor's veto.[48] Nevertheless, this legislative division allowed Folsom to impede for a time the racist tide.

During 1955, in a series of legislative sessions, Folsom pushed through substantial parts of his program and succeeded in preventing enactment of most of the segregationist bills introduced in the legislature. He ignored passage of a resolution calling upon Congress to curtail the power of the federal judiciary but threatened to veto any pronouncement actually censuring the Supreme Court.[49] He accepted but refused to sign a pupil placement bill, stating that he found nothing "seriously wrong with it."[50] He vetoed three anti-NAACP measures and characterized the one that was repassed over his veto as being "unjust, unfair and undemocratic."[51]

But during 1956 time ran out for racial moderation in Alabama. The first months of that year witnessed a climactic stage in the Montgomery bus boycott, the Autherine Lucy riots at the University of Alabama, a booming Citizens' Council movement, and a developing racial neurasthenia that was to dominate politics for the remainder of the decade. As governor, Folsom was of course partly responsible for the course of events, and most observers agreed "that his recent failures to act firmly and promptly have contributed to the difficulties now afflicting the state."[52] Most notably, the Folsom administration failed to take adequate pre-

---

[47] As quoted in *Southern School News*, October, 1954.

[48] Havens, *City Versus Farm?*, 45–58.

[49] *Southern School News*, July, 1955; Act. 48, Legislative Acts, Alabama, 1955 Special Sess., *Facts on Film*, Roll 3.

[50] As quoted in Atlanta *Journal*, June 28, 1955; *Race Relations Law Reporter*, I (February, 1956), 235–37.

[51] As quoted in *Southern School News*, September, 1955. The other two vetoes came too late in the session to permit lawmakers an opportunity to reconsider the bills.

[52] Wayne Phillips, in New York *Times*, February 25, 1956.

cautions against potential resistance to desegregation at the University of Alabama.[53] Folsom also made political errors, particularly in issuing a hospitable but impolitic invitation to visiting Negro Representative Adam Clayton Powell for a drink at the Alabama Governor's Mansion. The two men discussed civil rights, and later Powell used quotations from the conversation in a speech before a Negro group in Montgomery, attributing to the governor such statements as "Integration is inevitable. It is here now."[54] Shortly afterward, Alabama voters dealt a sharp blow to Folsom's prestige by overwhelmingly rejecting two administration amendments authorizing corporate and personal income taxes and a large school bond issue.[55]

In January, 1956, Folsom convened a special session to deal with constitutional revision. He won legislative endorsement for an amendment partially rectifying malapportionment, but restive lawmakers refused to adjourn before taking up segregationist measures. When the pro-Folsom speaker of the house declared the session ended, a house majority refused to depart, and Attorney General Patterson ruled that the legislature was still legally constituted. The lawmakers then approved a nullification resolution and other segregationist proposals.[56] Folsom likened the interposition resolution to "a hound dog baying at the moon and claiming it's got the moon treed,"[57] but he accepted the legislative measures, neither vetoing nor signing them. A short time later, at another special session, the legislature enacted two constitutional amendments which, among other things, permitted Alabama to abandon its public school system. Thus, while under sharp attack from the Citizens' Councils

[53] Folsom later explained: "That thing [the Lucy riots] slipped up on us or we would have called out the Guard. . . . I didn't realize the Highway Patrolmen we sent over there couldn't handle the situation alone." As quoted in Montgomery *Advertiser*, September 5, 1956.

[54] As quoted in Nashville *Tennessean*, November 4, 1955. In 1958 journalist Bob Ingram wrote: "Folsom has gotten away with a lot of things in and out of public office, but having a drink with Powell is as fresh on the minds of the people now as it was two and one-half years ago. For this he may never be pardoned." Montgomery *Advertiser*, June 8, 1958.

[55] Birmingham *News*, December 7, 1955.

[56] A similar confrontation took place in the senate. *Southern School News*, January, February, 1956; Rex Thomas, in Birmingham *News*, January 22, 1956; Havens, *City Versus Farm?*, 30-35.

[57] As quoted in Montgomery *Advertiser*, January 26, 1956. The governor's opposition to interposition was tempered by expediency. Since Folsom wanted a constitutional convention to rewrite Alabama's out-dated fundamental law, he stated that he would favor nullification if it was done by a constitutional convention. *Ibid.*; Birmingham *News*, January 25, 1956.

and the traditionally anti-Folsom urban press, the governor faced a rebellious legislature seemingly intent upon overthrowing executive leadership. Folsom commented: "Hell, I wouldn't run for dog catcher today. I'd get the hell beat out of me."[58]

Folsom fought back, initiating a series of moves in an effort to regain control of the Alabama political situation. He attempted to enlist support from state news media for a high-level interracial commission empowered to deal with racial problems "through a Christian approach."[59] Speaking before approximately seventy-five publishers and editors, the state legislature, and a packed gallery, Folsom called upon the newsmen to participate in establishing a commission sufficiently prestigious to command influence and to support its members in their efforts to combat developing racial tensions. Through such an institution, Folsom said, "the moderate, thinking people of both races can get together and iron out their differences."[60] Under the glare of live television coverage, the journalists and the legislators endorsed Folsom's plan by a voice vote.

The governor sought to counter the turbulent atmosphere engendered by the Montgomery bus boycott and the Lucy riots with a series of strong statements upholding law and order. "The state of Alabama," he declared, "is not going to submit to mob rule under any circumstances."[61] At the same time, Folsom tried to broaden his support by speaking more forthrightly in favor of segregation than he had done in the past. In April, 1956, he signed a segregationist bill passed by the legislature implementing the private school, "freedom of choice" amendment—the first time he had signed any anti-integration measure.[62]

Finally, Folsom launched a campaign to carry the fight to the people.

---

[58] *Southern School News*, March, 1956; *Race Relations Law Reporter*, I (April, 1956), 418, (August, 1956), 732–33. Folsom is quoted in Montgomery *Advertiser*, January 26, 1956.

[59] Birmingham *News*, February 24, 1956. See also the accounts by Taylor, in *ibid.;* Tom Yarbrough, in St. Louis *Post-Dispatch*, February 24, 1956; Ingram, in Montgomery *Advertiser*, February 25, 1956; and Wayne Phillips, in Chattanooga *Times*, February 25, 1956.

[60] As quoted in Montgomery *Advertiser*, February 27, 1956.

[61] As quoted in Birmingham *News*, February 27, 1956.

[62] *Race Relations Law Reporter*, I (August, 1956), 717. Folsom signed the bill, which permitted students to attend segregated schools if their guardians objected to integrated facilities, on the grounds that it was not a "force bill" and was workable. As quoted in Montgomery *Advertiser*, April 15, 1956. Albert Boutwell, state senator from Birmingham and author of the amendment, explained, however, that the measure "will let white children choose to go to white schools and Negro children choose to go to Negro schools." He added that "It does not provide for any freedom of choice for a Negro child to attend a white school or a white child to attend a Negro school." As quoted in *ibid.*, August 15, 1956.

On March 1, 1956, the governor addressed the legislature, convened for its fifth special session in fourteen months, and called for a sane approach to race relations and support for his biracial commission plan. The legislators answered by introducing a host of segregation measures. The senate unanimously called upon Congress to apportion Negroes equally among the states, and the house unanimously approved a resolution demanding an investigation of communism in Alabama, beginning with Autherine Lucy.[63] Folsom announced that he would seek the post of Democratic National Committeeman in the spring elections and would make a statewide speaking tour, a "report to the people." His chief opponent for national committeeman was Charles McKay, a little-known legislator making his first statewide campaign. He was chairman of a local Citizens' Council chapter and had introduced the Alabama inter-position resolution. A Folsom victory promised to restore the governor's legislative influence, enhance his prestige generally, and deal a sharp blow to the massive resistance forces.

Accompanied by a hillbilly band, Folsom appealed to the grass roots. He said that the main issue in Alabama politics was "democracy against mobocracy." Nullification, he stated, "means lawlessness, riots and dis-order," while the "nullicrat party," he continued, was nothing but a revival of the Dixiecrats.[64] During his report to the people, Folsom claimed that "by my personal efforts we have kept our school segregated." He tempered these statements with such remarks as: "You can call the Supreme Court justices harsh names if you want to, but that doesn't relieve southern officials sworn to uphold the constitution of their respon-sibility."[65]

McKay focused his campaign on white supremacy and attacked the Folsom administration's "waste and extravagance" and its "belated" support of segregation. The result of the election was a crushing defeat for Folsom. McKay won by a 3 to 1 majority, and, in the balloting for other offices, every candidate associated with the Folsom administration also went down to defeat.[66] In August, 1956, voters again returned to the

[63] Birmingham *News*, March 1, 1956; *Southern School News*, March, April, 1956.

[64] As quoted by Taylor, in Birmingham *News*, March 15, 1956, and Chattanooga *Times*, April 8, 1956. On the campaign and the basic issues involved, see Taylor, in Birmingham *News*, March 15, 19, April 1, May 2, 8, 1956, and Taylor, in Atlanta *Journal and Constitution*, April 1, 22, 29, May 6, 1956.

[65] As quoted in Birmingham *News*, April 1, 1956, and Chattanooga *Times*, March 19, 1956.

[66] Taylor, in Atlanta *Journal and Constitution*, April 29, 1956; Birmingham *News*, May 2, 8, 1956; Ingram, in Montgomery *Advertiser*, May 6, 1956.

polls to approve the two segregation amendments and to reject an administration-sponsored amendment permitting higher corporation taxes for education.[67]

Governor Folsom failed to awaken support for moderation, and, in this atmosphere, his biracial commission plan died. By 1957 few Alabama politicians were willing publicly to endorse anything less than massive resistance. An adviser quoted Folsom as commenting that "apparently a great majority of the people are for segregation, period."[68] In 1957 the governor signed a second interposition resolution once again nullifying the *Brown* decision, and he offered only limited resistance to segregationist activity in the legislature, which among other measures enacted a law permitting school closures.[69] The 1958 Alabama elections confirmed the political demise of moderation. Gubernatorial candidates anxiously strove to identify their opponents with "Folsomism," and a high percentage of the legislators who had supported the administration were unseated.[70]

Earl K. Long avoided some of Folsom's travail by refusing to oppose massive resistance. The Louisiana governor's democratic and reformist program was, however, fundamentally incompatible with the neobourbon aims of the Rainach, Leander Perez, and Citizens' Council forces. So long as the segregationists concentrated their efforts on maintaining racial separation in the schools, Long accepted their measures and avoided a direct confrontation. But when they focused their attention on Negro voter registration, Long took up the challenge. The fight broke into the open in 1958. Long attacked William Rainach for too zealously defending white supremacy.[71] When the Rainach forces carried their purge of voter registration rolls to Long's home parish, the governor vigorously denounced the action.[72] The issue came to a head in the 1959 legislative

[67] Birmingham *News*, August 29, 1956. In November, 1956, Alabama voters rejected Folsom's reapportionment amendment, presumably because malapportionment in the legislature was popularly associated with defense of segregation and more equitable apportionment was associated with the Folsom administration. *Ibid.*, November 7, 1956.

[68] As quoted by Rex Thomas, in Montgomery *Advertiser*, January 13, 1957.

[69] Acts 14 and 528, Legislative Acts, Alabama, 1957 Sess., *Facts on Film*, Reel 3. Folsom continued to act as a restraining force on Alabama segregationist activity and to use the pocket veto against white supremacy legislation. Chattanooga *Times*, September 29, 1957.

[70] Montgomery *Advertiser*, May 8, June 5, 1958. This was also a reaction to extravagance and spoils politics, but it appears that both Alabama politicians and Alabama voters associated "Folsomism" most directly to racial toleration.

[71] New Orleans *Times-Picayune*, June 27, 1958.

[72] *Ibid.*, September 10, 21, 1958. All of this took place against a background of factional politics. Long accused Rainach of initiating the purge in order to aid the anti-Long candidate in a congressional race in the governor's home district. The purge ended when

session. The Rainach group introduced legislation to restrict voter registration still further and the Long forces countered with a measure to protect registrants from future purges. During the heated legislative struggle, Long suffered his widely publicized breakdown.[73] The white supremacy issue and the governor's personal difficulties ultimately led to the collapse of the Long faction. For the first time since 1928, no Long candidate appeared in the 1960 gubernatorial primary runoff election.

The defeats suffered by the Long and Folsom factions and the election victories recorded by Lindsay Almond and Orval Faubus illustrated southern political currents in the aftermath of Little Rock. During 1958 five states in addition to Arkansas selected governors. Georgia voters chose Lieutenant Governor Ernest Vandiver, who promised to "oppose with every personal and governmental means at my command any breakdown at any time at any place in the existing pattern of segregation in Georgia."[74] In Alabama, Attorney General Patterson, one of the most intransigent in a field of fourteen segregationist candidates, emerged as the popular choice for chief executive.[75] Tennesseans elected Commissioner of Agriculture Buford Ellington, a self-proclaimed "old-fashioned segregationist." Although closely associated with the Clement faction in Tennessee politics, Ellington in his campaign placed much greater emphasis on the race issue than Clement ever had done. Stating that he was "unalterably opposed to the integration of our public schools," Ellington vowed to "propose legislation to avoid the mixing of the races in the public schools of our state."[76] South Carolina voters elevated Lieutenant

---

Long and Rainach arranged a truce that was followed by both the Rainach and Long forces turning on Democratic National Committeeman Camille Gravel, who had angered the governor by opposing the Long congressional candidate and Rainach by voicing liberal racial views. The political complexities are unraveled in Havard and Steamer, "Louisiana Secedes: Collapse of a Compromise," 134–46.

[73] Opotowsky, *The Longs of Louisiana*, 170ff.; Martin, *Dynasty: The Longs of Louisiana*, 201ff.; Leibling, *The Earl of Louisiana*. The last work is devoted entirely to this period.

[74] As quoted in Atlanta *Journal*, July 27, 1958.

[75] Birmingham *News*, June 8, 1958. One legacy of "Folsomism" in Alabama was that virtually every candidate endorsed the use of hillbilly and popular bands and entertainers. Jack Owen, for example, finished fourth in the primary election even though he brought to the voters Elvis Presley, Roy Acuff, Porter Waggoner, Marlin Greene, and Shorty Sullivan and his Confederate Colonels. George C. Wallace (supported by Minnie Pearl and Web Pierce) also conducted a racist campaign and went into the runoff primary against Patterson, but lost handily.

[76] As quoted in Nashville *Banner*, July 4, 1958, and Chattanooga *Times*, June 15, 1958. As governor, Ellington followed the moderate policy established by Clement, leading one observer to say: "Ellington is not as bad a governor as he *promised* to be!" As quoted in Nicholls, *Southern Tradition and Regional Progress*, 94.

Governor Ernest F. Hollings, and Texas voters returned Governor Price Daniel to the statehouse.

These elections evidenced the rightward trend of southern politics, but they did not, of course, indicate that racial issues were the only matters of interest to southern voters. William T. Bodenhamer, former executive secretary of the Georgia States' Rights Council, made white supremacy virtually his only campaign plank and lost to Vandiver. W. Lee O'Daniel finished third in the Texas Democratic gubernatorial primary although he was obviously the most segregationist of all the candidates. In senatorial races, Ralph W. Yarborough of Texas and Albert Gore of Tennessee bested opponents far more conservative on social and economic issues than themselves. Success with the electorate required something more than anti-Negroism. But, in the main, the campaigns of the late 1950's bolstered the massive resistance cause.[77]

In this political atmosphere, southern state legislatures continued to churn out segregationist legislation. During 1957 Alabama legislators enacted a law authorizing local school boards to close any school within its jurisdiction and adding militantly that such action was "final and not subject to review by any court or other authority." The 1958 Louisiana legislature empowered the governor "to close any racially mixed public school or any public school which is subject to a court order requiring it to admit students of both the negro [sic] and white races by a date certain. . . ." A Mississippi law, also passed in 1958, authorized the chief executive to close any school when such action would be "to the best interest of a majority of the educable children." In 1957 both Georgia and South Carolina granted their governors broad authority to assume emergency powers that included closing public facilities, calling out the militia, and utilizing all state law enforcement personnel.[78]

By the end of 1958 every southern state except Tennessee had enacted school-closing laws. In six states governors possessed authority to terminate

[77] *Southern School News,* July-September, 1958. Mississippi's selection of Ross R. Barnett as governor in 1959 and the election of Jimmie H. Davis and Farris Bryant as chief executives of Louisiana and Florida, respectively, in 1960 further demonstrated this trend. The chief exception was North Carolina, where Terry Sanford, a progressive and the leader of the Kerr Scott faction after Scott's death, was elected governor in 1960.

[78] Act 528, Section 3, Legislative Acts, Alabama, 1957 Sess., *Facts on Film,* Reel 3. For Louisiana, Mississippi, Georgia, and South Carolina see *Race Relations Law Reporter,* III (August, 1958), 778, (June, 1958), 553, II (April, 1957), 505–506, (August, 1957), 855–56. A previous Georgia law had empowered the chief executive to close any school by executive order. *Race Relations Law Reporter,* I (April, 1956), 418–19.

operations of public schools.[79] Two other states, Alabama and North Carolina, had authorized local option school closing.[80] Texas and Florida specifically provided for barring the doors of educational institutions only when federal troops were present. But an additional Texas law would terminate payment of state funds to any school that desegregated unless a plebiscite first established that a majority of the citizens in the community preferred an integrated educational system. Other Florida legislation granted the governor such broad emergency powers that school-closing authority seemed implied.[81] Four states completely prohibited the expenditure of state funds for desegregated education.[82]

Eight states had provisions for substituting private schools for desegregated public schools, and five states had made arrangements to sell, lease, or give away public school properties to private groups or individuals. The citizens of seven states had voted on constitutional amendments prejudicial to the public schools, and, without exception, the amendments had been approved. In four states, these constitutional changes authorized abandonment of public education.[83] In the three others, Louisiana, North Carolina, and Virginia, they represented potential threats to the public schools.[84] Ultimately all eleven states repealed or modified compulsory attendance laws, and six states weakened or eliminated teacher tenure provisions.[85] This mass of legislation was all damaging or potentially damaging to the public schools.

The Little Rock crisis, passage of the 1957 Civil Rights bill, and the continuing rightward drift of southern politics revived neobourbon interest in resuming the battle with the national Democratic Party. In

---

[79] Louisiana, Mississippi, Georgia, South Carolina, Arkansas, and Virginia.

[80] Act 528, Legislative Acts, Alabama, 1957 Sess., *Facts on Film*, Reel 3; *Race Relations Law Reporter*, I (October, 1956), 928–37.

[81] *Race Relations Law Reporter*, II (June, 1957), 695–96, I (October, 1956), 954–56.

[82] Georgia: Act 82, Georgia Acts and Resolves, 1955 Sess., in *Facts on Film*, Reel 3; *Race Relations Law Reporter*, I (April, 1956), 421–22; South Carolina: *ibid.* (February, 1956), 241; Virginia: *ibid.* (December, 1956), 1092–93; and Louisiana: *ibid.* (February, 1956), 239–40.

[83] Georgia: Act 653, Georgia Acts and Resolves, 1954 Sess., in *Facts on Film*, Reel 3; *Race Relations Law Reporter*, I (April, 1956), 420–22; Virginia: *ibid.* (December, 1956), 1091–1113; Alabama: *ibid.* (April, 1956), 417–18; North Carolina: *ibid.* (October, 1956), 928–37; Louisiana: *ibid.* (August, 1956), 728, III (August, 1958), 768–78, (October, 1958), 1062–65; Arkansas: *ibid.* (October, 1958), 1043–44; South Carolina: *ibid.*, I (February, 1956), 241; Mississippi: Chapter 39, Mississippi Legislative Acts, 1954 Special Sess., in *Fact on Film*, Reel 3.

[84] *Southern School News*, January, October, 1956; *Race Relations Law Reporter*, I (February, 1956), 241–42.

[85] *Southern School News*, May 17, 1964; Sarratt, *The Ordeal of Desegregation*, Appendix.

late September, 1957, former Governor Byrnes of South Carolina broke a long silence to call for the organization of "a united South."[86] Just afterward Senator Talmadge attacked both national parties for "seeking the minority vote in other sections of the country and . . . striving with each other to see who can conduct the most punitive campaign against the South."[87] Talmadge hinted that the South might be driven from the Democratic Party. Then, in a widely publicized speech in Rock Hill, South Carolina, Senator Thurmond declared that the "real Democrats" should "not hesitate to pursue whatever course is deemed to be in the best interests of the people of our State."[88] Former Governor Shivers of Texas, Governor Griffin of Georgia, Representative Williams of Mississippi, and others added their endorsement to southern independent political action in national politics.[89] But, as in 1956, powerful forces pulled against such a program. By March, 1958, when the South Carolina state Democratic convention chose a party loyalist as state chairman, third party sentiment had cooled considerably.[90] Continued agitation for an independent political movement came primarily from the Citizens' Councils and the aging Dixiecrat forces, who kept alive the campaign that ultimately was to deny the electoral votes of Mississippi and part of those of Alabama to either major party candidate in the 1960 election.[91]

More immediately menacing to the principle of the *Brown* decision was the attack on the Supreme Court in the United States Congress. Court action, particularly in cases defending the right of political dissent, upholding equality before the law, and broadening federal authority, had antagonized powerful interests and laid the groundwork for a formidable anti-Court alliance. "Segregationists and the ultra-security-conscious," as Walter F. Murphy characterized the heart of the coalition in his study of congressional politics and the Court during the 1950's, "had found a common foe in the Court and had found common ground for opposition in the concepts of states' rights and virulent anticommunism."[92] Joining the assault were such business groups as the National

---

[86] As quoted in *The State*, September 27, 1957. See the results of a South-wide survey of third party sentiment by William M. Bates, in Atlanta *Journal and Constitution*, October 6, 1957.

[87] As quoted in Atlanta *Journal*, October 9, 1957.

[88] As quoted in *The State*, October 18, 1957.

[89] Atlanta *Journal*, October 21, 1957; Birmingham *News*, October 23, 1957; *Delta Democrat-Times*, October 4, 1957.

[90] *The State*, March 26, 1958; Charleston *News and Courier*, March 26, 1958.

[91] Theodore H. White, *The Making of the President, 1960* (New York, 1961), 28, *passim*.

[92] Murphy, *Congress and the Court*, 88.

Association of Manufacturers, the United States Chamber of Commerce, and the American Farm Bureau Federation. Legal conservatives, including the National Association of Attorneys General, the Southern Regional Council of Attorneys General, the Conference of State Supreme Court Chief Justices, and, later, the American Bar Association, also became involved. The result was the rise of a formidable anti-Court congressional bloc, composed predominantly of southern Democrats and conservative Republicans. None of the legislation backed by the coalition referred directly to segregation, but all concerned the prestige of the Court and challenged the whole philosophy of judicial activism from which the *Brown* decision had in part emerged.[93]

The attack on the Court reached its height during 1958, when the House of Representatives passed five bills designed to curb the Court's authority. These measures failed to receive Senate approval, but the anti-Court coalition evidenced substantial strength in the upper chamber. During August, 1958, the Senate divided sharply on two broad Court-rebuking bills, tabling a measure to restrict the Court's appellate jurisdiction by a 49 to 41 vote and refusing to table a somewhat less extreme House bill by a 39 to 46 division. Only a hasty adjournment and some frantic maneuvering by Senate Majority Leader Lyndon B. Johnson finally suppressed the latter measure by a 41 to 40 vote.[94] When Congress adjourned later in the month, the Court's prestige was shaken but intact.

The militancy of the southern resistance to desegregation, the successes of white supremacy candidates below the Potomac, the mass of state anti-integration laws, school closures in Arkansas and Virginia, and the threat of school closures elsewhere combined with the anti-Court movement in Congress to bring the Supreme Court under the heaviest attack it had experienced since 1937. Against these pressures, the Court compromised. It vigorously reaffirmed the principle of the *Brown* decision in *Cooper v. Aaron* in 1958. But in *Shuttlesworth v. Birmingham*, also decided

[93] Murphy, *Congress and the Court*, and Pritchett, *Congress Versus the Supreme Court*, deal in depth with the congressional anti-Court movement and the basic issues involved.

[94] The first bill was S. 2646, the Jenner-Butler bill. The latter was H R. 3, the "second Smith Act." The cloakroom maneuvering and the role of Senator Johnson are examined in Murphy, *Congress and the Court*, 199–212, 249–61. For the roll call votes, see *Congressional Record*, 85th Cong., 2nd Sess. (August 20, 1958), 18687ff. On the 49 to 41 vote to table the Jenner-Butler bill, four southern senators, Gore and Kefauver of Tennessee and Johnson and Yarborough of Texas, voted with the majority. On the crucial 41 to 40 rejection of the Smith bill, three southern senators, Kefauver, Johnson, and Yarborough, voted with the majority.

in 1958, the Court upheld the Alabama pupil placement act, thus granting school officials almost unlimited authority over school enrollment.[95] This case legitimatized a tightly controlled tokenism, permitting states to approach desegregation on an individual pupil-at-a-time basis and bringing almost anything short of massive resistance within the bounds of the *Brown* decision. With massive resistance sweeping to a climax, the federal courts showed a willingness to compromise on integration and to concentrate on salvaging the principle of equal protection of the law in education.

The proponents of massive resistance had succeeded in uniting large portions of the South in defense of white supremacy and southern rural and small-town values. This accomplishment was not only a substantial feat of political leadership; it also partially hid the deep fissures in southern society.

---

[95] *Cooper v. Aaron*, in *Race Relations Law Reporter*, III (October, 1958), 855–67; *Shuttlesworth v. Birmingham Board of Education*, in *ibid*. (June, 1958), 425–34. A lower court had earlier upheld the North Carolina placement act. See *Carson v. Warlick*, in *ibid*., II (February, 1957), 16–21. The Court's retreat was a general one that included a less aggressive defense of security risk personnel as well as Negro rights. See Murphy, *Congress and the Court*, 245–65.

CHAPTER 16

SOUTHERN INSTITUTIONS

Writing more than a decade before the *Brown* decision, Gunnar Myrdal depicted the role of "huge institutional structures like the church, the school, the university, the foundation, the trade union," and others in furthering racial justice. Myrdal observed that on an individual basis intolerance seemed to spread more easily than tolerance. But the great institutions in society tended to be devoted to the American Creed, to "progress, liberty, equality, and humanitarianism." Here, "the American Creed has its instruments."[1]

By the 1950's such institutions in the South were oriented more toward national ideals than they had been when Myrdal wrote *An American Dilemma*. Churchmen continued to be influenced by modernist theology; educators, particularly on the college level, were often oriented toward the ideas expressed by Myrdal himself; the American labor movement maintained its political alliance with Negroes; and corporate business was even more national in scope. At least in the broadest sense, the church, the school, organized labor, and business were forces pulling the South toward conformity with American norms.

Yet, while exercising a restraining influence on white supremacy extremism, these institutions did not provide the stabilizing element for the early development of a viable alternative to massive resistance. Rather

---

[1] Myrdal, *An American Dilemma*, I, 80. The following examination of the interaction between racism and southern institutions should be regarded as a tentative interpretation. An in-depth analysis would require extensive research into church records, labor documents, and other materials. Indeed, the complex questions of race in regard to any of the institutions mentioned below will likely provide academicians with the subject matter for a great many future books. Some attempt to assess the role of such institutions in the politics of massive resistance seems mandatory, however. When possible, I have relied upon the findings of scholars who have specialized in these various fields.

than acting as "instruments" of "the American Creed," they placed immediate institutional concerns above all else and functioned more nearly as
observers than as movers of events. Only when the stability of southern
society and, consequently, their own vested interests were more threatened
by massive resistance than by token social change did these great institutions make a meaningful contribution to the course of southern politics.
Their failure to exert a more positive stabilizing influence was an integral
element in the rise of massive resistance.

Of all these institutions, the church was the most significant potential
threat to segregationist dreams for a solid South. As Citizens' Council
spokesmen were well aware, the major Protestant denominations in the
South—those that had supported slavery, secession, the Confederacy,
redemption, and segregation—had drifted far from their sectional
moorings.[2] During the late 1940's and early 1950's, Southern Baptists,
Methodists, and (Southern) Presbyterians had created or enlarged agencies to deal with secular social problems. By the time of the *Brown* decision,
these denominations and others were well along the way to establishing
social justice as formal church policy, at least on the highest hierarchal
levels.[3] Most Protestant denominations, along with Catholic and Jewish
agencies, promptly endorsed the desegregation decision and called upon
their members "to conduct themselves," as the Southern Baptist Convention phrased it, "in this period of adjustment in the spirit of Christ." A
significant number of state and district conventions and various other religious agencies and associations also joined in endorsing the desegregation
decision. Some of these pronouncements, however, were innocuous pleas
for humility, patience, and prayer.[4] Such activity was ample to antagonize
segregationists within and without the church, but, as Kenneth K. Bailey
has pointed out, "the appraisals and importunities of religious editors and
high denominational councils were not automatically recited in local con-

[2] On the changing nature of southern churches, see Kenneth K. Bailey, *Southern White
Protestantism in the Twentieth Century* (New York, 1964); on American Protestants and race
relations, see David M. Reimers, *White Protestantism and the Negro* (New York, 1965).

[3] Bailey, *Southern White Protestantism in the Twentieth Century*, 35ff. Southern Baptists,
Methodists, and Presbyterians were the three largest religious groups in the South, and
of these the most numerous by far were the Southern Baptists.

[4] The statement of the Southern Baptist Convention is quoted in *New South*, August,
1954. See also, Southern Regional Council, *Special Report: Religious Bodies and the Supreme
Court Decision* (Atlanta, 1957); "Protestantism Speaks on Justice and Integration,"
Christian Century, LXXV (February 5, 1958), 164–66; and Campbell and Pettigrew,
Christians in Racial Crisis, 1–15. The latter work perceptively summarizes the reaction of
southern churches to the *Brown* decision and includes a convenient collection of representative church statements on integration, reprinted in the Appendix, 137–70.

gregations."[5] Instead, internal dissension sapped the will of southern churches as they attempted to deal with the disrupting problems of social change in a rapidly changing region.

Divisions within the southern white Protestant religious establishment were numerous and complex. In the broadest sense, the most fundamental cleavage existed between the liberal clergy and their segregationist congregations, with integrationist sentiment far more commonly found in the upper rather than in the lower South. But these generalizations, while true, obscure as much as they illuminate. Racial issues tore through the fabric of southern churches along a variety of lines.

Generally, the academically trained denominational ministers were apt to be oriented toward a favorable view of integration.[6] This fact, along with considerations of prestige, intellectual respectability, and other institutional factors, accounted for the ready acceptance of the *Brown* decision on higher denominational levels. It largely explained why state councils of churches and similar groups often defended desegregation. But most of all, the urban, educated minister found a voice in the city ministerial association. In a number of southern cities, such groups publicly condemned segregationist practices and called for positive steps toward a desegregated society. In January, 1957, the Richmond Ministerial Association purchased advertisements in the city's newspapers to publicize a manifesto attacking Governor Stanley, the Virginia general assembly, and the whole massive resistance program. Signed by fifty-nine of the association's members, the "Statement of Conviction" was a forthright appeal for racial equality and the elimination of segregation. Later in the year, a larger group of Atlanta ministers released a six-point statement calling for a free atmosphere of debate, obedience to the law, preservation of the

---

[5] Bailey, *Southern White Protestantism in the Twentieth Century*, 137.

[6] In a poll of a selected cross section of southern Protestant denominational ministers, the *Pulpit Digest* found 78 percent taking a favorable attitude toward desegregation. In the peripheral states of North Carolina, Texas, and Virginia, 85 to 90 percent of ministers participating in the poll expressed pro-integration sentiments; respondents favoring desegregation in Alabama, Arkansas, Mississippi, and South Carolina, however, ranged from 50 to 54 percent. "Southern Ministers Speak Their Minds," *Pulpit Digest*, XXXIX (December, 1958), 13–17. The nature of the poll, a mail survey, may have exaggerated pro-integration sentiment, but there seems little reason to dispute the basic point that a substantial majority of denominational clergymen approved of the principle of the *Brown* decision. See Charles Y. Glock and Benjamin B. Ringer, "Church Policy and the Attitudes of Ministers and Parishioners on Social Issues," *American Sociological Review*, XXI (April, 1956), 148–56; Campbell and Pettigrew, *Christians in Racial Crisis*, 121, *passim;* John Wicklein, in New York *Times*, July 5, 1959 (which includes the results of a survey of Richmond ministers); and Stanley Rowland, Jr., in *ibid.*, April 3, 1957 (which reports on interviews with Virginia clergymen).

public schools, elimination of race-baiting, improved communications between races, and the "full privileges of first class citizenship" for all. The Atlanta proclamation was followed by similar statements in other southern cities.[7] These declarations and the denominational stands were the most notable demurs by predominantly white groups from segregationist demands for southern solidarity.

Yet, despite the significance of ministerial proclamations and the almost venerable church "custom of 'going on record' . . . for improved race relations,"[8] southern clergymen rarely went beyond these occasional group statements. Although it seems probable that a clear majority of denominational ministers approved of desegregation, galvanizing opinion into action was a peculiarly difficult chore. For just as some institutional factors promoted integrationist sentiment among ministers, other institutional tendencies retarded effective expression of such sentiment. Ernest Q. Campbell and Thomas F. Pettigrew of the Harvard University Laboratory of Social Relations have described the "basic 'Protestant dilemma'—a dilemma between the organizational concerns of money and members and the effective expression of principle . . . ." Ministers, after all, had a heavy institutional stake in their own churches, their plants—and agressive social action was disruptive, threatening attendance, donations, plans for expansion, indeed, the whole establishment. Most southern laymen were segregationists, some militantly so, and there is some evidence to suggest that the more conservative church members were most likely to be the church "pillars," the ones who attended most regularly, held lay positions most often, and generally contributed most (financially and otherwise) to the church's "success."[9] Consequently, the pastors of the largest churches or those who were engaged in fund-raising drives were normally most cautious in their advocacy of social justice. And, of course, any minister, no matter how small his plant, could recognize the fact that silence was golden, or at least that there was some

[7] The "Statement of Conviction" is printed in Richmond *News Leader*, January 28, 1957. The Richmond Association was not the first such organization to act in this manner. See *Southern School News*, September, 1954; Charlotte *Observer*, February 8, 1956; and Nashville *Tennessean*, January 10, 1957. The Atlanta Proclamation is reprinted in New York *Times*, November 3, 1957, and a second Atlanta declaration, which included the temporizing statement that "We do not believe in the wisdom of massive integration," is reprinted in New York *Times*, November 23, 1958. John Wicklein, in New York *Times*, July 5–8, 1959, is a good summary of church activity on the racial front.

[8] Myrdal, *An American Dilemma*, II, 869.

[9] Campbell and Pettigrew, *Christians in Racial Crisis*, viii, 11–12, 63–84; Rowland, in New York *Times*, April 3, 1957.

relationship between silence and gold. Furthermore, ministers trained in the intricacies of their own denominational dogmas had difficulty acting together even when they were so inclined.[10]

Finally, denominational hierarchies normally offered little support and a great deal of discouragement to ministerial activity in race relations. As Pettigrew and Campbell summarized this point, the church hierarchy

> does not like to see congregations divided, ministers alienated, membership reduced, or contributions decreased. Responsible as it is for the destiny of the denomination in a given territory, it compares the changing fortunes of the denomination with those of rival churches. . . . However exalted the moral virtue the minister expounds, the hierarchy does not wish him to damn his listeners to Hell unless somehow he gets them back in time to attend service each Sunday. His promotions are determined far less by the number of times he defends unpopular causes, however virtuous their merit, than by the state of the physical plant and the size of the coffer.[11]

Integrationist activity was not conducive to a smoothly functioning House of God in almost any part of the South; in some rural areas and in a few Deep South cities like Birmingham, crushing community pressures and a very real threat of Ku Klux Klan type of violence were further persuasive arguments for ministerial inactivity.

All of this is not intended to imply that there was any real shortage of clerical defenders of the established order. Such ministers were numerous, and sometimes they were men of considerable influence. In most southern cities the more prestigious ministers were normally inactive or cautiously oriented toward desegregation, but the exceptions were fairly numerous, particularly in the Deep South. In Montgomery, Dr. Henry L. Lyon, pastor of the Highland Baptist Church and twice state president of the Alabama Southern Baptist Convention, and Dr. G. Stanley Frazer, pastor of St. James Methodist Church and a long-time state leader of Alabama Methodists, were two of the most prominent ministers in the city and both were outspoken proponents of segregation. In Birmingham, Dr.

---

[10] Episcopal Bishop Robert R. Brown makes this point clear in his *Bigger than Little Rock*, 67. In describing "the admitted difficulty ministers have in establishing a unity among themselves," he writes: "A case in point is the recent meeting of only four clergymen to begin work on a 'Little Rock Manifesto' on the desegregation problem. Of the four, one was a legalist, one a perfectionist, one a neo-orthodox theologian, and one a biblical theologian. They worked for hours in an attempt to find some common basis upon which to begin a document which would be assured of acceptance by other ministers of the community—but without success."

[11] Campbell and Pettigrew, *Christians in Racial Crisis*, 20.

Guy McGowan's Highlands Methodist Church was a center for intradenominational segregationist activity, and Dr. John H. Buchanan,
pastor of Southside Baptist Church and Birmingham's Man of the Year
in 1956, pronounced that "the good Lord set up customs and practices
of segregation." Similar influential clergymen could be found in other
Deep South communities.[12]

But the most strident ministerial condemnations of integration came
from the sect clergymen, such as the Missionary Baptists, Primitive
Baptists, Southern Methodists, and other similar groups. These pastors,
normally graduates of unaccredited fundamentalist seminaries, ministered
primarily to lower- and working-class congregations. They were, Campbell and Pettigrew found in their study of Little Rock ministers, relatively
insulated by their "social and cultural milieu from the prevailing interpretations of the American Creed."[13] The formal policy of these churches
was militant segregation. The American Council of Christian Churches,
an alliance of some fifteen fundamentalist sects claiming a membership
of more than one million, proclaimed that integration "does violence to
the true gospel of Jesus Christ." The American Baptist Association Convention annually attacked the *Brown* decision and desegregation. The
Alabama American Baptist Convention linked "Communist sympathizers
in our nation" to desegregation.[14] In some cities, pastors from these
churches banded together to issue their own segregationist proclamations
in opposition to those released by ministerial associations. In at least two
cities, fundamentalist sect clergymen were centers of Citizens' Council
agitation.[15] The sect ministers were often vigorous and effective proponents
of segregation, and their influence could easily be underestimated. They
represented the voice of religion in thousands of churches scattered
through the towns and villages and lower-status urban areas of the
South.

Segregationist clergymen were numerous, but, as already indicated, the

[12] Montgomery *Advertiser*, June 1, 2, 1956, February 12, June 11, 1958. Dr. Buchanan
is quoted in Birmingham *News*, March 12, 1957. On Atlanta ministers and race relations,
see the series of published sermons in the Atlanta *Journal*, beginning October 13, 1957.
[13] Campbell and Pettigrew, *Christians in Racial Crisis*, 59.
[14] The American Council of Christian Churches is quoted by W. Thomas McMahan, in
The State, May 1, 1958; the Alabama American Baptist Association is quoted in Memphis
Commercial Appeal, October 5, 1959. The American Baptist Association and the North
American Baptist Association were popularly referred to as Missionary Baptists.
[15] Wicklein, in New York *Times*, July 6, 1959. On Little Rock, see Campbell and
Pettigrew, *Christians in Racial Crisis*, 41–62; on St. Petersburg, see St. Petersburg *Times*,
September 30, October 14, 19, 28, 1955, October 1, 1957.

denominational ministers were conspicuously more tolerant on racial matters than the laity whose souls they tended. Again, generalizations are difficult, and this one must be qualified by an important exception. Women's church groups, particularly the United Church Women, were sometimes positive proponents of social change.[16] Nevertheless, internal quarrels over church policy on racial problems could frequently be traced to a fundamental cleavage between pastor and flock. In Virginia the Episcopal Diocese divided clearly along lay-clerical lines during a long debate over whether to desegregate the church's Hemlock Haven Youth Conference. The same dialectic sundered South Carolina Methodists on the question of the conference's relations with the integrationist National Council of Churches.[17] Alabama legislative committee hearings on a proposed bill to facilitate the withdrawal of local churches from national denominational conferences "boiled down," as an Alabama journalist described it, "to a free-for-all between laymen and ministers of the Methodist Church."[18]

Other examples of the division between laity and clergy abounded. Normally segregationist churchmen directed their attention toward intradenominational matters, especially to threats of church desegregation, liberal religious literature, higher church pronouncements, and integrationist sentiment among local ministers. Most often, lay resistance was expressed in an *ad hoc* fashion and took such forms as protest resolutions by individual congregations or local church groups, segregationist opposition to liberal pronouncements by state denominational convocations, and the silencing or dismissal of unorthodox clergymen by local congregations.[19]

Citizens' Council spokesmen attempted to exploit this rift by encouraging lay members to coerce conformity on the part of their ministers. Speaking in New Orleans, Robert Patterson urged laymen to organize within their own churches and "bring pressure on ministers to support segregation and change the position of state and national church organiza-

[16] The fact that southern women were themselves struggling to escape a second-class citizenship role, the influence of the wives of ministers, and a historical tradition of opposition to racial injustice, especially lynching, presumably accounted for this deviate behavior. See Reimers, *White Protestantism and the Negro*, 91–92, and Peters, *The Southern Temper*, 21-38.

[17] Washington *Evening Star*, March 24, 1958, April 14, 1959; Richmond *Times-Dispatch*, May 18, 1958; Washington *Post*, May 23, 1958; Charleston *News and Courier*, June 26, 1959.

[18] Bob Ingram, in Montgomery *Advertiser*, August 7, 1959.

[19] Quint, *Profile in Black and White*, 55–70, is a good summary of this type of activity in South Carolina.

tions which have endorsed mixing of races."[20] In some areas Councils prompted church boards to issue segregationst statements, and they attempted to rally community pressure against integrationist clergymen. Segregationist politicians often added their voices to the condemnation of ministerial heresy, and the legislatures in Alabama and Mississippi enacted laws to assist local church rebellions against denominational stands on integration.[21] Generally, however, popular commitment to separation of church and state precluded effective state action in the religious field.

Encouraged by the massive resistance atmosphere and supported by the Councils, an organized lay opposition to denominational desegregation policies promptly emerged in the Deep South. The Methodist Church, in which agitation for jurisdictional desegregation kept the racial issue a pertinent denominational topic, spawned the first and the most persistent segregationist activity. In December, 1954, representatives from Alabama, Florida, Georgia, Mississippi, South Carolina, and Tennessee met at Birmingham's Highlands Methodist Church "to help set up an organization to deal effectively and rightly with radical attempts to break down Southern customs and tradition."[22] Titled the Association of Methodist Ministers and Laymen, the movement included several prominent ministers, notably Dr. Frazer of Montgomery and Dr. McGowan of Birmingham, and a number of well-known laymen, such as Attorney Sidney W. Smyer of Birmingham, among its organizers. The association held a second regional conference in the spring of 1955 to lament the "brainwashing" tactics employed by a few radical ministers in their efforts to subvert Methodist young people and to organize a speakers' bureau and an informational program.[23] The association attracted substantial support in Mississippi and nominally spread to other states, but Alabama was the center of its activities.

[20] As quoted in Will D. Campbell, *Race and the Renewal of the Church* (Philadelphia, 1962), 18.

[21] Montgomery *Advertiser*, August 15, 1959; Jackson *Daily News*, April 1, 1960.

[22] Birmingham *News*, December 8, 1954, quoting Dr. G. Stanley Frazer, co-chairman of the organizing committee. The Methodist Church was organized nationally into five geographical jurisdictions, with Negroes segregated in a separate administrative unit, the Central Jurisdiction. Church liberals demanded abolition of the Central Jurisdiction and its incorporation into the regular geographical units. Segregationists, of course, feared that this administrative change would open the way for eventual integration of local congregations.

[23] Birmingham *News*, May 12, 13, 1955. Association members had been angered by an Alabama Methodist Student Movement Conference's endorsement of desegregation earlier in the year. *Ibid.*, February 13, 1955.

As the movement gradually declined during the late 1950's, Alabama Methodists attempted to revive the campaign with a new and more militant organization composed entirely of laymen. Some 1,800 Alabama lay leaders, again gathering at the Highlands Methodist Church in Birmingham, formed the Methodist Laymen's Union in March, 1959. Like its predecessor, the Laymen's Union attracted impressive leadership and evidenced substantial popular support. The organization fought a series of successful engagements with the demon integration, playing major roles in the firing of a Methodist minister critical of the Union, revoking the credentials of another minister who was executive secretary of the Alabama Council on Human Relations, and drafting and seeing through the state legislature a bill to enable local churches withdrawing from the Methodist Conference to retain their church properties.[24] Again the Alabama initiative spurred some activity in neighboring states.

The most notable sponsors of lay resistance organizations were members of the Methodist Church in the Deep South, but other denominations were by no means immune from similar expressions of internal differences. The Baptist Laymen of Alabama attracted an impressive following, and groups like the Presbyterian Laymen for Sound Doctrine and Responsible Leadership, Inc., received more than local attention.[25] Other scattered organizations, most of which were short-lived and not particularly influential per se, represented potential threats to the institutional integrity of the denominations, and they offered yet further encouragement for caution and inactivity by ministers and church leaders. Even the Catholic Church, with its much firmer clerical control, faced a lay rebellion sufficiently potent to suspend church plans for desegregation of parochial schools in southern Louisiana.[26]

In some cases segregationist churchmen were able to win endorsement by state denominational conventions for their somewhat narrow conception of the brotherhood of man. South Carolina Episcopalians resolved in 1956 "that there is nothing morally wrong in a voluntary recognition

---

[24] Montgomery *Advertiser*, March 15, 1959, September 9, 1960; Birmingham *News*, March 15, 20, 22, May 26, July 10, 16, August 12, 1959; New York *Times*, July 7, 1959; Robert E. Baker, in Washington *Post*, September 29, 1959.

[25] Montgomery *Advertiser*, May 16, 1957, January 13, February 12, 1958; Charlotte *Observer*, October 20, 1959.

[26] Catholic segregationists, their dissatisfaction institutionalized for a time in the Association of Catholic Laymen, were assisted by threats from state legislators to punish parochial schools if desegregation were attempted. This long and often involved intra-Catholic controversy was well covered in the New Orleans press. See New Orleans *Times-Picayune*, May, 1954–December, 1960.

of racial differences and that voluntary alignment can be both natural and Christian." The Mississippi Synod of the Presbyterian Church announced that it could not "in good conscience" comply with denominational recommendations for church desegregation. In Alabama the annual Methodist Conference called upon the church hierarchy to avoid "interference with the right to maintain separate racial customs in churches, schools, colleges, assemblies and conferences within the Methodist Church."[27] Such pronouncements, however, were relatively unusual.

On the whole, segregationists did not so much demand that the church actively endorse racial separation as they did that the church remain aloof from "current social, political and economic problems" and concentrate on "its mission."[28] "This concession in itself," Campbell and Pettigrew observed in reference to Little Rock lay segregationists, "is tribute to the fact that they realize a religious defense of segregation from their clergy would be too much to expect."[29] By concentrating their efforts upon insuring that liberally inclined ministers merely held their peace, southern traditionalists conceded a past bulwark of white supremacy, but they also established an attainable goal—one which they substantially accomplished.

Many a southern minister, sometimes easing his guilt with occasional pious and ambiguous generalizations,[30] devoted his attention to sins about which there was a consensus and watched the South seek a political solution to its most pressing moral problem. When a group of church leaders organized an interracial Conference on Christian Faith and Human Relations and invited 4,500 southern ministers to attend, 4,200 rejected the invitation.[31] A poll of 21 Atlanta ministers in late September, 1957, disclosed that 18 had not found time to comment in the pulpit on the tumultuous Little Rock desegregation controversy.[32] A similar survey of

---

[27] The Episcopalian resolution is quoted in *The State*, April 19, 1956; the Presbyterian statement is reprinted in Jackson *Daily News*, November 5, 1954; and the Methodist pronouncement is reprinted in Chattanooga *Times*, June 3, 1955. For other examples of state-level church statements endorsing segregation, see *Southern School News*, November, 1954; New York *Times*, September 9, 1954; Montgomery *Advertiser*, June 1, 1956; and Richmond *Times-Dispatch*, April 15, 1956.

[28] From a statement released by the First Presbyterian Church, Jackson, Mississippi, reprinted in Jackson *Daily News*, June 6, 1957.

[29] Campbell and Pettigrew, *Christians in Racial Crisis*, 129.

[30] Limited information would seem to suggest that "significant evidence of guilt" among such ministers was not extensive. Ernest Q. Campbell, "Moral Discomfort and Racial Segregation—An Examination of the Myrdal Hypothesis," *Social Forces*, XXXIX (March, 1961), 228–34.

[31] James, "The South's Own Civil War," 28.

[32] Laura McGregor, in Atlanta *Journal*, September 30, 1957.

the sermons of Tuscaloosa ministers on Race Relations Sunday following the University of Alabama desegregation rioting reported that "much was hinted at, but little was said on the subject."[33]

Similarly, state denominational convocations frequently found in equivocal pronouncements a refuge from a subject too controversial and disruptive to be faced and yet too pressing to be ignored. The Virginia Methodist Conference resolved: "Let us realize that we cannot improve human relations by either forcing the matter or by avoiding responsibility. We can do too little too late as well as too much too soon, and God alone can cause us to see the fine distinction here."[34]

The Alabama Baptist Convention called for calm judgment during this "present state of intensity" and asked that "all parties concerned on both sides, and this means Negro and white, seek the will of the Lord in the particular matter confronting them, thus by-passing in doing so, if necessary, various extreme organizations."[35] In 1955 the Georgia Baptist Convention stated that "the upholding of the law and order is every citizen's duty" and added that "hurried and enforced adjustments hurt the harvest of good will."[36] The following year Georgia Baptists overwhelmingly rejected a report unequivocally endorsing the *Brown* decision. Such evasive action by southern denominational groups was common during the 1950's, especially in Deep South states.

But perhaps the Louisiana Baptist Convention of 1957 exemplified this procedure in its starkest form. A former missionary placed a rather moderate resolution before the convention tying Baptist missionary work amid nonwhite populations abroad with Negro rights domestically. The convention resolutions committee promptly killed the statement, but, with the issue publicly raised, the committee felt compelled to offer a substitute. The substitute resolution, which the convention approved, regretted that "certain of our Missionaries have difficulties arising out of publicity given to racial problems" and recommended as a solution that "our ministers at home and abroad give more emphasis to the good that is being done in these fields and that in the main the Negroes of Louisiana

[33] Wayne Phillips, in New York *Times*, February 13, 1956.
[34] Reprinted in Richmond *News Leader*, June 14, 1956.
[35] Reprinted in Birmingham *News*, November 17, 1955.
[36] Compare the choice of words in the clauses on race relations just quoted with the terminology used in another resolution passed by the same convention: "Never have the people of Georgia been so cruelly betrayed. The yazoo [sic] fraud is mild by comparison." These words referred to Governor Griffin's "treachery" in assisting a brewery to locate in Atlanta. See Atlanta *Journal*, November 17, 1955, November 14, 1956.

prefer to have schools and churches of their own."[37] A participant in these proceedings explained: "We would have preferred to remain silent."

The southern white church response to the *Brown* decision was varied and complex. In some cases, it was a voice of segregation. Sometimes it spoke for racial justice. More frequently, entrapped in the "Protestant dilemma," it buried the principle of the *Brown* decision in evasive pronouncements or drowned it in silence.

But, in the most fundamental sense, even those churchmen who did come to the support of the Supreme Court failed to accomplish a real confrontation between the church and white supremacy. Denominational and ministerial pronouncement often dwelled on the integrity of law and the duties of citizenship, not on the obligations of a Christian individual or the moral imperatives of the church in a segregated society. As Will D. Campbell of the Committee of Southern Churchmen has observed: "For the health of our own souls, it might have been better if the Supreme Court had not ruled favorably in 1954 on the subject of race. . . . Then we would have been forced to speak, if we spoke at all, from the vantage point of the Christian gospel. We would have been required to say: Thus saith the Lord! Not, Thus saith the Law!"[38] By frequently basing its pronouncements on secular appeals to law, citizenship, and fair play, the church did indeed sometimes deviate radically from Citizens' Council demands for southern solidarity, but it did not require its adherents to face the basic moral issues involved.

And again, these deviations were relatively infrequent on the local level. Individual clergymen did brave community pressure to state their views, and many lost their jobs or were transferred to other regions for their efforts,[39] but on the whole the church acted as a prosperous secular institution, unwilling to allow Christian principles to impede seriously its institutional success. Protestant churches themselves remained segregated. Less than two dozen out of almost 100,000 white churches in the South were known to have Negro members in 1959.[40] They lagged behind Catholic and state-supported colleges in dropping racial barriers in their

[37] Reprinted in New Orleans *Times-Picayune*, November 14, 1957.

[38] Campbell, *Race and the Renewal of the Church*, 5.

[39] For example, see James, "The South's Own Civil War," 25–26; Sarratt, *The Ordeal of Desegregation*, 266–73; and Campbell and Pettigrew, *Christians in Racial Crisis*, 110–13.

[40] New York *Times*, July 5, 1959. Like a good many other observations made in these pages, this was a national, not a southern phenomenon. See Samuel S. Hill, "Southern Protestantism and Racial Integration," *Religion in Life*, XXXIII (Summer, 1964), 421–29.

own educational institutions.[41] Protestant churches had little or no positive influence on the racial attitudes of even their most devoted laymen.[42] During the 1950's the churches largely remained a potential threat to white supremacy, and they did not confront white southerners with the moral aspects of white supremacy.

Labor unions offered a considerably less formidable threat to defenders of the southern caste system. Compared to the packed congregations in the churches, southern union halls were lonely gathering places. Union membership ranged from an estimated 9 percent of the nonagricultural work force in the Carolinas to an estimated 24 percent in Alabama.[43] These figures represented a total of some 1,500,000 southern members, approximately 17 percent of southern nonagricultural employees. A large majority of southern unionists belonged to craft unions affiliated, before 1955, with the American Federation of Labor, which traditionally had been less concerned with minority rights than the Congress of Industrial Organizations.[44] Where the churches enjoyed wide prestige and an historically established place in southern society, unions were relative newcomers to the South. And, in a region under the persistent influence of an agrarian tradition and New South values, the unions were often viewed as foreign intruders and threats to future southern industrial progress.[45] Right-to-work laws in ten of the eleven southern states hampered their effectiveness and symbolized public hostility.

Labor leaders, particularly those on higher bureaucratic levels, normally favored integration. Unions were institutionally oriented toward social reform, and union officials had long recognized the mutual benefits of

[41] Joseph B. Parham, "Halls of Ivy—Southern Exposure: In the Colleges," in Shoemaker (ed.), *With All Deliberate Speed*, 166; Bailey, *Southern White Protestantism in the Twentieth Century*, 147.

[42] William T. Liu, "The Community Reference System: Religiosity and Race Attitudes," *Social Forces*, XXXIX (May, 1961), 324–28; Tumin, *Desegregation*, 101.

[43] Labor statistics used in this discussion were supplied by the Labor Consultant Department of the Southern Regional Council. Ray Marshall, "Some Factors Influencing the Growth of Unions in the South," in Gerald G. Somers (ed.), *Proceedings of the Thirteenth Annual Meeting of the Industrial Relations Research Association, 1960* (Madison, 1961), 167, contains a state-by-state estimate of labor union membership in 1953.

[44] For differing evaluations of the labor record on minority rights, see Herbert Hill, "Labor Unions and the Negro," *Commentary*, XXVIII (December, 1959), 479–88, and Harry Fleishman, "Equality and the Unions," *Religion and Labor*, IV (February, 1961), 1–8.

[45] Cash, *The Mind of the South*, remains the best analysis of the southern outlook. On the South and attitudes toward labor in more recent years, see Marshall, "Some Factors Influencing the Growth of Unions in the South," 166–82, and Solomon Barkin, "Southern Views of Unions," *Labor Today* (Fall, 1962), 31–36.

labor-Negro political cooperation. Union leaders were also fully aware of the potential consequences of leaving Negroes outside the house of labor. Continuing pressure by Negro groups within and without the labor movement encouraged unions to remain attentive to problems of racial discrimination. Consequently, many union officials, agencies, and conventions endorsed the *Brown* decision and called for compliance. When the American Federation of Labor and the Congress of Industrial Organizations merged in 1955, the new federation placed an equal rights provision in its constitution and provided for a Civil Rights Committee to insure implementation of this aim. Although the committee lacked effective coercive powers, the AFL-CIO chose James B. Carey, president of the International Union of Electrical Workers and a long-time civil rights champion, as committee chairman and elected two Negro vice presidents.[46] Affiliated unions joined in endorsing the movement's commitment to racial justice. The Textile Workers' Union of America called upon President Eisenhower "to provide moral leadership for the peaceful and orderly transition to an unsegregated public school system."[47] Delegates representing southern districts of the United Packinghouse Workers of America, the most aggressively integrationist of all unions in the South, held a two-day conference "To examine all problems related to segregation and discrimination and to map out specific programs to bring about their destruction."[48] The convention adopted a resolution urging the AFL-CIO to undertake a $10 million drive against segregation. Some state AFL-CIO groups joined in support of the *Brown* decision and labor's official policy of nondiscrimination.[49]

But, like the members of church congregations, rank and file unionists were extremely reluctant to adopt their leaders' views as their own. Labor unions, by definition, appealed to that part of the population where attitude studies have located relatively high levels of intolerance on matters pertaining to civil and minority rights. Southern locals, particularly in the Birmingham area, were soon bombarding AFL-CIO President George Meany and other top labor officials with threats and protests against labor's pro-integration stand generally and labor's financial assistance to the NAACP in particular. Ninety-four members of the United Steel

[46] Ray Marshall, *The Negro and Organized Labor* (New York, 1965), 14–85.
[47] As quoted in Greensboro *Daily News*, May 19, 1956.
[48] Atlanta *Constitution*, March 25, 1955, quoting a UPWA spokesman.
[49] For examples, see Dallas *Morning News*, August 2, 1957; Chattanooga *Times*, April 8, 1956; and Muse, *Virginia's Massive Resistance*, 35–36.

Workers in Birmingham informed Meany by registered letter: "If we have to choose between staying in the union and seeing our segregated way of life destroyed, we will pull out and form our own unions."[50] Another group of union members stated in a telegram to AFL-CIO headquarters that "Unionism and integration are not synonymous."[51] During the period following a well-publicized AFL-CIO civil rights "progress report" in 1956, Meany received some two hundred letters of protest per day from unionists in the South.[52]

The clash between union rank and file and union leadership was graphically delineated in a controversy over school desegregation in Chattanooga, Tennessee. In July, 1955, the city school board announced its intention to work toward gradual compliance with the *Brown* decision. The Chattanooga Central Labor Union commended the board's "middle-of-the-road policy." City locals, led by Printing Pressmen's Local 165, answered with a spirited attack on the *Brown* decision, the school board, and the Central Labor Union. The latter agency attempted to quiet the storm of protests with a letter to all affiliated locals criticizing "Intemperate public statements" and urging unionists to "reserve judgment" until all the facts had been considered.[53] But opposition continued to grow throughout the late summer of 1955. Ten locals went on record against the Central Union's position, and a few seceded from the organization entirely. Arthur A. Canada, a member of the Printing Pressmen's Union, organized the Tennessee Society to Maintain Segregation, which became a focal point of resistance to social change in the city. By mid-September the Central Union had had enough. At a special meeting, the agency capitulated, retracting its original statement of support for eventual desegregation and, to avoid strife within the labor movement, adopting an official policy of neutrality.[54]

This intra-union clash formed the background for the first organized protest movement within the house of labor. A group of union members in the Chattanooga area created the Southern States Conference of Union People, with Arthur Canada as chairman. Conference organizers insisted

[50] As quoted in Birmingham *News*, February 23, 1956. Several hundred other steel workers later added their endorsement to this or a similar statement. *Ibid.*, April 5, 1956.

[51] Reprinted in *ibid.*, February 12, 1956.

[52] This apparently was the result of an organized campaign. See Marshall, *The Negro and Organized Labor*, 197.

[53] Reprinted in Chattanooga *Times*, July 26, August 18, 1955.

[54] *Southern School News*, August-October, 1955; Chattanooga *Times*, July 26–September 13, 1955.

that they did not favor withdrawing from the unions. They sought instead to form a segregationist pressure group within organized labor to counter integrationist tendencies, much in the same fashion as had lay church groups. Canada and his associates drafted a resolution and mailed some ten thousand copies to unionists throughout the South. Membership in the Southern States Conference, according to the resolution, was restricted to individuals who were both prosegregation and members of AFL-CIO unions.[55]

Soon afterward, however, the conference leadership assisted in the creation of a separate, southern segregationist union. This movement originated when a group of Birmingham workers at Haynes Aircraft Company formed the Southern Aircraft Workers, Inc., an independent union unattached to and in competition with the United Automobile Workers. Broadening its operation, the Southern Aircraft Workers sponsored an all-southern labor conference held in Birmingham in July, 1956. Labor representatives from ten states drew up a manifesto condemning the "horde of meddlers under the guise of friends of the colored citizens of our Southland" and created an executive committee, with Canada as chairman, to promote organization of a segregated southern union.[56] The result of the Birmingham meeting was the Southern Federation of Labor.

The Southern Federation was the first of a number of segregationist independents that appeared during the period. In some cases the proponents of dual unionism seemed well-financed—a factor perhaps not unrelated to the endorsement of right-to-work legislation and other basically anti-union programs by several of these fledging independents. None of these unions achieved a significant following. The Southern Federation of Labor disappeared after its base of operations, the Southern Aircraft Workers, failed to win bargaining rights at the Haynes plant.[57] Other groups struggled along through the 1950's, but they did not make serious inroads on AFL-CIO membership.

Citizens' Councils and Klan groups were more successful in recruiting working-class members. Both an AFL-CIO investigation in 1956 and a

---

[55] Wallace Westfeldt, in Nashville *Tennessean*, May 23, 1956; Henry L. Trewhitt, in Nashville *Banner*, October 9, 10, 1956.

[56] Birmingham *News*, July 22, 1956.

[57] Ray Marshall, "Union Racial Problems in the South," *Industrial Relations*, I (May, 1962), 122–23. On dual unionism in the South generally, see Marshall, *The Negro and Organized Labor*, 192–96.

Jewish Labor Committee survey in 1957 found a substantial Council following within southern unions, and informed observers generally endorsed the accuracy of this conclusion.[58] Klan recruiters were also active among union as well as unorganized workers, particularly in the Birmingham area and the Piedmont.

These events put considerable pressure on AFL-CIO leaders. The union leadership was not overly fearful of dual union groups in the South. Not infrequently the internationals, not the southern locals, held both local union assets and the contracts with management. In southern branch plants or subsidiaries of northern-based firms, southern locals owed much of their bargaining strength to stronger northern unions. National unions had far more to offer economically than the regional segregationist groups could ever hope to match.[59] Furthermore, the Jim Crow independents were badly led. Established southern labor officials and organizers remained loyal to the AFL-CIO, while men of the "promoter" type often provided the leadership for dual unionism.[60]

Council and Klan activity did cause serious concern among labor leaders. Union officials felt that the Council movement was directed as much against organized labor as it was against desegregation.[61] And, whether the Councils were consciously anti-union or not, the integrationist (and economically liberal) stand taken by unions and the racist (and economically conservative) position held by the segregationist organizations represented a profound clash of values which threatened the long-range stability of southern unions. Union leaders reacted by vigorously denouncing both the Councils and the Klan as anti-labor movements seeking the destruction of trade unions.[62] Furthermore, in areas where white supremacy sentiment was particularly pervasive, local labor officials sometimes displayed considerable adroitness in parrying segregationist criticism. As an Alabama labor spokesman explained: "According to the

[58] Mitchell, "On the Rise of the White Citizens Council and Its Ties with Anti-Labor Forces in the South," and Mitchell, "The White Citizens Councils vs. Southern Trade Unions," report the result of the labor study; Irving Spiegel, in New York *Times*, May 13, 1957, gives the Jewish Labor Committee conclusions; and see Ed Townsend, in *Christian Science Monitor*, April 19, 1956, and Bem Price, in *Arkansas Gazette*, July 1, 1956.

[59] See Townsend's articles on racism and the unions appearing in *Christian Science Monitor* during 1956, particularly his report of April 25, 1956.

[60] Marshall, "Union Racial Problems in the South," 121–26.

[61] Mitchell, "On the Rise of the White Citizens Council and Its Ties with Anti-Labor Forces in the South," and "The White Citizens Councils vs. Southern Trade Unions"; Townsend, in *Christian Science Monitor*, April 19, 1956.

[62] For examples, see New York *Times*, May 15, July 1, 1956.

best information I can get the NAACP is financed by a dozen or more
giant corporations that are also helping finance the Republican party.
. . . So far as I know there is no breach of the segregation principles of the
South occurring anywhere in organized labor. . . . It was money donated
by these Republican controlled corporations that financed the Autherine
Lucy incident at the University of Alabama."[63] Most of all, as various
studies have demonstrated, men can hold conflicting—indeed incompatible—views at the same time, and some white southern unionists apparently did precisely that.[64] By applying their values selectively, union
members could rely upon the Councils to protect their caste position and
upon the unions for their class position.

The racial clamor surrounding massive resistance did, of course, invite
anti-union propaganda campaigns that appealed to racial fears and
and hatreds. In some cases, employers or community anti-union groups
overtly used racial emotionalism in attempts to influence the outcome of
bargaining rights elections. For example, a picture of the president of the
International Union of Electrical Workers, James B. Carey, dancing with
a Negro woman was circulated widely among southern electrical workers
and was used as anti-union campaign literature in two Mississippi elections. Such activity contributed to the prevailing anti-labor climate of
opinion in the South, and some unions lost membership and even affiliated
locals. No doubt this atmosphere of white solidarity and racism undermined labor's appeal, but, as labor economist Ray Marshall concluded:
"While organizing has been complicated by racial conflict, this has
probably been exaggerated as a factor impeding southern union growth."[65]

Instead, labor's problem was more fundamental, involving the institutional future of unionized labor. Union leaders were convinced that the
movement had to appeal to both white and Negro workers. During the
1930's and in the years immediately following, the American proletariat
was influenced by a depression psychology and economic interests were
predominant over racial divisions. By the 1950's—as the Great Depression

---

[63] As quoted by Anthony, "A Survey of the Resistance Groups of Alabama," 27.
[64] See the discussion and references in Marian D. Irish and James W. Prothro, *The
Politics of American Democracy* (3rd ed.; Englewood Cliffs, 1965), 64–66.
[65] Marshall, "Union Racial Problems in the South," 117. See Donald F. Roy, "Change
and Resistance to Change in the Southern Labor Movement," in McKinney and
Thompson (eds.), *The South in Continuity and Change*, 242–43; Peters, *The Southern Temper*,
234–40; Marshall, *The Negro and Organized Labor*, 197–200, and "Some Factors Influencing the Growth of Unions in the South," 176–77; and New York *Times*, September
15, November 10, 1957, May 6, 1958.

faded into history—labor leaders faced the problem of making civil rights progress with sufficient dispatch to hold Negro members and attract new ones while at the same time moving slowly enough not to alienate white members, both actual and potential. This dilemma became acute at a time when shifts in the national economy, among other factors, had halted the growth of American unions. After 1955 union membership remained constant while the number of potentially organizable employees in the national work force continued to grow. Thus, the second half of the 1950's was a period of relative labor decline. Massive resistance, therefore, emerged at a time when labor was experiencing growing racial tensions and declining membership relative to over-all employment. These difficulties were far more national than southern, but they appeared in stark outline below the Potomac. During the late 1940's the AFL and the CIO each undertook major organizing drives to extend both the labor movement and the labor-Negro political coalition into the South. The drives were failures, and the limited gains that labor had made during the 1930's and 1940's were eroded during the 1950's.

ESTIMATED UNION MEMBERSHIPS*
Per Thousands of Workers (A) and
as Percentage of the Nonagricultural Work Force (B).

STATE	1939		1953		1966	
	(A)	(B)	(A)	(B)	(A)	(B)
Alabama	64	16.1	168	24.7	151	18.0
Arkansas	25	12.7	68	21.5	112	26.2
Florida	44	11.3	136	16.3	201	13.1
Georgia	36	7.0	136	14.3	150	12.7
Louisiana	38	9.6	136	19.5	147	17.1
Mississippi	13	6.5	50	14.7	53	11.6
North Carolina	26	4.2	84	8.3	89	6.7
South Carolina	12	4.0	50	9.4	52	7.9
Tennessee	71	15.3	187	22.5	184	17.6
Texas	111	10.3	375	16.8	370	13.3
Virginia	68	12.8	156	17.3	179	15.5
United States	6,518	21.5	17,860	34.1	17,187	29.5

* Figures for 1939 and 1953 were provided by the Southern Regional Council's Labor Consultant Department. The 1966 tabulations are from U.S. Department of Labor, *News*, January 19, 1966.

Against this background, the national leadership chose to move cautiously. Labor leaders sought to avoid being forced to choose between an aggressively integrationist policy that might undermine labor's appeal to whites and a policy too tolerant of segregation that might disrupt its Negro support and alienate its liberal allies. The union hierarchy therefore relied heavily upon persuasion and education to accomplish its integrationist policies. Only occasionally did parent unions discipline their affiliates for segregationist practices. These gradualist policies led to increasing dissension within the labor movement and threatened the Negro-labor coalition in the North.[66]

In the South, labor made some progress toward the elimination of Jim Crow practices within the unions themselves, but it did not offer significant opposition to massive resistance. Organized labor rarely undertook open political cooperation with urban Negro voters. Its refusal to promote civil rights actively and aggressively and its weakness frequently led Negroes to look elsewhere for protection. Rather than a Negro-labor coalition, white laborers often followed the political advocates of white supremacy while Negroes attached themselves to the racial "moderation" of business conservatism.[67] The unions did not provide the framework for a coalition of lower- and working-class people that cut across color lines.

These two southern institutions, the church and the union, rarely behaved as positive "instruments" of "the American Creed." The church, advocate of the brotherhood of man and acknowledged guardian of society's morals, failed to accomplish a real confrontation between white supremacy and moral justice. The unions, self-proclaimed vanguard of reform and the secular defender of the brotherhood of workingmen, failed to create the institutional foundation for the old populist dream of a fusion of the have-nots solidified behind a program of economic and social reform. These were the two major institutions committed to integration on principle. Their lack of success insured whatever social adjustments the South eventually would make would be underlaid with Snopesean ethics.

The weakness of organized labor in the South enhanced the already powerful voice of corporate business. Middle- and upper-class urban southerners, as Samuel Lubell has observed, identified "the South's

---

[66] Marshall, "Some Factors Influencing the Growth of Unions in the South," 166–82, "Union Racial Problems in the South," 128, and *The Negro and Organized Labor*, 53–85, 177–205; Townsend, in *Christian Science Monitor*, April 28, 1956; Lubell, *White and Black: Test of a Nation*, 72–88.

[67] See Lubell, *White and Black: Test of a Nation*, 72–88.

economic future with the interests of business."[68] Spokesmen for the region's expanding industrial economy were assured a respectful hearing.

Business leaders and corporation executives in the South differed widely in their attitudes toward social change. Like other people of higher socio-economic levels, they tended to be somewhat more tolerant on racial issues than the population at large. But beyond this, there were at least three broad categories of business leadership. The economic elites of such "Old South" cities as Charleston, New Orleans, and a great many smaller urban centers made up one such grouping. Its members tended to be profoundly reactionary. Tradition, respect for old wealth, concern for the style of social life, and an elitist outlook acted as barriers to changes in social and ideological outlook.[69]

A second category centered around the *nouveaux riches*. World War II and post-World War II economic expansion in the South created an entre-preneurial class that frequently showed little awareness of social responsi-bility. Members of this group frequently were lower class in socio-economic background and fundamentalist in religious training. Not infrequently, they had gained prosperity in locally oriented businesses or services. These *nouveaux riches* tended to be ultraconservative on virtually every issue, including racial matters. One investigator found economic leaders of this type particularly influential in such communities as Jackson, Mississippi; Birmingham, Alabama; and Shreveport and Monroe, Louisiana.[70]

Finally, a third category of southern businessmen revolved around enterprises that were relatively capital-intensive, scientific, and nationally oriented. Members of this type tended to be better educated, less provin-cial, and more sophisticated than their peers. Their spokesmen were the economic elites of such "New South" cities as Atlanta, Miami, Houston, and, to a lesser degree, Baton Rouge. While they were normally quite conservative in outlook, they placed far greater value on progress and economic advancement than on white supremacy. What Atlanta corporate leaders "seem to want most," one scholar concluded, "are stable condi-tions for business activity and protection against further governmental regulation and taxation."[71]

[68] *Ibid.*, 69.

[69] Crain and Inger, *School Desegregation in New Orleans*, 103–27; Hero, *The Southerner and World Affairs*, 34–36.

[70] Hero, *The Southerner and World Affairs*, 153–62, 302–309.

[71] Bernd, *Grass Roots Politics in Georgia*, 35. See Crain and Inger, *School Desegregation in New Orleans*, 118–38; Hero, *The Southerner and World Affairs*, 139–83; Soukup, McCleskey

The South's captains of industry and finance differed among themselves, but, like ministers and labor leaders, they generally evidenced a predominant concern for the success of their own institutions. They were, as Ralph McGill put it, "more influenced by the slowing of cash register bells than by morality."[72] This statement summarized the businessman's dilemma. He feared the more rabid forms of neobourbon extremism, particularly the threat of violence or the dismantling of the public school system. Yet he, too, wished to defend states' rights and oppose the extension of federal authority. And, significantly, the corporation, unlike the church or the union, was not institutionally committed to integration in principle.

Consequently, business organizations usually remained aloof from the massive resistance controversy. When they did speak on the subject, they tended during the early phases of massive resistance to cooperate with—or perhaps more correctly in some cases, to attempt to take advantage of —the neobourbon crusade. Specifically, business groups sought to check the liberal tendencies of the United States Supreme Court and to reinforce states' rights generally. Thus both the National Association of Manufacturers and the Chamber of Commerce lobbied in favor of congressional legislation restricting the Court's jurisdiction.[73] Thurman Sensing, executive vice president of the Southern States Industrial Council, was a leading proponent of massive resistance measures.[74] Various state groups, such as the Tennessee Business Men's Association, went on record in favor of interposition or other anti-integration proposals.[75] Semibusiness groups with close rural ties, such as state Farm Bureau Federations or Cattlemen's Associations, overwhelmingly aligned themselves with a vigorous defense of white supremacy.[76] Dissenters existed in the business community, but they were few and were far outnumbered by those who supported massive resistance, or who offered at least guarded support for it, or who, as individuals, joined the Citizens' Councils movement.

---

and Holloway, *Party and Factional Division in Texas*, 9–14; and M. Richard Cramer, "School Desegregation and New Industry: The Southern Community Leaders' Viewpoint," *Social Forces*, XLI (May, 1963), 384–89.

[72] McGill, *The South and the Southerner*, 229.

[73] Murphy, *Congress and the Court*, 248.

[74] Memphis *Commercial Appeal*, February 22, 1956; Nashville *Tennessean*, August 24, 1957.

[75] Nashville *Banner*, June 27, 1956; Atlanta *Constitution*, September 30, 1957; Birmingham *News*, November 20, 1957.

[76] Richmond *News Leader*, November 12, 1954; Charleston *News and Courier*, April 24, 1956; New Orleans *Times-Picayune*, July 24, 1958; Richmond *Times-Dispatch*, November 25–27, 1958; Birmingham *News*, January 29, 1956, January 20, 1957.

Most of all, southern business sought to avoid involvement in the controversy altogether. Southern business publications, one study reported, carefully circumvented "discussion of race relations lest the thought of racial discord discourage industry from moving South."[77] State Chambers of Commerce normally refused to take a stand, and businessmen's clubs like Kiwanis, Rotary, and Lions rarely voiced a position as organizations. The Nashville Kiwanis Club approved a resolution opposing desegregation in the city and calling upon public officials to prevent Negro enrollment in white schools. The club president told reporters immediately afterward: "Luncheon clubs should never get into a controversial matter and we shouldn't have gotten into this one."[78] The president had pretty well summed up the general business approach to social justice in the South.

Industrial spokesmen did, however, want to preserve the South's good business image and to convince prospective manufacturers that the land below the Potomac indeed offered the nation's foremost economic opportunity. They insisted that massive resistance would have no effect upon the region's industrial future. The Southern Association of State Planning and Development Agencies endorsed a resolution branding as "false propaganda" the charge that racial difficulties hindered southern industrial development.[79] Similar sentiments were echoed by business and industrial groups throughout the South. Such statements stood as assurances that the region could have both white supremacy and economic progress. Not until the closure of public schools in Virginia and Little Rock was this general business attitude seriously questioned.

Of all groups, southern educators found their institutional future most closely bound up with massive resistance. The Supreme Court had assigned school authorities "the primary responsibility for elucidating, assessing, and solving" the problems of desegregation.[80] Yet state legislators filled the law books with preventive or hindering legislation and the air with threats to abolish the schools altogether. The public school

---

[77] Irish, "Political Thought and Political Behavior in the South," 409.

[78] As quoted in Nashville *Tennessean*, August 24, 1957.

[79] Reprinted in Birmingham *News*, October 12, 1957. For public pronouncements in Alabama see the statements of General Lewis A. Pick, director of the State Industrial Development Board, in Birmingham *News*, April 12, 1956; L. M. Smith, president of Alabama Power Company, in *ibid.*, April 18, 1956; Tom Blake, director of the Industrial Division of the Montgomery Chamber of Commerce, in Montgomery *Advertiser*, October 3, 1957; and Carl Griffin, promotional representative for the State Planning and Industrial Development Board, in *ibid.*, April 29, 1960.

[80] *Brown v. Board of Education* (1955), in *Race Relations Law Reporter*, I (February, 1956), 11.

administrator was indeed the "Man in No Man's Land."[81] He had, of course, a most direct stake in the preservation of popular education, and his professional interests, like those of the denominational minister, encouraged an awareness of contemporary intellectual trends. At the same time strong forces pulled him toward a position of segregation or silence. Dependent on public funds and thus on the good will of the community and the state legislature, he was not in a strategically favorable position to take a stand opposing massive resistance, even if so inclined. As an East Texas school official explained, "Anti-integrationist feeling is extremely strong in this area. To advocate any plan toward integration would be committing professional suicide."[82] Normally, school boards only too clearly reflected popular hostility to desegregation. Limited evidence suggests that the boards, rather than professional educators, were most apt to formulate racial policies, and southern school boards (their membership usually elected) were often strongholds of segregationist sentiment.[83] Sharpening these influences were the efforts by Citizens' Councils and other groups to purge southern schools of liberal social teachings. Furthermore, dual school systems were part of the southern educational establishment and were institutionalized by separate faculties, buildings, and administrative procedures. Except in areas where Negro enrollment was negligible, virtually no southern educator seriously contemplated abandoning "Negro" and "white" facilities even when a few Negroes were necessarily admitted to "white" schools.

Given these pressures, the professional educator tended to be a cautious influence for moderation. While greeting the *Brown* decision with few signs of enthusiasm, leading school officials in the upper South endorsed the feasibility of gradual compliance. "If we must end segregation," Florida State School Superintendent Thomas D. Bailey said in a fairly typical pronouncement, "then we'll go about it with common sense and careful deliberation."[84] Similar statements by state and urban education officials were relatively common during the 1954–55 period, and the school boards in a number of peripheral-South cities publicly announced their intention to plan for eventual desegregation. In the Deep South public expressions of this nature were far less frequent, but, even there, such

[81] Glen Robinson, "Man in No Man's Land: The School Administrator," in Shoemaker (ed.), *With All Deliberate Speed*, 183–201.

[82] As quoted in Dallas *Morning News*, September 5, 1957.

[83] Crain and Inger, *School Desegregation in New Orleans*, 111, 162; Robinson, "Man in No Man's Land," 187–89.

[84] As quoted in *New South*, December, 1953.

actions were recorded. When the National Education Association approved a resolution favoring integration, only the delegates from Mississippi and South Carolina voted against the measure.[85]

As massive resistance gained momentum, public espousal of moderation sharply declined among schoolmen. Deep South educators aligned themselves generally with the defense of segregation. Delegates to the Georgia Education Association convention unanimously resolved their "belief in and desire for a continuation of equal but separate schools."[86] Most other white education groups in the Deep South took similar positions or refused to speak at all. Louisiana educators presented a particularly solid front in support of segregation, and their actions exemplified the tendency of schoolmen to think in terms of immediate institutional interests. In Louisiana the Rainach faction and the school forces were frequent allies.[87] Segregationists, seeking to dampen Negro militancy by improving educational facilities within the Jim Crow system, and educators, for obvious reasons, found common cause in the support of increased appropriations for teachers' salaries and schools generally. The Louisiana School Boards Association urged state officials to resist integration, and the state Teachers' Association lobbied in favor of legislation posing vast potential threats to public education.[88] The Louisiana Parent Teacher Association failed for a time to join the front, tabling a segregationist resolution in 1957.[89] In their 1958 convention, however, association members pledged their cooperation "in working toward retention of segregation in public schools."[90] Soon afterward—in what some political observers considered more than a coincidence—a number of legislators associated with Rainach joined with the Long forces in winning enactment of tax raises for teachers' salaries.[91] At no time during the 1950's did a Louisiana teachers' group offer support for the maintenance of public education in the state.

In the upper South public educators placed less emphasis on defense of segregation and demonstrated greater concern for the continuation of

[85] New York *Times*, July 3, 1954. See Edgar L. Jones, "City Limits: Segregation-Desegregation in the Cities," in Shoemaker (ed.), *With All Deliberate Speed*, 85; and *Southern School News*, September, October, 1954.

[86] Reprinted in Chattanooga *Times*, March 19, 1955.

[87] *Southern School News*, February-September, 1955; New Orleans *Times-Picayune*, May 20–24, 1955.

[88] New Orleans *Times-Picayune*, February 8, 1956, June 10, 1958; Chattanooga *Times*, June 19, 1958.

[89] New Orleans *Times-Picayune*, May 5, 1957.

[90] As quoted in *ibid.*, April 27, 1958.

[91] See James McLean, in *ibid.*, December 14, 1958.

public education. The Florida Education Association resolved that "no issue, however critical, should prevent our wholehearted support and maintenance of free public schools" and followed this pronouncement with active opposition to school-closing legislation.[92] In North Carolina the State Congress of Parents and Teachers led the unsuccessful fight against the Pearsall plan, which permitted local closure of schools.[93] Such positive action by school groups was relatively infrequent, however. Individual educators often opposed measures deemed damaging to the schools, but education organizations normally contented themselves with a plea for the preservation of public education, sometimes wording their entreaties equivocally to avoid openly criticizing state policy.[94] Rare indeed were pronouncements such as the platform plank adopted by the Florida Congress of Parents and Teachers: "We must move realistically toward state and community planning in the integration of our schools and toward the implementation of the law of the land."[95]

During the 1950's white educators evidenced little stomach for "elucidating, assessing, and solving" the problems of integration. Only a minuscule number of school districts abandoned Jim Crow facilities voluntarily. The Atlanta *Journal and Constitution* reported in 1961 that: "Somewhere along the way, the Atlanta [School] Board adopted the attitude that it would do no more about integration than compelled to by court order. That is its attitude to this day."[96] It was also an attitude widely held among school administrative officials generally. When schools were desegregated, school authorities showed an almost eager willingness to placate community sentiment by desegregating on the secondary level despite the hardships thus imposed on Negro pupils attending the "white" schools. Often school officials showed far more ingenuity in sharply limiting the number of Negro students involved than in dealing with the problems of education in a desegregated school.[97] Generally, southern educators

[92] Reprinted in Miami *Herald*, April 15, 1956; Atlanta *Journal and Constitution*, March 24, 1957.
[93] *Southern School News*, August, September, 1956.
[94] For examples, see Richmond *Times-Dispatch*, October 31, 1954; Washington *Post*, October 28, 1955; Washington *Evening Star*, August 11, 1956; and Richmond *Times-Dispatch*, November 4, 1956.
[95] Reprinted in Miami *Herald*, November 11, 1955.
[96] Atlanta *Journal and Constitution*, August 27, 1961.
[97] Vernon E. Jordan, Jr. and Marvin Wall, "Desegregation of Atlanta Schools— 1942 to Present" (unpublished Southern Regional Council report, 1966); Hugh Davis Graham, "Desegregation in Nashville: The Dynamics of Compliance," *Tennessee Historical Quarterly*, XXV (Summer, 1966), 135–54; Blossom, *It Has Happened Here;* Crain and Inger, *School Desegregation in New Orleans;* Sarratt, *Ordeal of Desegregation*, 75–114.

preferred to seek security by following community sentiment rather than to risk the perils of leadership.

These institutions—church, union, corporation, school—placed few significant impediments in the path of the rise of massive resistance. Within each of these institutions a wide variety of opinions found expression. But, most of all, ministers, labor leaders, businessmen, and educators shared a common concern for the immediate interests of their own institutions. Abstract theories of human justice, or democracy, or Christian brotherhood, or the sanctity of national law had limited observable effects on their activities. Eventually, however, the framework of conflict changed.

CHAPTER 17

A THERMIDOREAN REACTION

School closures in Arkansas and Virginia brought to a head the fundamental dilemma facing a region seeking both the maintenance of past customs and the advancement of economic and technological progress. The Supreme Court refused to surrender to southern opposition, and the Eisenhower administration's intervention in Little Rock demonstrated that southern state governments would not be permitted to ignore court orders. State officials could only close the schools and stand defiantly in the face of federal authority. Such a policy of calculated anarchy assaulted public education and threatened the whole structure of southern society, the region's economic future, and the vested interests of southern institutions. Thus the dialectic was once again rephrased, and the future of public education and the stability of the governmental process, rather than segregation and desegregation, became the central issues. This situation led to a general shift away from massive resistance, a shift that was conservative rather than reformist, that sought social stability rather than social change.

During the fall and winter of 1958–59, massive resistance lost the initiative in southern politics. For the first time, a broadly based Southwide opposition openly challenged the Citizens' Councils and their allies. A save-the-schools citizens' movement that institutionalized urban middle-class "moderation" emerged in the cities. Schoolmen came out tellingly for the integrity of public education. Business leaders cautiously placed their influence in opposition to massive resistance extremism. These developments provided politicians of moderate inclinations with an expanding base of popular support.

Virginia was the testing ground for the newly emerging balance of forces. In October, 1958, Governor J. Lindsay Almond vigorously defended his no quarter policy in a speech before the annual convention of the Virginia Congress of Parent Teacher Associations. Although Almond's address was well received, PTA delegates rejected by a 557–557 tie vote a resolution endorsing massive resistance. Then by a two-vote margin, 515–513, the convention called for an abandonment of interposition and the adoption of a local option policy on school segregation or desegregation.[1] Later in the same month delegates to the Virginia Education Association convention approved resolutions expressing deep concern over school closures and urging a special legislative session to enact laws preventing the disruption of public education.[2] For the first time, educators had openly challenged state policy and unequivocally had come to the defense of public education in Virginia.

Soon afterward, the urban press shifted away from interposition. On November 11, 1958, *News Leader* Editor James Jackson Kilpatrick, speaking before a Richmond luncheon club, called for a review of Virginia's antidesegregation policy and suggested a shift back to the original strategy conceived by the Gray Commission.[3] On the next day, the Richmond *Times-Dispatch* editorialized: "We must now find another position from which to fight, with ground for maneuver, to gather our strength and renew the battle." The editorial, written by *Times-Dispatch* Editor Virginius Dabney, called for more flexible opposition to social change.[4] Urban newspapers in Norfolk, Roanoke, and elsewhere recommended similar reevaluations of Virginia policy.[5] City ministerial associations, local PTA's, the League of Women Voters, and other groups became more openly critical of school closures.[6]

The Committee for Public Schools, an open-schools organization that originated in Arlington, spread to other Virginia cities. The Committee for Public Schools avoided the racial issue, taking its stand on a local option policy and upholding public education. In December, 1958, representatives from fourteen communities formed a state organization with offices in Richmond. The Committee, which drew its membership mainly from urban professional and white-collar groups, became a "respectable" political pressure group opposing massive resistance. Like

[1] New York *Times*, October 21–23, 1958.
[2] Richmond *Times-Dispatch*, October 29–31, 1958.
[3] Richmond *News Leader*, November 11, 12, 1958.
[4] Richmond *Times-Dispatch*, November 12, 1958.
[5] John D. Morris, in New York *Times*, November 16, 1958.
[6] *Southern School News*, October, 1958–January, 1959.

the Defenders, it spoke for a greater number of Virginians than its membership rolls implied.[7]

Eventually, businessmen also actively came to the defense of public education. Generally, business spokesmen were reluctant to express "moderate" views openly and relied instead upon behind the scenes political pressure. Most notably, twenty-nine of Virginia's leading industrial and financial titans met privately with Governor Almond and his administration leaders in December, 1958, to urge the abandonment of interposition.[8] Business leaders in Norfolk and Charlottesville brought their concern into the open during January, 1959, publishing newspaper advertisements calling for local option and open schools.[9] By the end of 1958, the Virginia Committee for Public Schools claimed fifteen thousand members, and the illusion of unity in Virginia had been effectively shattered.

The political atmosphere in Virginia changed gradually, and it did so against the uncompromising opposition of the massive resistance forces. In November, 1958, Senator Byrd won reelection by his usual 70 percent majority. The election, as a Virginia journalist observed, "failed to show anything that could be considered a significant protest against the massive resistance policy Byrd symbolizes."[10] Immediately thereafter, the senator reaffirmed his faith in massive resistance and called for continuing opposition to the Supreme Court.[11] The Defenders insisted that the Old Dominion must hold to its course. Since Virginia "is the battleground upon which the struggle for the eternal liberties of America must be waged," the organization's board of directors stated, "let us not falter, let us not yield."[12] Spokesmen for the Defenders pressed Governor Almond to stand firm in defense of white supremacy.

Governor Almond wavered, giving hope to, and provoking the suspicions of, both the moderates and the proponents of massive resistance. Almond had been a reluctant recruit into the massive resistance camp, but he had campaigned on an interposition platform and had committed himself to an unalterable defense of segregation. Now he waited for public

---

[7] *Ibid.;* Muse, *Virginia's Massive Resistance,* 56–58, 89–94.

[8] Muse, *Virginia's Massive Resistance,* 109–10.

[9] Norfolk *Ledger-Dispatch,* January 25, 1959; Charlottesville *Daily Progress,* January 31, 1959. In the latter city, a large number of "Independent Citizens" joined in endorsing the "Non-Political Statement" originated by the city's businessmen.

[10] Latimer, in Richmond *Times-Dispatch,* November 5, 1958.

[11] Morris, in New York *Times,* November 14, 1958.

[12] Richmond *Times-Dispatch,* December 4, 1958.

opinion either to frame a new mandate or to reaffirm the old one. The governor stated: "I have often said that in the final analysis, the people of Virginia will have to determine this grave issue. It may bring them to consideration of the total abandonment of public schools in many areas of Virginia."[13]

During the closing months of 1958 Almond waited for Virginians to reach a conclusion about the relative importance of undefiled white supremacy and public education. He vowed "in profound and pleading reverence" that he would defend segregation "so long as I have the support of the people of Virginia."[14] At the same time, he kept other options open. He refused to invoke the massive resistance legislation which permitted the governor to take control of closed schools in the name of the general assembly and to reopen them as segregated institutions despite court orders to the contrary. He directed his attorney general to bring a test case seeking a state court ruling on the validity of the school-closing and funds-withholding laws under the Virginia constitution. The laws were already being challenged in federal courts, and Almond presumably felt that, if the measures were to be struck down, the massive resistance forces were more likely to accept such a decree from a state court than from the federal bench.[15] The governor continued to condemn the "nine fawning puppets of political pressure groups" who sat on the United States Supreme Court and to refuse to "concede an opinion of the Supreme Court to be the law of the land."[16] But he also failed to consult with Senator Byrd as previous governors normally had done,[17] and his statements and actions suggested a flexibility that set him apart from the more determined massive resistance forces.

Almond awaited the decision of the courts and of the general will of Virginia. The courts were the first to speak. On January 19, 1959, the Virginia Supreme Court of Appeals ruled that the closing of the schools and the withholding of state funds were violations of the state constitution.[18] On the same day a three-judge federal district court decision held that both measures also conflicted with the United States Constitution.[19]

---

13 As quoted in Washington *Post*, October 5, 1958.
14 As quoted in New York *Times*, October 21, 1958.
15 Muse, *Virginia's Massive Resistance*, 85; Richmond *News Leader*, November 1, 1958.
16 As quoted in Richmond *Times-Dispatch*, November 24, 1958.
17 Muse, *Virginia's Massive Resistance*, 99.
18 *Harrison v. Day*, in *Race Relations Law Reporter*, IV (Spring, 1959), 65–78.
19 *James v. Almond*, in *ibid.*, 45–54.

Virginia's key massive resistance laws had been invalidated, and the schools remained under court order to desegregate.

The court rulings required Virginia to make a decision, but the state's white citizenry had not yet reached a consensus, and Almond, himself, sometimes seemed none too sure about the proper course to follow. Nevertheless, the governor's actions showed a certain logical consistency. He endeavored to protect his own segregationist-states' rights credentials and, at the same time, maneuvered toward a more flexible policy. Such an approach permitted the massive resistance forces, as well as segregationists generally, to accept the shift with as little loss of face as possible. Insofar as this course of action represented Almond's premeditated strategy, it underestimated the depth of the neobourbon commitment to massive resistance.

On the day after the court actions, Governor Almond answered with a fiery radio and television call to arms. He declared that Virginia "will not abandon or compromise with principle to have it lost never to be regained." He made "it abundantly clear for the record now and hereafter, as Governor of this state, I will not yield to that which I know to be wrong . . . ." He stated that he would appoint a commission to study the entire situation and called upon Virginians "to stand firmly with me in this struggle."[20] Senator Byrd promptly endorsed the governor's "notable speech," and the Defenders called for a special legislative session to shore up the massive resistance structure.[21]

Almond convened the special session (which met later in January, 1959), but in his address to the legislature the governor cautiously sounded the call for a retreat from massive resistance. "The time has arrived," he stated, "to take a new, thorough, and long look at the situation which confronts us." He asked for measures enacting a new tuition-grant system and repealing compulsory attendance laws. He called upon the legislature to approve these measures and to await the report of the study commission.[22] The special session was short, and the massive resistance forces were slow to comprehend the full significance of Almond's proposals. The governor got the legislation that he had requested; the closed schools reopened; and, shortly afterward, three Virginia cities desegregated. The legislative session became increasingly acrimonious as the proponents

[20] Reprinted in Richmond *Times-Dispatch*, January 21, 1959.
[21] William B. Foster, Jr., in Richmond *News Leader*, January 21, 1959; *Southern School News*, February, 1959.
[22] Reprinted in Richmond *News Leader*, January 28, 1959.

of massive resistance regrouped in the face of this unexpected turn of events. The massive resistance bloc centered around such close friends of Harry Flood Byrd as Garland Gray, E. Blackburn Moore, Mills E. Godwin, and Harry F. Byrd, Jr., who substantially represented the hard core of the Byrd organization. But now organization stalwarts found the state executive power in unfriendly hands. Almond won the support of a number of the more moderate members of the organization and combined their votes with those of anti-organization Democrats and several Republicans. The legislature rejected all the defiant measures introduced by the extreme segregationists.[23] Arlington, Norfolk, and Alexandria admitted Negro students to formerly all-white schools without incident.

The massive resistance forces fought to regain control of state policy. Southside flamed with revolt, and town councils censured Almond and his policies. The Defenders spread the demand for a return to the principle of interposition, sponsoring protest meetings across the state and organizing a mass pressure group movement called the "Bill of Rights Crusade."[24] William Old, the original propagandist for interposition in Virginia, circulated a new constitutional treatise calling upon the state legislature to "screw up its courage to the sticking point" and to "refuse to submit to the unconstitutional rulings of the Federal courts."[25]

Governor Almond awaited the report of his study commission. Packed by the governor with moderate legislators and headed by State Senator Mosby G. Perrow, Jr., the Commission on Education conducted public hearings and generally took a long-range look at the problem. Its conclusions were essentially not unlike those of the 1955 Gray Commission. The Perrow Commission recommended a local option policy that sought to hold desegregation to token levels while offering white students as much "freedom of choice" as possible.[26]

The legislature convened in April, 1959, to take up the fifteen-bill program recommended by the Perrow Commission. Almond vigorously endorsed the report, stating that it dealt with facts rather than fiction and

---

[23] Muse, *Virginia's Massive Resistance*, 126–43; *Southern School News*, February, March, 1959. The laws passed by the legislature are reprinted in *Race Relations Law Reporter*, IV (Spring, 1959), 188–90.

[24] Richmond *Times-Dispatch*, February 10–April 7, 1959; Richmond *News Leader*, February 10–April 7, 1959.

[25] William Old, *The Segregation Issue As It Appears Now* (privately printed, 1959), 23–24.

[26] "Report of the Perrow Commission," in *Race Relations Law Reporter*, IV (Summer, 1959), 392–408.

reality rather than wishful thinking. "It represents the next best step in determined continuation of our struggle, under the Polar Star of honor and within the framework of law, in defense of our rights," Almond told the legislators. "In design, purpose and content it bears no semblance of surrender."[27] A Bill of Rights Crusade rally on the opening day of the session sought to call the legislators back to a massive resistance course. The Committee for Public Schools lobbied effectively for the Perrow plan. The session developed into a bitter struggle between two almost evenly balanced legislative blocs. House Speaker Moore and State Senator Harry F. Byrd, Jr., led a determined drive to block the Perrow plan and to enact extreme measures. The machine was now split, and the organization's hard core was in the minority; yet its members fought stubbornly on. Governor Almond and Lieutenant Governor A. E. S. Stevens marshaled the administration forces and held together a narrow majority. The Perrow Commission's recommendations were enacted into law.[28]

The Virginia primary elections in July, 1959, confirmed the demise of massive resistance. The Defenders campaigned for the defeat of a sufficient number of pro-administration members to reestablish a massive resistance majority in the legislature. Candidates supported by the Defenders did make limited gains in the house, but their gains were small, and, in the all-important senate races, the diehard segregationists failed to unseat their major targets.[29] Virginians gradually became accustomed to token desegregation, and the policy of interposition faded once again into Virginia's past.

The Byrd organization's dogged defense of massive resistance had endangered its own existence, and the breach within the Virginia Democratic Party hardened during the remaining years of Almond's governorship. At his annual apple orchard picnic in August, 1959, Senator Byrd said: "I stand now as I stood when I first urged massive resistance."[30] Byrd made it clear that the governor and his allies would not be forgiven for their betrayal of the cause. The organization forces fought the administration's tax policies and its other major programs; Almond purged pro-Byrd appointees from state patronage positions and openly attacked

---

[27] Reprinted in Richmond *Times-Dispatch*, April 7, 1959.
[28] *Race Relations Law Reporter*, IV (Summer, 1959), 411–39; *Southern School News*, May, June, 1959; Muse, *Virginia's Massive Resistance*, 160–64.
[29] Muse, in Washington *Post*, July 19, 1959; *Southern School News*, August, 1959.
[30] As quoted by Laurence Stern, in Washington *Post*, August 30, 1959.

Harry F. Byrd, Jr., and, by implication, the senator himself.[31] In the Democratic primary elections of 1961, supporters of the Almond administration fielded a formidable anti-organization ticket led by Lieutenant Governor Stevens. The Byrd organization, admitting defeat on the massive resistance issue, selected Attorney General Albertis S. Harrison, who was not identified with the resistance-to-the-bitter-end movement, as its gubernatorial nominee. It chose, however, former massive resistance stalwarts as candidates for lieutenant governor and attorney general.[32] The election symbolized the conservative nature of the shift away from massive resistance. Almond had led Virginians through the crisis, and now Virginians reestablished the old regime by nominating, and later electing, Harrison and his ticket.[33]

Events in Arkansas confirmed the defeat of massive resistance in the upper South. As in Virginia, a coalition of educators, friends-of-the-schools citizens groups, and business spokesmen led a general swing in popular sentiment away from the scorched earth strategy of massive resistance. Again, the balance of political pressures was narrow. The proponents of massive resistance remained militant and unreconstructed, as the Arkansas Education Association was to learn.

In November, 1958, the Arkansas Education Association convention, the largest adult convention in the state, resolved its firm support for the preservation of public education. Association delegates went on to recommend the formation of a coalition of its chapters, PTA's, and interested citizens to keep watch on state legislators and to press for open-school legislation.[34] Such impertinence on the part of school teachers brought instant retaliation from the state legislature. The Legislative Council, which included the state's most powerful legislators among its membership, unanimously voted to postpone indefinitely any action on the Department of Education's budget request, to turn all documents approved by the association convention over to the Committee on Subversion in Education, to order a poll of all association members on their attitudes toward the organization's policies, and to review that part of the state sales tax earmarked for teachers' salaries.[35] The legislators

[31] Richmond *Times-Dispatch*, February 20, 1960; Robert E. Baker, in Washington *Post*, December 17, 1961.
[32] State Senators Mills E. Godwin and Robert Y. Button respectively.
[33] *Southern School News*, August, 1961; Baker, in Washington *Post*, January 21, 1962.
[34] *Arkansas Gazette*, November 7, 1958.
[35] Roy Reed, in *ibid.*, November 8, 1958.

eventually subsided, and these measures were forgotten. The episode, however, served as a clear warning of the perils of moderation. Other potentially moderate groups in Arkansas were noticeably reluctant to speak until, eventually, the excesses of massive resistance provoked a reaction in Little Rock.

Governor Orval Faubus had closed the high schools in the state capital in September, 1958. Later in that month the city's voters endorsed the governor's action in a special election. Less than 30 percent favored "For racial integration of all schools within the Little Rock School District," as the option for reopening the closed schools was listed on the ballot.[36] Faubus assured voters that the high schools could be promptly reopened as segregated, private institutions, but federal district and circuit court injunctions prohibited transfer of the school buildings and equipment to private groups.[37] The circuit court order, handed down on November 10, 1958, followed close upon the heels of Representative Brooks Hays's failure to win reelection in the Little Rock congressional district. These events convinced five of the six members of the Little Rock school board of "the utter hopelessness, helplessness and frustration of our present position."[38] After buying up Superintendent Virgil Blossom's contract, all the board members except Congressman-elect Dale Alford resigned. In December, 1958, Little Rock elected a new school board. The massive resistance forces, led by the Capital Citizens' Council and supported by Governor Faubus, put up one slate of candidates. A group of Little Rock businessmen recruited an alternate ticket, which took a more "moderate" segregationist position in the campaign. The voters chose three board members from each group.[39] The new board was hopelessly divided, and Little Rock, as one scholar observed, "was being torn apart over the question of whether it wished to obey or to defy an objectionable ruling of the Supreme Court."[40]

During the early months of 1959, Little Rock drifted—its high schools closed and its citizens torn between the racial extremism institutionalized by the Capital Citizens' Council and a growing voice of moderation. Then, on May 5, the school board held a fateful session that was to revitalize the moderate cause in Arkansas. For some weeks persistent rumors had

[36] Reprinted in *ibid.*, September 27, 1958.
[37] *Aaron v. Cooper,* in *Race Relations Law Reporter,* III (December, 1958), 1135–44.
[38] *Southern School News,* December, 1958, quoting from the statement of resignation.
[39] *Southern School News,* January, 1959.
[40] Silverman, *The Little Rock Story,* 31.

circulated in Little Rock that the extreme segregationists were demanding a purge of school employees.[41] A number of teachers and administrators had incurred the wrath of white supremacy elements due to their generous treatment of Negro students at Central High School during the previous school year. Faubus said that these educators had done "everything they could to discriminate against white students . . . ."[42] A segregationist leader on the school board said: "We do not want teachers in our schools teaching our children alien racial doctrines."[43] A later investigation by the Arkansas Education Association and the Classroom Teachers' Association found the accused teachers guilty of enforcing class discipline, permitting Negro students to take regular turns in reading the Bible, and in general, dealing fairly with all students. A segregationist group answered that the teachers' offenses included: "Teaching alien doctrines, incompetency, . . . improper punishment, intimidation of students, [and] immorality."[44] The school board took up the question of teacher contracts at its May 5, 1959, meeting. The three segregationist members wanted to dismiss the offending employees; the three moderate members favored rehiring all school personnel. After a lengthly and fruitless argument, the three moderates walked out, stating that their departure left the meeting without a quorum. The segregationist threesome unanimously concluded, however, that the session began with a quorum and remained legally constituted. They settled down to a long afternoon's work that included disapproving the contracts of thirty-four teachers, two principals, five other administrative officials, and three secretaries.[45]

Little Rock moderates, having failed to rally effectively behind the cause of public education, now had a new issue. The city PTA Council, composed of representatives of local white PTA's in Little Rock, initiated the antipurge movement. The council resolved "that board members who attempt such highhanded tactics are not qualified to hold offices of such great responsibility"[46] and sponsored nightly protest meetings throughout the city. Local PTA's, other school organizations, and the Women's Emergency Committee to Open Our Schools joined the drive. The Women's Emergency Committee, a middle-class organization formed to

[41] The proposed purge was first disclosed by the *Arkansas Gazette*, February 8, 1959.

[42] As quoted by *Southern School News*, February, 1959. Faubus was referring to three administrative officials at Central High School.

[43] *Arkansas Gazette*, May 20, 1959, quoting Ed I. McKinley.

[44] As quoted in *Southern School News*, June, 1959.

[45] *Arkansas Gazette*, May 6, 1959.

[46] Reprinted in *ibid.*, May 7, 1959.

support an open-schools vote in the September referendum, now numbered more than a thousand members. Important Little Rock business leaders were already publicly committed to the reopening of schools, and they gave strong support to the antipurge movement. By early 1959, the material costs of overt defiance and locked schoolhouses were becoming painfully obvious. Although ten new industries had located in Little Rock during the two years prior to September, 1957, the city had won not a single new industrial commitment since that date.[47] A number of individual businessmen, led by the former industrial director of the Little Rock Chamber of Commerce, had participated in the December school board elections. The Chamber of Commerce itself took note that something was wrong in January, 1959, just seventeen months after the city had become an international symbol of racial controversy and five months after the high schools had been closed. Two months later, in March, 1959, the Little Rock Chamber of Commerce released a formal statement of policy. While expressing faith in segregation, the statement defended the rule of law and the importance of public education. It called for the schools to be reopened on a desegregated basis.[48] Three days after the purge of the school teachers, 179 Little Rock business and civic leaders organized the Committee to Stop This Outrageous Purge (STOP). The group issued a statement demanding the recall of the three segregationist board members and undertook to circulate recall petitions.[49]

The Capital Citizens' Council, the Mothers' League, and the newly formed States' Rights Council countered by circulating petitions for the recall of the three moderate board members. Within days both STOP and the segregationists had enough signatures to force elections for all six seats. STOP led the moderate campaign; the segregationists created the Committee to Retain Our Segregated Schools (CROSS) to lead their voter drive. The recall campaign was hotly contested. CROSS insisted that the election gave voters a choice between integration and segregation; STOP reiterated its contention that the election had nothing to do with race but instead involved honesty and fair play toward the teachers. Governor Faubus intervened late in the campaign on the side of the

---

[47] *Arkansas Gazette, A Selection of Editorials: Crisis in the South, The Little Rock Story* (Little Rock, 1959), 81; *Arkansas Gazette*, January 27, June 25, 28, August 2, December 31, 1959; Women's Emergency Committee to Open Our Schools, *Little Rock Report: The City, Its People, Its Business, 1957–1959* (Little Rock, 1959).

[48] Reprinted in Record and Record (eds.), *Little Rock U.S.A.*, 139–42.

[49] *Southern School News*, June, 1959; Silverman, *The Little Rock Story*, 31.

segregationists, warning the "good, hard-working, honest people" to beware of the "charge of the Cadillac brigade."[50]

The election was close, but nevertheless it marked a decisive victory for the moderates. The three anti-Faubus board members retained their seats; the three segregationist members were recalled.[51] For the first time Governor Faubus had been clearly beaten on a matter pertaining to race and the schools. Little Rock's civic and business leadership and a considerable number of private citizens had become actively involved on the side of moderation in the city's desegregation controversy. They acted not for the most part, it should be stressed, as defenders of human equality or social justice but merely as proponents of order, stability, and new factories in Little Rock.

During June, 1959, the Little Rock school board, now composed of the three moderates and two new members appointed by the county board of education, voted to strike the May 5 session completely from the record and discussed reopening the high schools in the fall. At its next meeting the board announced formally that the schools would be reopened on a basis acceptable to the federal courts. On June 18 a three-judge federal district court declared the Arkansas school-closing and funds-withholding laws unconstitutional and ordered the city school board to proceed with its original desegregation plan. Governor Faubus stated that he remained opposed to "forced" desegregation.[52]

Little Rock peacefully desegregated its white public high schools in August, 1959. The atmosphere was tense. The segregationist opposition remained strong, and Governor Faubus represented a distinctly unpredictable element. But in 1959 Little Rock was prepared for desegregation. The school board received organized public support. The city government, breaking a long silence, announced that disorder and lawlessness would not be tolerated. The police department, now capably led and properly prepared, dealt firmly and promptly with public disturbances.[53] The Little Rock desegregation crisis came to an end.

The 1960 elections in Arkansas ratified the moderate victory in Little Rock. Attorney General Bruce Bennett challenged Governor Faubus for the Democratic gubernatorial nomination. Bennett had championed his

---

[50] As quoted in *Arkansas Gazette*, May 23, 1959.

[51] *Southern School News*, June, 1959.

[52] *Ibid.*, July, 1959; and *Aaron v. McKinley*, in *Race Relations Law Reporter*, IV (Fall, 1959), 543–50.

[53] *Southern School News*, September, 1959.

"Southern Plan for Peace," made war on the NAACP, and searched for Communists. He had, so the *Arkansas Gazette* felt, sought "to stake out a stronger position on the race issue than that held, to good profit, by Orval Faubus. This is not easy to do, of course, and Mr. Bennett has had to make his headlines by resorting to the phony investigation and the calculated smear."[54] In his campaign for the governorship, the attorney general called for a return to massive resistance and promised to "de-integrate" Arkansas. "The best defense is a good offense," he declared. "Six other Southern states don't have integration and I'm intent on making Arkansas the seventh." Faubus conducted a relatively moderate campaign. He spoke of peace and order and of the gains accomplished "by working together, not by fighting, not by yielding to the agitators of whatever race or creed." The governor won renomination for a fourth gubernatorial term by a large majority. In the November general elections, Arkansas voters overwhelmingly rejected a constitutional amendment eliminating requirements for the state to provide public schools and permitting local option school closures.[55] It was the only time during the period that a southern statewide electorate defeated a measure threatening the public schools. Arkansas citizens had accepted token desegregation.

Events in Virginia and Arkansas broke the massive resistance front and demonstrated the essential nature of the shift from the principle of inter-position. In the fall of 1959 a Miami school district admitted Negro pupils to a formerly all-white school, and in the fall of 1960 a ruling by the Texas attorney general permitted Houston to desegregate without the loss of state funds. These developments confined the interposition front to the five states of the Deep South, and desegregation in Atlanta and New Orleans during the early 1960's marked the final demise of the massive resistance stage of southern politics. The same forces that undermined massive reistance in the upper South were present in the Deep South, but neobourbon influence was also greater; thus the shift to a nominal accept-ance of the validity of the *Brown* decision was in some cases a traumatic and violent process.

Georgia followed the example of the upper South. The New South leadership in Atlanta was fully aware of the economic consequences of racial turmoil in Little Rock, and, well before the city desegregated in the

<hr>

[54] *Arkansas Gazette*, January 18, 1959.
[55] Quotations are from *ibid.*, February 25, May 23, 1960. On the election, see *Southern School News*, August, December, 1960.

fall of 1961, its leaders were maneuvering frantically to protect the city's progressive image from the type of publicity that racial hysteria had earned for Little Rock and New Orleans. By the time the Atlanta school board presented an acceptable desegregation plan to the federal district court in January, 1960, the city had already effectively shifted from Georgia's massive resistance stance. Mayor William B. Hartsfield vigorously and ably promoted an open-schools policy. The Atlanta board of aldermen pledged "our support to the Board of Education of the City of Atlanta in its announced determination to maintain a system of public education in the City of Atlanta."[56] Help Our Public Education (HOPE), the Atlanta-based save-the-schools citizens group, claimed thirty thousand members and was a dynamic and influential force in urban affairs. The League of Women Voters, *ad hoc* professional groups, PTA's and other school organizations, church groups, civic organizations, the Atlanta *Constitution*—virtually the united voice of respectability in the metropolitan area—demanded that the city be permitted to comply with court orders without state interference.[57] Business leaders, hesitantly but influentially, became publicly involved, particularly after the Atlanta Chamber of Commerce selected a new president who insisted that "Atlanta's public schools must stay open and the Chamber should provide its share of vigorous leadership in seeing that they do."[58] Though centered in Atlanta, the open-schools campaign won support in other Georgia cities and gained the important endorsement of the Georgia Education Association.[59]

Political leaders on the state level found themselves in an untenable position. They were committed to interposition, yet they would have to risk closing all of the state's schools in order to deny a school board the right to obey a court order. And Atlanta, despite the county-unit system and malapportionment, was a formidable economic and demographic entity for the state legislature to attempt to crush. Georgia's political solidarity began to crack under the pressure. In January, 1959, Herman Talmadge said on the Senate floor that "the Supreme Court's school decision is an accomplished fact which will remain so until it either is reversed by the Court itself or is nullified or modified by Congress or the

[56] Reprinted in Atlanta *Constitution*, January 5, 1960.
[57] *Southern School News*, February, March, May, 1960; Jordan and Wall, "Desegregation of Atlanta Schools—1942 to Present," 18–21.
[58] Atlanta *Constitution*, November 29, 1960, quoting Chamber President and later Mayor Ivan Allen, Jr.
[59] Atlanta *Journal*, March 19, 1960.

people."[60] It was the first time that Talmadge had hinted that the *Brown* decision might have to be recognized as a legitimate expression of the nation's highest Court. Talmadge criticized the decision as usual, but he also stressed the importance of public education. The senator's remarks stimulated a more realistic discussion of antidesegregation policy in Georgia, and the reevaluation process was hastened when former Governor Ellis G. Arnall suddenly emerged from political retirement to announce: "Unless the public schools are kept open or some worthy candidate comes forth, I will be a candidate for governor in 1962, and I will be elected."[61] In speeches, statements, and public letters, Arnall stated that "Open schools can be maintained with maximum segregation through a strong pupil placement act, local option, and grants-in-aid."[62] He also called attention to the obvious fact that "You can't turn out into the streets a million school children, 48,000 teachers, 6,000 bus drivers and 17,000 other school employees."[63] Governor Ernest Vandiver denounced Arnall's "open invitation to the NAACP to file a school suit in every county in Georgia,"[64] but the logic of Arnall's position was not ignored by his old political enemies. By early 1960 the possibility that a voter reaction to school closures might permit Arnall's reentry into Georgia politics was being discussed by high-level political friends of Senator Talmadge and Governor Vandiver.[65] While Vandiver himself remained adamant in his public statements, his legislative leaders spoke in favor of open schools in a series of Legislative Forums sponsored by the state Chamber of Commerce, and the legislature in its 1960 session created the Committee on Schools to restudy the segregation question.[66] This committee, headed appropriately enough by Atlanta banker John A. Sibley, was the Georgia equivalent of Virginia's Perrow Commission. The Sibley Committee held hearings in every Georgia congressional district, heard more than eighteen hundred witnesses, and delivered a report recommending the abandonment of massive resistance.[67]

Georgia felt its way toward a new policy, but it did so against the determined opposition of the more recalcitrant massive resistance forces.

[60] Reprinted in Atlanta *Journal*, January 27, 1959.
[61] As quoted by Joseph H. Baird, in *Christian Science Monitor*, April 20, 1959.
[62] As quoted by Margaret Shannon, in Atlanta *Journal*, May 20, 1959.
[63] As quoted by Claude Sitton, in Chattanooga *Times*, July 19, 1959.
[64] As quoted in Atlanta *Journal*, April 15, 1959.
[65] See Charles Pou, in Atlanta *Journal*, January 18, 1960.
[66] Jordan and Wall, "Desegregation of Atlanta Schools—1942 to Present," 16–20.
[67] *Race Relations Law Reporter*, V (Summer, 1960), 509–20.

Opinion in Georgia was deeply divided, when, unexpectedly, a federal district court ordered the admission of two Negro students to the University of Georgia.[68] Their enrollment in January, 1961, touched off a campus riot, and Governor Vandiver was required by law to prohibit the payment of state funds to the university. The disorder and the prospect of closing not only one of the nation's oldest state universities but also the alma mater of a large number of Georgia politicians sharply undermined the massive resistance appeal. Vandiver called a special legislative session, and the legislators passed the Sibley Committee's recommendations.[69] Atlanta, having thoroughly prepared for desegregation, did so without incident in September, 1961.

The policy of interposition was not truly tested until desegregation came to New Orleans in the fall of 1960. For four months, from November, 1960, to February, 1961, the government of Louisiana fought a tense duel with the federal courts, enacting new massive resistance legislation as the courts struck down the old. Again and again, the legislature re-interposed the state government between the courts and the city by taking direct control of the New Orleans schools. It sought to abolish the two desegregated schools by refusing to pay the salaries of teachers and administrators. It encouraged white boycotts of the schools, disrupted the city's entire educational establishment, and made a mockery of the legislative process. Ultimately, however, even the defenders of white supremacy in the Louisiana legislature stopped short of directly violating a federal court injunction and thus stepping across the line into criminal contempt and, very possibly, into jail.[70]

The origins of the New Orleans desegregation crisis revolved around absence of the open-schools coalition that had effectively led the retreat from massive resistance in Virginia, Arkansas, and Georgia. In Louisiana, teachers' organizations and other education groups did not come to the defense of education. During the winter of 1960–61 the Louisiana Teachers' Association supported the state government in its fight to prevent desegre-

---

[68] *Holmes v. Danner*, 191 F. Supp. 394.

[69] *Southern School News*, February, 1961.

[70] Louisiana Attorney General Jack P. F. Gremillion was cited for contempt of court and sentenced to confinement for sixty days, although the federal judge commuted the sentence to an eighteen-month probationary period. *Race Relations Law Reporter*, V (Fall, 1960), 668; *Southern School News*, November, 1960. This episode, which occurred early in the battle, served as a warning to other Louisiana politicians. Crain and Inger, *School Desegregation in New Orleans*, and Louisiana State Advisory Committee, *The New Orleans School Crisis*, are detailed and perceptive studies of the New Orleans desegregation crisis.

gation in New Orleans, and the Louisiana School Boards Association not only endorsed the state's efforts but also expelled from its membership the four moderate members of the New Orleans school board who had attempted to keep the schools open.[71] The New Orleans PTA Council in June, 1960, resolved support for open schools even if some desegregation were necessary. At the council's next meeting one week later, however, a larger group of PTA delegates reconsidered and promptly abrogated the resolution and threatened to expel any local PTA that endorsed it.[72] Except for the relatively uninfluential New Orleans Classroom Teachers' Federation and a few Local PTA's, school groups in Louisiana remained silent or supported the bitter-end segregationists.[73]

New Orleans did nurture a citizens save-the-schools movement, but it arrived too late and failed to become an effective rallying point for middle-class white moderates. Save Our Schools (SOS), which appeared publicly in April, 1960, made an energetic effort to arouse concern for public education. The SOS membership, however, included a disproportionate number of Tulane University faculty members, social workers, and other "radicals." It was, as one study characterized it, "full of Jews, integrationist Catholics and nonsoutherners" and consequently was regarded with suspicion in New Orleans.[74]

More in tune with the city's mood was the Committee for Public Education, formed in June, 1960. The committee was a more conservative group that preferred cautious, behind-the-scenes activity to public stands.[75] Finally, the previously potent, but long inactive, Independent Women's Organization came out for open schools in August, 1960.[76] None of these groups achieved apparent influence. The economic and civic leadership in the city remained aloof from the developing crisis.[77] New Orleans was dominated by a traditional elite that was out of sympathy with "progress" generally, and younger business leaders were divided on the wisdom of defending public education. During the summer of 1960 the Junior Chamber of Commerce endorsed open schools; the Young Men's Business Club voted down an open-schools resolution.[78]

[71] *Southern School News*, January, February, 1961.
[72] New Orleans *Times-Picayune*, June 1, 9, 1960.
[73] Louisiana Advisory Committee, *The New Orleans School Crisis*, 12–20.
[74] Crain and Inger, *School Desegregation in New Orleans*, 34.
[75] *Ibid.*, 38–42.
[76] *Southern School News*, September, 1960.
[77] This point is the central thesis of Crain and Inger, *School Desegregation in New Orleans*.
[78] Louisiana Advisory Committee, *The New Orleans School Crisis*, 8–10.

Eventually, after the Louisiana legislature demonstrated its inability to face down the federal judiciary and rioting and disorder threatened the city with chaos, businessmen and civic groups were to become more active in defense of order and stability.

New Orleans in 1960 thus resembled Little Rock in 1957. The New Orleans school board failed to rally support or to provide leadership. As in Little Rock, the board chose schools in lower-income white districts for the desegregation experiment. The New Orleans government sought to ignore the whole problem. While his city was under court order to desegregate, Mayor deLesseps S. Morrison ran for governor. During the campaign Morrison proposed a considerably more moderate program on racial matters than did his chief opponents, and the mayor attracted substantial support from Negroes, business conservatives, and liberal whites. Nevertheless, he ran on a segregationist platform, and after the election he refused to support any action that would place him in an integrationist position. Mobs effectively enforced a white boycott of the city's two desegregated schools (and at the same time entertained the nation's television audiences) for a full school year without the city government's even attempting to disperse them.[79] Public authority failed to offer leadership, and private groups were equally ineffective. The open-schools coalition failed to emerge, and "the expected moral example of the Catholic Church never materialized."[80] New Orleans had no *Arkansas Gazette* or Atlanta *Constitution* to keep responsible alternatives before the public view. In this atmosphere, the Greater New Orleans Citizens' Council gained enormous influence, and, as in Arkansas, the vacuum of responsible leadership invited state intervention. Unlike the situation in Arkansas, many Louisiana state officials were only too eager to fight a second Battle of New Orleans.

Country-musician Jimmie H. Davis became governor of Louisiana for a second time in 1960. During the first Democratic primary election in late 1959, Davis finished second behind Mayor Morrison. William Rainach ran third. Davis advanced from a "100 percent" segregationist to a "1,000 percent" segregationist during the first primary. After that,

[79] For a critique of Morrison's performance, see Crain and Inger, *School Desegregation in New Orleans*, 17–28, 77–81.

[80] *Ibid.*, 30. Indeed, lay Catholics in the Deep South evidenced a far greater willingness to permanently close the public schools than did lay Protestants. See Division of Scientific Research, American Jewish Committee Institute of Human Relations, "Research Reports: The Nationwide Poll of March, 1959" (unpublished survey conducted for the American Jewish Committee by Gallup Organization, Inc., 1959), 20–31.

he concluded a deal with Rainach, and, now stoutly supported by the Citizens' Council forces, he reached out avidly and successfully for the hard-core segregationist vote. In the second primary election, Davis won sixteen parishes carried by Rainach and the Democratic nomination.[81] Davis was a friendly person who liked to write and sing country music (of which his "You Are My Sunshine" is a classic) and shake hands with people. "A generally well meaning individual," Harnett T. Kane has described him, "he almost never demonstrated definite convictions about anything."[82] Yet he was deeply committed to the segregationists, and the federal courts were forcing New Orleans to desegregate. In June, 1960, the New Orleans school board appealed to the governor to interpose the sovereignty of the state between the federal judiciary and Louisiana's citizenry. At first Davis refused, but, as the pressure from the Rainach-Perez-Citizens' Council forces mounted, he seized control of the New Orleans schools in mid-August, 1960, and ordered the superintendent of schools to maintain the segregated system.[83] The governor's intervention was immediately challenged in federal court, and a period of comic relief followed as Davis sought to evade service of the court summons. Nevertheless, the governor was enjoined from further obstructing desegregation in the city.[84] Although restrained himself, Davis gave the legislators an opportunity to stand in the front lines of the battle against federal encroachments in a series of special sessions during the winter of 1960–61. During the struggle, a three-judge federal court ruled directly on interposition: "The conclusion is clear that interposition is not a constitutional doctrine. If taken seriously, it is illegal defiance of constitutional authority."[85]

But by this time the framework of racial conflict was being reshaped by other forces. In February, 1960, the sit-in movement began, and the great neobourbon crusade gradually passed into the broader stream of the white reaction to the Negro revolution. The 1950's opened with a growing southern white rebellion against social change; the 1960's began with a growing southern Negro protest demanding social change. During the 1950's southern neobourbons had launched a militant effort to suppress

---

[81] New Orleans *Times-Picayune*, November 4, 19, December 19, 1959, January 10, 11, 1960.

[82] Harnett T. Kane, in *New York Times Magazine*, January 1, 1961.

[83] *Southern School News*, July, September, 1960.

[84] *Bush v. Orleans Parish School Board; Williams v. Davis*, in *Race Relations Law Reporter*, V (Fall, 1960), 666–70.

[85] *Orleans Parish v. Bush; United States v. Louisiana*, in *ibid.* (Winter, 1960), 1008.

social and ideological progress, but their movement eventually came to pose a far more serious danger to social stability than did token social change, and, increasingly, it threatened the region's economic progress. At this point, the established order in the South turned against massive resistance fanaticism. The inauguration of President John F. Kennedy in January, 1961, and the involvement of the Negro masses in the civil rights movement further doomed neobourbon dreams of defeating the principle of the *Brown* decision. Massive resistance passed into history, and the central question now came to be whether nominal acceptance of the validity of desegregation would mean an integrated society or a less institutionalized form of white supremacy.

"Massive Is in the Cold, Cold Ground." Newton Pratt in McClatchy Newspapers.

CHAPTER 18

LOOKING BACK: AN EVALUATION OF
MASSIVE RESISTANCE

Massive resistance failed to achieve the most cherished aims of its neo-bourbon proponents. The movement did not hold the South to an unde-viating adherence to the caste system; it did not reestablish a pre-Civil War concept of states' rights; and it did not insulate the region from the intrusion of new ideas and social practices. Yet the real significance of massive resistance was not its failure, but the success it enjoyed in stabiliz-ing political patterns.

Southern traditionalists challenged some of the main social and intel-lectual currents of mid-twentieth century America. The forces set loose by a changed intellectual climate, the depression, World War II, urbaniza-tion, industrialization, and the emergence of the Second Reconstruction threatened southern rural and small-town values. Against these trends, neobourbon southerners mounted a determined drive to restore and defend conventional beliefs and practices. The Dixiecrats of 1948 were the harbin-gers of massive resistance. They recognized the growing threat to southern traditions, and they represented a broad and purposive, if somewhat premature, resurgence of the old order. In 1950 the *Sweatt* and *McLaurin* decisions and the NAACP's legal attack on the separate but equal doctrine in public education intensified neobourbon fears. Herman E. Talmadge of Georgia and James F. Byrnes of South Carolina emerged as the spokesmen for white reaction, while the defeats of Senators Frank P. Graham of North Carolina and Claude Pepper of Florida signalized a conservative shift on the part of southern voters. The presidential election of 1952 indicated that sustained popular concern for white supremacy was concentrated largely in the Deep South, and only in the Deep South did state governments enact legislation to prevent desegregation prior to the *Brown* decision. Georgia, Mississippi, and South Carolina made early

preparations to defend institutionalized white supremacy from an adverse
Supreme Court ruling and thus initiated the movement later to be termed
"massive resistance."

Brown v. Board of Education sharpened the politics of race in the Deep
South, while the states of the upper South drifted indecisively, taking no
major steps either to comply with the Court ruling or overtly to defy it.
The southern mood leaned toward social reaction, however, and during
the year following the second *Brown* decision of May, 1955, massive resistance grew to maturity. The Citizens' Councils spread through the South
and provided grass roots organizational support for the resistance. Important southern politicians, led by Senators Harry F. Byrd of Virginia and
James O. Eastland of Mississippi, took a determined stand against implementation of the desegregation decision. The massive resistance forces
sought to draw the line sharply between segregation and integration, and
they developed a comprehensive resistance program. During 1956
Virginia joined the states of the Deep South in adopting interposition
as state policy, and other states of the peripheral South shifted toward
more aggressively segregationist positions. The period following the Little
Rock crisis of 1957 marked the climax of the massive resistance movement. For a time it seemed that the neobourbon South might achieve
regional unity and succeed in facing down the federal courts and defeating
the principle of the *Brown* decision. But, ultimately, total resistance to
desegregation required closing the public schools, and school closures in
Arkansas and Virginia threatened the material progress of the region and
the future of entrenched southern institutions. During the winter of
1958–59 massive resistance lost the initiative in southern politics. First
in the upper South and then, during the early 1960's, in the Deep
South, the massive resistance front gradually collapsed.

The demise of massive resistance did not herald the inauguration of a
new political order in the South. The 1950's began with Herman Talmadge shouting defiance in Georgia; the 1960's opened with one of
Talmadge's close political friends in the Georgia governorship. James
F. Byrnes rallied the resistance to desegregation during the early 1950's;
his friend and former law partner took over the South Carolina governorship in the early 1960's. The vulnerability of Frank Graham and Claude
Pepper in the 1950 senatorial primary elections in North Carolina and
Florida had focused attention on the political perils of liberalism. During
the 1964 gubernatorial primary the traditional organization in North
Carolina once again turned successfully to a politics of white supremacy

as an expedient method to promote conservative rule in the state.[1] In
Florida, Farris Bryant, a leading proponent of interposition in the Florida
legislature, and Haydon Burns, who attacked his runoff opponent as the
"candidate of the NAACP,"[2] were the successful aspirants to the governorship during the early 1960's. The Byrd organization weathered another
threat and resumed its rule of Virginia although changing conditions and
the advancing age of Senator Byrd were gradually modifying, or perhaps
even undermining, the organization's reign. In Alabama and Louisiana,
the "common man" appeal of James Folsom and Earl Long had given
way to the "white common man" appeal of George C. Wallace and John
J. McKeithen. The South's political leadership had for the most part
accepted the inevitability of token desegregation, but, on the whole, it had
changed remarkably little during a decade of economic and demographic
upheaval.

Wilbur J. Cash, broadly surveying the southern political scene at the
end of the 1930's, wrote: "By and large, however, the scene is pretty
barren—is made up on the one hand of honest but complacent Tories and
too few men of liberal sympathy to have much practical effect, and on the
other of a horde of outright demagogues. . . ."[3] Cash's observation still had
some validity at the end of the 1950's. To be sure, politicians of business
conservative inclinations challenged the Tories and demagogues, and
a growing, if still very small, number of Negro political leaders participated
in southern politics. The business conservatives, themselves often "honest
but complacent," and the newly emerging Negro spokesmen offered the
best hope for a more progressive politics in the South. But Toryism and
demagoguery remained major threads in the southern political fabric, and
the region still lacked a liberal alternative. Indeed, the politics of the
1950's had taken a heavy toll from rural liberalism, and any danger of
a more liberal politics growing out of the New Deal experience had been
effectively crushed. The acceptance of token desegregation was a conser-

---

[1] In 1960 the anti-organization candidate, Terry Sanford, entered the Democratic
gubernatorial runoff against I. Beverly Lake, an extreme neobourbon proponent of
white southern rights. The uncompromising position symbolized by Lake threatened the
state's industrial stability, and the traditional organization, led by Governor Luther
Hodges, supported Sanford's successful candidacy as the lesser of two evils. The organization's role in Sanford's election represented the state's conservative reaction to massive
resistance extremism. In 1964, however, Lake was eliminated in the first gubernatorial
primary, and organization and anti-organization candidates went into the runoff.
Organization spokesmen reached an accord with the Lake forces, received Lake's support
in the campaign, and won the election in a blaze of social conservatism.

[2] As quoted in Sarratt, The Ordeal of Desegregation, 24.

[3] Cash, The Mind of the South, 421.

vative reaction in defense of southern continuity and represented no real break with the past.

But, at the same time, the South was clearly plunging through a period of sweeping change. The shift toward urbanization and industrialization continued unabated into the 1960's and the changing southern environment combined with other factors to pull toward a different political order. Supreme Court decisions undermined rural and small-town domination of the legislative process, offering the opportunity for politics to adjust to economic and demographic reality. A growing Republican Party promised a more structured politics. The continuing decline of overt white supremacy that the opinion polls reflected, the increasing number of Negro voters, and more positive policies on the part of the federal government outwardly pointed toward a politics less anchored to racism. Similarly, the grass roots, civil rights protest movement made a substantial and not easily forgotten impact. These and other factors offered unmistakable evidence of a politics in transition.

Massive resistance was a part of this paradoxical pattern of continuity and change. The politics of massive resistance pulled the southern political spectrum far to the right and oriented political transition toward the more conservative aspects of the southern tradition. For the most part, the give and take of the political process during the period occurred within a white supremacy context. Even the more progressively oriented "moderates" usually felt compelled to avow their devotion to segregation before timidly suggesting token alternatives. And token efforts to comply nominally with the letter of the law of the land, while often evading its spirit, came to be hailed as "progress." The racial emotionalism effectively impeded the development of a constructive moderation and contributed to the absence of a viable liberal voice within the white community. To a striking degree, southern neobourbons were not only able to define the issues and structure the political debate during the 1950's but also to hold many of the substantive aspects of southern political transition in abeyance.

The Citizens' Councils and their allies stabilized racial customs during a period of change by sharply defining the lines over which both whites and Negroes stepped only at great peril. Segregationist demands for white solidarity in defense of the social status quo served to consolidate the sense of white community while at the same time undermining Negro confidence in the white community's commitment to good will, fair play, and justice.[4]

---

[4] See Louis E. Lomax, *The Negro Revolt* (New York, 1962), 74ff.

Discussing white racists during an earlier period of American history, I. A. Newby wrote: "Despite their inability to solve the problem, however, they could and did prevent others from solving, or at least ameliorating it."[5] This statement was also applicable to the 1950's. Massive resistance contributed to making the early stages of the Negro Revolution a period of regression rather than a period of adjustment.

The tactics of the proponents of massive resistance further blurred the lines between legality and illegality in a region already possessing an historical strain of violence and disrespect for law.[6] Southern legislatures so perverted the law to accomplish illegal ends that the whole process made a mockery of justice. The willingness of political leaders to resort to chicanery and suppression and the willingness of the white community not only to tolerate but often to cooperate with the extralegal vigilante activities of the Citizens' Councils and other groups evidenced a widespread lack of public commitment to the rule of law and public ethics. These activities simultaneously contributed to a declining confidence in law within the Negro community. One of the linguistic ironies of the saga of massive resistance was the fact that white efforts to subvert duly constituted authority, an action generally termed "revolutionary," was now normally called "conservative." And Negroes were branded as "revolutionary" or "subversive" for seeking enforcement of law.

To be sure, the problems of race relations were not confined to the South and, for the most part, the imperfections of southern society were aberrations from national norms more in degree than in substance. Broadly speaking, massive resistance was a part of a national reaction by white citizens to the changing position of Negroes in American society. As the civil rights movement spread North during the 1960's, talk of a "white backlash" became increasingly common. During the period between President Truman's civil rights recommendations to Congress and the mid-1960's, however, the South occupied the center of the minority rights debate, and the nation's civil rights idealism was absorbed in the struggle against *de jure* segregation below the Potomac. The South once again served as the nation's conscience, while many of the more fundamental problems of Negro Americans festered substantially undisturbed.

It would be comforting to assign the rise of massive resistance to a

---

[5] Newby, *Jim Crow's Defense*, 189.

[6] See Myrdal, *An American Dilemma*, I, 441–51, for a perceptive discussion of this tradition.

default of southern political leadership, and in one sense it was. The neobourbon power structure did provide much of the thrust for massive resistance. But at the same time a significant number of politicians evidenced a genuine desire to act as responsibly as their constituents would allow, and a few went beyond what their constituents would allow and suffered politically. More fundamentally, the rise of massive resistance rested upon the failure of southern institutions and southern society to support a responsible alternative. Even the eventual abandonment of massive resistance rested upon pocketbook ethics and conservative inclinations. The white South was yet to face the "American dilemma" or to demonstrate confidence in the principles of liberal democracy. The willingness of white southern society to allow its leaders seriously to contemplate abolition of the public schools and to tolerate racism, chicanery, and suppression of dissent was the symptom of a none too healthy society. The South was changing, and some of these changes were pointed in constructive directions. At the same time, however, optimistic forecasts that the South, having accepted token desegregation, might exercise a more responsible role in national affairs found little support in the politics of massive resistance.

CRITICAL ESSAY ON AUTHORITIES

This bibliographical essay is limited to those materials that the author found useful. Serious students of recent southern history should also consult Elizabeth W. Miller, *The Negro in America: A Bibliography* (Cambridge, Mass., 1966), and Arthur S. Link and Rembert W. Patrick (eds.), *Writing Southern History: Essays in Historiography in Honor of Fletcher M. Green* (Baton Rouge, 1965), especially the chapter entitled "The Twentieth-Century South" written by Dewey W. Grantham, Jr.

NEWSPAPER SOURCES

The most important sources for factual data on the southern reaction to school desegregation are the newspaper clipping files of the Southern Education Reporting Service in Nashville and the Southern Regional Council in Atlanta. Established in the fall of 1954, the Southern Education Reporting Service clipped a wide variety of newspapers within and outside the South. The Southern Education Reporting Service dropped and added newspaper subscriptions on a flexible basis depending upon the development of events, but for the period 1954–62 its files include at least one newspaper from every southern state at all times and in eight of the eleven southern states at least two newspapers at all times. Virtually all of the materials in the Southern Education Reporting Service Library are available on microfilm: Southern Education Reporting Service (ed.), *Facts on Film* (164 rolls in 8 series, 1958–66). The Southern Regional Council files cover the period from the mid-1940's to the present. The Southern Regional Council clipped a number of newspapers on a regular basis, and its library contains (in addition to the *Facts on Film* microfilm) a large volume of incidental clippings gathered largely by its Human

Relations Council affiliates. These libraries also contain the bulk of the pamphlets and unpublished sources used in this study. In both libraries, newspaper clippings are filed according to subject.

A chronological perspective and a clearer view of the relationship between events can best be obtained from *Southern School News*, the New York *Times*, and *New South*. *Southern School News*, published monthly from September, 1954, through June, 1965, by the Southern Education Reporting Service, sought with substantial success to report accurately and objectively the developments that flowed from the 1954 *Brown v. Board of Education* decision. State correspondents for *Southern School News* included some of the South's most capable journalists, and the publication is the best guide to events concerning the school segregation-desegregation controversy. *Southern School News* does suffer, however, from the space limitations inherent to a monthly publication of limited size and from its somewhat narrow focus. The New York *Times*, once again living up to its reputation, provides better coverage of racial and political developments in the South than any other daily newspaper. *New South*, which the Southern Regional Council published monthly (sometimes bimonthly during summer months) beginning in January, 1946 (and quarterly beginning with the Winter, 1966, edition), comments perceptively, if often subjectively, on the southern social and political scene.

DOCUMENTARY SOURCES

The most important source for documentary evidence is *Race Relations Law Reporter*, edited by the Vanderbilt University School of Law and published bimonthly February, 1956–Winter, 1967. The editors of the *Race Relations Law Reporter* proficiently performed an invaluable service by reprinting state and federal judicial and legislative materials relating to racial matters. The journal contains a substantially, though not entirely, complete record of such documents as state and federal court decisions and state laws and resolutions pertaining to race relations for the period following January, 1956. Its early editions include materials from the 1953–55 period, but the *Race Relations Law Reporter* must be supplemented with Southern Education Reporting Service (ed.), *Legislative Acts, 1954–1957*, Roll 3 of *Facts on Film*. Also helpful are Pauli Murray (ed.), *States' Laws on Race and Color* (1950), and Verge Lake and Pauli Murray, *States' Laws on Race and Color: 1955 Supplement* (1955), both published in Cincinnati by the Woman's Division of Christian

Service of the Methodist Church. Eugene Cook (ed.), *Compilation of Georgia Laws and Opinions of the Attorney General Relating to Segregation of the Races* (Atlanta, 1956), is a thorough state collection. The *Congressional Record* (Washington, 1948–61) is an important source not only for speeches delivered by southern congressmen on the chamber floors but for the variety of materials that senators and representatives have read into the *Record*.

SOUTHERN POLITICS

The starting point for any examination of recent political trends in the South is, of course, V. O. Key, Jr., with the assistance of Alexander Heard, *Southern Politics in State and Nation* (New York, 1949). For the most part, Key's observations about the politics of the 1940's remained valid for the 1950's. Supplementing Key's work is Heard, *A Two-Party South?* (Chapel Hill, 1952). Also of basic significance to an understanding of the political South are Dewey W. Grantham, Jr., *The Democratic South* (Athens, Ga., 1963), an important interpretive study of southern political development; William H. Nicholls, *Southern Tradition and Regional Progress* (Chapel Hill, 1960), a graphic depiction of the conflict between tradition and economic advancement in the South; and Samuel Lubell, *The Future of American Politics* (2nd ed. rev.; Garden City, N.Y., 1956), *Revolt of the Moderates* (New York, 1956), and *White and Black: Test of a Nation* (New York, 1964), all of which comment perceptively on the forces shaping modern southern politics. W. J. Cash, *The Mind of the South* (New York, 1941) and C. Vann Woodward, *The Burden of Southern History* (Baton Rouge, 1960), are provocative examinations of the historical experiences that shaped southern attitudes. William C. Havard and Loren P. Beth, *The Politics of Mis-Representation: Rural-Urban Conflict in the Florida Legislature* (Baton Rouge, 1962), a model study of the politics and politicians in the Florida legislature, contains important implications about the nature of southern politics generally. Francis Butler Simkins, *The Everlasting South* (Baton Rouge, 1963), discusses the conservative tradition in the South; and Jasper Berry Shannon, *Toward a New Politics in the South* (Knoxville, 1949), pens the classic portrait of the "county-seat governing class." T. Harry Williams, *Romance and Realism in Southern Politics* (Athens, Ga., 1961), concludes that a refusal to recognize reality has frequently influenced southern political behavior. Other suggestive interpretations are Keith F. McKean, *Cross Currents in the South* (Denver,

1960), and Howard Zinn, *The Southern Mystique* (New York, 1964). Helpful recent surveys of the post-Civil War South are John Samuel Ezell, *The South Since 1865* (New York, 1963), and Thomas D. Clark and Albert D. Kirwan, *The South Since Appomattox: A Century of Regional Change* (New York, 1967). The most important in-depth studies of the making of the New South are C. Vann Woodward, *Origins of the New South, 1877–1913* (Baton Rouge, 1951), and George Brown Tindall, *The Emergence of the New South, 1913–1945* (Baton Rouge, 1967). These two works comprise Volumes IX and X of Wendell Holmes Stephenson and E. Merton Coulter (eds.), *A History of the South*.

Dewey W. Grantham, Jr., (ed.), *The South and the Sectional Image: The Sectional Theme Since Reconstruction* (New York, 1967); Frank E. Vandiver (ed.), *The Idea of the South: Pursuit of a Central Theme* (Chicago, 1964); and Charles Grier Sellers (ed.), *The Southerner as American* (Chapel Hill, 1960), include important interpretive essays that delve into the essential nature of the South and southerners. Willie Morris (ed.), *The South Today: 100 Years After Appomattox* (New York, 1965), contains revisions of essays that first appeared in the April, 1965, edition of *Harper's Magazine*. Allan P. Sindler (ed.), *Change in the Contemporary South* (Durham, N.C., 1963), is a well-conceived collection of interpretive essays stressing political change in the South. Composed of essays that first appeared in special issues of the *Journal of Politics*, Taylor Cole and John H. Hallowell (eds.), *The Southern Political Scene, 1938–1948* (Gainesville, Fla., 1948), and Avery Leiserson (ed.), *The American South in the 1960's* (New York, 1964), examine various aspects of southern politics.

Other pertinent studies of southern political tendencies include Manning J. Dauer, "Recent Southern Political Thought," *Journal of Politics*, X (May, 1948), 327–53; two articles by Marian D. Irish, "Recent Political Thought in the South," *American Political Science Review*, XLVI (March, 1952), 121–41, and "Political Thought and Political Behavior in the South," *Western Political Quarterly*, XIII (June, 1960), 406–20; and two unsigned articles that appeared in the *Congressional Quarterly Almanac*, "North-South Political Alliance," 84th Cong., 2nd Sess., XII (1956), 587–88, and "How Big Is the North-South Democratic Split?" 85th Cong., 1st Sess., XIII (1957), 813–17. Of importance also are Donald R. Matthews and James W. Prothro, "Southern Images of Political Parties: An Analysis of White and Negro Attitudes," *Journal of Politics*, XXVI (February, 1964), 82–111; James W. Prothro, Ernest Q. Campbell, and Charles M. Grigg, "Two-Party Voting in the South: Class vs.

Party Identification," *American Political Science Review*, LII (March, 1958), 131–39; Dewey W. Grantham, Jr., "The South and the Reconstruction of American Politics," *Journal of American History*, XIII (September, 1966), 227–46; and Norman I. Lustig, "The Relationships Between Demographic Characteristics and Pro-Integration Vote of White Precincts in a Metropolitan Southern Community," *Social Forces*, XL (March, 1962), 205–208. Cortez A. M. Ewing, *Primary Elections in the South: A Study in Uniparty Politics* (Norman, Okla., 1953), is a good introduction to the intricacies of primary elections politics in one-party states.

The most convenient source for pre-1950 election returns is Alexander Heard and Donald S. Strong (eds.), *Southern Primaries and Elections, 1920–1949* (University, Ala., 1950). Richard M. Scammon (comp.), *America Votes: A Handbook of Contemporary American Election Statistics* (7 vols; New York, 1956, 1958; Pittsburgh, 1959, 1962, 1964; Washington, 1966, 1968) contains presidential, gubernatorial, and senatorial general election returns (no primary returns included) for elections held during the 1950's. The only general collection of southern primary election statistics for this period is Richard M. Scammon (comp.), *Southern Primaries '58* (Washington, 1959), which contains the results of major primary elections for the years 1957–58. In most, but not all, southern states, the secretaries of state (state departments of archives and history in Alabama and Georgia) periodically publish county election returns, including those for primary races, in works variously titled *Official and Statistical Register*, *Report of the Secretary of State* . . . , *Roster of Officials*, *Manual*, and *Blue Book*. In Arkansas and Texas, this function is performed by the *Arkansas Almanac*, published biennially by the Arkansas Almanac Company in Little Rock, and the *Texas Almanac*, published biennially by the Dallas *Morning News*. There is no convenient source for primary election statistics for the states of South Carolina and Virginia. The states' *Registers* and *Almanacs* list only numerical returns, and consequently a real need exists for works similar to Annie Mary Hartsfield and Elston E. Roady (comps.), *Florida Votes, 1920–1962* (Tallahassee, 1963), which includes major primary and general statewide election returns with county percentages calculated for each candidate. Tip H. Allen, Jr., *Mississippi Votes: The Presidential and Gubernatorial Elections, 1947–64* (State College, Miss., 1967), lists county election returns but not percentages; and Donald R. Matthews and Associates (comps.), *North Carolina Votes: General Election Returns, by County, for President of the United States, 1868–1960, Governor of North Carolina, 1868–1960, United States Senator from North Carolina, 1914–1960*

(Chapel Hill, 1962), and Texas Election Research Project Committee, *Texas Votes: Selected General and Special Election Statistics, 1944–1963* (Austin, 1964), do not include primary election returns and therefore add little to material already published.

The South is, of course, more American than anything else, and studies concerned with national politics often shed important light on the nature of southern politics. Among such works is James MacGregor Burns, *The Deadlock of Democracy: Four-Party Politics in America* (Englewood Cliffs, N.J., 1963), a revealing analysis of the persistent cleavage between executive and congressional authority. Angus Campbell, Philip E. Converse, Warren E. Miller, and Donald E. Stokes, *The American Voter* (New York, 1960), is an impressive study of voting behavior. Also suggestive is Leon J. Epstein, "Size and Place of the Two-Party Vote," *Western Political Quarterly*, IX (March, 1956), 138–50. Malapportionment in state legislatures, which was of basic importance in the politics of the South and of the nation during the 1950's, is examined in Paul T. David and Ralph Eisenberg, *Devaluation of the Urban and Suburban Vote: A Statistical Investigation of Long-Term Trends in State Legislative Representation* (Charlottesville, Va., 1961), and Gordon Baker, *Rural Versus Urban Political Power: The Nature and Consequences of Unbalanced Representation* (Garden City, N.Y., 1955). Although *Southern Politics in State and Nation* was V. O. Key's greatest contribution to scholarship concerning the South, his *American State Politics: An Introduction* (New York, 1956), and *Public Opinion and American Democracy* (New York, 1961), effectively demonstrate that southern political problems generally differed from national problems more in degree than in substance. Self-explanatory are the titles of Kirk H. Porter and Donald Bruce Johnson (eds.), *National Party Platforms, 1840–1960* (2nd ed.; Urbana, Ill., 1961), and Richard C. Bain, *Convention Decisions and Voting Records* (Washington, 1960). Helpful for comparative purposes is John H. Fenton, *Politics in the Border States: A Study of the Patterns of Political Organization and Political Change, Common to the Border States—Maryland, West Virginia, Kentucky and Missouri* (New Orleans, 1957).

POPULATION AND ECONOMICS

John C. McKinney and Edgar T. Thompson (eds.), *The South in Continuity and Change* (Durham, N.C., 1965), is an outstanding example of interdisciplinary collaborative scholarship. Ranging over a wide variety of subjects, the twenty-two essays in this volume present a well-rounded assessment of the southern states. Rupert B. Vance and Nicholas J. Demerath, with the assistance of Sara Smith and Elizabeth M. Fink (eds.), *The Urban South* (Chapel Hill, 1954), and Robert B. Highsaw (ed.), *The Deep South in Transformation: A Symposium* (University, Ala., 1964), stress the impact of economic and demographic change. John M. Maclachlan and Joe S. Floyd, Jr., *This Changing South* (Gainesville, Fla., 1956), is an in-depth statistical study of population shifts in the South. Trends in the regional economy are examined in Melvin L. Greenhut and W. Tate Whitman (eds.), *Essays in Southern Economic Development* (Chapel Hill, 1964); and United States Senate, 85th Cong., 2nd Sess., *Selected Materials on the Economy of the South: Report of the Committee on Banking and Currency* (Washington, 1956), contains relevant statistics concerning the southern economy in the mid-1950's. Hammer and Company, *Post-War Industrial Development in the South* (Atlanta, 1956); James W. Martin and Glenn D. Morrow, *Taxation of Manufacturing in the South* (University, Ala., 1948); and James H. Street, *The New Revolution in the Cotton Economy: Mechanization and Its Consequences* (Chapel Hill, 1957), deal with significant aspects of southern economic development. Thomas D. Clark examines the inter-relationship between racial and political developments on the one hand and economic and demographic change on the other in *The Emerging South* (New York, 1961).

ATTITUDES AND OPINIONS

Contrasting with the rapid material changes taking place in the South was the persistence of traditional attitudes. The best starting point for examining the racial views of southern whites is John Dollard, *Caste and Class in a Southern Town* (New Haven, 1937), which is the classic study of the attitudes and social patterns prevalent in a small southern town. Alfred O. Hero, *The Southerner and World Affairs* (Baton Rouge, 1965), is a major attitudinal study that ranges over a wider scope of topics than the title implies. Melvin M. Tumin and others, *Desegregation: Resistance and Readiness* (Princeton, N.J., 1958), analyzes white attitudes toward public school desegregation; and Ernest Q. Campbell, with the assistance of Charles E. Bowerman and Daniel O. Price, *When a City Closes Its Schools* (Chapel Hill, 1960), reports on the opinions of white residents of a southern city in which public schools were closed to prevent desegregation. Donald R. Matthews and James W. Prothro of the Institute for Research in Social Science have presented the results of their extensive investigations of southern attitudes in *Negroes and the New Southern Politics* (New York, 1966). Particularly significant to an understanding of the dynamics of massive resistance is their examination of "Southern Racial Attitudes: Conflict, Awareness, and Political Change," *Annals of the American Academy of Political and Social Science*, CCCXLIV (November, 1962), 108–21. Samuel A. Stouffer, *Communism, Conformity and Civil Liberties: A Cross-Section of the Nation Speaks Its Mind* (Garden City, N.Y., 1955), includes important information about the opinions of southerners, as do two works by William Brink and Louis Harris, *The Negro Revolution in America* (New York, 1964) and *Black and White: A Study of U. S. Racial Attitudes Today* (New York, 1967).

Newspapers are the best source for following the shifting patterns recorded by the public opinion polls; however, Hazel Gaudet Erskine, "The Polls: Race Relations," *Public Opinion Quarterly*, XXVI (Spring, 1962), 137–48, is a convenient collection of the more important opinion surveys concerning race relations. Paul B. Sheatsley, "White Attitudes Toward the Negro," *Daedalus*, XCV (Winter, 1966), 217–38; Herbert H. Hyman and Paul B. Sheatsley, "Attitudes Toward Desegregation," *Scientific American*, CXCV (December, 1956), 35–39; and Hyman and Sheatsley, "Attitudes Toward Desegregation," *Scientific American*, CCXI (July, 1964), 2–9, are perceptive discussions of the long-term trends in white racial attitudes. Seymour Martin Lipset, "Democracy and Working-Class Authoritarianism," *American Sociological Review*, XXIV (August, 1959), 482–501, documents the tendency toward intolerance among lower-class groups, while Charles H. Stember, *Education and Attitude Change: The Effect of Schooling on Prejudice Against Minority Groups* (New York, 1961), suggests that latent intolerance among the better educated and more affluent is greater than opinion polls indicate. The Division of Scientific Research, American Jewish Committee Institute of Human Relations, "Research Reports: The Nationwide Poll of March, 1959" (unpublished poll conducted by Gallup Organization, Inc., for the American Jewish Committee, Southern Regional Council Files), contains important data on opinions toward desegregation held by members of various white religious groups. The attitudes of white school children attending desegregated classrooms for the first time in a southern city are probed in Robert Coles, *The Desegregation of Southern Schools: A Psychiatric Study* (Atlanta, 1963). James W. Vander Zanden, *American Minority Relations: The Sociology of Race and Ethnic Groups* (2nd ed.; New York, 1966), is an excellent general examination of the roots of prejudice and discrimination by a scholar well-known for his research in southern race relations.

RACE RELATIONS

Although now dated, Gunnar Myrdal, *An American Dilemma: The Negro Problem and Modern Democracy* (2 vols.; New York, 1944), remains the essential beginning point for examining the evolving social position of southern Negroes. Few observers have been able to match Myrdal's perceptive insights into southern and American racial culture. C. Vann Woodward's provocative and still somewhat controversial *The Strange Career of Jim Crow* (2nd ed. rev.; New York, 1966), describes the changing patterns of southern racial practices since Reconstruction. The standard history of Negroes in the United States is John Hope Franklin, *From Slavery to Freedom: A History of American Negroes* (2nd ed.; New York, 1956). This work emphasizes the earlier phases of Negro history and is complemented by E. Franklin Frazier, *The Negro in the United States* (rev. ed.; New York, 1957), which is oriented toward a more contemporary period. John Hope Franklin and Isidore Starr (eds.), *The Negro in Twentieth Century America: A Reader on the Struggle for Civil Rights* (New York, 1967), is a well-selected series of readings; and Charles E. Wynes (ed.), *The Negro in the South Since 1865: Selected Essays in American Negro History* (University, Ala., 1965), is a helpful essay collection.

Testifying in part to the success of southern white traditionalists in preventing constructive action in the field of race relations, many indicators of Negro progress registered declines during the 1950's. Vivian W. Henderson, *The Economic Status of Negroes: In the Nation and in the South* (Atlanta, 1963), and James D. Cowhig and Calvin L. Beale, "Relative Socio-economic Status of Southern Whites and Nonwhites, 1950 and 1960," *Southwestern Social Science Quarterly*, XLV (September, 1964), 113–24, demonstrate that the economic position of Negroes declined in comparison to that of whites, especially in the South. The national failure to achieve meaningful public school integration in the period following the *Brown* decision is documented in U.S. Commission on Civil Rights, *Racial Isolation in the Public Schools* (2 vols.; Washington, 1967). Office of Policy Planning and Research, United States Department of Labor, *The Negro Family: The Case for National Action* (Washington, 1965), written by Daniel Patrick Moynihan, calls attention to the deterioration of Negro family stability. The severe identity problems that centuries of oppression have created for Negro Americans and the psychological stresses that fall upon Negroes in our own time are examined in Thomas F. Pettigrew, *A Profile of the Negro American* (Princeton, N.J., 1964). *Report of the National Advisory Commission on Civil Disorders* (Washington, 1968) concludes that the deepening racial divisions in American society represent a frighteningly real threat to basic democratic values. Reflecting this pessimistic trend are such interpretive studies as Lubell, *White and Black: Test of a Nation* (previously cited); Oscar Handlin, *Fire-Bell in the Night: The Crisis in Civil Rights* (Boston, 1964); Charles E. Silberman, *Crisis in Black and White* (New York, 1964); and Lewis Killian and Charles Grigg, *Racial Crisis in America: Leadership in Conflict* (Englewood Cliffs, N.J., 1964).

In a less pessimistic vein, Matthews and Prothro, *Negroes and the New Southern Politics* (previously cited), is a thoroughly documented study of the reemergence of Negroes as an important voting force in the South. Pat Watters and Reece Cleghorn, *Climbing Jacob's Ladder: The Arrival of Negroes in Southern Politics* (New York, 1967), analyzes the complexities and shifting crosscurrents of the civil rights struggle of the early 1960's and succeeds in capturing the mood of the "movement." A good popular history of the same period is Louis E. Lomax, *The Negro Revolt* (New York, 1962). Collected readings on the civil rights controversy are Daniel Bradford (ed.), *Black, White and Gray* (New York, 1964); Hubert H. Humphrey (ed.), *Integration vs. Segregation: The Crisis in our Schools as Viewed by 17 Outstanding Commentators* (New York, 1964); and Alan F. Westin (ed.), *Freedom Now!: The Civil Rights Struggle in America* (New York, 1964).

SOUTHERNERS ON THE SOUTH

A number of important books have been written by southerners who have sought to explain their region's behavior. Essentially subjective in nature and resting at least in part on the writers' own observations and experiences, these works have not infrequently shown unusual perception and insight. Ralph McGill, *The South and the Southerner* (Boston, 1963), Harry S. Ashmore, *An Epitaph for Dixie* (New York, 1958), and Hodding Carter, *Southern Legacy* (Baton Rouge, 1950), record the reflections of three of the South's best-known journalists. V. M. Newton, Jr., managing editor of a leading Florida newspaper, relates his experiences in *Crusade for Democracy* (Ames, Iowa, 1961); and Carl T. Rowan, a northern journalist and one-time head of the USIA, presents his bitingly critical review of the southern scene in *Go South to Sorrow* (New York, 1957). Robert Penn Warren, a leading southern literary figure, relates his impressions in *Segregation: The Inner Conflict in the South* (New York, 1956), and reflects on the significance of the "Lost Cause" in *The Legacy of the Civil War: Meditations on the Centennial* (New York, 1964). Other important interpretations include James McBride Dabbs, *The Southern Heritage* (New York, 1958), and *Who Speaks for the South?* (New York, 1964); Wilma Dykeman and James Stokely, *Neither Black Nor White* (New York, 1957); Thomas J. Woofter, *Southern Race Progress: The Wavering Color Line* (Washington, 1957); and Henry Savage, Jr., *Seeds of Time: The Background of Southern Thinking* (New York, 1959). Lillian Smith, *Killers of the Dream* (New York, 1949), and Sarah Patton Boyle, *The Desegregated Heart: A Virginian's Stand in Time of Transition* (New York, 1962), are representative of the views of southern white liberals.

The memoirs of several southern political figures are recorded in Brooks Hays, *A Southern Moderate Speaks* (Chapel Hill, 1959); Luther H. Hodges, *Businessman in the Statehouse: Six Years as Governor of North Carolina* (Chapel Hill, 1962); Frank E. Smith, *Congressman from Mississippi* (New York, 1964); James F. Byrnes, *All in One Lifetime* (New York, 1958); Charles Longstreet Weltner, *Southerner* (Philadelphia, 1966); and Ellis Gibbs Arnall, *The Shore Dimly Seen* (New York, 1946), and *What the People Want* (Philadelphia, 1948).

NEWSPAPER REPORTERS

Whatever merit the preceding pages possess is to a considerable extent due to the day-to-day work of newspaper reporters in the South, and it seems only fitting to include in this bibliographical essay a comment about the journalists who covered the southern beat during the 1950's. Forced to record complex events in the face of ever-pressing deadlines, some of these reporters compiled an admirable record for insight and accuracy. Among the best were those who wrote for the New York *Times*. The *Times'* successive southern correspondents, John N. Popham and Claude Sitton, were outstanding, as were Wayne Phillips and several other journalists associated with the *Times* or with the New York *Times* News Service. Bem Price of the Associated Press; Robert S. Bird, whose by-line appeared in several major newspapers; Robert S. Baker of the Washington *Post;* and Max K. Gilstrap, Joseph H. Baird, Ed Townsend, and Bicknell Eubanks, all of whom wrote for the *Christian Science Monitor*, were consistently perceptive in their selection, description, and analysis of newsworthy events. A number of important southern journalists who tended to limit their attention to developments in their home states will be mentioned later.

ALABAMA

An extremely valuable body of literature concerns individual southern states. On Alabama, newspaper sources are especially important, since a recent history of the state is yet to be written. Fortunately, some of the South's most perceptive journalists covered the Alabama beat. Among them, Fred Taylor of the Birmingham *News* was preeminent. His columns constitute a penetrating analysis of the political scene in Alabama. Also excellent was the reporting of Bob Ingram of the Montgomery *Advertiser* and Rex Thomas, Alabama correspondent for the Associated Press. Hugh Sparrow of the Birmingham *News* and John Temple Graves of the Birmingham *Post-Herald* reflect the views of Alabama traditionalists. This is especially true of Graves, who was closely associated with the Citizens' Councils and with the resistance generally. The editorials of Grover C. Hall, Jr., editor of the Montgomery *Advertiser*, were influential in Alabama. The *Publish It Not in the Streets of Askelon* series, written by Hall and Tom Johnson, was published in pamphlet form by the *Advertiser* in 1956. Patrick Earl McCauley, a Southern Education Reporting Service staff member and an experienced Alabama journalist, has written an unusually able Masters Thesis, "Political Implications in Alabama of the School Segregation Decisions" (Vanderbilt University, 1957), which includes the results of interviews with leading Alabama political figures. Charles Morgan, Jr., *A Time to Speak* (New York, 1964), records the dilemma faced by white liberals in Alabama and comments knowledgeably on the political trends in the state. Murray Clark Havens provides valuable insights into the nature of Alabama politics in his *City Versus Farm?: Urban-Rural Conflict in the Alabama Legislature* (Tuscaloosa, Ala., 1957), a study of factional divisions within the state legislature. Donald S. Strong, *Registration of Voters in Alabama* (University, Ala., 1956), is a good examination of the impediments faced by prospective voters; and James E. Larson, *Reapportionment in Alabama* (University, Ala., 1955), documents the gross inequality of representation in the state legislature. W. Bradley Twitty, *Y'All Come* (Nashville, 1962), is an uncritical campaign biography of Governor James E. Folsom. National Education Association Commission on Professional Rights and Responsibilities, *Report of an Investigation: Wilcox County, Alabama, A Study of Social, Economic, and Educational Bankruptcy* (Washington, 1967), is a revealing portrait of a black-belt Alabama county.

ARKANSAS AND LITTLE ROCK

Much of the published material concerning political and racial developments in Arkansas concentrates upon the Little Rock desegregation controversy. Corinne Silverman, *The Little Rock Story* (rev. ed.; University, Ala., 1959), is a factual, noninterpretive narrative of events; and Wilson Record and Jane Cassels Record (eds.), *Little Rock, U.S.A.: Materials for Analysis* (San Francisco, 1960), is a well-chosen selection of readings about the Little Rock episode and about the segregation-desegregation controversy generally. These two works are an excellent introduction to the complexities of the events at Little Rock. Virgil T. Blossom, Little Rock superintendent of schools, presents the standard interpretation in *It Has Happened Here* (New York, 1959). Blossom defends the actions of Little Rock school officials and is critical of many of the other participants in the controversy, placing primary responsibility for disrupting the city's transition to a desegregated school system upon Governor Orval E. Faubus. In general agreement with Blossom is Woodrow Wilson Mann, mayor of Little Rock during the crisis, who records his version of the affair in a twelve-part series published in the New York *Herald-Tribune*, January 19–31, 1958. Mann castigates the governor as an opportunist who deliberately perpetrated a racial confrontation for personal political gain. A similar account is presented by Warren Olney III, "A Government Lawyer Looks at Little Rock," *Congressional Record*, 85th Cong., 2nd Sess. (March 24, 1958), 5090–92, which might be considered the Eisenhower administration's version. While also critical of Faubus' performance, Numan V. Bartley, "Looking Back at Little Rock," *Arkansas Historical Quarterly*, XXV (Summer, 1966), 101–16, stresses the failure of public officials and civic leaders in Little Rock to prepare the city for desegregation and the ineptness of the Eisenhower administration in the period prior to the crisis. Faubus justifies his use of the national guard to block desegregation as a necessary measure to prevent violence in the city in "The Story of Little Rock—As Governor Faubus Tells It," *U.S. News and World Report*, XLIV (June 20, 1958), 101–106. Dale and L'Moore Alford, *The Case of the Sleeping People (Finally Awakened by Little Rock School Frustrations)* (Little Rock, 1959), offers an extreme segregationist view; and Daisy Bates, an NAACP leader, recounts events from the perspective of the city's Negro community in *The Long Shadow of Little Rock: A Memoir* (New York, 1962). Colbert S. Cartwright, a Little Rock minister and a perceptive observer, comments on the evolution of the crisis and criticizes the local leadership in the city in "Lesson from Little Rock," *Christian Century*, LXXIV (October 9, 1957), 1193–94, and "The Improbable Demagogue of Little Rock, Ark.," *Reporter*, XVII (October 17, 1957), 23–25. Episcopal Bishop Robert R. Brown, *Bigger than Little Rock* (Greenwich, Conn., 1958), concentrates on the role of the church during the controversy, as does Ernest Q. Campbell and Thomas F. Pettigrew, *Christians in Racial Crisis: A Study of Little Rock's Ministry, Including Statements on Desegregation and Race Relations by the Leading Religious Denominations of the United States* (Washington, 1959), which is also extremely valuable for its insights into Little Rock and southern society generally. Fletcher Knebel, "The Real Little Rock Story," *Look*, XXI (November 12, 1957), 31–33, and "Georgia: Rallying Point of Defiance," *Look*, XXI (November 12, 1957), 34, contain important interviews with leading participants in the controversy. Women's Emergency Committee to Open Our Schools, *Little Rock Report: The City, Its People, Its Business, 1957–1959* (Little Rock, 1959), documents the economic losses suffered by the city due to the tumultuous racial situation. *Arkansas Gazette, Crisis in the South: The Little Rock Story* (Little Rock, 1959), is a collection of the newspaper editorials that won for the *Gazette* a Pulitzer Prize for public service.

The best general study of Arkansas politics is Boyce Alexander Drummond, Jr., "Arkansas Politics: A Study of a One-Party System" (Ph.D. dissertation, University of Chicago, 1957). Covering the years 1932–56, Drummond's study generally supports the conclusions previously drawn about the nature of Arkansas politics by V. O. Key in his *Southern Politics* (previously cited). Thomas F. Pettigrew and Ernest Q. Campbell, "Faubus and Segregation: An Analysis of Arkansas Voting," *Public Opinion Quarterly*, XXIV (Fall, 1960), 436–47, is an important analysis of voting patterns. Perhaps most significant of all in contributing to an understanding of both the Little Rock crisis and Arkansas state politics is the *Arkansas Gazette*. With Hugh B. Patterson, Jr., as publisher and Harry S. Ashmore as executive editor, the *Gazette* consistently provided perceptive and in-depth coverage of political and racial events during the 1950's. Also helpful are the columns of Kenneth Johnson of the Memphis *Commercial Appeal*.

FLORIDA

Two excellent studies analyze political developments in Florida. Hugh Douglas Price, *The Negro and Southern Politics: A Chapter of Florida History* (New York, 1957), concentrates on the impact of increased Negro voter registration in the state, while Havard and Beth, *The Politics of Mis-Representation: Rural-Urban Conflict in the Florida Legislature* (previously cited), dissects Florida politics by focusing upon the structure of the state legislature. Also helpful is National Commission on Professional Rights and Responsibilities of the National Education Association of the United States, *Report of an Investigation: Florida, A Study of Political Atmosphere as It Affects Public Education* (Washington, 1966). Among a number of competent journalists who helped to clarify the complexities of Florida's unstructured politics in the 1950's were Bert Collier, Miami *Herald* staff writer and Florida correspondent for the Southern Education Reporting Service's *Southern School News;* John B. McDermott, political writer for the Miami *Herald;* Allen Morris, columnist for the St. Petersburg *Times;* and Frank Trippett, political writer for the St. Petersburg *Times.*

GEORGIA

The most penetrating discussion of Georgia politics is Joseph L. Bernd, *Grass Roots Politics in Georgia: The County Unit System and the Importance of the Individual Voting Community in Bifactional Elections, 1942–1954* (Atlanta, 1960). Bernd combines an analysis of election returns with the results of interviews and other research to produce a well-balanced appraisal of Georgia political developments. The functioning of the county unit system is critically examined in Louis T. Rigdon II, *Georgia's County Unit System* (Decatur, Ga., 1961); R. Carter Pittman, a states' rights leader, defends the system in *"The County Unit System Prevents City Political Machines Controlling the State of Georgia" (Address to the Associated Industries of Georgia at Rome, Georgia, August 5, 1959)* (Atlanta, 1959). Efforts to prevent the expansion of Negro voter registration are scrutinized in Joseph L. Bernd and Lynwood M. Holland, "Recent Restrictions upon Negro Suffrage: The Case of Georgia," *Journal of Politics,* XXI (August, 1959), 487–513. John C. Meadows, *Modern Georgia* (rev. ed.; Athens, Ga., 1954), is a good general history. The two Atlanta dailies, the *Constitution* and the *Journal,* provided day-to-day coverage of racial and political events in the state.

LOUISIANA

Louisiana ranks as the most thoroughly studied of southern states for the decade of the 1950's. Perry H. Howard, *Political Tendencies in Louisiana, 1812–1952* (Baton Rouge, 1957), stresses the continuity of political alignments in the state and places the development of Long and anti-Long factions in the state Democratic Party in an historical perspective. Howard takes an essentially favorable view toward the Long faction. Allan P. Sindler, on the other hand, is critical of the Long leadership in his heavily documented *Huey Long's Louisiana: State Politics, 1920–1952* (Baltimore, 1956). Among popular treatments of Governor Earl K. Long are Stan Opotowsky, *The Longs of Louisiana* (New York, 1960), which is sympathetic; Thomas Martin, *Dynasty: The Longs of Louisiana* (New York, 1960), which is hostile; and A. J. Liebling, *The Earl of Louisiana* (New York, 1961), a witty and decidedly partisan account that praises Earl Long and captures the mood of the Long leadership. William C. Havard and Robert F. Steamer unravel some of the factional complexities of Louisiana Democratic politics in "Louisiana Secedes: Collapse of a Compromise," *Massachusetts Review*, I (October, 1959), 134–46. L. Vaughan Howard and David R. Deener, *Presidential Politics in Louisiana, 1952* (New Orleans, 1954), is a good study of the 1952 election campaign; and William C. Havard, Rudolf Heberle, and Perry H. Howard, *The Louisiana Elections of 1960* (Baton Rouge, 1963), is a broader analysis of state political trends than the title implies. Alden L. Powell and Emmett Asseff, *Party Organization and Nominations in Louisiana* (Baton Rouge, 1952), is a short but helpful examination of the organization and function of party politics in a one-party state. Garnie William McGinty, *A History of Louisiana* (New York, 1951); Louisiana Legislative Council, *Louisiana: Its History, People, Government and Economy* (Baton Rouge, 1955); and T. Lynn Smith and Homer L. Hitt, *The People of Louisiana* (Baton Rouge, 1952), are general studies. Two excellent books examine the New Orleans desegregation crisis. Louisiana State Advisory Committee, *The New Orleans School Crisis: Report to the United States Commission on Civil Rights* (New Orleans, 1961), is a valuable summary of this tangled affair; and Robert L. Crain and Morton Inger, with the assistance of Gerald A. McWorter, *School Desegregation in New Orleans: A Comparative Study of the Failure of Social Control* (Chicago, 1966), is an interpretive account sharply critical of the local New Orleans leadership. Crain and Inger studied the "power elite" of a number of other cities for comparative purposes, and their book is therefore helpful on southern urban politics generally.

MISSISSIPPI

James W. Silver, *Mississippi: The Closed Society* (New York, 1964), is an angry and brilliant analysis weaving together the historical and cultural factors that contributed to the creation of a "closed society." Parts of the work are based on Silver's experiences as a faculty member at the University of Mississippi. In a similar vein is Russell H. Barrett, *Integration at Ole Miss* (Chicago, 1965), also written by an University of Mississippi professor. Like Silver, Barrett describes the totalitarian tendencies of a society dominated by racism. A well-written popular account that covers some of the same material is Walter Lord, *The Past That Would Not Die* (New York, 1965). Hodding Carter III, editor-publisher of the Greenville, Mississippi, *Delta Democrat-Times*, examines the rise of the Citizens' Councils as a political force in Mississippi and lucidly reviews state politics during the governorship of James P. Coleman in *The South Strikes Back* (Garden City, N.Y., 1959). Two other works by Carter are *First Person Plural* (Garden City, N.Y., 1963) and *So the Heffners Left McComb* (Garden City, N.Y., 1965). Extremely valuable on racial and political developments in Mississippi during the 1950's is the reportorial work of Kenneth Toler, head of the Memphis *Commercial Appeal*'s Mississippi Bureau and Mississippi correspondent for *Southern School News;* Jay Milner, managing editor of the *Delta Democrat-Times;* and John Herbers of the *Delta Democrat-Times.* Such writers as Jimmy Ward, columnist for the Jackson *Daily News;* Tom Ethridge, columnist for the Jackson *Clarion-Ledger;* and Charles M. Hills of the *Daily News* reflected the ultraconservative (or, more correctly, the ultrareactionary) views that helped to make Mississippi a "closed society." United States Commission on Civil Rights, *Voting in Mississippi* (Washington, 1965), is a good survey of white resistance to Negro voter registration in the state. Edward H. Hobbs, *Legislative Apportionment in Mississippi* (University, Miss., 1956), is helpful on the structure of politics and demonstrates that legislative malapportionment was less severe in Mississippi than in other southern states. John K. Bettersworth, *Mississippi: A History* (Austin, 1959), is a good general reference work despite the author's uncritical orientation toward defense of "the southern way of life." The civil rights movement of the 1960's has spawned numerous books that in one way or another relate the experiences and impressions of the participants, and the "Freedom Summer" of 1964 was particularly prolific. Although this bibliography has generally excluded works that deal only with the post-1950's period, a sampling of this material does contribute to a broader understanding of the dynamics of racial politics in the South. Among pro-civil rights books that resulted from the Mississippi "Freedom Summer" project are Sally Belfrage, *Freedom Summer* (New York, 1965); Len Holt, *The Summer That Didn't End* (New York, 1965); William Bradford Huie, *Three Lives for Mississippi* (New York, 1965); William McCord, *Mississippi: The Long Hot Summer* (New York, 1965); and Elizabeth Sutherland (ed.), *Letters From Mississippi* (New York, 1965).

NORTH CAROLINA

Easily the best source for racial and political developments in North Carolina during the 1950's is the writing of Jay Jenkins, North Carolina correspondent for *Southern School News* and staff writer for the Raleigh *News and Observer* during the early 1950's and for the Charlotte *Observer* during the latter half of the decade. Hugh Talmage Lefler and Albert Ray Newsome, *North Carolina: The History of a Southern State* (rev. ed.; Chapel Hill, 1963), is an ably done general history that may be supplemented by S. Huntington Hobbs, Jr., *North Carolina: An Economic and Social Profile* (Chapel Hill, 1958). Since Luther H. Hodges was governor of North Carolina during the massive resistance period, his *Businessman in the Statehouse* (previously cited) is extremely valuable. Capus M. Waynick, John C. Brooks, and Elsie W. Pitts (eds.), *North Carolina and the Negro* (Raleigh, 1964), is well worth reading although it is concerned with racial progress during the 1960's.

SOUTH CAROLINA

The politics of massive resistance in South Carolina is competently examined in Howard H. Quint, *Profile in Black and White: A Frank Portrait of South Carolina* (Washington, 1959), which stresses the pervasive influence of racism on virtually every phase of social and political life in the state. Ernest McPherson Lander, Jr., *A History of South Carolina, 1865–1960* (Chapel Hill, 1960), a concise and penetrating overview, is valuable for its analysis of factional political divisions. William Francis

Guess, *South Carolina: Annals of Pride and Protest* (New York, 1960), is a popular general history. Informed and reliable newspaper commentary can be found in articles by Bob Pierce, state news editor of the (Columbia) *State*, and S. L. Latimer, Jr., editor of the *State*. The Charleston *News and Courier* was a persistent defender of traditional white southern values; however, William D. Workman, Jr., of the *News and Courier* was somewhat of a rarity in that he was both an active proponent of massive resistance and at the same time a journalist who had established a deserved reputation for balanced and incisive reporting. *We Take Our Stand*, published by the *News and Courier* in 1956, offers a sampling of editorials that illustrate the newspaper's enthusiasm for the massive resistance position.

TENNESSEE

Hugh Davis Graham, *Crisis in Print: Desegregation and the Press in Tennessee* (Nashville, 1967), a study of the editorial reaction of Tennessee newspapers to desegregation, is the best guide to events in Tennessee during the 1950's. Also valuable is Norman L. Parks, "Tennessee Politics Since Kefauver and Reece: A 'Generalist' View," *Journal of Politics*, XXVIII (February, 1966), 144–68, which analyzes recent political trends in the state. William Goodman, *Inherited Domain: Political Parties in Tennessee* (Knoxville, 1954), provides some background on Tennessee politics in the early 1950's. The much-maligned Highlander Folk School is examined in H. Glyn Thomas, "The Highlander Folk School: The Depression Years," *Tennessee Historical Quarterly*, XXIII (December, 1964), 358–71. As in other southern states Tennessee newspapers are among the best sources not only for factual data but also for knowledgeable analysis of events. Noteworthy are the articles by Morris Cunningham of the Memphis *Commercial Appeal*, Joe Hatcher and Wallace Westfeldt of the Nashville *Tennessean*, and Fred Travis of the Chattanooga *Times*.

TEXAS

The complexities of Texas politics are deftly unraveled in James R. Soukup, Clifton McCleskey, and Harry Holloway, *Party and Factional Division in Texas* (Austin, 1964). Combining standard research in periodicals and documentary materials with interviews and an analysis of election returns, this work is among the best studies of a southern state. *Party and Factional Division in Texas* should be supplemented by two excellent books by O. Douglas Weeks, *Texas Presidential Politics in 1952* (Austin, 1953) and *Texas One-Party Politics in 1956* (Austin, 1957). The latter work is particularly valuable for its perceptive analysis of factional struggles within the Texas Democratic Party during the mid-1950's. Day-to-day developments pertaining to race relations are recorded in articles written by Richard M. Morehead, head of the Capital Bureau of the Dallas *Morning News* and Texas correspondent for *Southern School News*, and Robert M. Hayes, head of the Dallas *Morning News'* East Texas Bureau.

VIRGINIA

Events in Virginia were crucial to the rise of massive resistance in the South, and the evolution of a program based on the theory of interposition in that state is examined by Robbins L. Gates, *The Making of Massive Resistance: Virginia's Politics of Public School Desegregation, 1954–1956* (Chapel Hill, 1962), and Benjamin Muse, *Virginia's Massive Resistance* (Blooming-ton, Ind., 1961). Gates's factual and well-documented study catalogues the success enjoyed by the Byrd organization and representatives of black-belt areas in institutionalizing their program despite the wide diversity of attitudes within the state. Muse, a Washington *Post* journalist, similarly points out the absence of a consensus among Virginians and emphasizes the role of Senator Byrd and spokesmen for the Southside Fifth Congressional District in creating the massive resistance crisis. Muse also describes the impact of school closings in the state and the gradual abandonment of interposition as state policy. Marshall W. Fishwick, *Virginia: A New Look at the Old Dominion* (New York, 1959), is an interpretive state history stressing the popular attachment to past values prevalent in the Old Dominion. The presence of reporters of the caliber of James Latimer and L. M. Wright, Jr., of the Richmond *Times-Dispatch* and Edward T. Folliard and Benjamin Muse of the Washington *Post* assured outstanding newspaper coverage of racial politics in Virginia during the 1950's. Richmond *News Leader, Interposition: Editorials and Editorial Page Presentations* (Richmond, 1956), includes many of the editorials printed in that important editorial crusade.

CASE STUDIES

On the local level, the following case studies present helpful information about the dynamics of desegregation and the opposition to desegregation: Omer Carmichael and Weldon James, *The Louisville Story* (New York, 1957); Bonita H. Valien, *The St. Louis Story* (New York, 1956); Elinor Pancoast and others, *Report of a Study on Desegregation in the Baltimore City Schools* (Baltimore, 1956); Irene Osborne and Richard K. Bennett, "Eliminating Educational Segregation in the Nation's Capital, 1951–1955," *Annals of the American Academy of Political and Social Science*, CCCIV (March, 1956), 98–108; Roscoe Griffin, *Sturgis, Kentucky: A Tentative Description and Analysis of the School Desegregation Crisis* (New York, 1958); Hugh Davis Graham, "Desegregation in Nashville: The Dynamics of Compliance," *Tennessee Historical Quarterly*, XXV (Summer, 1966), 135–54; Anna Holden, Bonita Valien, Preston Valien, and Francis Manis, *Clinton, Tennessee: A Tentative Description and Analysis of the School Desegregation Crisis* (New York, n.d.); Margaret Anderson, *The Children of the South* (New York, 1966), which deals with desegregation in Clinton, Tennessee; John Howard Griffin and Theodore Freedman, *Mansfield, Texas: A Report on the Crisis Situation Resulting from Efforts to Desegregate the School System* (New York, 1957); Warren Breed, *Beaumont, Texas: College Desegregation Without Popular Support* (New York, 1957); Bob Smith, *They Closed Their Schools: Prince Edward County, Virginia, 1951–1964* (Chapel Hill, 1965); Paul M. Gaston and Thomas T. Hammond, "Public School Desegregation: Charlottesville, Virginia, 1955–62" (Unpublished report presented to the Nashville Conference on "The South: The Ethical Demands of Integration," a consultation sponsored by the Southern Regional Council and the Fellowship of Southern Churchmen, December 28, 1962); and Vernon E. Jordan, Jr., and Marvin Wall, "Desegregation of Atlanta Schools—1942 to Present" (Unpublished Southern Regional Council report, 1966). Other important case studies, including examinations of school desegregation crises in Little Rock, New Orleans, and Oxford, Mississippi, are listed elsewhere in this bibliography.

THE LAW AND THE SCHOOLS

An impressive body of literature has examined the legal aspects of the *Brown* decision and of equal protection of the laws generally. Among historical inquiries, the following studies are excellent: Robert J. Harris, *The Quest for Equality: The Constitution, Congress and the Supreme Court*

(Baton Rouge, 1960); Alexander M. Bickel, *The Least Dangerous Branch: The Supreme Court at the Bar of Politics* (Indianapolis, 1962); United States Commission on Civil Rights, *Equal Protection of the Laws in Public Education* (Washington, 1960); Joseph B. James, *The Framing of the Fourteenth Amendment* (Urbana, Ill., 1956); Bernard H. Nelson, *The Fourteenth Amendment and the Negro Since 1920* (New York, 1946); and Loren Miller, *The Petitioners: The Story of the Supreme Court of the United States and the Negro* (New York, 1966). Important works dealing with segregation and desegregation during the 1950's include Albert P. Blaustein and Clarence Clyde Ferguson, Jr., *Desegregation and the Law: The Meaning and Effect of the School Segregation Cases* (2nd ed. rev.; New York, 1962); Alexander M. Bickel, *Politics and the Warren Court* (New York, 1965); Jack Greenberg, *Race Relations and American Law* (New York, 1959); and Daniel M. Berman, *It Is So Ordered: The Supreme Court Rules on School Segregation* (New York, 1966). Kenneth N. Vines, "Federal District Judges and Race Relations in the South," *Journal of Politics*, XXVI (May, 1964), 337–57; George W. Spicer, "The Federal Judiciary and Political Change in the South," *Journal of Politics*, XXVI (February, 1964), 154–76; and J. W. Peltason, *Fifty-Eight Lonely Men: Southern Federal Judges and School Desegregation* (New York, 1962), are significant investigations of the performance of federal judges in the South. Walter F. Murphy, *Congress and the Court: A Case Study in the American Political Process* (Chicago, 1962), is an admirable analysis of congressional opposition to the liberal tendencies of the Warren Court; and C. Herman Pritchett, *Congress Versus the Supreme Court, 1957–1960* (Minneapolis, 1961), is also helpful.

Contributing significantly to an understanding of the background of the school desegregation controversy in the South are Robin M. Williams, Jr., and Margaret W. Ryan (eds.), *Schools in Transition: Community Experiences in Desegregation* (Chapel Hill, 1954), and Harry S. Ashmore, *The Negro and the Schools* (Chapel Hill, 1954), which describe the national trend away from coerced segregation in public school facilities prior to the *Brown* decision. Ashmore's *The Negro and the Schools* and Truman M. Pierce and others, *White and Negro Schools in the South: An Analysis of Biracial Education* (Englewood Cliffs, N.J., 1955), document the gross inequities in educational opportunity provided by separate but equal facilities. Patrick E. McCauley and Edward D. Ball (eds.), *Southern Schools: Progress and Problems* (Nashville, 1959), further documents this same fact while providing valuable statistical materials relating generally to education in the South.

NEGRO VOTER REGISTRATION

The uneven growth of Negro voter registration and the persistence of white resistance to black suffrage in many areas of the region are surveyed in Margaret Price, *The Negro Voter in the South* (Atlanta, 1957), and Price, *The Negro and the Ballot* (Atlanta, 1959). The decline of the white Democratic primary and the poll tax as effective guardians of politics for white people only are scrutinized in O. Douglas Weeks, "The White Primary, 1944–1948," *American Political Science Review*, XLII (June, 1948), 500–10, and Frederick D. Ogden, *The Poll Tax in the South* (University, Ala., 1958). Alfred B. Clubok, John M. DeGrove, and Charles D. Farris demonstrate that the increasing number of Negro voters did not always use the ballot as an instrument for political change in "The Manipulated Negro Vote: Some Pre-Conditions and Consequences," *Journal of Politics*, XXVI (February, 1964), 112–29. As noted earlier, Matthews and Prothro, *Negroes and the New Southern Politics*, and Watters and Cleghorn, *Climbing Jacob's Ladder: The Arrival of Negroes in Southern Politics*, are thoughtful studies of the impact of Negro voting on southern politics.

THE DIXIECRATS

Reacting to the changing role of Negroes in American life, real and threatened, the States' Rights Democrats of 1948 expressed the same emotional and ideological orientation that was to motivate massive resistance. Indispensable on the Dixiecrats are Key, *Southern Politics in State and Nation*, and Heard, *A Two-Party South?* (both cited previously). Emile B. Ader, *The Dixiecrat Movement: Its Role in Third Party Politics* (Washington, 1955); Ader, "Why the Dixiecrats Failed," *Journal of Politics*, XV (August, 1953), 356–69; Sarah McCulloh Lemmon, "The Ideology of the 'Dixiecrat' Movement," *Social Forces*, XXX (December, 1951), 162–71; David M. Heer, "The Sentiment of White Supremacy: An Ecological Study," *American Journal of Sociology*, LXIV (May, 1959), 592–98; and William G. Carleton, "The Fate of Our Fourth Party," *Yale Review*, XXXVIII (March, 1949), 449–59, offer important insights into the nature and aims of the movement. *To Secure These Rights: The Report of the President's Committee on Civil Rights* (New York, 1947) presents the program that the Dixiecrats found so objectionable. The growth of southern sectional consciousness generally is surveyed in Fletcher M. Green, "Resurgent Southern Sectionalism, 1933–1955," *North Carolina Historical Review*, XXXIII (April, 1956), 222–40.

PRESIDENTIAL POLITICS

The most detailed published analyses of the presidential elections of 1952 and 1956 in the South are two works by Donald S. Strong, *The 1952 Presidential Election in the South* (University, Ala., 1955) and *Urban Republicanism in the South* (University, Ala., 1960). These studies are particularly valuable for their identification of the sources of the Republican Party's new-found presidential following. Samuel Lubell comments perceptively on southern voting trends in *Revolt of the Moderates, The Future of American Politics,* and *White and Black: Test of a Nation* (all mentioned previously). Paul T. David, Malcolm Moos, and Ralph M. Goldman (eds.), *Presidential Nominating Politics in 1952* (5 vols.; Baltimore, 1954), is a thorough examination of the 1952 party conventions, although Allan P. Sindler, "The Unsolid South: A Challenge to the Democratic National Party," in Alan F. Westin (ed.), *The Uses of Power: 7 Cases in American Politics* (New York, 1962), 229–83, an excellent account of the political infighting at the Democratic convention, should also be consulted.

THE DESEGREGATION CONTROVERSY

The most thorough examinations of white southern resistance to school desegregation are Reed Sarratt, *The Ordeal of Desegregation: The First Decade* (New York, 1966), and Benjamin Muse, *Ten Years of Prelude: The Story of Integration Since the Supreme Court's 1954 Decision* (New York, 1964). Both works are reportorial decennial reviews of the progress—or, more correctly, the frequent lack of progress—toward desegregation during the period between the *Brown* decision of 1954 and the civil rights act of 1964. Sarratt's *Ordeal* is organized topically, with such chapter titles as "The Governors," "The Legislators," "The Schoolmen," "The Lawyers," and "The Editors." This organizational approach contributes to the book's value as a reference work, but it hampers the flow of the narrative. The book was sponsored by the Southern Education Reporting Service, where Sarratt served as executive director. Although both works are important, Muse's study, which was sponsored by the Southern Regional Council, is perhaps the more valuable of the two. It is more readable and contains a wealth of factual material. Don Shoemaker (ed.), *With All Deliberate Speed: Segregation-Desegregation in Southern Schools* (New York, 1957), is an earlier Southern Education Reporting Service-sponsored survey of the school desegregation controversy in the South. Written largely by Southern Education Service state correspondents and staff members, the essays in this work present a useful summary of racial developments. Also important is William Peters, *The Southern Temper* (Garden City, N.Y., 1959). A free-lance writer, Peters bases much of his narrative on interviews conducted during a lengthy tour of the South. While dealing perceptively with various phases of the white southern resistance, he focuses his narrative on those individuals who actively favored social change or who were willing to accept it passively. Less valuable is Anthony Lewis, *Portrait of a Decade: The Second American Revolution* (New York, 1964), a popular account interspersed with articles and stories from the New York *Times*. James W. Vander Zanden, *Race Relations in Transition: The Segregation Crisis in the South* (New York, 1965), is a brief but incisive work. *Report of the United States Commission on Civil Rights, 1959* (Washington, 1959) is an excellent summary of civil rights developments. Especially pertinent is Part Three entitled "Public Education." Peltason, *Fifty-Eight Lonely Men* (mentioned previously), concentrates on the role of federal judges in the South, but it also offers perceptive insights into the resistance to court-ordained social change.

THE EISENHOWER ADMINISTRATION

Several of the books mentioned in the preceding paragraph evaluate the performance of the Eisenhower administration in the segregation-desegregation controversy. The general consensus is critical of the President's cautious and noncommittal leadership. Supporting this view is Emmet John Hughes, *The Ordeal of Power: A Political Memoir of the Eisenhower Years* (New York, 1963). Written by one of Eisenhower's advisors, Hughes' work is valuable for its effectiveness in recreating the milieu of the Republican leadership and for its insights into the processes of decision making during the Eisenhower years. Also finding White House personnel inclined to discuss the problems of race relations and to discover reasons not to face or act upon them is E. Frederic Morrow, *Black Man in the White House: A Diary of the Eisenhower Years by the Administrative Officer for Special Projects, The White House, 1955–1961* (New York, 1963). Dwight D. Eisenhower, *The White House Years: Mandate for Change, 1953–1956* and *The White House Years: Waging Peace, 1956–1961* (Garden City, N.Y., 1963, 1965), are not as candid nor as valuable as they might have been, but these works are helpful on the President's concept of leadership and his views toward the racial events of the 1950's.

Sherman Adams, *Firsthand Report: The Story of the Eisenhower Administration* (New York, 1961), is friendly toward Eisenhower. John W. Anderson, *Eisenhower, Brownell and the Congress: The Tangled Origin of the Civil Rights Bill of 1956–1957* (University, Ala., 1964), is an excellent study of the Republican administration's rather inept dealings with Congress over the civil rights act of 1957.

THE CITIZENS' COUNCILS

The Citizens' Councils have occupied the attention of a number of writers. John Bartlow Martin achieves a considerable degree of insight and objectivity in *The Deep South Says "Never"* (New York, 1957). Martin's journalistic account is based primarily on interviews with segregationist leaders. Similar books are James Graham Cook, *The Segregationists* (New York, 1962), a thoughtful and well-constructed survey of segregationist groups generally; and Dan Wakefield, *Revolt in the South* (New York, 1960), which is helpful but evidences signs of hasty preparation. Among significant articles dealing with the Councils are: James W. Vander Zanden, "The Citizens' Councils," *Alpha Kappa Deltan*, XXIX (Spring, 1959), 3–9, and "A Note on the Theory of Social Movements," *Sociology and Social Research*, XLIV (September-October, 1959), 3–7; Paul Anthony, "Resistance!" *Research in Action* (published by the Louisiana Council on Human Relations), I (November, 1956), 1–6; Frederick B. Routh and Paul Anthony, "Southern Resistance Forces," *Phylon Quarterly*, XVIII (First Quarter, 1957), 50–58; Harold C. Fleming, "Resistance Movements and Racial Desegregation," *Annals of the American Academy of Political and Social Science*, CCCIV (March, 1956), 44–52; David Halberstam, "The White Citizens Councils: Respectable Means for Unrespectable Ends," *Commentary*, XXII (October, 1956), 293–302; Samuel DuBois Cook, "Political Movements and Organizations," *Journal of Politics*, XXVI (February, 1964), 130–53; Anti-Defamation League of B'nai B'rith, "The Citizens Councils and Anti-Semitism," *Facts*, XI (January, 1956), 67–70; and Alabama Council on Human Relations, "Pro-Segregation Group Trends," *Alabama Council Newsletter*, III (June, 1957), 1–5. Southern Regional Council, *Special Report: Pro-Segregation Groups in the South* (Atlanta, 1956), is an important survey that has served as the standard reference for the numerical strength of the resistance movement. Among the many works cited elsewhere in this bibliography that include significant material on the Councils are such state studies as Carter, *The*

South Strikes Back, and Quint, *Profile in Black and White: A Frank Portrait of South Carolina*, and such general works as Vander Zanden, *Race Relations in Transition: The Segregation Crisis in the South*, and Muse, *Ten Years of Prelude: The Story of Integration Since the Supreme Court's 1954 Decision*. Also valuable on the Councils are several unpublished sources located in the Southern Regional Council library. H. L. Mitchell, "On the Rise of the White Citizens Council and Its Ties with Anti-Labor Forces in the South" and "The White Citizens Councils vs. Southern Trade Unions" (Confidential AFL-CIO reports, January 30, 1956, March 12, 1956), investigate the Councils' growing influence vis-a-vis organized labor in the South. Paul Anthony, "A Survey of the Resistance Groups of Alabama" (Southern Regional Council field report, 1956); "Patriots of North Carolina, Inc." (Southern Regional Council field report, 1956); and "The Resistance Groups of South Carolina" (Southern Regional Council field report, 1956) evaluate the Councils in these three states.

The *Annual Reports* published by the Association of Citizens' Councils of Mississippi (Winona, Miss., 1955; Greenwood, Miss., 1956–) are important summaries of events by Council leaders. *The Citizens' Council* (Greenwood, Miss., n.d.), *The Educational Fund of the Citizens' Councils* (Greenwood, Miss., n.d.), and *The Citizens' Council: The South's Only Answer* (Montgomery, Ala., n.d.) reflect the Council organizers' professed views of their movement's aims and methods. Similar information concerning the Federation for Constitutional Government is presented in *Federation for Constitutional Government* (New Orleans, n.d.). An important resistance leader describes some of the Councils' activities in *The Mid-West Hears the South's Story: An Address by William J. Simmons Before the Oakland Farmers-Merchants Annual Banquet, Oakland, Iowa, Feb. 3, 1958* (Greenwood, Miss., n.d.) and *Citizens' Council Forum* (Jackson, Miss., 1958). Extremely valuable are the editorials and stories in *The Citizens' Council*, published monthly in Jackson by the Association of Citizens' Councils of Mississippi from October, 1955, through October, 1956, and by the Citizens' Councils of America thereafter. In September, 1961, the newspaper format of *The Citizens' Council* was abandoned, and the publication became a monthly magazine. At the same time the title was changed to *The Citizen*. Also helpful are *The Defenders' News and Views*, published by the Defenders of State Sovereignty and Individual Liberties (publication dates vary), and *Arkansas Faith*, published irregularly by the White Citizens' Council of Arkansas.

THE KU KLUX KLAN

The Ku Klux Klan in the South is inspected in three recent books. David M. Chalmers, *Hooded Americanism: The First Century of the Ku Klux Klan, 1865–1965* (New York, 1965), is a detailed study that emphasizes the activities of the Klan during the 1920's but devotes adequate attention to more recent developments. Arnold S. Rice, *The Ku Klux Klan in American Politics* (Washington, 1962), is a helpful survey that suffers from its somewhat narrow focus. William Peirce Randel, *The Ku Klux Klan: A Century of Infamy* (New York, 1965), is a popular work of limited value. James W. Vander Zanden, "The Klan Revival," *American Journal of Sociology*, LXV (March, 1960), 456–62, is a revealing analysis of the social and psychological factors that have contributed to the Klan's appeal and influenced its behavior. David M. Chalmers, "The Ku Klux Klan and the Radical Right," in *The Radical Right: Proceedings of the Sixth Annual Intergroup Relations Conference at the University of Houston, Houston, Texas, March 27, 1965* (n.p., n.d.), 3–9, should also be consulted. Robert S. Bird's series on the Ku Klux Klan in the *Herald-Tribune*, April 14–28, 1958, is an excellent report. Epitomizing the mentality symbolized by the Ku Klux Klan was the frequent resort to racial violence by white southerners, which is surveyed in Southeastern Office, American Friends Service Committee, Department of Racial and Cultural Relations, National Council of Churches of Christ in the United States of America, and Southern Regional Council, *Intimidation, Reprisal and Violence in the South's Racial Crisis* (Atlanta, 1959), and Southern Regional Council and the American Jewish Committee, *The Continuing Crisis: An Assessment of New Racial Tensions in the South* (Atlanta, 1966).

STATE ACTION

Massive resistance legislation and the activities of state officials designed to hamper, harass, or destroy the NAACP and other proponents of social change are discussed in American Jewish Congress, *Assault Upon Freedom of Association: A Study of the Southern Attack on the National Association for the Advancement of Colored People* (New York, 1957); Walter F. Murphy, "The South Counterattacks: The Anti-NAACP Laws," *Western Political Quarterly*, XII (June, 1959), 371–90; Vanderbilt University School of Law, "Inciting Litigation," *Race Relations Law Reporter*, III (December, 1958), 1257–77; Joseph B. Robinson, "Protection of Associations from

Compulsory Disclosure of Membership," *Columbia Law Review*, LVIII (May, 1958), 614–49; Vanderbilt University School of Law, "Freedom of Association," *Race Relations Law Reporter*, IV (Spring, 1959), 207–36; and Robert B. McKay, "The Repression of Civil Rights as an Aftermath of the School Segregation Cases," *Howard Law Journal*, IV (January, 1958), 9–35. Arthur Garfield Hays Memorial Fund, "Racial Integration and Academic Freedom: Part I," *New York University Law Review*, XXXIV (April, 1959), 727–52, discusses state laws relating to the advocacy of desegregation by state employees. Jack Nelson and Gene Roberts, Jr., *The Censors and the Schools* (Boston, 1963), and Willis Moore, "Causal Factors in the Current Attack on Education," *AAUP Bulletin*, XLI (Winter, 1955), 621–28, are helpful in assessing the health of academic freedom in the South; and Paul Oberst and Loyd D. Easton, "Alabama Polytechnic Institute," *AAUP Bulletin*, XLIV (Spring, 1958), 158–69, and an unsigned article, "Academic Freedom and Tenure: Allen University and Benedict College," *AAUP Bulletin*, XLVI (Spring, 1960), 87–104, are case studies of invasions of academic freedom. Louisiana Joint Legislative Committee, *Subversion in Racial Unrest* (2 pts.; Baton Rouge, 1957); General Legislative Investigating Committee, *Report to the 1962 Regular Session, Mississippi State Legislature, On the Investigation of Un-American Activities in the State of Mississippi* (Jackson, 1962); and Georgia Commission on Education (comp.), *Communism and the NAACP* (2 vols.; Atlanta, n.d.) (a report of public hearings before the Florida Legislative Investigation Committee, February, 1958) are reports of investigations by state legislative committees into the "subversive" activities of the NAACP.

Massive resistance laws relating to the assignment of pupils, the conversion of public schools to private schools, and the closing of schools threatened with desegregation are examined in Daniel J. Meador, "The Constitution and the Assignment of Pupils to Public Schools," *Virginia Law Review*, XLV (May, 1959), 517–71; Ralph Lee Smith, "The South's Pupil Placement Laws: Newest Weapon Against Integration," *Commentary*, XXX (October, 1960), 326–29; Jay W. Murphy, "Can Public Schools Be 'Private'?" *Alabama Law Review*, VII (Fall, 1954), 48–73; Walter F. Murphy, "Private Education with Public Funds?" *Journal of Politics*, XX (November, 1958), 635–54; and Vanderbilt University School of Law, "School Closing Plans," *Race Relations Law Reporter*, III (August, 1958), 807–40.

SOUTHERN TRADITIONALISTS

A vast body of literature presents the views of southern traditionalists. William D. Workman, Jr., *The Case for the South* (New York, 1960), is a balanced work that rallies states' rights, conservative jurisprudence, and Sumnerian social philosophy to the defense of segregation. James F. Byrnes explains why "The Supreme Court Must be Curbed" and why "Guns and Bayonets Cannot Promote Education" in *U.S. News and World Report*, XL (May 18, 1956), 50–58, and XLI (October 5, 1956), 100–104. R. Carter Pittman, "Equality Versus Liberty: The Eternal Conflict," *American Bar Association Journal*, XLVI (August, 1960), 873–80, is an interesting discussion that associates "equality" with communist ideology and places "liberty" in the Western and American tradition. William Old, one of the original popularizers of interposition in the 1950's, vigorously asserts the sovereignty of states in *The Segregation Issue: Suggestions Regarding the Maintenance of State Autonomy* (privately printed, 1955) and *The Segregation Issue: As It Appears Now* (privately printed, 1959). The Richmond *News Leader* reprints many of the editorials and documents from its editorial crusade in support of interposition in *Interposition: Editorials and Editorial Page Presentations* (previously cited). Among other works stressing a states' rights defense of segregation are Charles P. Bloch, *State Rights: The Law of the Land* (Atlanta, 1958), and Eugene Cook and William I. Potter, "The School Segregation Cases: Opposing the Opinion of the Supreme Court," *American Bar Association Journal*, XLII (April, 1956), 313–17. James Jackson Kilpatrick, editor of the Richmond *News Leader*, combines constitutional and states' rights arguments with evidence purporting to suggest the inferiority of Negroes in his *The Sovereign States: Notes of a Citizen of Virginia* (Chicago, 1957) and *The Southern Case for School Segregation* (New York, 1962). A well-articulated though simplistic work that achieved considerable popularity is Carleton Putnam, *Race and Reason: A Yankee View* (Washington, 1961), which emphasizes asserted innate racial differences between Negroes and whites in such areas as achievement and intellect. Thomas R. Waring, "The Southern Case Against Segregation," *Harper's Magazine*, CCXII (January, 1956), 39–45; Herbert Ravenel Sass, "Mixed Schools and Mixed Blood," *Atlantic Monthly*, CXCVIII (November, 1956), 45–49; Peter A. Carmichael, *The South and Segregation* (Washington, 1965); and Nathaniel Weyl, *The Negro in American Civilization* (Washington, 1960), are other important expressions of the segregationist position, which is pushed to its outer limits in Herman E. Talmadge, *You and Segregation* (Birmingham, Ala., 1955), and Judge Tom P. Brady, *Black Monday* (Winona, Miss., 1955). Manning Johnson, *Color, Communism and Common Sense* (New York, 1958), is representative of works that visualize Negro civil rights progress as the result of communist subversion. Among the mass of material circulated by the Citizens' Councils, the following pamphlets were significant: *"We've Reached Era of Judicial Tyranny": An Address by Senator James O. Eastland Before the Statewide Convention of the Association of Citizens' Councils of Mississippi, Held in Jackson, December 1, 1955* (Winona, Miss., n.d.); *The Ugly Truth about the NAACP: An Address by Attorney General Eugene Cook Before the 55th Annual Convention of the Peace Officers Association of Georgia* (Greenwood, Miss., n.d.); and Georgia Commission on Education, *Highlander Folk School: Communist Training School, Monteagle, Tenn.* (Atlanta, n.d.).

A growing body of literature has sought to demonstrate empirically the assumption upon which most of the works listed in the paragraph above are at least in part based—that Negroes are innately inferior to whites. Wesley C. George, *The Race Problem from the Standpoint of One Who Is Concerned About the Evils of Miscegenation* (Birmingham, Ala., 1955), a well-written and documented work based on questionable scientific authority, concludes that Negroes are biologically inferior. Other works by George include *Race Heredity and Civilization* (Norfolk, Va., n.d.) and *"Human Progress and the Race Problem": An Address Given at Dartmouth College, Hanover, New Hampshire, Oct. 12, 1956* (Atlanta, n.d.). Audrey M. Shuey impressively marshals evidence purporting to demonstrate "the presence of some native differences between Negroes and whites as determined by intelligence tests" in *The Testing of Negro Intelligence* (Lynchburg, Va., 1958). Representative works by other important contributors to this school of literature are Frank McGurk, "Psychological Tests: A Scientist's Report on Race Differences," *U.S. News and World Report*, XLI (September 21, 1956), 92–96, and Henry E. Garrett, "One Psychologist's View of 'Equality of the Races,'" *U.S. News and World Report*, LI (August 14, 1961), 72–74.

An excellent critique of the work of the "scientific racists" is I. A. Newby, *Challenge to the Court: Social Scientists and the Defense of Segregation, 1954–1966* (Baton Rouge, 1967). Newby's *Jim Crow's Defense: Anti-Negro Thought in America, 1900–1930* (Baton Rouge, 1965) provides significant background for placing the views of southern segregationists in an historical perspective. James W. Vander Zanden, "The Ideology of

White Supremacy," *Journal of the History of Ideas*, XX (June-September, 1959), 385–402, and Victor C. Ferkiss, "Political and Intellectual Origins of Americanism, Right and Left," *Annals of the American Academy of Political and Social Science*, CCCXLIV (November, 1962), 1–12, provide helpful insights into the rationale of white supremacy. Ronald Harry Denison, "A Rhetorical Analysis of Speeches by Segregationists in the Deep South" (Ph.D. dissertation, Purdue University, 1961), and Paul Anthony, "An Analysis of the Hate Literature of Resistance Groups of the South" (Unpublished Southern Regional Council memorandum, 1956), are critical examinations of segregationist oratory and literature.

THE CHURCH

The best introduction to the role of the church during the massive resistance phase of southern race relations is Kenneth K. Bailey, *Southern White Protestantism in the Twentieth Century* (New York, 1964), a judicious and lucid survey of the changing positions of the three major denominational churches in the South. Campbell and Pettigrew, *Christians in Racial Crisis: A Study of Little Rock's Ministry* (previously cited), is an indispensable case study that perceptively examines the "basic 'Protestant dilemma'—a dilemma between the organizational concerns of money and members and the effective expression of principle." Also important are Charles Y. Glock and Benjamin B. Ringer, "Church Policy and the Attitudes of Ministers and Parishioners on Social Issues," *American Sociological Review*, XXI (April, 1956), 148–56; William T. Liu, "The Community Reference System, Religiosity, and Race Attitudes," *Social Forces*, XXXIX (May, 1961), 324–28; Ernest Q. Campbell, "Moral Discomfort and Racial Segregation—An Examination of the Myrdal Hypothesis," *Social Forces*, XXXIX (March, 1961), 228–34; and Samuel S. Hill, "Southern Protestantism and Racial Integration," *Religion in Life*, XXXIII (Summer, 1964), 421–29. "Southern Ministers Speak Their Minds," *Pulpit Digest*, XXXIX (December, 1958), 13–17, reports the results of a broadly based poll concerning the racial views of denominational ministers. Will D. Campbell, *Race and the Renewal of the Church* (Philadelphia, 1962), is a penetrating discussion by a white southern churchman who has practiced what he has preached. A convenient compilation of statements relating to the *Brown* decision by major religious groups is Birmingham Council on Human Relations (comp.), *Special Report: Religious Bodies and the Supreme Court Decision* (Atlanta, 1957).

David M. Reimers, *White Protestantism and the Negro* (New York, 1965), surveys the depressing national performance of the institutionalized expression of the lily-white brotherhood of man.

THE UNIONS

An interesting comparison of the similarities between church and union is Broadus Mitchell, "Labor Unions and Churches," *Christian Century*, LXIII (November 13, 1946), 1369–71. Ray Marshall, *The Negro and Organized Labor* (New York, 1965), is the most complete examination of the role of labor in the South's racial controversy. Solomon Barkin, "Southern Views of Unions," *Labor Today* (Fall, 1962), 31–36, and Ray Marshall, "Some Factors Influencing the Growth of Unions in the South," *Proceedings of the Thirteenth Annual Meeting of the Industrial Relations Research Association, 1960* (Madison, Wis., 1961), 166–82, are perceptive discussions of the difficulties faced by union organizers. Other valuable articles that delve into various aspects of organized labor's failure to achieve a brotherhood of working men are: Ray Marshall, "Union Racial Problems in the South," *Industrial Relations*, I (May, 1962), 117–28; Solomon Barkin, "Organization of the Unorganized," *Proceedings of the Ninth Annual Meeting of the Industrial Relations Research Association* (Madison, Wis., 1957), 232–37; and Herbert Hill, "Labor Unions and the Negro," *Commentary*, XXVIII (December, 1959), 479–88.

BUSINESS

Surprisingly little has been written about the role of business leaders. M. Richard Cramer, "School Desegregation and New Industry: The Southern Community Leaders' Viewpoint," *Social Forces*, XLI (May, 1963), 384–89, demonstrates that there was no direct correlation between enthusiasm for new industry and racial moderation among community leaders. Hero, *The Southerner and World Affairs*, and Crain and Inger, *School Desegregation in New Orleans* (both cited previously) include valuable data on the attitudes of business leaders. Eli Ginzberg (ed.), *The Negro Challenge to the Business Community* (New York, 1964), should also be consulted.

THE PRESS

Walter Spearman and Sylvan Meyer, *Racial Crisis and the Press* (Atlanta, 1960), is a good evaluation of the performance of southern newspapers that should be supplemented with Roy E. Carter, "Segregation and the News: A Regional Content Study," *Journalism Quarterly*, XXXIV (Winter, 1957), 3–18, and Carter, "Racial Identification Effects upon the News Story Writer," *Journalism Quarterly*, XXXVI (Summer, 1959), 284–90. Graham, *Crisis in Print: Desegregation and the Press in Tennessee* (previously noted), analyzes the response of Tennessee newspapers to the unfolding racial controversy. Collectively, these works demonstrate that while southern newspapers failed in some areas—especially in interpreting the meaning of events deemed newsworthy—they did provide factual and conscientious coverage of racial events in the South.

And, appropriately enough, the Southern Regional Council has just released a *Special Report* entitled *Lawlessness and Disorder: Fourteen Years of Failure in Southern School Desegregation* (Atlanta, 1968).

INDEX

Abbitt, Watkins M.: attends segregationist conference, 94; supports massive resistance, 110, 112; and Federation for Constitutional Government, 123

Ader, Emile B., 37

Advisory Committee on Segregation in the Public Schools: created in Texas, 79; report of, 140–41

Alabama: malapportionment in, 18; opposition to Negro suffrage in, 30; loyalist Democrats win in, 36; elections in, 49, 50, 158, 162, 168, 285, 287; segregationist legislation proposed in, 56; Citizens' Councils in, 87–90, 105; interposition policy in, 131, 132, 135; segregationist legislation in, 135, 282, 283–84, 286; propaganda activity in, 177–79; political questionnaires in, 198; Ku Klux Klan in, 201–202, 203–204, 206; anti-NAACP activity in, 215–16, 220–21; academic freedom in, 227–28, 232–33; demand for censorship in, 234; segregation ordinance in, 236

Alabama Polytechnic Institute: professor fired at, 227–28

Alabama State College: faculty member dismissed at, 232–33

Alcorn A. and M. College: dismissals at, 233

Alford, Dale, 259n, 273, 328

Allen University: faculty members dismissed at, 231–32

Almond, J. Lindsay, Jr.: on segregation strategy, 112; in 1957 gubernatorial campaign, 271–72; recommends segregationist legislation, 272–73; closes schools, 275; leads retreat from massive resistance, 320–27

American Association for the Preservation of State Government and Racial Integrity, 91

American Federation of Labor. *See* Labor Unions

American States Rights Association, 87–88

Andrews, T. Coleman: as third party candidate, 163–65

Arkansas: desegregation in, 7, 262; elections in, 48, 142, 162, 168, 261, 273, 331–32; White America in, 100–101; White Citizens' Councils in, 100–101; and interposition, 131, 132, 137, 144n; segregationist legislation in, 143, 261, 262, 274; anti-NAACP activity in, 187, 214, 217–22 *passim*; Ku Klux Klan in, 203

Arkansas Education Association: supports open schools, 327; attacked in legislature, 327

Arkansas Faith. See White Citizens' Council

Arkansas Gazette, 174, 269. *See also* Little Rock

Arnall, Ellis G., 69, 334

Ashmore, Harry S., 8, 73, 117

Association of Methodist Ministers and Laymen, 300

Atlanta: ministerial statement in, 295–96; support for open schools in, 333; desegregation in, 334–35

Attitudes: of southern whites, 12–16; toward desegregation, 276–77

Bailey, Kenneth K., 294

Bailey, Thomas D., 316

Barnett, Ross R.: Citizens' Council member, 86; and State Sovereignty Commission, 181–82; on moderation, 246

Barr, John U.: as Dixiecrat, 34; as Federation for Constitutional Government leader, 122, 123; seeks national coalition, 149; as third party leader, 163–64

Bates, Jeff B., 157

Bates, Lester, 70